D0759255

PHILOSOPHICAL
DICTIONARY

Enlarged Edition

Other books by Mario Bunge

Causality and Modern Science

Finding Philosophy in Social Science

Foundations of Biophilosophy

Foundations of Physics

The Mind-Body Problem

Philosophy in Crisis

Philosophy of Physics

Philosophy of Psychology

Philosophy of Science, 2 volumes

Social Science Under Debate

Treatise on Basic Philosophy, 8 volumes

PHILOSOPHICAL
DICTIONARY
Enlarged Edition

MARIO BUNGE

 **Prometheus Books**

59 John Glenn Drive
Amherst, New York 14228-2197

CHABOT COLLEGE LIBRARY

Published 2003 by Prometheus Books

Dictionary of Philosophy. Copyright © 2003 by Mario Bunge. All rights reserved. No part of this publication may be reproduced, stored in a retrieval system, or transmitted in any form or by any means, digital, electronic, mechanical, photocopying, recording, or otherwise, or conveyed via the Internet or a Web site without prior written permission of the publisher, except in the case of brief quotations embodied in critical articles and reviews.

Inquiries should be addressed to
Prometheus Books
59 John Glenn Drive
Amherst, New York 14228–2197
VOICE: 716–691–0133, ext. 207
FAX: 716–564–2711
WWW.PROMETHEUSBOOKS.COM

07 06 05 04 03   5 4 3 2 1

Library of Congress Cataloging-in-Publication Data

Bunge, Mario Augusto.
    Philosophical dictionary / Mario Bunge.—Enl. ed.
        p. cm.
    ISBN 1–59102–037–9 (alk. paper)
    1. Philosophy, Modern—Dictionaries. I. Title.
B791.B765 2002
190'.3—dc21   2002031911

Printed in the United States of America on acid-free paper

FOREWORD

This is a lexicon of modern philosophical concepts, problems, principles, and theories. It is limited to modern Western philosophy. Far from being neutral, it adopts a humanist and scientistic standpoint. But then, the competition too is biased in its choice of terms, authors, and analyses—only, covertly so in most cases.

Three warnings are in order. First, the entries are uneven in length: whereas most are short, a few are minipapers on important topics that, in my opinion, have not been handled correctly in the literature. Second, some entries contain technical matter that the nonspecialist may skip or leave for later. Third, I have eschewed solemnity, because it belongs in mummified, not in living, philosophy; and somberness is best left to hell-mongers. Philosophy should lighten, not burden; and enlighten, not obscure.

The choice of philosophical terms has been dictated by usage, usefulness, and enduring value rather than trendiness. Fashions are, by definition, local and short-lived. This is why such traditional terms as 'thing', 'change', 'test', 'truth', and 'good' occur here, whereas 'abduction', 'anomalous monism', 'logical atomism', 'prehension', 'rigid designator', 'strict implication', and other archaisms or short-lived curios do not.

The reader interested in further ideas or different approaches should consult longer dictionaries or my *Treatise on Basic Philosophy* (8 volumes, Dordrecht-Boston: Reidel/Kluwer, 1974–89). My *Philosophy in Crisis: The Need for Reconstruction*, and *Scientific Realism: Selected Essays of Mario Bunge*, edited by Martin Mahner, both published by Prometheus Books in 2001, should also be helpful.

This is the second, revised, and considerably enlarged version of the edition first published in 1999.

I am very grateful to Martin Mahner for his numerous constructive criticisms, as well as to Mary A. Read for her intelligent copyediting.

I dedicate this book to Marta, my beloved wife of over four decades.

Mario Bunge
Department of Philosophy
McGill University
Montréal

CONVENTIONS

↑X = See entry X

Ant = Antonym

Syn = Synonym

LHS = left-hand side

RHS = right-hand side

w.r.t. = with respect to

=df = Identical by definition

iff = if and only if

¬p = not-p

$p \lor q$ = p or q

p & q = p and q

$p \Rightarrow q$ = if p, then q

$p \Leftrightarrow q$ = p if and only if q

$p, q \vdash r$ = p and q jointly entail r. **Syn** ∴

$\{x \in A| Px\}$ = the set of objects in set A that possess property P

$a \in S$ individual a belongs to set S

∅ the empty set

$\mathbb{N}$ = the set of natural numbers: 0, 1, 2, . . .

$\mathbb{R}$ = the set of real numbers, such as 1, ½, $\sqrt{2}$, π, and e

$f: A \rightarrow B$ the function f maps the set A (domain) into the set B (codomain)

A = A Traditional formalization of the logical principle of ↑**identity**: Every object is identical to itself. Equivalent formulation: For all x, $x = x$, or $\forall x \, (x = x)$. This principle has often been misunderstood as denying the possibility of change. Actually it states only that, in the respect that is being considered, every object remains identical to itself. Moreover, the principle is necessary to state that a given thing undergoes certain changes. For instance, "personal identity" does not mean that persons do not change, but that they continue to be the same in some important respects throughout their changes. The principle is also useful in some mathematical proofs: if one reaches a conclusion of the form "$A \neq A$," one knows that at least one of the premises is false, and must thus be altered or dropped.

ABOUT X is about Y = X refers to Y = X concerns Y = X deals with Y = X relates to Y. A key semantic concept. Examples: logic is about the form of arguments; historiography is about the past. ↑**Reference**. Sometimes confused with ↑**intentionality**, a psychological concept.

ABSOLUTE / RELATIVE A fact that happens relative to all reference frames, or a proposition that holds regardless of context, can be said to be absolute. Ant ↑**relative**. For example, a light beam striking a retina is an absolute fact. By contrast, the value of the wavelength is relative to a frame of reference; and the color sensation it causes is relative to (depends on) the subject's state and her surrounding. Mathematical truths are relative, in that they exist and hold only within definite contexts rather than across contexts. (For example, the equality "$12 + 1 = 1$" holds in clock arithmetic, not in number theory.) By contrast, many factual statements are absolutely true because they adequately represent absolute facts. Examples: "This is a book," "Water is composed of oxygen and hydrogen." Objective properties that are invariant with respect to changes in reference frame may be said to be absolute. Examples: electric charge, number of components, chemical composition, and social structure. Likewise objective patterns (↑**laws**$_1$) that are the same in all reference frames may be said to be absolute. 'Absolute', like 'relative', is an adjective, for it represents a property. When ↑**reified**, it becomes 'the Absolute', a favorite with mystics, theologians, and traditional metaphysicians. Nobody knows for sure what this expression means. The expression 'absolute truth' is sometimes intended to mean total (by contrast to partial) truth, as in the statement that the progress of science consists in going from relative to absolute truths. This usage is confusing. ↑**Partial truth**.

ABSOLUTISM The view that existence, knowledge, or morals are independent of the knower-actor as well as of circumstances. **Ant** ↑**relativism**.

ABSTRACT a Semantics A construct or symbol is *semantically abstract* if it does not refer to anything definite. All the constructs of logic and abstract algebra are semantically abstract. The more abstract constructs are the more general. Hence they are the more portable from one discipline to another. Empiricists and vulgar materialists (e.g., nominalists) refuse to admit them, just as subjective idealists mistrust, despise, or even reject everything ↑**concrete**. **b Epistemology** A construct or symbol is *epistemologically abstract* if it does not evoke any perceptions. Examples: the highest-level concepts of mathematics and theoretical science, such as those of function, infinity, energy, gene, evolution, ecological niche, and risk.

ABSTRACTION The operation of rendering something ↑**abstract**. The dual of ↑**interpretation**. Example: one of the possible interpretations of the abstract algebraic formula "$a \circ b$," where a and b designate nondescript individuals, and $\circ$ stands for an unspecified associative operation, is the arithmetic formula "$a + b$," where a and b designate numbers and $+$ stands for ordinary addition. Abstraction is a gate to generalization.

ABSURD Nonsensical or false. According to Schopenhauer, Kierkegaard, Sartre, and other writers, the world, or at least human life, is absurd, hence it cannot be accounted for in rational terms. Therefore these writers cannot help us understand reality, let alone cope with it in an effective manner. Moreover, their thesis is itself absurd, because absurdity can be predicated only of symbols or ideas, never of concrete items such as the world. Nor should 'absurd' be used as a noun, as in 'the absurd', because it designates a property, not an entity.

ABUSE The cheapest, most common, and most persuasive form of ↑**criticism**. Thus, secular humanists are routinely accused of ignoring the spiritual dimension of human life, and materialists of being crass, narrow-minded, and dogmatic.

ACADEMIC A piece of intellectual work of very limited interest, and that is more likely to advance its author's career than human knowledge. When a significant number of scholars engage in work of this kind, one faces an academic ↑**industry**.

ACCIDENT Unforeseen crossing of initially independent lines, as in meeting without premeditation a long-lost friend. Individual accidents exhibit no patterns, hence are unpredictable. Biological and social evolution are littered with accidents, whence they cannot be understood exclusively in terms of patterns (laws). By contrast, large collections of accidents of the same kind, such as automobile crashes and unintentional fires, exhibit definite statistical patterns. Thus what is accidental on one ↑**level** may become lawful on the next. This is why insurance companies make money insuring against such accidents. By the same token they refuse to compensate for the accidents called Acts of God. ↑**Chance**.

ACCIDENTAL a Event An ↑ **accident**. **b Property** An unimportant property: one whose absence would not essentially alter the thing concerned. Example: someone's skin color or having a beard. **Ant ↑essential.**

ACCOUNT ↑Description or **↑explanation** of some **↑facts.**

ACTION a General (ontological) concept What one thing does to another. Possible formalization: The action that thing x exerts on thing y equals the set-theoretic difference between the history of y in the presence of x, and the history of y in the absence of x. **b Human action** is whatever humans do. **Syn ↑praxis.** The ultimate source of social life. Some human actions are deliberate: they are preceded by the design of a **↑plan.** There are several sources or triggers: habit, coercion, passion, compassion, interest, reason, and combinations of two or more of the preceding. Exclusive focus on any of these gives rise to a one-sided theory of action, such as **↑behaviorism, ↑emotivism,** and **↑rational-choice theory.** Action theory = **↑praxiology.**

ACTIVE / PASSIVE ↑Agent / patient.

ACTUAL a Ontology Real, as opposed to both potential and virtual. **b Mathematics** An *actual infinity* is an infinite set as determined by some predicate, such as the set of points inside a circle. Dual: *potential infinity*, constructed step by step according to a rule such as a recursive definition. Example: Peano's axiomatic definition of the concept of natural number.

ACTUALISM The ontological view that all possibility is unreal or subjective, hence all dispositions are imaginary, and all possibility statements are metaphysical or arbitrary. **Ant ↑possibilism.** Actualism is falsified by any theory in factual science or technology, for any such theory refers not only to actuals but also to possibles—such as possible antennas and the fields they would emit. This is made clear by the **↑state-space** representation, where all the possible (lawful) states of things of a kind are represented. It is even more obvious in the case of probabilistic factual theories, such as quantum mechanics and genetics. In short, all factual knowledge is about possibles as well as actuals. This explains why **↑modal logic** is useless in science. Caution: 'actualism' is also a misnomer for activism, the pragmatist thesis that everything revolves around action.

ACTUALITY Reality, concrete **↑existence.** The dual of **↑possibility.**

ACTUALIZATION Transformation of **↑possibility** into **↑actuality.** Example: the occurrence of any possible change, such as motion and a firm's reorganization. A key concept in Aristotle's philosophy.

ADAPTATIONISM The exaggeration of the role of adaptation in evolution, based on the assumption that natural selection "chooses" among alternative "designs" on the basis of how well they function. A tenet of pop evolutionary biology, **↑evolutionary epistemology, ↑evolutionary psychology,** and evolutionary medicine. Even diseases as disabling as depression would ultimately be good for us. Adaptationism is an exaggeration of the truism that well-adapted organisms can outreproduce ill-adapted ones. And it overlooks the occurrence of plenty of biologically neutral items, such as "junk" DNA (nearly 99 percent of our genome), and traits, such as eye color and ear shape.

ADDITION a Logic The principle of addition states that any proposition p entails a proposition $p \lor q$, where q need not bear any relation to p. This principle is both generous and treacherous. It is generous because it allows for the deduction of infinitely many propositions from any given proposition. This ensures that even the humblest of assumptions entails infinitely many possible consequences. But the principle is treacherous because it allows for the intrusion of total strangers into any formally valid argument. For example, let p be a theorem in some mathematical theory, and q = "God is vindictive." Since p entails p or q, it is correctly concluded that, if God is not vindictive, then p. (This by virtue of the logical truths: $p \lor q = p \lor \neg\neg q = \neg\neg q \lor p = \neg q \Rightarrow p$.) Thus the appearance is created that theology has mathematical consequences. The previous argument must then be regarded as being logically valid but semantically fallacious, for mixing disjoint ↑**universes of discourse**. The only way to avoid this fallacy is to impose the condition that the two propositions share at least one predicate. This ensures that both are ↑**coreferential**. ↑**Relevance logic** was introduced to avoid the intrusion of irrelevancies in a discourse. But it fails to do so because it keeps the addition principle. By contrast, ↑**axiomatization** blocks trespassers. **b Mathematics** The addition, logical sum, or union of two sets is the set comprised of all the elements in both sets. Symbol: ∪. 'Addition' takes on different meanings for other mathematical objects, such as numbers, functions, and operators. **c Science and Ontology** Concrete things may add up in at least two different ways: juxtaposition and combination. The juxtaposition, aggregation, or physical addition of two or more things of the same kind results in another thing of the same kind. The combination of two or more things of any kind results in a third thing with some new (↑**emergent**) properties, that is, properties not possessed by its components or precursors.

AD HOC HYPOTHESIS A hypothesis devised either to "cover" a narrow range of data or to save another hypothesis from adverse evidence. Ad hoc hypotheses of the first kind have a very restricted explanatory or predictive power, for they are tied to a small and fixed body of data. The distinction between ordinary and ad hoc hypotheses parallels that between two sorts of marksmanship. The honest marksman puts up a target and then shoots. The dishonest one shoots first and then draws concentric circles around the bullet's hole. Ad hoc hypotheses of the second kind, i.e., those aiming at protecting other hypotheses, are in turn of two sorts: in good and in bad faith. A *bona fide* ad hoc hypothesis is independently testable, a *mala fide* one is not. A classical example of a bona fide ad hoc hypothesis is William Harvey's conjecture of the existence of capillaries bridging the arteries to the veins visible to the naked eye. The capillaries were eventually seen through the microscope. A classical example of a mala fide ad hoc hypothesis is Sigmund Freud's repression hypothesis, designed to protect the Oedipus complex and other fantasies. For example, if a man does not ostensibly hate his father, he has only repressed his hatred. And if this particular dream does not have an overt sexual content, it must have a covert ("latent") one.

AD HOMINEM a Argument Defense or attack of a doctrine on the strength of the prestige or discredit of its proponents. Examples: *tu quoque* (you too) and "X-ism is right (wrong) because it is held by the great (miserable) Y." Ad hominem arguments are fallacious because there is no necessary connection between a person's views and his character. They are usually resorted to when no genuine arguments come to mind. However, they may induce us to watch out for hidden presuppositions or agendas. Besides, they can be effective silencers. **b Explanation** Account of a person's views in terms of his background or interests. Example: "The ambiguity of Kant's ethics is due to his being a subject of the Prussian state, and yet in sympathy with the Enlightenment and the French Revolution." By contrast to arguments ad hominem, ad hominem ↑**explanations** may have some merit.

AESTHETICISM The opinion that beauty is the overriding value. Not a popular view among those who have to work for a living, or who devote themselves to the search for truth.

AESTHETICS a Philosophical The philosophy of art. It pivots around the general concepts of work of art, representational / abstract, style, and beautiful / ugly. The status of this field is uncertain because there are no known objective standards, hence transpersonal and cross-cultural ones, for evaluating works of art—particularly in our time, when even a capricious collage and an arbitrary sequence of noises will pass for works of art if suitably marketed. As a consequence, although there are plenty of aesthetic opinions, definitions, and classifications, there seem to be no testable aesthetic hypotheses, let alone hypothetico-deductive systems (theories). Still, the analysis and interrelation of aesthetic concepts is a legitimate endeavor, that may be called 'analytical aesthetics'. **b Scientific** The experimental psychology of art appreciation.

AFTERLIFE Life after life—an oxymoron. Belief in afterlife is common to most religions, which have exploited it in return for meek behavior and resignation in the face of injustice. The worst deal: pay now, enjoy later (maybe). Only an idealist philosophy of mind can be compatible with belief in the afterlife. However, most contemporary idealist philosophies are nonreligious.

AGATHONISM The ethical component of ↑**systemism**. According to it we must seek the good for self and others. Maximal postulate: "Enjoy life and help live an enjoyable life." This principle combines selfishness with altruism. Agathonism posits further that rights and duties come in pairs; that actions must be morally justified; and that moral principles should be evaluated by their consequences. Agathonism combines features of both Kantianism and utilitarianism. ↑**Principlism** in ↑**bioethics** is very close to agathonism.

AGENCY Human ↑**action**. Often opposed to (social) structure, while actually the latter is both an outcome of previous agency and a constraint upon it. Indeed, we are all born into a preexisting society that has a definite (but changing) structure, and which we may alter to some extent or other through our social behavior. For example, even the mere addition or withdrawal of a single person makes a difference to the structure of a family.

AGENT / PATIENT The relata of the ↑**action** relation. If x acts upon y, then x is called the *agent* and y the *patient*. However, the patient may react back on the agent that initiated the process. In this case both entities ↑**interact**, and the agent/patient distinction evaporates except for practical purposes.

AGNOSIA Ignorance. The initial state of exploration and research. According to radical ↑**skepticism**, ignorance is also the final stage of inquiry.

AGNOSTICISM a Epistemology Denial of the possibility of knowing facts as they really are, or even whether there are facts outside the knower. A version of ↑**skepticism**. Sextus Empiricus, Francisco Sánches, Hume, Kant, Mill, and Spencer were epistemological agnostics. **b Philosophy of religion** Suspension of all religious belief. A religious agnostic is likely to be a shame-faced atheist afraid that he might be wrong, accused of dogmatism, or discriminated against. Agnosticism is part of radical (or systematic) ↑**skepticism**. It is usually defended on the strength of either or all of the following views: (1) ↑**anything is possible**; (2) the hypothesis of the existence of the supernatural can be neither proved nor disproved by empirical means, precisely because the supernatural is inaccessible to the senses; (3) good scientists must never make categorical statements: the most they can responsibly state is that the hypothesis in question is either extremely plausible or implausible; (4) agnosticism makes no difference to scientific research, whereas atheism narrows its range. Let us examine these views. The first view is wrong, for possibilities are constrained by ↑**laws**. The second view holds only on the empiricist assumption that experience is the sole source of knowledge. But ↑**empiricism** is too narrow a philosophical framework for a science that studies radio waves, genes, hominids, nations, anomie, political discontent, inflation, and other unobservables. Science also predicts the impossibility of certain things and processes, such as human immortality and reincarnation (since brain death is accompanied by the cessation of mental processes). As for the ban on categorical statements, it is actually ignored in science. For example, biologists reject the possibility of reversing any long evolutionary line, because of (a) the randomness of genetic mutations; and (b) the second law of thermodynamics, that excludes the recurrence of exactly the same environmental conditions prevailing in the past. Extreme caution is indicated only in matters of detail, such as the nth decimal figure of the value of a parameter. And the fourth plea for agnosticism, though the most subtle of all, holds no water either. Indeed, consider the following test cases: cosmology, evolution, and the soul. The agnostic must admit the possibility that the universe was created and may be destroyed by divine fiat. But this admission subjects science to theology. As for evolution, the agnostic must be prepared to admit that any gap in the paleontological record may be a practical joke of the Creator. Consequently he will be tempted to give up further search for fossils of the same stage, or else to give up any attempt to explain their disappearance. Finally, an agnostic will not regard research on the ghostly as a waste of time, which it is if ↑**cognitive neuroscience** is taken seriously. ↑**Atheism** has none of these flaws.

AGONISM The worldview according to which conflict is what keeps the world going. Held by Heraclitus, Hobbes, Hegel, and Marx. ↑**Dialectics**, ↑**Hobbesianism**. Agonism

Algorithm 13

is only partially true, because ↑**cooperation**, whether deliberate or not, is just as pervasive as conflict.

AKRASIA Weakness of will: doing what one knows not to be the best. Some philosophers are puzzled by such behavior, which they regard as irrational. However, there are often good reasons for not doing the best, from compassion and fear of consequences to prudence. In general, there is seldom a single reason for taking action, and ↑**utility** maximization is not always practically or morally advisable.

ALCHEMY, EPISTEMIC The attempt to transmute ignorance into knowledge with the help of symbols. Because of the latter, the illusions of knowledge and perhaps even exactness are created. A few academic industries and many scholarly reputations have been built in this manner. Example 1: Assign (subjective) ↑**probabilities** to possibilities of unknown outcomes or to untested hunches, and set in motion the machinery of the calculus of probability. ↑**Probabilistic philosophy** (in particular ontology), ↑**Bayesianism**, ↑**rational-choice** theories. Example 2: Attribute (subjective) ↑**utilities** to the outcomes of any action. Example 3: Equate anything you like with ↑**information**, and put the statistical theory of information to use. All three are examples of ↑**pseudoexactness**.

ALETHIC Having to do with truth. ↑**Logic** in the strict sense, unlike ↑**model** theory, is alethically neutral, because logical validity concerns form, not content nor, a fortiori, truth. So much so, that none of the axioms in any logical theory contains a truth concept. Truth and falsity occur only in the heuristics of logic, such as the soundness requirement, that true premises should not entail false conclusions. Those concepts also occur in the didactics of logic, particularly in the use of the ↑**truth table** as a ↑**decision** procedure.

ALGEBRA The study of algebraic systems, such as Boolean algebras, lattices, groups, and vector spaces. In turn, an algebraic system may be defined as a set together with one or more operations among members of the set, and some laws governing these operations. Algebra has applications in logic, mathematics, science, and ↑**exact philosophy**.

ALGORITHM Foolproof ("mechanical") computational procedure, such as long division and the method for extracting square roots. This intuitive concept is exactified by those of ↑**computability** and ↑**Turing machine**. Algorithms are precise and effective rules for operating on symbols to solve well-posed problems of a restricted kind with the help of a body of knowledge. Since only direct problems can be well posed, in general no algorithms to solve↑**inverse problems** are possible. The concept is central to mathematics, computer science, knowledge engineering (in particular artificial intelligence), cognitive psychology, and the philosophy of mind. It also occurs in two quaint ideas. One is the rather popular thesis that all mental processes are algorithmic, whence computers can think whatever humans can. This view is false because most mental processes are noncomputational: think, e.g., of emotion, perception, identification, comparison, problem detection, guess, convention, evaluation, and invention. ↑**Com-**

putationism Another misuse of the concept occurs in the view that biological evolution is algorithmic. This idea is triply wrong: (a) it overlooks the key roles of opportunity (e.g., the appearance of a new kind of food), accident (e.g., a draught), chance (e.g., a mutation), and creativity (e.g., a new use of an environmental item); (b) it ignores the emergence of qualitative novelty; and (c) it confuses ↑**law** with ↑**rule**. Only a few artificial items can be subjected to algorithms: nature and society are nonalgorithmic. There can be no algorithms for the production of radically new items (ideas, organisms, artifacts, organizations, etc.), because (a) the design of an algorithm involves a piece of original research; and (b) an algorithm specifies exactly and in advance every stage of the process and, in particular, the kind of result it is intended to obtain. Shorter: original ↑**creation** is nonalgorithmic; only routines are algorithmic. In particular, the design of algorithms is nonalgorithmic. True, there are flexible algorithms (or programs), such as the so-called genetic ones, that incorporate chance and selection. However, they too proceed blindly, without conscious choice. A flexible program is still a program. Originality and initiative are in the programmer, not in the program. ↑**Artificial intelligence**, ↑**artificial life**.

ALL IS ONE Everything is interconnected, nothing is isolated—except for the ↑**universe** as a whole. The formula of radical ↑**holism**. It is true that everything is connected to something else. But not all bonds among things are equally strong, and most of them decrease rapidly with distance. In particular, the bonds among the components of a ↑**system** are stronger than the ties between the system and its environment—otherwise there would be no distinct systems. ↑**Systemism**.

ALL / SOME The quantifiers ∀ (all) and ∃ (some). Relation between the two in classical logic: For any predicate F: $\forall x\, Fx = \neg\exists x \neg Fx$. Trading ∀ for ∃ in this formula yields $\exists x\, Fx = \neg\forall x \neg Fx$. This is why the two quantifiers are mutually ↑**dual** (not opposite). In ordinary language these quantifiers do not always occur explicitly. For example, the sentence 'Mathematics studies unreal things' must be understood as stating that mathematics studies *some* fictions, whereas 'Mathematics studies numbers' must be understood as asserting that mathematics studies *all* numbers. Even standard mathematical texts omit some quantifiers. For example, in most cases, a formula of the form "$f(x) = 0$" is understood to hold only for some values of x, that is, as "$\exists x\, [f(x) = 0]$."

ALOOFNESS / ENGAGEMENT Ever since Aristophanes placed Socrates in a cloud, philosophers have had a reputation for aloofness w.r.t. wordly affairs. Arguably, logicians and semanticists can afford to remain aloof, because they deal in pure ideas. By contrast, ontologists, epistemologists, philosophers of science and technology, and ethicists, as well as legal and political philosophers, must face the real world if their ideas are to be realistic and of interest to nonphilosophers. However, curiosity about wordly affairs does not entail narrow partisanship. On the contrary, such engagement is detrimental to philosophizing because it restricts freedom of thought. Still, indifference to needless suffering and unwillingness to do anything about it are the mark of pettiness, not of full dedication to lofty matters.

ALTRUISM Selflessness, generosity: doing good without expecting a reward. Ant ↑**ego-**

ism, selfishness. Utilitarians hold that altruism is nothing but enlightened selfishness. This only holds for reciprocal altruism or *quid pro quo* (you scratch my back and I scratch yours). Normal people engage in both spontaneous and calculated altruism. Every moral code worth its name includes altruistic norms. And no social system is viable without a modicum of altruism.

AMBIGUITY, LEXICAL A ↑**sign** is said to be ambiguous if it designates or denotes more than one object. Example: 'ring' (wedding ring, telephone ring, algebraic ring, etc.). In natural languages ambiguities are tolerable, nay unavoidable, but they are inexcusable in scientific texts. And yet they often do occur in the latter. Examples: the terms 'information', 'species', 'genome', 'genotype', and 'phenotyope' in contemporary biology.

AMORAL Independent of morality. Not to be confused with "immoral," or contrary to received morality. Examples: mathematics and basic science are amoral. By contrast, technology and ethics are morally committed because of their power to affect life. A classical problem is whether the social studies are morally committed. This problem evaporates upon distinguishing ↑**basic social science**, such as sociology, from ↑**social technology**, such as normative macroeconomics. Indeed, only the latter is intent on altering society, and is therefore in agreement or in violation with some moral norms. Still, a good case may be made for the thesis that morality is relevant to all human activities. In particular, the search for truth involves honesty, and that of efficiency requires concern for others.

AMORALISM The collection of doctrines that denies the legitimacy of moral norms and, in general, value judgments. Examples: ethical ↑**emotivism** and ↑**nihilism**. Ant ↑**moralism**.

ANALOGY Similarity in some respect. Analogy can be substantial, formal, or both. Two objects are *substantially* analogous to each other iff they are composed of the same "stuff." Example: all social systems are substantially analogous in being composed of people. Two objects are *formally* analogous iff there is a correspondence between either their parts or their properties. Examples: the sets of integers and of even integers; human and ion migration. Two particularly important cases are when the objects concerned are either sets or systems. Analogy between sets comes in different strengths. The weakest obtains when there is an *injective* mapping from one set into the other, that is, when every element of a set has a partner in the other. The strongest is *isomorphism*, which obtains when every element and every operation in one of the sets is mirrored in the other. Being the strongest, isomorphism is the less common. (Incidentally, the rather popular claim that true knowledge is isomorphic to the real world is mistaken, if only because the real world is not a set.) Two concrete ↑**systems** can be analogous in any of five ways: with respect to composition, environment, structure, function, or history. Thus all social systems are composition-wise analogous, in that they are composed of people; all rural communities are environment-wise analogous in that they are embedded in agricultural settings; all schools are structurally analogous in that they are held together by the learning bond; all states are functionally analogous in that they maintain security; and all banks are historically analogous in that they are generated by trade. The concept of functional analogy is unimportant in biology. For example, not much can be made out of the fact that the wings of bats and birds are functionally analogous. By contrast, the concept of historical analogy is particularly important in biology, where it is called *homology*. Example: the forelimbs of terrestrial animals are historically analogous to the flippers of aquatic animals in having common ancestors. Analogies can be shallow or deep. If the former, they may mislead. If deep, they suggest pattern (law). Currently fashionable examples of superficial misleading analogies: genetics-linguistics, mind-computer, cultural transmission-genome.

ANALYSIS Breaking down a whole into its components and their mutual relations. **Ant** ↑**synthesis**. Analysis can be conceptual, empirical, or both. Conceptual analysis distinguishes without dismantling, whereas empirical analysis consists in separating the components of a concrete whole. A prism analyzes white light into waves of different frequencies; Fourier analysis does the same conceptually. Critical thinking starts by analyzing ideas and procedures, and culminates in such syntheses as classifications, theories, experimental designs, and plans. Analysis may have any of the following results: dissolution of ill-conceived problems; clear restatement of ill-posed problems; disclosure of presuppositions; elucidation; definition; deduction; proof of consistency or inconsistency; proof of compatibility or incompatibility with some body of knowledge; reduction; bridge building—and more. Analysis is a mark of conceptual ↑**rationality**. Accordingly, the family of philosophies may be split into analytic or rationalist, and antianalytic or irrationalist. Not surprisingly, whereas there is little variety in the antianalytic camp, the analytic camp is characterized by diversity. The various analytic schools can be ordered in several ways, among them according to depth. The shallowest of them all is ordinary-language philosophy, which employs only common sense and shuns the entire traditional problematics of philosophy. Next comes ↑**exact philosophy**, which may or may not tackle important problems, but at least it handles them with the help of logical and mathematical tools. The deepest philosophies combine potent analytic tools with scientific and technological knowledge to tackle interesting and often tough philosophical problems. However, there is no deep analysis outside some ↑**theory** (hypothetico-deductive system).

ANALYSIS OF VARIANCE Analysis of the variance (scatter around the average) of a trait in a population. Standard abbreviation: ANOVA. Widely believed to point to causal factors—as when it is stated that heredity "explains" 80 percent of the variance in the IQ of a human population, the remaining 20 percent being due to (caused by) random environmental factors. This belief is wrong, because a variance (or "variability") need not result from any variation of a property over time or space, such as an acceleration or a density gradient. Therefore, no statistical analysis of an array of observational data can establish ↑**causation**. Two traits can be associated (e.g., statistically correlated) more or less strongly, but no trait, such as the possession of a certain gene, can cause another trait. Only ↑**experiment** can establish causation, by checking the effect of actual changes (variations) in the values of the independent variable(s) upon the dependent one. For example, genetic manipulation may eventually cause changes in some mental abilities. Until that happens, and until we understand what 'intelligence' means, we should abstain from stating that good genes cause intelligence. ↑**Nature / nurture**.

ANALYTIC PHILOSOPHY a Broad sense The philosophical approach that seeks clarity through conceptual ↑**analysis**. It is an approach, not a doctrine. ↑**Ordinary-language philosophy. b Narrow sense** The examination of the usage of ordinary-language words and locutions, as well as of some philosophical problems in the light of popular wisdom. **Syn** ↑**linguistic philosophy**, Oxford philosophy, Wittgensteinian philosophy.

ANALYTIC / SYNTHETIC DIVIDE The traditional view that every proposition is either analytic in the narrow sense (i.e., logically true and uninformative) or synthetic (i.e., empirical and informative). A cornerstone of both ↑**logical positivism** and Wittgenstein's philosophy. This view is false because the strictly mathematical propositions, such as "There are infinitely many prime numbers," belong neither in logic nor in factual science. The correct dichotomy is↑**formal / factual**.

ANALYTICITY This word designates several concepts, among them Kant's vague notion, and that of a tautology. **a Kant's notion** According to Kant, a proposition is analytic if its predicate is included in its subject. (Presupposition: all predicates are unary, like "is young.") Taken literally, this definition is absurd. Consider the proposition "God is omnipotent," which may be symbolized as "Og." There is no way the subject g can be included in the predicate O. The best we can do is to reanalyze the given proposition as "If g is godlike, then g is omnipotent." The hypothesis that omnipotence is one of the attributes of the divinity amounts to the assertion that the predicate "omnipotent" is a member of the ↑**intension** of the predicate "is godlike," along with "ubiquitous," "omniscient," "all-merciful," and the like. This is the closest we can get to Kant's notion of analyticity. It involves the notion of set membership, not that of inclusion, and it uses a semantic tool, namely the present author's theory of ↑**intension**. Hence it is unrelated to the logical notion of an analytic proposition. It is just a historical curiosity. This is why it is standard fare in history of philosophy courses. **b Logic** An *analytic proposition* is the same as a ↑**tautology**: a composite formula that is true regardless of the meanings and truth values of its (atomic) constituents. Example: "p or not-p" in classical logic. The analytic propositions are included in the class of formal or a priori ↑**truths**, that is, propositions which are true not because they match facts but by virtue of their ↑**coherence** with other propositions in the same body of knowledge. In the case of tautologies this coherence is assured by the mutual equivalence of all tautologies. Warning 1: Different logical theories may have different but partially overlapping sets of tautologies. Warning 2: Tautologies are not meaningless: they just do not have any specific meanings: they do not "say" anything special about anything in particular.

ANARCHISM a Epistemology Radical ↑**skepticism**: the opinion that all beliefs are equivalent, in that none of them has more legitimate claims to truth or efficiency than its rivals. **Syn:** ↑**relativism**. Thus, creationism would be just as legitimate as evolutionary biology, and faith healing just as good as medicine. Epistemological anarchists preach tolerance to anything but rigorous standards: it thus condones intellectual sloth, imposture, and irresponsibility. **b Political philosophy** The doctrine and movement that seeks to abolish the state. Leftist anarchism promotes an egalitarian federation of cooperatives. Right-wing anarchism advocates the reduction of the state to the law-enforcement agencies.

AND Ordinary-language designation of the conjunction, as in the predicate "general & deep," and in the proposition "Molecular biology is general & molecular biology is deep." Relation to ↑**disjunction**: $\neg\,(\neg\,p\,\&\,\neg\,q) = p \vee q$. Standard symbols: $\wedge$ and &. The ontic counterpart of disjunction is ↑**juxtaposition**.

ANIMAL RIGHTS The doctrine that all animals have the right to life. Strictly speaking, animals have no rights, since they have neither moral qualms that they could debate rationally, nor duties other than those that we impose on some of them, such as pack mules and watchdogs. The so-called animal rights are actually obligations we impose upon ourselves to ease the unnecessary suffering of animals and enhance their welfare. We do this out of empathy, to check our own cruelty, and to assuage our conscience— or else to increase the quality and quantity of animal activities or products. Philosophers can help nonhuman animals in two ways. One is by incorporating into moral philosophy the duty to treat animals in a humane way. (This injunction has already had a positive impact on applied ethology.) The other is by criticizing animal experimentation of the trial-and-error kind, that is, without a clue as to what type of stimuli might produce interesting responses—with the accompanying waste of life.

ANIMISM The doctrine that all things, or all things of some kind, are animated, i.e., inhabited by immaterial ↑**spirits**, which would rule them. Example: The metaphor that the soul governs the body, just as the pilot steers the boat (Plato). Syn: ↑**panpsychism**.

ANNIHILATION The conversion of something into nothing. An impossible event according to the laws of conservation of energy and momentum. What often does happen is a qualitative transformation whereby some properties submerge. Example: the so-called annihilation of an electron pair consists in its conversion into a photon; in this process, mass and charge disappear but the total energy, total charge (nil), and total spin (one) are conserved.

ANOMALY A fact or idea that is out of the ordinary, that contradicts an accepted generalization, or that falls under no known law. Initially, discrepancies from received views are accounted for by patching up the received view with ↑**ad hoc hypotheses**. Should these pile up or turn out not to be independently corroborated, the view in question is replaced with a more comprehensive one that "covers" (accounts for) the anomaly in question. Thus, the discovery of anomalies is an important motivator for theory change. But, contrary to popular belief, a scientific ↑**revolution** takes much more than the discovery of a few anomalies.

ANTECEDENT / CONSEQUENT In a conditional proposition "If p then q" (or "$p \Rightarrow q$" for short), p is called the antecedent and q the consequent. Warning: The consequent q is not the consequence of p, unless p is independently asserted. ↑**Modus ponens**.

ANTECEDENT KNOWLEDGE Body of knowledge available at the time of the start of a research project. Some such knowledge is necessary to pose any new problem. ↑**Background knowledge**.

ANTHROPIC HYPOTHESIS The hypothesis that the universe was designed so that eventually it would possess all the necessary and sufficient conditions for the emergence of human life. Wrong logic: all that follows from the fact that humans emerged at the place and time they did, and not somewhere else at a different time, or not at all, is that it was possible, not necessary, for our species to appear there and then.

ANTHROPOCENTRIC View regarding human beings as either the creators, centers, or beneficiaries of the world. Examples: Judaism, Christianity, Islam, subjective ↑**idealism**, ontological ↑**constructivism** and ↑**phenomenalism**, the ↑**anthropic hypothesis**.

ANTHROPOLOGY a Scientific The most basic and comprehensive of all the sciences of man. It studies social systems of all kinds and sizes, at all times, and in all respects: environmental, biological, economic, political, and cultural. It is one of the ↑**biosocial** (or socionatural) sciences. It is so far lacking in theoretical sophistication—largely in reaction to the anthropological speculations of philosophers. **b Philosophical** The branch of ↑**ontology** that deals with human beings in general rather than with any particular human group. Because of its apriorism, it has been in decline since the birth of scientific anthropology at the end of the nineteenth century. It remains to be seen whether a philosophical anthropology consistent with scientific anthropology is viable.

ANTHROPOMORPHIC Metaphor that assigns human features to nonhuman objects. Examples: imagining personal gods, identifying computers with brains, and attributing goals to firms.

ANTI-INTELLECTUALISM Rejection or subordination of the intellect, and the concomitant overrating of passion, feeling, intuition, or action. Examples: mysticism, vitalism, emotivism, intuitionism, romanticism, pragmatism, existentialism, postmodernism, back-to-nature movement, New Age, and vulgar red-neckism. Anti-intellectualism implies ↑**antiphilosophy**, but the converse is false. **Ant** ↑**intellectualism**.

ANTINOMIANISM a Theology and ethics Belief in the existence of chosen people above moral bonds. Practiced by all tyrants and some intellectuals. **b Philosophy of biology** Disbelief in the existence of biological laws. Falsified by the existence of genetic, embryological, physiological, and other laws. **c Philosophy of social science** Disbelief in the existence of historical laws. Falsified by the existence of such laws as: "All social systems deteriorate unless overhauled from time to time," "No institution discharges exactly the tasks it was originally set up to do," and "The diffusion curve of any cultural novelty is roughly sigmoid."

ANTINOMY A pair of mutually contradictory hypotheses, each of which is confirmed by a different body of knowledge. Example: "Space is infinitely divisible" and "Space is not infinitely divisible." Kant regarded this particular antinomy as insoluble. But the hypothesis of space (and time) quantization is inconsistent with all contemporary physical theories. Indeed, in all of these the space-time manifold is assumed to be continuous. ↑**Scientism** denies the existence of insoluble antinomies.

ANTIPHILOSOPHY The collection of views that, like irrationalism and radical skepticism, deny the possibility or desirability of rational discussion or of knowledge, or that regard philosophizing as a waste of time or as an affliction resulting from language mistakes, hence as curable with a dose of linguistic analysis. ↑**Linguistic philosophy.**

ANTIREALISM The opposite of ↑**realism.** The denial of objective reality, or the mistaking of fiction for fact. Characteristic of ↑**subjective idealism** as well as of schizophrenics.

ANTISCIENCE The belief system openly hostile to science. Examples: alternative medicine, "humanistic" (armchair) psychology and sociology, phenomenology, and existentialism.

ANTITHESIS The negation of a thesis, as in "Irrationalism is the antithesis of rationalism." If two propositions are mutually antithetical, and one of them is true, then its antithesis is false. A key term in Hegelian and Marxist ↑**dialectics,** where theses and antitheses are ↑**reified** and said to interpenetrate and combine into syntheses—a prime example of muddled thinking.

ANY An arbitrary item. To be distinguished from "all," as in the logical truth: What holds for any holds for all (If Fx, then $\forall x\ Fx$).

ANYTHING GOES Believe and do whatever you want. The slogan of ↑**epistemological anarchism.**

ANYTHING IS POSSIBLE This view is often associated with the scientific attitude. Actually scientists hold that certain entities, properties, or events are impossible for violating certain deeply entrenched scientific laws. For example, any scientist will deny that there can be light, chemical reactions, or life inside a compact rock. Likewise, a physiological psychologist will deny the possibility of telepathy or psychokinesis; an anthropologist will deny the possibility that a tribe of gatherer-hunters can design, let alone build, a nuclear reactor; and an economist will deny the possibility of industrialization without natural resources and skilled labor. In each of these cases certain necessary conditions for the existence of some object are not met. The philosophical principle of the universality of the fundamental laws of physics reinforces the case against the view that anything is possible. Indeed, according to the former, it is impossible that in some region of the universe the force of gravity be different from what it is in the known part of the universe, or that a body could reverse its direction of motion without first stopping, or that it could overtake light in the void. The case is further reinforced by the ontological principle of ↑**lawfulness.** Indeed, according to the latter there can be no lawless events, such as miracles: there can only be events that satisfy unknown laws, and even so provided the latter do not violate any of the reasonably well-confirmed law-statements.

APODEICTIC Doubtless. Logically necessary (tautologous). ↑**Necessity a Logic.**

APORIA Conceptual difficulty, perplexity, dilemma, blind alley. In particular, unsolved contradiction between theses that at first sight are equally plausible. Examples: Zeno's paradoxes of motion, Epimenides' Liar paradox, and such dilemmas as atomism v. plenism, individualism v. holism, rationalism v. empiricism, and deontologism v. utilitarianism. ↑**Antinomy**. The radical skeptic takes pleasure in aporias because they seem to make his point. Others see them as challenges, since they can only be solved by further inquiry.

APPEARANCE Fact as perceived or imagined by some animal. **Syn** ↑**phenomenon**. In other words: x is an appearance to y =df y perceives or imagines x. Examples: stellar constellations appear to be systems but are not such; hypocrites appear to be what they are not. Appearances, unlike objective facts, are context-dependent. Hence "appears" is a quaternary relation: In circumstance w, fact x appears to animal y as z. In the philosophical tradition appearance is the opposite of reality. This is mistaken, for an appearance is a process occurring in the nervous system of some animal, hence it is just as much of a fact as an external event. Appearances constitute just facts of a special kind: they occur, so to speak, in the subject/object (or inquirer-external thing) interface. What is true is that, unlike external facts, appearances do not occur by themselves, independently of cognitive subjects. Whereas in business and politics appearance is everything, in science it only raises the problem of its explanation. The philosophical school that holds that only appearances exist or can be known is ↑**phenomenalism**. ↑**Thing in itself**.

APPLIED PHILOSOPHY The motley collection of applications of philosophical ideas to some of the strategy, policy, and decision problems raised by science, technology, and social practice. Examples: environmental and business ethics, legal and political philosophy, bioethics, and the philosophy of education.

APPREHEND Grasp, understand. The word is misleading, because it suggests Plato's ready-made realm of ideas rather than either learning or fresh construction.

APPROACH Way of looking at things or handling them. Manner in which a problem (cognitive, practical, or moral) is tackled. Examples: commonsensical or scientific, down-to-earth or philosophical, sectoral or systemic, prudential or moral, medical or legal. In general, an approach $\mathcal{A}$ may be construed as a body B of background knowledge together with a set P of problems (problematics), a set A of aims, and a set M of methods (methodics): $\mathcal{A} = <B, P, A, M>$. Unlike a ↑**paradigm**, an approach is not committed to any particular hypotheses other than those in B.

APPROACH, PHILOSOPHICAL a Ordinary knowledge Resignation. **b Philosophy** A philosophical approach is general (rather than limited to a few cases), universal (cross-cultural), radical (rather than superficial), global (rather nonsectoral), and critical (nondogmatic).

APPROXIMATION An approximately true proposition is one that is closer to the ↑**truth** than to falsity. For example, the statement that the Earth is spherical is approximately true, and the statement that it is ellipsoidal is an even better approximation to the truth. Another example: 3 is a first approximation to the value of π, 3.1 a second-order approximation, 3.14 a third-order one, and so on. Approximation theory is the branch of mathematics that studies methods of successive approximations to solve problems that, like most nonlinear differential equations, lack closed-form (exact) solutions. In particular, interpolation methods, series expansions, and the calculus of perturbations allow for successive approximations. Likewise, ever more refined experimental techniques yield increasingly true values of ↑**magnitudes**. The pervasiveness of approximation techniques in applied mathematics, science, and technology underlines the importance of the concept of ↑**partial truth**—a concept overlooked by most philosophers.

A PRIORI / A POSTERIORI A priori = prior to or independent of experience. A posteriori = following or dependent upon experience. The mathematical and theological propositions are a priori. A priori ideas are of two kinds: formal (or propositions of reason) and factual (ordinary guesses or scientific hypotheses). Ordinary knowledge, science, and technology blend a priori ideas (hypotheses) with a posteriori ones (data).

APRIORISM The view that the world can be known by either intuition or pure reason, without observation and experiment. Radical ↑**intuitionism** and radical ↑**rationalism** are aprioristic. This is why neither of them has inspired any scientific discoveries or technological designs.

ARBITRARY a Logic and mathematics An arbitrary member of a set, or argument of a function, is an unspecified one. Example: the individual variable x in "x is young," and the predicate variable F in "America is F." **b Praxiology and politology** A capricious decision or action: one that does not abide by any generally recognized rule.

ARGENTINE ROOM A test of creative intelligence. A person is locked up in a room during twenty-four hours, without access to any documents or computers, and is asked to come up with a couple of new nontrivial problems in a field of her choice. The answer is examined by a panel of peers. If they rule that the problem is indeed novel and interesting, the subject is declared to possess an original brain rather than either an imitative or an algorithmic (machinelike) one. Whereas some people will pass this test, no computers will, because they all work to rule, and problem-invention is not subject to rules (or ↑**algorithms**). This test is to be compared with both the ↑**Turing** and the ↑**Chinese room** tests, neither of which sets the task of coming up with new problems.

ARGUMENT a Ordinary language Dispute, debate, controversy. **b Logic** Reasoning (valid or invalid) from premises to conclusion. The only valid arguments are deductive. Logical validity depends exclusively on form. Thus "All melons are virtuous; this is a melon; hence this melon is virtuous" is formally valid. Regardless of their validity, arguments can be fruitful or barren. If invalid yet fruitful, they may be called seductive. Example: a statistical inference of sample to population. Nondeductive arguments depend on their content. Hence the project of building inductive or analogical logics is wrongheaded. The study of nondeductive arguments belongs in cognitive psychology and epistemology, not logic. Analogical and inductive arguments, however fruitful, are logically invalid.

ARGUMENT, FOR THE SAKE OF A proposition is asserted for the sake of argument if the goal is to find out the truth value of its logical consequences.

ARISTOTELIAN In accordance with Aristotle's teachings. Example: Thomism revived and reformed Aristotelianism.

ARROW OF TIME The mistaken idea that time "flows" from past to future. It is often held that irreversible processes, such as heat transfer, the mixing of liquids, aging, and the expansion of the universe, exhibit or even define the arrow of time. This is an unfortunate metaphor, for the "arrow" or directionality in question is inherent in irreversible processes, not in time. If time had an arrow it would be represented, like a force, by a vector; but as a matter of fact the time variable is a scalar. And if time flowed, it would have to move at the speed of one second per second—a meaningless expression. What is true is that the time interval between any two events e and e', relative to the same reference frame f, changes sign when the events are traded. That is, $T(e,e',f) = -T(e',e,f)$. However, this is not a law but a convention useful to distinguish "before" from "after." ↑**Time**.

ART a Aesthetics The transmutation of feelings, images, and ideas into words, figures, sounds, or bodily movements. Artists are expected to give pleasures, to self or others, other than the so-called pleasures of the flesh. The object of ↑**aesthetics**. **b Epistemology** Some products of scientific and technological research are more than valid, true, or efficient: they are also regarded as beautiful (or ugly), and elegant (or clumsy). Moreover, it is generally agreed that scientific research is an art rather than a science. However, there is no consensus on the meanings of these terms. Hence all arguments about aesthetic qualities are inconclusive. ↑**Aesthetics**, ↑**beauty**.

ARTIFACT Man-made object. Examples: Symbols, machines, industrial processes, formal organizations, social movements. Unlike natural entities, artifacts obey ↑**rules** in addition to ↑**laws**.

ARTIFICIAL / NATURAL Artificial = man-made, natural = nonartificial. Obvious examples: computers and stars respectively. Subjectivists, in particular constructivists, tacitly reject this dichotomy: they deny the existence of autonomous nature. But they do not even attempt to explain why, if this is so, the natural sciences do not contain any of the typical notions of social science or technology, such as those of price, policy, and automation. What is true is that all typically human traits and activities are at least partly artificial, for they are invented or learned. Examples: ideation, speech, tool design, computation, romantic love, moral norms, social conventions. Human nature is thus largely artificial. Therefore, with reference to humans, the concepts of state of nature (prior to society) and natural law are only philosophical fantasies. And "natural deduction" is a misnomer, because logic is so unnatural that it did not even exist twenty-five centuries ago.

ARTIFICIAL INTELLIGENCE (AI) The branch of engineering devoted to the design of information processors and robots. Two versions: weak and strong. *Weak* AI assumes that such machines can only mimic some mental processes, namely those that are subject to explicit computation rules (↑**algorithm**). *Strong* AI holds that some digital computers have or can be made to acquire a mind. This belief is mistaken if only because there are plenty of nonalgorithmic (non-rule-directed) cognitive processes, such as concept formation, guessing, and criticism—not to speak of feelings and emotions. Besides, programmed machines are not expected to have initiative, in particular to do things that have not been programmed, such as having original ideas and rebelling. ↑**Cognitive science**.

ARTIFICIAL LIFE (AL) There are currently two research projects: weak and strong AL. The goal of the *weak* (or classical, or wet) AL project is to synthesize cells out of their abiotic components, starting by assembling organelles and making intensive use of biochemistry. This is a scientific project. The *strong* (or dry) AL project is the attempt to mimic some life processes on computers, instead of studying them in vivo. The basic assumption of strong AL is that life is solely characterized by organization: that carbon, water, and things do not matter any more than chemical reactions. This is a project of information technologists.

AS IF Pretense or fiction, as in "Mainstream economic theory assumes that individuals behave as if they maximized their expected utilities." The trademark of ↑**fictionism**.

ASEITY Uncaused, self-caused. Said of God by religionists, and of the universe by naturalists.

ASSERTION To assert a proposition is to state it and affirm that it is true. That is, an assertion is actualy the conjunction of two propositions: *p* and *p* is true. The distinction between stating a proposition and asserting it (as true) helps to understand why a proposition is neither true nor false before being put to the test. Stating a proposition carries no truth commitment. By contrast, asserting it can be legitimately made only either on the strength of proof or strong evidence, or for the sake of argument.

ASSOCIATION a Ontology Objects of all kinds can associate, spontaneously or artificially, to form objects of the same or different kinds. Symbols, concepts, atoms, cells, parts of machines, persons, social systems, and the like, associate to form either aggregates or systems. The resulting object may or may not have ↑**emergent** properties. If it has any, it qualifies as a ↑**system**. **b Mathematics** Any two given attributes of a given object are either mutually independent or associated in some way. If the latter, they are associated with some strength or other. Functional dependence is the strongest. Statistical correlation, a far weaker association, ranges between weak and strong, and it is measured by a number comprised betwen -1 and +1. A strong statistical correlation suggests a functional dependence masked by noise (random fluctuation) of some kind.

ASSOCIATIONISM The eighteenth- and nineteenth-centuries psychological school that held that all mental processes consist in the association of elementary ideas, whence psychology would be a sort of mental chemistry. Behaviorism confirmed this view with regard to simple stimuli, but it failed to account for the emergence of radically new ideas, whether simple or complex, that do not result from putting together two or more simple ideas. For instance, the concepts of chance, mass, electromagnetic field, DNA, and anomie were not arrived at by combining previously known notions. Yet, associationism is back in fashion among the philosophers of mind and evolutionary psychologists who hold that our basic ideas are innate.

ASSOCIATIVITY Property of the combination of symbols and constructs of some kinds. Examples: word concatenation, number addition, and physical juxtaposition. A set S together with a binary associative operation $\oplus$ is called a semigroup. It is defined by the associative law: For all x, y, and z in S, $x \oplus (y \oplus z) = (x \oplus y) \oplus z$. Semigroups are useful in ↑**exact philosophy** because they are qualitative and occur in nearly all domains. Examples: the definitions of ↑**language** and of the ↑**part-whole** relation.

ASSUMPTION ↑ **Premise,** ↑ **hypothesis, posit.** Assumptions need not be known to be true: they can be posited for the sake of argument, that is, to find out their logical consequences and thus evaluate them.

ATHEISM Disbelief in deities. Not to be confused with ↑**agnosticism,** which is merely suspension of belief in the supernatural. Atheism cannot be proved except indirectly. However, it does not call for proof. Indeed, the ↑**burden of proof** of the existence of any X rests on those who claim that X exists. However, the refutation of any particular version of deism or theism constitutes an indirect partial proof of atheism. Indirect because, in ordinary logic, refuting a proposition p amounts to proving not-p. And the refutation is partial because it concerns only a particular kind of deism or theism at a time. Thus a refutation of the tenets of any of the Christian religions does not refute those of Hinduism or conversely. The refutation of any belief in deities of a certain kind may proceed in two ways: empirically and rationally. The former consists in pointing to (a) the lack of positive evidence for religion; and (b) the abundance of evidence contrary to the predictions of religionists—e.g., that lightning will strike the blasphemer. The rational method consists in noting contradictions among religious dogmas. For example, if God is both omnipotent and good, why does he tolerate congenital diseases and war? If God is both omnipotent and omniscient, why has he created species condemned to extinction? Atheism is supported by modern science and technology in several ways. Indeed, modern science and technology involve no supernatural entities, and deny the possibility of miracles. Consequently scientific research, which is largely the search for objective pattern, is hindered by deism and theism. Examples of research on problems actively discouraged by organized religion: nature and origins of life, mind, and religion.

ATOM a Logic Atomic formula = formula that contains no logical functors ("not," "or," "and," "if . . . then"). Example: "0 is a number." **b Semantics** Unit of meaning. ↑**Concept,** ↑**proposition.** Example: "object." **c Ontology** Unit of being, or indivisible thing. Example: ↑**elementary** particles such as electrons.

ATOMISM Any view that objects of some kind are either indivisible or aggregates or combinations of indivisibles (individuals, atoms). The ontology underlying radical ↑**individualism**. Ancient Greek and Indian atomism was perhaps the earliest naturalist and nonanthropomorphic worldview. It was also the most comprehensive and rational one, for it purported to understand everything concrete, whether physical, chemical, biological, or social, without invoking any supernatural and therefore unintelligible forces. Admittedly, ancient atomism was qualitative and totally speculative. It became quantitative and testable only after the work of Dalton, Avogadro, and Cannizzaro in chemistry, and Boltzmann in physics. But it was not until the beginning of the twentieth century that the atomic hypothesis was experimentally confirmed and incorporated into full-fledged theories. ↑**Quantum mechanics**. However, this was somewhat of a Pyrrhic victory, for atoms proved to be divisible after all. Still, according to modern physics there are indivisible material things, such as quarks, electrons, and photons. Even so, the current view of the basic bricks of the universe is different from that of ancient atomism. Indeed, according to quantum physics the elementary "particles" are not pellets but rather fuzzy entities. Moreover, they interact mainly through fields, which are not corpuscular. So, without fields atoms would neither exist nor combine. As well, there is no total vacuum: even in places where there are neither "particles" nor field quanta, there is a fluctuating electromagnetic field that can act on any incoming piece of matter. "Empty" space is thus never totally empty, and it has physical properties such as polarization. ↑**Plenism**, defended by Aristotle and Descartes, has thus been vindicated by modern physics as much as atomism. Atomism spilled over into other sciences. For example, biologists found that the cell is the atom or unit of life. The associationist psychologists, from Berkeley to Mill to Wundt, were atomists in positing that all mental processes are combinations of simple sensations or ideas. For a time there was even talk of mental chemistry. Atomism has been somewhat more successful in social studies. For example, Adam Smith modeled the economy as the aggregate of producers and consumers acting independently from one another. All contemporary ↑**rational-choice** theories are atomistic. Indeed, they all claim to explain social facts in a bottom-up fashion, i.e., starting from individual valuations, decisions, and actions. Finally, atomism is strong in moral philosophy. Witness Kantianism, utilitarianism, contractarianism, and libertarianism: all of them start from the fiction of the totally free or autonomous individual. There are, then, physical, biological, and social atoms, but none of these is isolated. Every single entity except for the universe as a whole is a component of some ↑**system**. The free electron or photon, the isolated cell, and the isolated person are idealizations, ↑**ideal types**, or fictions. Still, the connections among things are not always as strong as assumed by ↑**holism**. If they were, the cosmos could not be analyzed and science would be impossible, for we would have to know the whole in order to know every single part of it—as Pascal realized. Though very potent, atomism is limited. For example, not even ↑**quantum mechanics** can dispense with macro-objects when describing micro-objects. Indeed, any well-posed problem in quantum mechanics involves a description of the boundary conditions which constitute an idealized representation of the macrophysical environment of the thing of interest. The importance of the environment is, if anything, even more obvious in social matters. For example, an individual's actions are unintelligible except when placed in the physical environment and the social systems he is a part of. What holds for social science holds, a fortiori, for moral philosophy. In this field atomism is radically false, for every moral problem arises from our living in society and being able to engage in either prosocial or antisocial behavior. But, since there is some truth to atomism, as well as to holism, we need a sort of synthesis of the two whereby both are transformed. This synthesis is ↑**systemism**.

ATTRIBUTE a Ordinary language Synonym of property. **b Philosophy** Predicate, i.e., function from individuals of some kind to propositions, as in Hot: Bodies → All the propositions containing "hot." The generalization to higher-order attributes is immediate: ↑**Predicate**.

AUTHORITARIANISM Submission to authority, hence proscription of criticism and protest in epistemic, educational, moral, economic, or political matters. A component of all undemocratic ideologies and political regimes, as well as of traditional teaching methods. It also occurs in ↑**intuitionism** and in school philosophies.

AUTHORITY Legitimate power. Two kinds of power are of interest with reference to scholarly communities: intellectual and moral. A person exerts **intellectual authority** in a research team or a field of study if his or her intellectual superiority in the matter is acknowledged in the group, regardless of any legal or moral authority. And anyone acting with unselfish motives and consistent integrity enjoys **moral authority**. The two kinds of authority are mutually independent: eminent researchers may be morally slack, whereas moral role-models may be intellectually mediocre. Scientific communities are classless, but they have a status structure in that their leaders are freely recognized as the most intelligent, insightful, or productive of the group: their authority derives entirely from their "nose" for good problems and originality, and their ability to attract coworkers and train students.

AUTONOMY/ HETERONOMY a Ontology and science Autonomous = independent, self-determined, self-governing. Heteronomous = dependent, other-determined, other-governed. A system is the more autonomous, the more stable against external disturbances. Such stability or homeostasis is achieved through self-regulation mechanisms. **b Praxiology and ethics** The injunction to behave as autonomous beings is laudable but not fully viable because no one is totally self-sufficient and free from social burdens. Real human beings are partially autonomous in some respects and partially heteronomous in others. Not even autocrats can do everything they would like to, and not even slaves are totally deprived of initiative.

AXIOLOGY ↑ Value theory.

AXIOM Explicit assumption. In a theory, initial and therefore unprovable hypothesis. **Syn** ↑**postulate**. In ancient philosophy and ordinary language, "axiomatic" amounts to "self-evident." The contemporary concept of an axiom does not involve the idea that it is a self-evident or intuitive proposition. In fact, the axioms (postulates) of most scientific theories are highly counterintuitive. Nor is it required that they be true. Thus, the axioms of an abstract (uninterpreted) mathematical theory are neither true nor false, and those of a factual theory may be partially true or even just plausible. Axioms are not provable but they are justifiable by their consequences. ↑**Axiomatics**.

AXIOMATICS Any reasonably clear ↑**theory** can be axiomatized, that is, organized in the axiom-definition-theorem format. Since axiomatization concerns not content but architecture or organization, it can be carried out in all fields of inquiry, from mathematics and factual science to philosophy. The main points of axiomatics are rigor and systemicity. Rigor, because it requires exhibiting the underlying logic as well as presuppositions, and distinguishing defined from undefinable, and deduced from assumed. And systemicity (hence avoidance of irrelevancy) because all the predicates are required to be ↑**coreferential**, and because all the statements "hang together" by virtue of the implication relation. Contrary to widespread opinion, axiomatization does not bring rigidity. On the contrary, by exhibiting the assumptions explicitly and orderly, axiomatics facilitates correction and deepening. Moreover, in principle any given axiomatization can be replaced with a more precise or a deeper one. It is often stated that ↑**Gödel's incompleteness theorem** dashed Hilbert's optimism concerning the scope of axiomatics. Actually all the theorem did was to prove that there can be no perfect (complete) axiomatic system. It did not prove that more inclusive systems are impossible. Example of an axiomatic system: the socioeconomics of the arms race. Axiom 1: The sum of civilian and military investments is constant. Axiom 2: The rate of technological innovation is an increasing function of investment in R&D. Axiom 3: Commercial competitiveness is an increasing function of technological innovation. Axiom 4: The standard of living is an increasing function of civilian investment. Some consequences follow. Theorem 1: The greater the military expenditures, the smaller the civilian ones (from Axiom 1). Theorem 2: As civilian investment decreases relative to military investment, the rate of technological innovation declines (from Axiom 2 and Theorem 1). Theorem 3: Commercial competitiveness declines with increasing military expenditures (from Axiom 3 and Theorem 2). Theorem 4: The standard of living declines with increasing military expenditures (from Axioms 1 and 4).

B TEST A test of the worth of a philosophy. According to it, a good philosophy is (a) clear and internally consistent; (b) compatible with the bulk of the knowledge of its time; (c) helpful in identifying new interesting philosophical problems; (d) instrumental in evaluating philosophical ideas; (d) helpful in clarifying and systematizing key philosophical concepts; (e) instrumental in advancing research both in and out of philosophy; (f) capable of participating competently, and sometimes constructively, in some of the scientific, moral, or political controversies of its day; (g) helpful in identifying bunk; and (h) characterized by a low word-to-thought ratio. Aristotle would have passed the B test with flying colors in his time. By contrast, Hume's empiricism, Hegel's idealism, Nietzsche's vitalism, Bergson's intuitionism, Husserl's phenomenology, and Heidegger's existentialism flunk the B test.

BABBLE Platitudinous, enigmatic, or incoherent talk. Examples: psychobabble (pop psychology), sociobabble (pop sociology), ↑**existentialism**, and much contemporary literary "theory," in particular deconstructionism. ↑**Gobbledygook.**

BACKGROUND OF A RESEARCH FIELD The body of knowledge used, and taken for granted until new notice, in an inquiry. ↑**Antecedent knowledge.** Some philosophers, such as Bacon, Descartes, and Husserl, recommended that nothing be presupposed when initiating an inquiry. But this is impossible, because every inquiry is triggered by some problem, which is discovered in the pertinent background knowledge. Moreover, problems cannot even be stated, let alone examined, in a knowledge vacuum: there are no absolute beginnings in research. A correct methodological maxim is not to ignore the background knowledge but to reexamine and repair some of its components whenever they look defective. Another is to keep an ↑**open mind**—never an empty one.

BACONIAN In accordance with Francis Bacon's epistemology. This was ↑**empiricist**, in particular ↑**inductivist.** Consequently, it cannot account for nonobservational concepts and generalizations, such as those occurring in dynamics and history.

BAROQUE PHILOSOPHY Rhetorical (empty and convoluted) form of philosophizing that specializes in ↑**miniproblems** and ↑**pseudoproblems.**

BASIC a Logic *Basic concept:* undefined (or primitive) concept in a given context. *Basic assumption*: unproved premise (↑**axiom**, postulate) in a given context. What is basic in one context may be derived in an alternative one. **b Epistemology** Sense datum, description of perceived item, or protocol statement. Only empiricists, in particular logical positivists, regard such statements as basic, or constitutive of the "empirical basis of science." Working scientists check data, and they value general and deep hypotheses as much as, or even more so than, well-confirmed but narrow or shallow theories. **c Ontology** Elementary (indivisible) thing or constituent of things. Examples: electrons, quarks, and photons. Warning 1: Whether things of a given kind are actually basic, or only undivided until now, is for empirical research to determine. Warning 2: "Basic" is not the same as "simple." Indeed, basic things, such as electrons, have a rather complex behavior, whence they are described by extremely complex theories such as relativistic ↑**quantum mechanics.**

BASIS Premises of an argument or evidence in support of a hypothesis. **Syn** ground.

BAYESIANISM School that upholds the subjective interpretation of ↑**probability** as credence or degree of certainty. **Syn personalism.**The gist of Bayesianism is the interpretation of the arguments occurring in the probability functions as propositions and, in particular, hypotheses and data, and of the probabilities themselves as credences (degrees of credibility or certainty). This interpretation is untenable because (a) the mathematical formalism does not contain variables interpretable as persons; (b) the concept of credibility is neither mathematical nor methodological, but psychological; (c) even assuming that they are meaningful, the prior probability $P(h)$ of a hypothesis and its posterior probability $P(h|e)$ are unknowable; and (d) no list of hypotheses compatible with a given body of data can be exhaustive and mutually exclusive, so that the sum taken over all of them equals unity—as required by the definition of a probability function. ↑**Academic industry,** ↑**alchemy, epistemic,** ↑**Bayes's theorem,** ↑**probability paradoxes b,** ↑**probability, subjective.**

BAYES'S THEOREM The theorem that relates the conditional probabilities $P(A|B)$ and $P(B|A)$. In mainstream probability theory and statistics, the arguments A and B denote either arbitrary sets or facts (states or events). The interpretation of A and B as propositions (in particular hypotheses and data) is fraught with paradox. ↑**Bayesianism, probability paradoxes.**

BEAUTY What everyone seeks and enjoys but nobody seems to know. Axiological absolutists regard beauty as objective and cross-cultural, whereas subjectivists declare it to lie in the eyes of the beholder, hence relative to subject and culture. Presumably, this question can be settled only by anthropology and experimental ↑**aesthetics.**

BECOMING Change, process. The central concept in any processual ontology, just as that of being, is pivotal to any static ontology. ↑**Processualism.** However, becoming and being are not mutually exclusive, for to be ↑**material** is to be able to change.

BEGGING THE QUESTION Fallacy consisting in assuming what is to be proved. Examples: Bodies cannot think because they are physical things; markets cannot lie because they are always in or near equilibrium. **Syn** ↑*petitio principii.*

BEHAVIORISM The psychological school that studies only overt behavior. **Syn** S-R (stimulus-response) psychology. Two varieties: methodological and ontological. The former does not deny the occurrence of mental processes but decrees that they are not scientifically studiable. By contrast, ontological behaviorism denies the reality of the mental. Obviously, the second entails the first. What makes behaviorism philosophically interesting is that it was inspired by empiricism. However, the empty-organism and mindless approach to psychology is now all but dead. Its main legacies are experimental rigor, behavior therapy, and distrust of empty talk about the soul. Its contemporary successor is ↑**functionalism**.

BEING a Individual existent, as in "human being." **Syn** ↑**entity**. **b** ↑**Existence**, as in "There are stones" (factual existence) and "There exist irrational numbers" (formal existence).

BELIEF A state of mind, or mental process, consisting in giving assent to a proposition or a set of propositions. These are accepted for being regarded as true, practical, or moral. Thus, the concept of belief is a ternary predicate: x believes y on ground z [authority, evidence, etc.]. In everyday matters belief is often independent of truth. In mathematics, science, technology, and philosophy proper, one believes only what can be proved either conclusively or plausibly, or what entails true propositions. In other domains, particularly religion and politics, most people believe uncritically what they have been taught: they rarely bother to find out whether it is true or efficient. Belief is thus a psychological category, not a semantic or epistemological one. However, this is not to belittle the importance of justifiable (well-grounded) belief in all fields of knowledge and action. For example, researchers believe that it is worthwhile to redo certain observations or to put certain hunches to the test; and citizens will mobilize only if they believe that their interests are at stake, or are made to believe certain slogans. ↑**Justification**.

BELIEF SYSTEM The collection of beliefs held at a given time by an individual or shared by the members of a social group. Such beliefs are more or less strongly held, some of them change over time, and they constitute a system—though not necessarily a consistent one.

BENEVOLENCE Disposition to do good. **Ant** malevolence. Benevolence can be spontaneous or calculated (rational). Either is necessary for coexistence.

BEPC SKETCH The view that society is a supersystem composed of four coupled subsystems: the biological (B), economic (E), political (P), and cultural (C). A ↑**systemist** alternative to both ↑**individualism** and ↑**holism**. A practical consequence of it is that authentic and sustainable social development is at once biological, economic, political, and cultural.

BICONDITIONAL A proposition of the form "If p then q and conversely." That is, $p \Leftrightarrow q =_{df} (p \Rightarrow q)$ & $(q \Rightarrow p)$. Standard abbreviations: $p \equiv q$, p iff q. A biconditional is true iff both constituents are either true or false in the same degree.

BIG BANG The hypothesis of the start of the expansion of the universe. Not to be con-fused with the beginning of the universe, much less with its divine creation. Physics makes no room for an absolute and unique beginning, since any value of the time vari-able is arbitrary: the laws of physics are not dated.

BIG QUESTIONS Important and long-lasting questions, some of which are asked by philosophers, scientists, and religionists, who treat them differently and seldom answer in the same way. Examples: What is time, and does it exist by itself? What is chance, and is it any different from ignorance of the real causes? Did the universe have an ori-gin, and will it have an end, or is it eternal? How did life originate: by divine fiat or from prebiotic matter, and if so how? What is mind: immaterial stuff or brain process? Does God exist or is it a fiction? Some of these questions constitute the partial over-lap between science and religion. ↑**Double-truth doctrine**.

BIOETHICS The branch of ↑**ethics** that investigates the moral problems raised by med-icine, biotechnology, social medicine, and normative demography. Sample of prob-lematics: whether a person begins at birth or at conception; the moral legitimacy of the death penalty, assisted suicide, and human cloning; and the right to patent genes. The bulk of current bioethics focuses on problems concerning individuals, such as surro-gate motherhood and the right to decline medical treatment. It neglects the problem-atics of social medicine and public-health policies, such as restrictions on reproduc-tive freedom, universal health care, the disease-poverty connection, the insufficient funding of public-health care, and the private appropriation of biological knowledge. Some bioethical problems belong also in ↑**environmental ethics**,↑**nomoethics**, or ↑**technoethics**. Examples: the status of the right to reproduce in an overpopulated world; the risks of letting loose genetically engineered organisms; and the duty to pro-tect the environment. Bioethics is one of the most active fields of contemporary phi-losophy, and the battleground among all the major moral philosophies. However, among caregivers and public health-care managers, a consensus is emerging around ↑**principlism**.

BIOLOGISM The program of reducing all the social sciences to biology, in particular genetics and evolutionary biology. The gist of human sociobiology. The program can-not be carried through because (a) one and the same group of people can organize it-self into different social systems; (b) the laws of nature constrain but do not entail so-cial conventions; and (c) social change need not have biological motivations. Still, sociobiology has had the merit of reminding social scientists that people are not just bundles of intentions, values, and norms: that they have biological needs and drives, and are subject to evolution. ↑**Evolutionary psychology**.

BIOLOGY a Science The scientific study of living beings present and past. Like all fac-tual sciences, biology is at once theoretical and empirical. Since the inception of evo-lutionary ideas, biology has been a historical science along with cosmology, geology, and historiography. ↑**Evolution**. **b Philosophy of** The philosophical investigation of problems raised by biological research, such as those of the peculiarities of organisms, the nature of biospecies, the scope of teleology, the structure of evolutionary theory, the possibility of reducing biology to physics and chemistry, the prospects of ↑**artificial life**, and the relations between ethics and biology.

BIOSOCIAL SCIENCES Sciences that study the links between biological and social features. Examples: anthropology, social psychology, human geography, demography, biosociology (as different from sociobiology). The very existence of such hybrids falsifies the Kantian and ↑**hermeneutic** dogma of the dichotomy between the natural and the social sciences.

BIVALENCE The principle that every proposition is either true or false. Not to be confused with the law of ↑**excluded middle**. The latter is not a law in intuitionistic logic, which abides by bivalence. Obviously, bivalence does not hold in ↑**many-valued** logics. Moreover, classical logic is consistent with any number of theories that admit more than two truth values, as well as with those that admit propositions with no truth value. ↑**Truth-gap theory**, ↑**partial truth-value**.

BLACK BOX Input-output ↑**schema**: ↑**model** or ↑**theory** of a thing that focuses on what it does, while disregarding its "works" or mechanism. **Syn** ↑**functional** or ↑**phenomenological** model or theory. Examples: classical thermodynamics, behaviorist learning theory, computationist psychology, and descriptive sociology. Black boxes are necessary but insufficient, for they do not supply ↑**explanations** proper. ↑**Mechanism**.

BLACK-BOXISM The philosophical prescription that the innards (stuff and structure) of things should not be exposed, much less conjectured. **Syn** ↑**descriptionism**, ↑**functionalism**. Philosophical underpinning: ↑**positivism**, ↑**phenomenalism**.

BLAME A central concept in legal theory and practice, deontological ethics, religion, and politics. It is peripheral in humanist ethics, which emphasizes personal responsibility and rehabilitation rather than guilt and punishment. Apportioning blame is a favorite occupation of the bad losers and the self-righteous.

BODY a Science and ontology Macrophysical thing endowed with mass. Examples: grains of sands, planets, cells, and forests. ↑**Idealism** conceives of concrete things as embodiments of ideas, and places the human body under the mind. ↑**Materialism** regards mental functions as processes in the brain. Since the latter is part of the body, the mental turns out to be bodily. Thus the idealist (and theological) contrast between body and mind disappears. ↑**Mind-body problem. b Epistemology and semantics** A body of knowledge is a set of more or less closely related ideas, intermediate between a random collection and a system. Examples: the background knowledge of a discipline, the legal corpus of a society.

BOND or LINK Two things are bonded, linked, or coupled, if there is a relation between them that makes a difference to them. Examples: physical force, chemical bond, friendship, business relation. Relations may then be divided into *bonding* and *nonbonding*. The spatiotemporal relations are nonbonding. However, they may render bonds possible or impossible. Examples: proximity, betweenness, and temporal succession.

BOOLEAN ALGEBRA An ↑**abstract** mathematical system described by the corresponding abstract theory. The system $\beta = \langle S, \cup, \cap, ', 0, 1 \rangle$ is a Boolean algebra if S is a set, $\cup$ (union or join) and $\cap$ (intersection or meet) are binary operations in S, ' is a unary operation in S, and 0 and 1 are distinct members of S, such that each operation is associative and commutative, and distributes over the other, and, for all a in S, $a \cup 0 = a$, $a \cap 1 = a$, $a \cup a' = 1$, $a \cap a' = 0$. Boolean algebras are of interest to philosophy on several counts: (a) they are abstract, hence they can be interpreted in an unlimited number of ways: i.e., they have any number of ↑**models**; (b) the propositional calculus is a model (example) of a Boolean algebra; and (c) if t is a theorem in the theory of Boolean algebras, then its dual too is a theorem, where the dual of t is obtained by exchanging $\cup$ for $\cap$, and 0 for 1—which constitutes a ↑ **metatheorem**.

BOTTOM-UP / TOP-DOWN Two research strategies used to tackle multilevel systems. A bottom-up or synthetic study moves upward from the lower-level components, attempting to assemble a system from them, and a macroprocess from lower-level processes. Its dual is the top-down or analytic study, that decomposes a system or a process into its lower-level components. The two strategies are mutually complementary rather than mutually exclusive. For example, the proper study of memory, perception, imagery, and other mental processes is conducted on both the macro- or phenomenological level, and its lower-level components. Thus, the study of memory leads to inquiring into its neural mechanisms, which in turn poses the problem of finding the molecules that facilitate and those that inhibit the consolidation of memories. Again, the study of social cohesion and disintegration leads to inquiries into individual actions, which are in turn stimulated or constrained by institutions.

BOUDON-COLEMAN DIAGRAM Diagram linking macro- to microprocesses, and thus contribute to explaining both. Example:

Macro-level	Raise in employment rate → Stock-market fall
	↓ ↑
Micro-level	Fear of inflation → Shareholders' panic

BRAIN The control center of behavior and the organ of the mind. The human brain is likely to be the most complex and intriguing thing in the world. It is investigated by neuroscience and cognitive psychology, but ignored by behaviorists, psychoanalysts, and traditional philosophers of mind.

BRAIN / MIND An unnecessary hybrid in the same bag as "leg / walk." A more reasonable expression would be "the minding brain."

BREADTH / DEPTH Breadth (or ↑**coverage**) and ↑**depth** are usually regarded as being inversely related. However, depth is often attained only through ↑**cross-disciplinarity**. And one of the merits of a philosophical approach is that it combines previously disconnected items.

BREAKTHROUGH A radically new discovery or invention. Examples: the inventions of the microscope, the atomic hypothesis, and mathematical proof. An epistemic ↑**revo-lution**, such as the seventeenth-century Scientific Revolution, is a bundle (system) of epistemic breakthroughs in a number of research fields—never in all.

BURDEN OF PROOF Whoever proffers a conjecture, norm, or method has the moral obligation to justify it. For example, whoever advances a nonbiological account of the mental, or a biological account of the social, has the duty to exhibit evidence for it. By contrast, scientists and technologists are in no obligation to check the wild fantasies of pseudoscientists: they have enough work of their own. Likewise, detectives have no obligation to disproof claims to alien abduction; biomedical researchers do not have the duty to check every alleged case of faith healing; and engineers do not have the duty to examine every new design of a perpetual motion machine. **Syn** ↑*onus probandi.*

BUSINESS ETHICS Ethics applied to business transactions. Example of problems: Is honesty always good business, as Ben Franklin claimed? Is the market a school of morality, as the free-marketeers maintain? Is it moral to market whatever can sell, regardless of its noxious effects? Is it right to patent genes, by contrast to GMOs (genetically modified organisms)? Is it moral to market GMOs without a license based on tests? Is it morally justified to privatize such public services as jails and the water supply? Is it moral to lend money to oppressive and corrupt governments? In general, which are the moral limits to the market forces, and who is to set them?

CALCULUS a In logic, a theory of deductive reasoning, such as the propositional and the predicate calculi. **b** In mathematics, a theory involving one or more ↑**algorithms**, such as the infinitesimal (differential and integral) calculus.

CARDINAL / ORDINAL Cardinality of a set = numerosity of its membership. Cardinal magnitude (or "scale"): one with numerical values. Examples: length, age, population. Ordinal magnitude: one whose degrees can be ordered as to more or less, but not assigned numerical values. Examples: awareness, subjective utility, plausibility, aesthetic satisfaction.

CARTESIAN PRODUCT The cartesian product of two sets equals the set whose members are the ordered pairs of members of the given sets: $A \times B = \{<a,b> \mid a \in A \& b \in B\}$. If A and B are intervals of the real line, $A \times B$ can be visualized as the rectangle of base A and height B. Clearly, $A \times B \neq B \times A$. The cartesian product of n sets is the set whose members are the ↑**ordered n-tuples** of members of the given sets. The main interest of the cartesian product to philosophy is that it occurs in the standard definition of the concepts of ↑**relation** and ↑**function**, which in turn occur in the definition of plenty of philosophical concepts, such as those of ↑**predicate**, ↑**extension**, and ↑**reference**.

CASUISTRY a Ordinary language Sophistry. **b Ethics** The opinion that there are no universal moral norms, hence every case must be judged on its own merits. **Syn** case-based moral reasoning.

CATEGORICAL IMPERATIVE Kant's principle that all rules of conduct should be universalizable, i.e., applicable to everyone. Contrary to popular belief, and Kant's own, this is not a moral maxim but a ↑**metaethical** principle, hence a metarule. The principle is a pillar of ↑**humanism** and democratic political philosophy. To reject it is to condone the practice of having one morality for the rulers and another for the ruled. But Kant's claim, that the principle is a priori and rational, is false. If it were, it would have been formulated at least three millennia earlier, when rational thinking emerged.

CATEGORIZATION The grouping of items into ↑**categories** or kinds, such as "alive," "food," "friendly," and "abstract," regardless of the peculiarities of the individual members. A basic mode of cognition of higher animals.

CATEGORY a Philosophy An extremely broad concept. Examples: construct, abstract, change, existence, kind, generality, law, matter, meaning, mental, social, space, system, thing, time. **b Mathematics** A construct consisting of objects and arrows (mappings) between them satisfying certain axioms. For example, sets and functions constitute a category. Other examples arise in specific branches of mathematics. Category theory provides an alternative and deeper foundation for mathematics than does set theory.

CATEGORY MISTAKE Presentation of an object of a certain kind as belonging to another. Examples: confusing free will with predictability; speaking of "collective memory" and "the meaning of an action"; conflating constructs (such as propositions) with linguistic expressions (such as sentences); and confusing objective patterns with their conceptualizations (law statements).

CAUSA CESSANTE, CESSAT EFFECTUS If the cause ceases, so does its effect. A central maxim of the Aristotelian theory of change. It holds only for chemical reactions: they cease when the supply of reagents stops. But it fails in most other cases, in particular for the motion of bodies and photons, since they keep moving until stopped by something else, without anything pushing them. ↑**Inertia**.

CAUSAL ANALYSIS Analysis of two or more events to find out whether they are causally related. Two main types: qualitative and functional. If the events are given only global descriptions, such as "the patient responded favorably to the treatment," one starts by setting up a ↑**two-by-two** experimental or statistical design such as

$$CE \quad C\bar{E}$$
$$\bar{C}E \quad \bar{C}\bar{E}$$

where C and E name the events in question, whereas $\bar{C}$ and $\bar{E}$ stand for the nonoccurrence of C and E respectively. C will be said to be a cause of E if the entries in the main diagonal are occupied whereas the remaining entries are empty. A statistical analysis will yield a numerical value for the C-E correlation. If this value is high, a causal relation is likely to obtain, but must still be established by wiggling C and E in a controlled (experimental) fashion. The ideal case is that where C and E are not coarse dichotomic (yes-no) variables, but numerical variables related by a function of the form $y = f(x)$. In this case, the events will be changes (increments or decrements) in x and y. These changes will be approximately related by $\Delta y = f'(x) \cdot \Delta x$, where $f'(x)$ is the value of the slope of the graph of f at x. Note that this is a factual (or empirical) interpretation of the mathematical formula in question. And the relation will be causal if the formula (as interpreted) is empirically corroborated. The so-called counterfactual analysis of causation, favored by the ↑**plurality of worlds** metaphysicians, is utterly different from the above standard analyses in science. Indeed, it is roughly the following: If C had not occurred, E would not have occurred either. This is just the translation, to the subjunctive mode, of the indicative C E that occurs in the two-by-two matrix above. Moreover, it does not help the causal analysis of functional relations.

CAUSALISM The ontological thesis according to which ↑**causation** is the only mode of becoming. Falsified by radioactivity, the spontaneous discharge of neurons, and ↑**self-assembly**. ↑**Determinism**.

CAUSATION. An ↑**event** (change of state) c is said to be *the* cause of another event e if and only if c is sufficient for that of e. Example: the Earth's spinning is the cause of the alternation of days and nights. If on the other hand c can happen without the occurrence of e—i.e., if c is necessary but not sufficient for e— then c is said to be *a* cause of e. Example: HIV infection is a cause of AIDS. A necessary but insufficient cause is called a *contributory* cause. Most if not all social events have multiple contributory causes. Another important distinction is that between linear and nonlinear causal relations. A *linear* causal relation is one where the size of the effect is commensurate to that of the cause. Example: the flow of water that moves an alternator, which in turn generates electricity. In a *nonlinear* causal relation, the size of the effect is many times that of the cause. Example: giving an order to fire a gun or an employee. The first is a case of energy transfer, the second one of triggering. The causal relation (or nexus) holds exclusively between events. Hence, to say that a thing causes another, or that it causes a process (as when the brain is said to cause the mind), involves misusing the word 'cause'. Empiricists have always mistrusted the concept of causation because the causal relation is imperceptible. In fact, at best a cause and its effect can be perceived, but their relation must be guessed. This is why empiricists have proposed replacing causation with constant conjunction (Hume) or with function (Mach). But constant conjunction or concomitance can occur without causation. And a functional relation, being purely mathematical, has no ontological commitment; besides, most functions can be inverted, which is not the case with most causal relations; furthermore, if the independent variable in a functional relation is time, a causal interpretation of it is out of the question, because instants are not events. Although causal relations are imperceptible, they can be checked experimentally by wiggling the cause. For example, the hypothesis that electric currents generate magnetic fields is confirmed by varying the current intensity and measuring the intensity of the magnetic field. Caution: only events or processes can be causally related. Hence it is just as mistaken to assert that the brain causes the mind as it is to say that the legs cause the walking. The correct statement of the psychoneural identity thesis is that all mental processes are brain processes, and that some of them can cause other processes in the brain or in another part of the body, as when a sudden emotion stops a train of thought.

CAUSE / EFFECT The terms of the causal relation. ↑**Causation**.

CAVE, PLATO'S Plato claimed that the inquiring subject is like a prisoner chained in a cave, who can only see the flitting and ambiguous shadows cast by the things outside. A metaphor intended to convey the idea that our knowledge of the external world, unlike that of ideas, is necessarily superficial and uncertain. This idea has been falsified by modern science and technology. For example, we know the chemistry of the fire in Plato's cave, as well as the optics of the light it gives out.

CERTAINTY Certainty is the state of mind or mental process that involves no wavering. It is a desirable state as long as it is not regarded as final. **Ant** ↑**doubt**. Like doubt, certainty is a psychological category, not an epistemological one: all certainty is certainty of someone about something. In fact, an inquirer may be certain about a falsity and uncertain about a truth. Moreover, certainty comes in degrees. However, the attempt to equate degree of certainty with ↑**probability** is misguided, because changes in certainty are not known to be chance events: most of them result from learning. ↑**Uncertainty**.

CESM MODEL The ↑**sketch** of a ↑**system** as the ordered quadruple $\mathcal{M}$ = < Composition, Environment, Structure, Mechanism(s)>. Example: a manufacturing plant is composed of workers, engineers, and managers; its environment is a market; it is held together by contracts and relations of communication and command; and its mechanisms are those of manufacturing, trading, borrowing, and marketing. If the mechanism of a system is either unknown or ignorable, the mechanismic CESM sketch reduces to a ↑**functional** CES sketch.

CETERIS PARIBUS Other things being equal, or the other variables being ignored or held constant. A common simplifying condition or assumption in all disciplines, from mathematics to medicine. Examples: the concepts of partial derivative and of isolation in some respect (e.g., thermal). However, it is often wrongly held that the ceteris paribus condition is typical of the social sciences.

CHAIN (OR LADDER) OF BEING The Neoplatonic worldview that ranked all beings, real or imaginary, in a hierarchy from higher to lower. Contemporary secular version: the ↑**level** structure of reality, or ordering of levels of organization. Unlike the chain of being, whose order relations are those of closeness to God and domination (or subordination), the collection of levels of organization is ordered by the relation "emerges from" or "evolves from." Besides, it does not include immaterial objects such as souls and supernatural entities.

CHANCE There are essentially two concepts of chance: the traditional or epistemological one, and the ontological or modern one. **a Epistemological** Chance = unpredictable, unanticipated, or uncertain. Examples: the accidental collision of two cars, and the accidental stumbling on a fact of a previously unknown kind. Presumably, an omniscient being would not need this concept. Mechanism has no use for it either. Recall Laplace's thesis: If we knew all the causes, and all the antecedent conditions, we would be able to predict the entire future. Hence the epistemological concept of chance is but a name for ignorance. **b Ontological**. Chance event = event belonging to a random sequence, i.e., one every member of which has a definite ↑**probability**. Examples: radioactive decay, random shuffling of a pack of cards, random choice of a number, random mating of insects. Ontological chance is objective: random events have definite ↑**propensities** independent of the knowing subject. These objective propensities have nothing to do with uncertainty, which is a state of mind. We may be uncertain about an objective probability value, but the latter is a property of real states or changes of state (events). Moreover, these are objective properties of individuals, not of collectives. For example, an atom in an excited state has a definite probability of emitting a photon within the next second. Consequently, different atoms of the same kind, all in the same excited state, will decay at different times. By virtue of the probability law those times will not be scattered wildly but will fit a pattern. Thus ontological chance, far from being the same as indeterminacy, is a type of lawfulness or determination. In other words, there are laws of chance. Related but different concept: ↑**accident**.

CHANGE Any alteration or variation in one or more properties of a thing. The peculiarity of ↑**material objects**. *Quantitative* change = change in the value of one or more properties. Examples: motion, accretion, population increase. *Qualitative* change = the ↑**emergence** or submergence of one or more properties of a thing. Examples: "creation" and "annihilation" of electron pairs; transmutation of atomic nuclei; chemical combinations and dissociations; birth and death of organisms; structural changes in social systems. *Evolutionary change* = the emergence of a whole new kind (species) or of things. Examples: formation of new biospecies and of new institutions. Ontological principle: Every change causes some other change(s).

CHAOS a Traditional or nontechnical concept: Chaotic = lawless. Example: The things in a municipal garbage dump are scattered chaotically. **b Contemporary** or technical concept: Chaotic = fitting a pattern represented by a nonlinear finite difference of differential equation of a certain type. Best-known example: the logistic equation $x_n = kx_n(1 - x_n)$. As the value of the parameter (or "knob variable") k takes certain values, the solution x_n changes abruptly. Since these processes are perfectly lawful, the word 'chaotic' is inappropriate. Moreover, it is misleading, for it has suggested to many a nonmathematical author that any apparently disorderly process, such as political turbulence, must fit chaos theory.

CHARLACANISM The literary genre introduced by the French psychoanalyst Jacques Lacan, who admitted that psychoanalysis is not a science but *"l'art du bavardage."*

CHEMISTRY The science of molecular composition and transformation. A *chemical system* or reactor is a system where chemical reactions occur. If all of these cease, for example, as a result of either very low or very high temperatures, the system becomes a physical system. The logical relation between chemistry and physics is still a matter of controversy. The majority view is that chemistry has been converted into a chapter of physics and, more particularly, of ↑**quantum mechanics**. However, a detailed analysis of present-day quantum chemistry shows that the very statement of a problem in this field presupposes such supraphysical concepts as chemical reaction, and the macrochemical theory of chemical kinetics.

CHICKEN-AND-EGG PROBLEM A problem of the same kind as "What was first, the chicken or the egg?" Earlier thought to be insoluble riddles, these problems are now seen in the light of evolution. For example, the egg I just had for breakfast came from a hen that came from a different egg, that was laid by a somewhat different hen, and so on—all the way back to a dinosaur's egg. Chicken-and-egg problems must not be confused with problems such as "What came first, matter or space-time, nature or nurture, player or rule of the game, social stratification or the state?" These other problems are caused by a false tacit assumption, namely, that one of the disjuncts had to precede the other, while actually both come together.

CHINESE ROOM ARGUMENT John Searle's thought-experiment suggesting, by analogy, that computers only perform mindless symbol-processings, so that they do not understand what they do. Simplified version: A person who knows no Chinese is locked in a room and given two stacks of cards written in Chinese, along with instructions in English. These specify that every card in the first stack containing a Chinese character with a certain shape is to be exchanged for a card in the second stack containing another designated ideogram, also recognizable by its shape. The mindless execution of this task amounts to a mechanical computation. The operator has performed it without understanding the ideograms. However, this argument cuts no ice with the eliminative materialist, who would argue that this is exactly how brains proceed, namely, as programmed computers. An experienced teacher would argue that a standard school examination involving nonalgorithmic operations is a more adequate test of understanding. ↑**Argentine room**.

CHOICE Key concept in ethics, psychology, and social science. It occurs, for instance, in the philosophico-scientific problem of whether choice is completely free, partly free, or totally determined by the past and by external circumstances. ↑**Free will**, ↑**rational-choice theory**.

CHOICE, AXIOM OF Given any family F of nonempty sets, there exists a function f that "chooses" one representative of each member of F—i.e., that assigns to each member A of F a unique element $f(A)$ of F. This axiom of standard set theory is one of the most hotly debated axioms of contemporary mathematics. Mathematical intuitionists reject it because it is not constructive, i.e., it does not define the choice function but only states its existence. ↑**Intuitionism, a mathematical**, ↑**set theory**.

CHUTZPAH, PHILOSOPHICAL Cheek, nerve. The one commodity that has never been in short supply in the philosophical community. Few philosophers have been known to refrain from pontificating on subjects about which they did not have the dimmest idea. Examples: Kant's, Engels's, and Wittgenstein's pronouncements on mathematics; Hegel's on chemistry and biology; Bergson's on relativity theory; and Heidegger's on ontology and technology.

CIRCLE, VICIOUS / VIRTUOUS a Logic *Vicious circle*: repetition of the defined concept in the defining clause, or of the conclusion among the premises. Example: "People can speak because they are endowed with a language acquisition device" (N. Chomsky). *Virtuous circle*: process of successive approximations, whereby a finding is used to improve on it. Example: the validity of mathematics consists in its abidance by logic, which in turn is tested and challenged by mathematics. **b Ontology** Feedback loop. ↑**Cybernetics**. Example of material vicious circle: poverty breeds ignorance, which in turn fosters poverty. Example of material virtuous circle: good wages increase productivity, which in turn makes wage raises possible.

CLARITY, SEMANTIC Having a precise ↑**meaning**, being minimally vague or fuzzy. For an idea to be clear it suffices that it be well defined, either explicitly or by means of a set of postulates. Clarity is the very first requirement of rational discourse and a necessary condition for civilized and fruitful dialogue. Some ideas, such as those of holy trinity, absolute, dialectical contradiction, transcendence, id, and ↑*Dasein*, are intrinsically unclear (obscure). Others are initially somewhat unclear but are gradually elucidated through exemplification, analysis, or ↑**theorification**. This has been the case with the ideas of set, function, energy, evolution, and uncounted others.

CLASS Collection (in particular set) defined by a (simple or complex) predicate. **Syn** kind, type, sort. Algebra of classes: the branch of logic that handles sets as wholes (individuals), and investigates their union, intersection, and complement.

CLASSIFICATION Exhaustive partition of a collection into mutually disjoint subsets (species), and grouping of the latter into higher-rank classes (taxa) such as genera. Two logical relations are involved in a classification: those of membership (∈) of an individual in a class, and of inclusion (⊆) of a class in a higher-rank class. Hence every classification is a ↑**model** (example) of set theory. ↑**Taxonomy**.

CLOSURE A set of well-formed formulas is *syntactically closed* (or closed under deduction) if every member of the set is either an assumption or a logical consequence of one or more assumptions. A set of well-formed formulas is *semantically closed* if all of them are ↑**coreferential**. The only way to achieve at once syntactical and semantical closure is to use the ↑**axiomatic** method, including at least one ↑**semantic** assumption per primitive (undefined) concept, so as to prevent the smuggling in of interlopers.

CODE a Applied mathematics A one-to-one correspondence between any two sets, at least one of which is composed of artificial signs, such as numerals, letters, words, or figures. Examples: the Morse code, traffic lights, and the semantic assumptions in a theory. The mathematical structure of codes is studied by coding theory, a chapter of ↑**information** theory. **b Philosophy** ↑**Semantics** is interested in the codes constituting the ↑**semantic assumptions** enabling one to interpret ("read") a mathematical formalism in factual terms, such as "Let 'p' and 'q' represent the price and quantity of a good respectively." The occurrence of an explicit code in a text is a mark of its ↑**exactness**. Its absence condones or even encourages arbitrary ↑**interpretations**, such as those of dreams, tea leaves at the bottom of a cup, and social facts. The so-called **genetic code** is a correspondence between nucleic acids and proteins. This correspondence is not a code proper because it does not involve signs, and because it is many-to-one rather than one-to-one. Hence, knowledge of the structure of a protein is insufficient to infer the structure of the RNA molecule involved in its synthesis: this is an ↑**inverse problem** with multiple possible solutions.

COEXTENSIVE Two ↑**predicates** are *strictly* coextensive if their ↑**extensions** coincide, and *partially* coextensive if they overlap only in part. Example of the former: "body" and "massive." Example of the latter: "artificial" and "made."

COGITO, ERGO SUM I think, therefore I am. A principle of Descartes's, who took it to be self-evident. It has been interpreted and reinterpreted to death over nearly four centuries. Sometimes it is believed to encapsulate the idealist doctrine that ideas precede existence. However, taken literally it asserts, on the contrary, that existence is necessary for (hence precedes) thinking. Indeed, in the conditional "$C \Rightarrow S$," C is sufficient for *S*, and *S* necessary for *C*. A more plausible interpretation is that Descartes starts his inquiry by doubting everything except that he is thinking at the moment.

COGNITION Process leading to ↑**knowledge**. Perception, exploration, imagination, reasoning, criticism, and testing are cognitive processes. Cognition is studied by cognitive ↑**psychology**, and cognitive neuroscience, whereas knowledge is studied primarily by ↑**epistemology** and knowledge engineering.

COGNITIVE NEUROSCIENCE The merger of neuroscience and ↑**psychology**: the study of the brain processes that we feel introspectively as mental. Examples: the location and identification of the neural processes triggered by a luminous signal or a word; the search for the place and mechanism of the binding of the various features of vision (shape, color, movement, and texture); the neurophysiological study of intention and volition in the prefrontal cortex; the study or control of schizophrenic or paranoiac episodes as brain processes. The underlying philosophy of mind is centered on the materialist hypothesis that mental processes are brain processes. ↑**Mind-body problem**, ↑**cognitive science**.

COGNITIVE SCIENCE The alliance of cognitive ↑**psychology**, ↑**linguistics**, and ↑**Artificial Intelligence**. This alliance is based on the hypotheses that all mental processes are cognitive; that these are immaterial (substrate-free); and moreover that they are computational, whence they can be "instantiated" in either brains or computers. Clearly, this dualistic and mechanistic philosophy of mind is at variance with that underlying ↑**cognitive neuroscience**. ↑**Artificial intelligence**.

COGNITIVISM The family of axiological and ethical doctrines that assert the relevance of knowledge to value judgments and moral norms. Ant ↑**emotivism**, ↑**intuitionism**.

COHERENCE ↑**Consistency**.

COHERENCE THEORY OF TRUTH The thesis (rather than theory) that a proposition is true, without further ado, just in case it coheres (is ↑**consistent**) with every other proposition in the body of knowledge under consideration. Obviously, this holds only for formal truths. Factual ↑**truth** is more demanding. A body of knowledge concerning facts of some kind is expected not only to be coherent (internally consistent), but also to match the facts it refers to. That is, in factual science and technology coherence is necessary but insufficient.

COINTENSIVE Two predicates are cointensive if their ↑**intensions** (or senses or connotations) coincide totally or in part. Examples: "mass" and "weight," "book" and "booklet," "dependent" and "linearly dependent," "supernaturalist" and "religious."

COLLECTION A group of objects, gathered either arbitrarily or because they have some property in common. A collection with fixed membership is a ↑**set** in the mathematical sense of the word. For example, humankind is a collection with variable membership, whereas the collection of all humans alive at a given time is a set.

COLLECTIVISM The ontological and epistemological thesis, found in the philosophy of social studies, that social wholes always precede and condition their individual constituents.
Syn ↑**holism**. Collectivism is true insofar as every individual is born into a preexisting society and can never free himself entirely from it. But it is false in denying that individual
actions, sometimes against the prevailing current, are what keep or alter social wholes. **Ant**
↑**individualism**. ↑**Systemism** is the alternative to both collectivism and individualism.

COMBINATORIAL An association of items that does not alter their nature and satisfies the
laws of combinatorics. For instance, n items can be ordered linearly in $n! = 1.2 \ldots n$ different ways (permutations); and the number of sets of r different items deriving from a
total of n individuals is the binomial coefficient. Combinatorial associations are exceptional because, when two or more items come together, they are likely to constitute a
↑**system** with ↑**emergent properties**. Examples: the meaningless letters d, g, o associate into the meaningful words 'dog' and 'god'; and two hydrogen atoms combine into
a hydrogen molecule with properties of its own, such as a dissociation energy and a band
(as opposite to a line) spectrum.

COMMANDMENT ↑**Imperative**. Example: "Thou shalt be precise."

COMMITMENT, ONTOLOGICAL W. v. O. Quine's thesis that the occurrence of the ↑**"existential" quantifier** ∃ in logic shows that this science, far from being ontologically
neutral, is committed to the existence of things of some kind. But this interpretation
of ∃ is mistaken, since it is best read as "for some." An affirmation of existence,
whether conceptual or material, calls for the use of the ↑**existence predicate**.

COMMON GOOD The good or wealth shared by everyone or nearly everyone in a society. Examples: security, peace, clean air, universal health care, public parks, muse-
ums. The unavoidable, but in principle soluble, conflicts between public and private
interests are studied by moral philosophers and social scientists and technologists, and
are managed by statesmen, judges, and government bureaucrats.

COMMON SENSE Faculty or judgment lying between wild speculation on the one
hand and well-grounded assertion and educated guess on the other. Common sense,
which involves both ordinary knowledge and rationality, is a point of departure: science, technology, and philosophy start where common sense proves insufficient. Recourse to common sense is double-edged: it can discourage serious research as well as
nonsense. For example, linguistic philosophy—a commonsense philosophy—has
served both as an antidote to idealist extravagances, and as a deterrent to exact and scientific philosophizing. ↑**Analytic philosophy**, ↑**antiphilosophy**.

COMMONSENSE REALISM Naive or uncritical ↑**realism**. Effective against both wild
fantasy and radical skepticism, but insufficient to cope with the unobservables that are
peculiar to science and technology.

COMMUNICATION The transmission of a cognitively meaningful signal or message,
that is, one involving some knowledge, as is the case with data, conjectures, questions,

instructions, and commands. When two or more things communicate, either in one way only or reciprocally, they constitute a *communication system*. More precisely, a communication system may be characterized as a concrete (material) system composed of animals of the same or different species, as well as nonliving things, in some (natural or social) environment, and whose structure includes signals of one or more kinds— visual, acoustic, electromagnetic, chemical, etc. The propagation of such signals is typically subject to distortions due to uncontrolled (often random) changes in the communication channel. Communication engineers, ethologists, sociolinguists, linguists, and others study, design, maintain, or repair communication systems, such as TV networks, the Internet, and linguistic communities. The latter are the units of study of the sociolinguist. ↑**Linguistics d**.

COMMUNISM The kind of ↑**egalitarianism** that advocates a classless society through the socialization of the means of production by violent means. Communism has been practiced in all primitive societies. Modern or Soviet communism succeeded in decreasing income inequalities and raising the cultural level. Ultimately it failed because it betrayed the original ideal: it was a dictatorship that destroyed social bonds, invaded the private sphere, and discouraged individual initiative; it confused socialization with state ownership, and imposed an obsolete philosophy as part of intellectual censorship.↑**Marxism**.

COMMUNITARIANISM Moral and social philosophy that stresses solidarity, community efforts, and social values. **Ant** ↑**individualism**. According to it (a) values and norms are somehow exuded by communities, hence they can be neither grounded nor disputed; (b) all values and norms are local, none is universal; (c) different cultures (societies), in particular their value systems, are equivalent and mutually "incommensurable"; (d) the individual is thoroughly shaped by his community (or collectivity, or society), to which he owes allegiance; (e) the community as a whole must care for the individual in a paternalistic fashion. A component of ↑**holism**, cultural ↑**relativism**, and ↑**nationalism**. From a sociological viewpoint, communitarianism is a natural product of either small, isolated, and stagnant rural communities, or oppressed ethnic minorities. An obvious flaw of this doctrine is that it underplays individual differences, interests, aspirations, and even rights. Because it punishes dissent, communitarianism is basically conservative when not reactionary. Its merits are that (a) contrary to ↑individualism, it reminds us that we all have some duties, and it emphasizes certain social values, chief among them social cohesion and solidarity; and (b) it calls for a vision of the good society, i.e., the community capable of attaining or preserving the ↑**common good** from individual greed. ↑**Agathonism** is expected to combine the positive aspects of communitarianism and individualism.

COMPARATIVE JUDGMENT A description of the outcome of a ↑**comparison**. Examples: "A is larger than B," "Whereas A is smooth, B is rugged," "Bread loaves are incomparable with symphonies." As regards precision, comparative statements are comprised between qualitative and quantitative statements.

COMPARATIVE METHOD No such thing: there are no general rules for drawing ↑**comparisons**. The reason is that different comparisons are elicited by different questions or hypotheses. For example, two biospecies may be compared with respect to either common ancestors or adaptedness, and two artifacts as to either efficiency or cost.

COMPARISON a Broad sense Search for similarities and differences between two or more objects. A basic cognitive operation. If conscious, a comparison may result either in a ↑**comparative judgment** or in a denial that the objects under consideration are comparable in a given respect, such as usefulness or beauty. **b Narrow sense** Checking whether a ↑**comparison relation** holds between two objects.

COMPARISON RELATION A reflexive, antisymmetric, and transitive relation. A relation, such as $\leq$ and $\subseteq$, as in "Big events are less frequent than small ones," and "The human species is included in the primate genus."

COMPATIBILITY Two or more propositions are mutually compatible if neither denies any of the other(s). Compatibility does not require that all the propositions in question be true. This condition is too strong because, before inquiring into the truth of a set of propositions, it is advisable to check whether they are mutually compatible. **Ant** incompatibility. The concept of incompatibility may be adopted as the single primitive (undefined) logical operation (Sheffer's stroke). ↑**Consistency.**

COMPETITION A pervasive mode of interaction, mostly unwitting, found on all levels. Examples: competition between two chemical reactions for a reagent; among plants for nutrients or sunshine; and among siblings for parental attention and affection. Competition in some respects is compatible with cooperation in others, as in the cases of communities of apes and scientists. Individualists exalt competition, holists exaggerate cooperation, and systemists admit both modes of interaction. ↑**Cooperation.**

COMPLEMENT The complement of a set S relative to its universe of discourse U is the set of all the elements of U that are not in S. Symbols: $U, U \setminus S$. **Syn** set-theoretic difference. Example: physical fields constitute the complement of the collection of bodies in the collection of all material things: $F = M \setminus B$, whence $M = B \cup F$.

COMPLEMENTARITY, PRINCIPLE OF Niels Bohr's hypothesis that every thing, property, and concept has a dual or complement; and that, the more precise or better known one of them, the fuzzier or less well known its "complement." A failed generalization of ↑**Heisenberg's inequalities**. Genuine examples: position and momentum, angle and angular momentum of a ↑**quanton**. Spurious examples proposed by Bohr himself: energy and time, truth and depth, psychology and physiology.

COMPLETENESS A ↑**theory** is complete if every formula of it is either a postulate or a valid logical consequence of its postulates. Hence a complete theory cannot be enriched without introducing a contradiction in it. First-order predicate logic and a few simple mathematical theories have proved to be complete. By contrast, any theory containing a fragment of number theory is necessarily incomplete. ↑**Gödel's incompleteness theorem.**

COMPLEXITY A complex object is one with two or more components. **Ant** ↑**simplicity**. Conceptual examples: all of the defined concepts, all propositions, all theories, and all methods are complex to some extent or other. Factual examples: atoms, molecules, cells, social systems. However, complexity on one ↑**level** of organization may coexist with simplicity on another, as exemplified by the laws of gases vis à vis their molecular constituents. Since every ↑**system** can be analyzed into its composition, environment, structure, and mechanism (↑**CESM**), four kinds of complexity must be distinguished. These are compositional (number and types of components); environmental (number, types, and intensities of links with items in the environment); structural (number, types, and intensities of bonds among the components); and mechanismic (types of process that makes the system "tick").

COMPOSITION a System The collection of parts of a system. Since a system may have parts on several levels (e.g., atoms, molecules, cells, organs, persons, etc.), it is necessary to indicate the level at which the composition is being thought of. Examples: composition at the atomic level, at the level of the person (in the case of a social system), at the level of the firm (in the case of an economic system). The definition of the concept of composition $C_L(s)$ of a system s at level L is straightforward: it is the intersection of $C(s)$ with L, i.e., $C_L(s) = C(s) \cap L$, i.e., the collection of Ls that are parts of s. **b Fallacy** The ontological fallacy consisting in attributing to a whole (collection or system) all the properties of its parts. Example: "That species lives on termites." This fallacy originates in the denial of ↑**emergence**. Radical ↑**reductionism** involves the fallacy of composition. Ontological ↑**individualists**, particularly in the social sciences, are particularly prone to that fallacy.

COMPUTATION a Broad Sense Processing information in accordance with a fixed set of rules (↑**algorithms**). ↑**Computationism. b Strict sense** Finding the value of a function for one or more values of its argument(s). A function f is said to be computable if there exists a rule (or instruction, or algorithm) to obtain its value $f(x)$ for any value of x. Computability (in this narrow technical sense) is the exception rather than the rule, if only because it is restricted to recursive functions, which are defined on the set of natural numbers. Hence, it does not cover the overwhelming majority of functions nor, a fortiori, the most important numerical functions that occur in science and technology, namely the real-valued and complex-valued functions. For example, not even the trigonometric functions, such as the sine function, are computable in the strict technical sense, although every calculus student is expected to be able to find any value of them to any desired approximation. A fortiori, computability theory cannot handle functions involving the imaginary unit $i = \sqrt{-1}$, such as, e.g., $i^i = (\exp i\pi/2)^i = \exp (i^2 \pi/2) = \exp (-\pi/2) \approx .208$.

COMPUTATIONISM The thesis that the ↑**mind** is a collection of computer programs. Equivalently: the thesis that all mental operations are computations in accordance with ↑**algorithms**. This thesis underpins the uncritical enthusiasm for ↑**artificial intelligence**. By the same token, it has impoverished psychology and misguided the philosophy of mind. Indeed, it has led to neglecting such nonalgorithmic processes as those of posing new problems and forming new concepts, hypotheses, and rules (such as algorithms). Besides, it has reinforced the idealist myth that the mental is stuff-neutral, so that it can be studied in isolation from both neuroscience and social psychology. Finally, computationism has artificially cut the links between intelligence and emotion—despite the well-known fact that the corresponding organs are anatomically linked, and that learning requires motivation.

COMPUTER Symbol-processing ↑**machine**. An artifact that can be operated, in particular programmed, to undergo processes whose inputs and outputs are surrogates of ideas. There are two main genera of computers: analogical and digital. The former consist of continuous physical (e.g., hydrodynamic or electromagnetic) processes, and consequently are slow. By contrast, digital computers operate on a small number of symbols, such as the numerals 0 and 1. Digital computers are so fast that they can accomplish in a second the analogs of mental operations that would take thousands of people thousands of years to perform. On the other hand, because computers run on ↑**programs**, they have neither initiative nor creativity.

COMPUTER MODEL A computer model of a thing or process is a ↑**program** that mimics or simulates the original object in some respects, in such a way that its behavior under certain stimuli can be found out.

COMPUTER MODEL OF THE BRAIN The view that human brains are computers or very similar to them. This analogy is biologically untenable because of the radically different kinds of stuff (hence processes) that brains and computers are made of. In particular, the hardware/software distinction makes no sense with reference to brains. Obviously, the analogy holds up to a point for algorithmic ("mechanical") operations: if fed a suitable program, a computer will carry out operations that only brains could perform in the past. But the parallel breaks down for all the other mental operations, in particular for the invention of theories and the design of algorithms. Besides, computers operate with symbols, such as numerals, not with concepts, such as numbers. And they are devoid of initiative, creativity, and judgment. Last, but not least, computers do not feel emotions, not even enthusiasm when working well, or sadness when attacked by a "virus." Still, given any process, whether physical, chemical, biological, or social, some of its features can be simulated on a computer—provided something is known about them, and this knowledge is combined with an algorithm.

COMPUTER PROGRAM A sequence of instructions for the automatic and sequential transformation of symbols by a ↑**computer**. The concept of a computer program is central in the psychological theories and philosophies of mind that postulate that the mind is a set of computer programs. ↑**Computationism**, ↑**mind-body problem**.

COMPUTER WORSHIP The wild overrating of the ability of computers. Computer worship is evident in strong ↑ **artificial intelligence**, ↑**artificial life**, and ↑**computationism**. It also occurs in daily life, when the verdicts of computers are regarded as unappealable.

CONCEIT, PHILOSOPHER'S The belief that philosophers are competent to make pronouncements about the nature of things without using any scientific or technological findings. Examples: the philosophies of nature of Schelling and Hegel, phenomenology, philosophical anthropology, philosophy of mind, and the philosophies of science or technology that pay no attention to either. ↑**Navel contemplation.**

CONCEPT Simple idea, unit of ↑**meaning**, building block of a ↑ **proposition**. Examples: "individual," "species," "hard," "harder," "=," "between." Every concept can be symbolized by a term, but the converse is false. Indeed, some ↑**symbols**, such as 'it' and 'of', are ↑**syncategorematic**, and others denote concrete things or properties thereof. Concepts can be grouped into two large genera: ↑**sets** and ↑**predicates** of different degrees (unary, binary, etc.). These concepts are implicitly defined in set theory and predicate logic respectively. Since names are neither predicates nor sets, they are not concepts, even though some of them designate concepts. ↑**Nominalism** denies the existence of concepts for fear of Platonism. But, ironically, the very statement "There are no concepts" involves the concepts of existence, negation, and concept.

CONCEPT FORMATION Invention, ↑**definition**, or ↑**elucidation** of concepts.

CONCLUSION The last line of a deductive argument such as a proof. In ordinary language and the scientific literature, a far more lax acceptation occurs. Here a hypothesis suggested by a set of data is often called a conclusion. So much so that the last paragraph or section of a research paper is usually called 'conclusion' even if it only summarizes the hypotheses in the paper or evaluates the evidence for or against them. It should be called 'evaluation' or 'summary' instead.

CONCRETE Material. Ant ↑**abstract**. All concrete objects are individual. Hence Hegel's "concrete universal" is an oxymoron.

CONDITION a Logic The necessary condition for the truth of the antecedent p of the ↑**conditional** statement "If p, then q" is that its consequent q be true. The *sufficient* condition for q to be true is that p be true. **b Ontology** A *necessary* (or contributory) ↑**cause** of an event is an event without which the effect would not happen. Example: the presence of a thing at some time is necessary for its correct perception. (Caution: the perceived thing may have disappeared by the time it has been perceived. Examples: "dead" stars and phantom limbs.) A *sufficient* cause of an event is one that is alone necessary to bring it about. For example, intake of peyote suffices to cause hallucinations.

CONDITIONAL a Logic A proposition of the form "If p, then q," or "$p \Rightarrow q$" . Standard definitions: $p \Rightarrow q =_{df} \neg p/q = \neg(p \,\&\, \neg q)$. **b Mathematics** The *conditional probability* of y given x (i. e., assuming that x is the case) is $P(y \mid x) =_{df} P(x \,\&\, y)/P(x)$. Upon trading x for y, $P(x \mid y)$ results. And dividing the two conditional probabilities one obtains *Bayes's theorem*: $P(x \mid y) = P(y \mid x) \cdot P(y)/P(x)$. **c Philosophy** The previous valid mathematical result has been misinterpreted in terms of cause and effect, and in terms of hypothesis and evidence. According to the former interpretation, the probability that event c causes event e is $P(c \mid e) = P(e \mid c) \, P(e)/P(c)$. In the second interpretation, the probability of the hypothesis h given the evidence e is $P(h \mid e) = P(e \mid h) \, P(e)/P(h)$. In the first case the prior probability $P(c)$ of the cause, and in the second case the prior probability $P(h)$ of the hypothesis, must be posited. If such probabilities were known, empirical investigation would be dispensable. Since this is not the case, both interpretations are wrong. The first interpretation is also wrong for assuming tacitly that all events are random, and the second for assuming that propositions can be assigned ↑**probabilities**. ↑**Bayesianism**.

CONFIRMATION a Ordinary knowledge An empirical generalization is confirmed by its instances. Example: "All adult dogs can bark" is confirmed by Rover's and Fido's barkings. This is the kind of unproblematic and therefore uninteresting hypotheses studied in ↑**inductive logic**. ↑**Paradox**. **b Science** A scientific generalization is a hypothesis that may not have instances because it contains predicates that represent things or properties inaccessible to the unaided senses, such as molecules and nations. Examples: "Decision making is a specific function of the frontal lobes"; "Overpopulation generates poverty." A hypothesis of this kind is confirmed by a set of empirical data if these are predicted or retrodicted with its help. Caution 1: Since normally ↑**forecasts** and ↑**hindcasts** involve not only the hypotheses under test but also subsidiary assumptions and data, contrary evidence may be debilitating but not damning. Caution 2: Empirical confirmation is necessary but insufficient for attributing truth. First, because it often happens that a scientific hypothesis is initially confirmed, but falsified by further tests. Second, because hypotheses come in bunches, not in isolation, they should be compatible with their partners. ↑**Consistency, external**. In principle, a proposition can be confirmed (or refuted) in a definitive way. By contrast, a ↑**theory** (hypothetico-deductive system) can never be so confirmed because it contains infinitely many propositions. The best one can do is (a) check whether the theory as a whole (as represented by its axioms) is compatible with the background knowledge; and (b) subject a representative sample of the propositions of the theory to rigorous empirical tests. The degree of confirmation of a hypothesis h by a set of n observations, m of which are positive, is $C_n(h) = m/n$. The formal similarity of this formula with the elementary (and controversial) definition of probability has suggested to some philosophers the possibility of interpreting probabilities as degrees of confirmation. This project cannot be completed for two reasons: (a) the above ratio does not equal a mathematically well-defined function approaching a limit when n tends to infinity—unlike, say, the ratio $n/n+1$; and (b) there is nothing random about the distribution of positive test results in a run of observations. ↑**Probability**.

CONFLICT a Ontology Opposition, incompatibility, struggle. A key concept of ↑**agonism**. **b Ethics** Conflict between either two moral norms (e.g., sincerity and benevolence) or between these and prudential (practical) considerations. Moral conflicts are the sources of all moral problems. **c Law** Conflict between rights, e.g., between freedom of speech and security; or between individual rights and civil duties; or between the (real or invented) rights of different parties. Arguably, a moral conflict underlies every legal conflict.

CONJUNCTION The formal counterpart of the ordinary-knowledge "and." The conjunction of the propositions p and q is the proposition p & q that is true if both p and q (the conjuncts) are true. If at least one of the conjuncts is only partially true, the truth value of their conjunction may be taken to equal either the average or the smallest of the two truth values. In ordinary logic, conjunction is commutative, that is, p & $q = q$ & p. Not so in ordinary language. Example: Beautiful but dumb ≠ dumb but beautiful. ↑**Subtlety**. Relation to ↑**disjunction** in ordinary (classical) logic: $p \wedge q = \neg(\neg p \vee \neg q)$.

CONNECTIVE, LOGICAL Any of the functions that map propositions, or pairs of propositions, into propositions: $\wedge$, $\vee$, $\neg$, $\Rightarrow$, $\Leftrightarrow$. Of these, only conjunction ($\wedge$ or &) has an ontic counterpart, namely ↑**juxtaposition**. In particular, there are neither disjunctive nor negative facts.

CONNOTATION / DENOTATION Properties of ↑**predicates** and, by extension, of the corresponding symbols. Connotation = ↑**sense**. **Syn** ↑**content**. Denotation = ↑**reference**. The two together constitute ↑**meaning**. Example 1: In number theory, "even" connotes divisibility by 2, and denotes the integers. Example 2: "Life" connotes (inter alia) metabolism, and denotes the totality of living beings. Example 3: "Anomie" connotes mismatch between aspirations and attainments, and denotes people.

CONSCIENCE, MORAL Moral responsibility: the ability to identify moral problems and do the right thing about them.

CONSCIOUSNESS A polysemous term that denotes at least the following brain states or processes: (a) *sensitivity* (or reactivity), e.g., to a pinch; (b) *awareness* of external or internal stimuli, as in seeing someone; (c) *self-awareness*: awareness of what one is feeling or doing; (d) *consciousness*: awareness of what one is perceiving or thinking; (e) *self-consciousness*: reflection upon one's own perceptions or thoughts, concurrent, past, or future, without attributing them to someone else. Neglected until recently, consciousness is now an object of some scientific research and much wild speculation. Two of the problems addressed by consciousness researchers are the identification of the self-awareness neural systems and mechanisms, and whether nonhuman animals can be conscious and in particular self-conscious.

CONSENSUS Unanimity on certain opinions or principles. Rational debate requires a modicum of consensus on certain principles and definitions: logical (mainly non-contradiction and the idea of a test or proof), semantic (sticking to the point, and some notion of truth), epistemological (nature of problem and evidence), and moral (neither withholding information nor cheating). However, rationalists do not bow blindly to consensus. In science, consensus is taken as a fallible ↑**truth** indicator; and in moral matters it is a weak indicator of ↑**justice**. In a community of rational persons, consensus follows the recognition of truth or justice, not the other way round. ↑**Sociologism**, ↑**conventionalism**, and ↑**relativism** conflate truth and justice with consensus. Hence they are epistemologically, morally, and politically conformist, despite the revolutionary rhetoric of some of them.

CONSEQUENCE a Logic In ordinary parlance, "consequence" and "deduction" are synonymous. In ↑**model theory** (a part of logic), the notion of consequence is defined in a formal theory (or "formalized language"), namely thus: A proposition C is a consequence of a set P of premises if C is true under every interpretation on which every member of P is ↑**satisfied**. ↑**Entailment**. **b Ontology** Consequence of an event or process = effect, outcome, result. **c Methodology** The testable (or observable) consequences of a factual theory are those that can be confronted with empirical data. Strictly speaking, the high-level theories, such as classical mechanics and quantum mechanics, have no testable consequences by themselves. To face the pertinent facts, a logical consequence of the postulates of such a theory has got to be enriched with a model of the thing being observed, the appropriate indicator hypotheses (or unobservable-observable links), and some empirical data. Since any of these components may be false, the empirical test may be inconclusive. **d Praxiology** Consequence of a human action = effect, result, or outcome of the action. Rules or maxims, whether technical, legal, or moral, have consequences in the derivative sense that they steer actions with outcomes. Every human ↑**action** has ↑**unanticipated consequences**, some favorable and others unfavorable ("perverse").

CONSEQUENTIALISM The family of ethical theories according to which consequences should matter in taking action and in evaluating moral decisions and norms. An extreme version of consequentialism is ↑**utilitarianism**, according to which only consequences matter. ↑**Agathonism** involves moderate consequentialism, for it makes room for actions with inevitable negative consequences to self or others. **Ant** ↑**deontologism**.

CONSERVATION LAWS Scientific laws that state the constancy or permanence of certain features alongside changes in others. Examples: conservation of energy, electric charge, and total angular momentum. In principle, every conservation law is deducible from a set of equations of motion or field equations.

CONSERVATISM Attachment to received principles or methods even in the face of their failure. **Ant** ↑**revisionism**, reformism, progressivism. Whereas dogmatism is conservative, truth-seeking research is revisionist.

CONSILIENCE The unification, systematization, or theorification of previously unrelated hypotheses. ↑**Convergence, interdiscipline**.

CONSISTENCY a Logic A set of propositions is said to be *internally consistent*, or *coherent*, if no two members of it are mutually contradictory. **Ant** ↑**inconsistency**. Consistency is as valuable as truth, because contradictions are false and they imply arbitrary (i.e., irrelevant) propositions: ↑*Ex falso quodlibet sequitur*. **b Epistemology** A theory is said to be *externally consistent* if it is compatible with the bulk of background knowledge, particularly with the other theories about the same or related things. Examples: unlike alchemy, modern chemistry is consistent with physics; neuropsychology, unlike computationist psychology, is consistent with neuroscience; and scientific realism, unlike rival epistemologies, is consistent with the practice of science and technology. **c Praxiology and ethics** To be viable, any system of norms must be internally consistent. Indeed, a pair of mutually contradictory rules, such as "If f happens do g," and "If f happens do not do g," leads to apraxia. **d Psychology and sociology** A person's social behavior is said to be consistent if it abides by the same set of social norms in all circumstances.

CONSTANT CONJUNCTION Hume's view of causation as the temporal and spatial co-incidence of events, rather than as the production of one event by another. This is not the concept of causation used in science and technology, both of which search for the consequence (effect) of varying a variable representing a property. ↑**Causation**.

CONSTITUTIVE / REGULATIVE Whereas a constitutive proposition encapsulates a bit of knowledge, a regulative proposition is either a heuristic tip or a norm for the search for knowledge. A useful distinction due to Kant.

CONSTRUAL Conception, version, or interpretation, as in "the hermeneutic construal of 'meaning' as goal." A term best handled with care due to its ambiguity.

CONSTRUCT A ↑**concept**, ↑**proposition**, or set of propositions, such as a ↑**classification**, a ↑**theory**, or a moral or legal code. **Ant** ↑**fact**. Example: a boiling kettle is an objective fact, feeling it hot is an experience, and the concepts of temperature, quantity of heat, and specific heat are constructs. Warning: Constructs are not to be confused with the ↑**symbols** that designate them. For example, concept ≠ term, and proposition ≠ sentence. The reason is that the choice of symbols is conventional, whereas that of constructs is a part of the search for either truth, efficiency, or good.

CONSTRUCTIVISM a Broad sense The view that objects of certain kinds, or of all kinds, are human constructions. **b Mathematics** The view that only effectively constructible concepts and effectively computable procedures are admissible in mathematics. Akin to mathematical ↑**intuitionism**. Mathematical constructivism places severe restrictions on mathematical research, and is therefore a minority party. Still, it is sound practice to construct as much as possible. **c Psychology and epistemology** The thesis that ideas, rather than either being innate or found ready-made in experience, are constructed. Developmental psychologists and ratioempiricist philosophers nod. To avoid confusion with the idealist theses to be examined in **e** and **f**, the term 'constructionism' might be preferable. **d Pedagogy** The opinion that the student, even in elementary school, can reconstruct by himself, without assistance, everything he is expected to learn. This quaint opinion, an offshoot of ↑**nativism**, is falsified every day in the classroom. Hence anyone who holds it disqualifies himself as a teacher. **e Ontology** The view that the world is a human construction: that there are no ↑**things in themselves** but only things for us. According to this view, nature has no independent existence. This thesis is in violent conflict with everything we know about the world before the emergence of human beings. What is true is that ideas, artifacts, and social facts are human creations, though not always deliberate ones. **f Sociology of knowledge** The doctrine that all "scientific facts" are constructions and, in particular, the product of scientific communities. Thus stars and atoms, genes and dinosaurs would be social constructions. In fact, the whole of nature would be a cultural construction. This view is a wild exaggeration of the platitude that scientists are creative, construct all constructs, and do not work in a social vacuum. In denying the possibility of objective truth, and thus the universality of science, the social constructivists inadvertently condone the subjection of scientific research and scholarship to the political powers that be, as demanded by totalitarianism. ↑**Relativism**, ↑**sociologism**.

CONTEMPLATION Passive viewing (perceptual, conceptual, or both). Together with uncontrolled speculation, the characteristic mode of prescientific thinking. **Ant** intervention.

CONTENT ↑**Connotation**, ↑**sense**.

CONTENT / CONTEXT Students of ideas are roughly divided into those who focus on ideas themselves, and those who stress their social context. Both perspectives are legitimate. However, content precedes context: the social and historical place of an idea cannot be evaluated unless the idea is formulated and understood.

CONTENT / FORM A classical distinction in philosophy, aesthetics, and other fields, as in "formal logic holds regardless of content or meaning," "in factual matters content is more important than form," and "abstract art is devoid of content."

CONTEXT Any domain or universe of discourse in which a given item belongs, or in which it is embedded. Examples: the context of "contradiction" is logic, not ontology; that of "turbulence" is fluid dynamics, not politology (except metaphorically). More precisely, a context may be characterized as the ordered triple: C = <Statements, Predicates occurring in these statements, Domain of such predicates >, or C = <S, P, D> for short. P and D are listed separately because one and the same set P of (formal) propositions may be assigned now one reference class, now another. A context is a system proper only if its component propositions have at least one common referent, for in this case they are related by the equivalence relation of sharing a nonempty reference class. (This relation, then, is the structure of a context.) Indication of context is important because, although a construct may make sense in one context, it may be meaningless in other contexts. So much so, that a common if dishonest rhetorical trick is to quote sentences out of context.

CONTEXT, IN / OUT OF The very first step to take when researching a problem is to put it in context—i.e., to find out whether the problem is conceptual or empirical, ontological or epistemological, practical or moral, etc. Placing in context is nearly automatic in the mature sciences. By contrast, many a failure in philosophy has been due to a wrong choice of context—e.g., treating the mind-body problem as a linguistic question, or the freewill question as one consisting in predictability. Warning: contexts are not rigid, since a change in viewpoint or in data may force a change (usually an expansion) of the context. For example, a problem initially seen as unidisciplinary may turn out to be cross-disciplinary.

CONTINENTAL PHILOSOPHY The family of philosophies that developed in western continental Europe during the nineteenth and twentieth centuries. A phase of the ↑**Counter-Enlightenment**, and source of ↑**postmodernism**. Characterized by intuitionism, idealism, subjectivism, an opaque prose, and, by and large, also hostility to science, positivism, and analytic philosophy. Some of its earliest, most characteristic and influential representatives were Wilhelm Dilthey, Henri Bergson, Benedetto Croce, Giovanni Gentile, the later Edmund Husserl, the early Max Scheler and Nicolai Hartmann, and Martin Heidegger. By contrast, Emile Meyerson, the neo-Kantians (particularly Paul Natorp and Ernst Cassirer), Gaston Bachelard, and the later Nicolai Hartmann wrote clearly and in sympathy with science. Nowadays most Continental philosophy is done in North America, whereas the Europeans are catching up with analytic philosophy.

CONTINGENCY a Logic and semantics Not logically ↑**necessary. Syn** of 'factual', as in 'the truths of geology are contingent'. **b Ontology** Not necessary, or that may or may not happen. Examples: names, future events, and ↑**accidents.** Contingency plays an important role in biological and social evolution. **Syn** fortuitous. **Ant** ↑**necessary.** An ambiguous word in English, where it is also used as a synonym for 'conditional', as in 'buying that book is contingent upon obtaining those funds'.

CONTINUUM a Mathematics Roughly, smooth or nondenumerable. Examples: the real line (set of real numbers) and the Euclidean plane. **b Science** Empty space and the physical fields (of force) are three-dimensional real continua. **c Ontology** Some ↑**cosmologies** assume, against ↑**atomism,** that the world is a continuum or plenum: ↑**plenism.** Ironically, contemporary physics confirms plenism, in regarding fields as the basic stuff, particles as their quanta (units), and "empty" space as filled with the fluctuating electromagnetic vacuum.

CONTINUUM HYPOTHESIS Cantor's conjecture that the cardinality (numerosity) of the ↑**continuum** comes next to the cardinality of the set of natural numbers. (That is, $2^{\aleph_0}$ = $\aleph$.) This conjecture is neither deducible nor refutable on the axioms of standard (Cantorian) set theory. In alternative theories Cantor's conjecture does not hold. (In them, $\aleph_0 < 2^{\aleph_0} < \aleph_1$.) The invention of any nonstandard set theory is a serious blow to mathematical ↑**Platonism,** according to which mathematics, in particular set theory, describes a definite reality. For, if this were so, there should be no mutually inconsistent yet equally valid (because internally consistent) set theories.

CONTRACT A tacit or explicit agreement among two or more individuals, whereby each promises to give something to the other in exchange for something else. However legally binding a contract may be, from a moral viewpoint it can be undone if it is unfair, as is often the case with contracts between unequally powerful parties, such as firms and employees.

CONTRACT, SOCIAL The fiction that the democratic social order rests on a freely agreed-on yet tacit contract among equals, never on the exploitative or despotic domination of one of them. A useful metaphor at the time of the French Revolution, because it replaced the ideas of absolute monarchy and the divine right of kings with an agreement among equals. It has since lost its appeal in view of the persistence of social inequalities of various kinds. Still, a tacit social contract prevails in the scientific community, based on a commitment to the search for and sharing of truth. ↑**Contractualism.**

CONTRACTUALISM or CONTRACTARIANISM a Ethics The doctrine that morality is part of a ↑**social contract**, hence a social convention that may be altered as a consequence of a power struggle. Although this view has a grain of truth, it makes no room for empathy and compassion, and it does not explain the emergence of moral norms (such as that of reciprocity) in childhood. **b Social philosophy** The view that all social relations are contracts among equal and free agents. This view is an extrapolation of the market transactions among equally powerful (or powerless) agents. It covers only a small part of social life, because it overlooks the many social relations of dependence and domination. Thus the relations of loving, parenting, helping, teaching, and communicating are rarely ruled by contracts. And the employer-employed, teacher-student, and candidate-voter relations, though tacitly contractual to a point, are not contracts between equally powerful agents. Moreover, they are not absolutely binding, as shown by strikes, lockouts, student truancy, and voter abstention.

CONTRADICTION a Logic A contradiction is a formula of the form "*p* and not-*p*," where '*p*' stands for either a predicate or a proposition. Examples: "Wet and dry," "Though very corrupt, he is basically honest." Only clear predicates and propositions can be negated. Hence irrationalist discourses are bound to contain sentences that are not even contradictions in terms. A contradiction implies any number of propositions, relevant or irrelevant, true or false (↑*ex falso quodlibet sequitur*). In other words, contradictions are excessively fertile. **b Semantics** A contradictory proposition is completely false if its elementary constituent *p* can only take the truth values T and F. But if *p* is a half-truth, as is the case with "Canada is inhabitable," then "*p* and not-*p*" too is half-true. Thus, as truth weakens, so does the sting of contradiction. In general, the precise truth value of a contradiction depends on that of its constituent *p*, as well as upon the theory of partial truth one adopts. ↑**Truth. c Epistemology** Contradictions are to be avoided because they are false, and research is the search for (maximal) truth. But of course contradiction is a fact of life, so it had better be faced and fought when it raises its head. Besides, it plays an important role in all proofs by ↑*reductio ad absurdum*. Thus, logical falsity can be a tool for discovering truth. Moreover, the study of mutually contradictory hypotheses is an important task for epistemologists, particularly when the empirical evidence is so restricted that it does not suffice to reject either of the competing conjectures. **d Ontology** The principle of noncontradiction has been widely misunderstood as disallowing change. It has been argued that, while a thing changes, it is and is not at the same time. (Thus, Hegel held that becoming is the synthesis of being and nothingness.) This belief is mistaken because the principle refers to predicates and propositions, not to concrete things. Moreover, the laws of change, such as the laws of motion and the equations of chemical reactions, are consistent and do not involve the concept of negation. The principle would have to be invoked only if someone stated, e.g., that hydrogen and oxygen at once combine and do not combine into water: this would be a logical falsity purporting to represent an impossible chemical situation. In ↑**dialectics**, whether Hegel's or Marx's, 'contradiction' denotes mutually opposed entities, features, or processes. In such theories ontic contradiction, i.e., opposition or conflict, is assumed to be the ultimate source of all change, in particular of all social progress. Any case of (deliberate or unwitting) cooperation, as in the cases of chemical syntheses and political coalitions, contradicts that sweeping assumption. **e Action theory** Two actions may be said to be mutually contradictory (or, better, mutually opposed) if they cannot be performed at the same time, or if their separate consequences are mutually exclusive. Examples: walking and lying down, building and destroying the same thing, competing and cooperating in the same respect.

CONTRAPOSITION The contrapositive of "If p, then q" is "If not-q, then not-p." A proposition and its contrapositive are equivalent: $(p \Rightarrow q) \Leftrightarrow (\neg q \Rightarrow \neg p)$. Hence they follow immediately from each other.

CONTROL a Ontology Regulation of a variable of a system, either spontaneously or deliberately, as in 'automatic control' and 'out of control'. A key concept in cybernetics, biology, engineering, and management science. A typical control device is of the negative feedback type, where the difference between the actual and the desired output activates a mechanism that regulates the input. ↑**Cybernetics**. Another typical control mechanism, used in the quality control of manufactured goods, is a selection whereby the defective items are discarded. Selection can be applied either to every item or to random samples. According to ↑**pragmatism**, the aim of science is control rather than truth—a thesis that betrays confusion between science and technology. **b Methodology** The experimental method involves setting up a control group for every group whose members are subjected to the stimulus of interest. Statistical methods are employed to find out whether the difference in the behavior of the two groups is significant, so that a causal relation between stimulus and response can be established.

CONTROVERSY, PHILOSOPHICAL Argument about the adequacy of different approaches, principles, or methods. Philosophical controversies abound in science as well as in philosophy. Examples: the idealism-materialism, rationalism-empiricism, subjectivism-realism, individualism-collectivism, creationism-evolutionism, computationism-cognitive neuroscience, and Keynesianism-neoliberalism controversies. Some of the great controversies in the history of science have had a philosophical component. For instance, one of the main points of the dispute between Galileo and his prosecutors was the realism-conventionalism dilemma; the evolutionism-creationism conflict is over the reliability of theological dicta; and the controversy over Keynesianism is largely a debate over the immorality of involuntary unemployment. There are controversies in every field of research. As some of them cease, at least for a while, new ones emerge. An uncontroversial field is one where no new big problems are being tackled and no new approaches are being tried. In mathematics, science, technology, and the humanities, most controversies are terminated by recourse to reason, empirical evidence, or both. By contrast, in theology and politics most controversies are terminated by recourse to authority. This second procedure was also employed in the trials of Giordano Bruno and Galileo Galilei, and in the confrontation between Lysenko and genetics.

CONVENTION An explicit or tacit agreement to assume, use, or do (or abstain from doing) something. Examples: linguistic conventions, notational conventions, definitions, units of measurement, etiquette rules, contracts, and social norms. Conventions are not natural or lawful, yet they rule reasoning and action, so much so that the price for violating linguistic or conceptual conventions is error or confusion; and the violation of so-cial norms is sanctioned to some degree or other, from rebuke to prison or worse. More-over, not all conventions are arbitrary: some are adopted for the sake of convenience, others are backed by principles, and still others by special interests. For example, the decimal metric system has been adopted almost universally for convenience. By con-trast, the convention about the zero of the Kelvin temperature scale is backed by the pos-tulate that there is no molecular motion below $0^O K$. Likewise, the convention that bans smoking in public places is based on the finding that secondhand smoking is harzardous to health, which renders smoking in public an antisocial activity. By contrast, the social norms involved in slavery, gender discrimination, and compulsory religious worship rest on class interests. Hence it is naive to suppose, as Hume and the utilitarians do, that all conventions are adopted because they enhance everybody's welfare.

CONVENTIONALISM The epistemological thesis that all truth is conventional, hence im-pregnable to empirical testing. A form of idealism. Conventionalism is false even of mathematics, where notational and definitional conventions are expendable, and care-fully distinguished from both postulates and theorems. It is even more false of factual science and technology, where conventions, unlike hypotheses and methods, are not subjected to empirical testing. ↑**Realism** is decidedly anticonventionalist.

CONVERGENCE a Mathematics A ↑**sequence** (of, e.g., points, numbers, or proposi-tions) is said to be convergent if it has a limit value; that is, if its successive terms x_n approach the limit as n approaches a certain value (in particular, as $n \to \infty$). Conver-gence can be uniform or in the long run. Mathematical analysis contains convergence tests or ↑**criteria** to check whether infinite sequences and series are convergent or di-vergent. And approximation theory, a branch of mathematics, contains ↑**algorithms** for computing successive approximations of functions that converge to the desired exact value. **b Biology** Convergent evolution: the evolution of two populations of different species toward species with more features in common, usually under the pressure of environmental factors and natural selection. **c Epistemology** 'Convergence' has two main epistemological senses. One of them is the rapprochement of approaches, hy-potheses, or fields of inquiry, as in "Philosophy and mathematics converge in exact phi-losophy," "Psychology and neuroscience converge in cognitive neuroscience," and "Economics and sociology converge in socioeconomics." ↑**Cross-disciplinary**. The other sense is the thesis of ↑**scientism** that, barring the neglect of a research project for lack of interest or funds, its findings can be made to converge to exact truths—though not necessarily in real time. This principle can be confirmed but not falsified.

CONVICTION Firmly held ↑**belief**. It is generally considered bad form for academic philosophers to hold convictions even while studying other people's convictions. They are expected to learn about other people's beliefs and to comment on them in a de-tached manner. The philosophers with convictions risk being branded as 'opinionated', 'dogmatic', or even 'philosophers' rather than 'philosophy professors'.

COOPERATION The joining together of two or more entities or processes to effect some-thing that neither of them could achieve separately. **Ant** ↑**competition**. Cooperation, mostly unwitting, is conspicuous on all levels. Witness the self-assembly of particles, atoms, molecules, and cells; the chemical reactions that cooperate in the production of a compound; the cooperation among genes during the construction of an organism; the formation of social systems, and intellectual collaboration. ↑**Self-assembly**.

COPENHAGEN INTERPRETATION of quantum mechanics. The opinion according to which the entities referred to by ↑**quantum mechanics** have no properties of their own, but acquire the properties that the experimenter decides to attribute to them. The sources of this interpretation are (a) Berkeley's subjectivist empiricism: ↑**to be is to perceive or to be perceived**; (b) the confusion between objective existence and our knowledge of it; and (c) the fact that, in some cases (e.g., the velocity of an electron), though not in others (e.g., the velocity of the Sun), the very act of measuring alters the state of the mensurandum.

COPERNICAN REVOLUTION a Astronomy The replacement of the geocentric (or Ptolemaic) planetary model with the heliocentric (or Copernican) one. **b Philosophy** Kant's name for his own replacement of ↑**objectivism** (or realism) with ↑**subjectivism** (or idealism). This was a misnomer, because Kant's subject-centered worldview was a retreat from the ↑**realism** advocated by Galileo and his followers. Moreover, it was analogous to pre-Copernican planetary astronomy. Hence, "Kant's Ptolemaic counterrevolution" would be a more adequate designation.

COREFERENTIAL Two constructs or symbols are *strictly* coreferential if they share all their referents, and *partially* coreferential if they share some referents. Examples of strict coreference: in 'Jane said that she is home,' 'Jane' and 'she' are coreferential; 'mass' and 'electric charge' have exactly the same referents, namely, bodies. Example of partial coreference: "human" and "primate." (The reference class of the former is included in that of the latter.)

CORRELATION, STATISTICAL Association or concomitance of attributes. A correlation coefficient is a numerical measure of the strength of such association. The range of correlation coefficients is the real-number interval $[-1, +1]$. A strong (positive or negative) correlation value, that is, one near either $+1$ or -1, suggests but does not establish a possible causal link. Any such suggestion is weak, because causal relations hold only among events (changes of state). Thus, weight and height may be strongly correlated in a given human population, but neither can be the cause of the other. Even strong correlations can be spurious, that is, the effect of a third variable. For example, schoolchildren who wear uniforms do better than those who don't. This is not because dress makes smart, but because uniforms are required in schools attended by children of well-off parents, who can afford to invest more time and money on their education. This should suffice to discourage the wasteful search for mindless correlations.

CORRESPONDENCE, PRINCIPLE OF The metatheoretical rule according to which a necessary condition for a new scientific theory to be preferred over an older one is that it yields, perhaps in some limit, the same true results of its ancestor. The principle, widely used in physics, is metatheoretical and heuristic, and it serves to reject offhand any theories that account for far less than the incumbents.

CORRESPONDENCE RULE Theoretical-empirical link. ↑**Indicator hypothesis**, ↑**operational definition**.

CORRESPONDENCE THEORY OF TRUTH The thesis (not yet a theory) that the truth of a factual statement consists in its correspondence with, or adequacy to, the fact(s) it refers to. For example, the statement "It is raining" is true if and only if it is actually raining. In general, a proposition asserting that "fact f is the case" is true if and only if f is really (actually, in fact) the case. In science and technology, hypotheses and theories are confronted not with facts, but with empirical data relevant to the former conjoined with ↑**indicator hypotheses**. In these cases, and when the hypothesis h in question is quantitative, one may stipulate that

h is true with respect to datum e and up to error $\varepsilon =_{df}$ the discrepancy between h and e is less than ε.

However, empirical confirmation is necessary only to attribute truth to a hypothesis. External ↑**consistency** (compatibility with the bulk of the background knowledge) is required as well.

CORRIGIBILITY The property of being subject to possible emendation or even falsification. Just as the mark of dogma is incorrigibility, that of factual science and technology is corrigibility. ↑**Falsifiability**.

COSMOLOGY a Scientific Megaphysics: the branch of physics that seeks to model the universe and its evolution. Because this science is a branch of physics, the cosmologist is expected to abide by the known physical laws, and to seek for empirical evidence. However, this rule is often broken, as when the ↑**Big Bang** is identified with the creation of the world, and the ↑**anthropic principle** is taken seriously. As a result, cosmology is the most speculative, as well as the most fascinating, branch of physics. Cosmology raises several problems of philosophical interest, and in turn it can make contributions to philosophy. Sample: Is the universe spatially finite or infinite? Did the universe have an origin, and will it have an end? Can human existence have any cosmological significance? **b Philosophical** The branch of ↑**ontology** that inquires into the basic constituents and patterns of the universe. Examples: atomism, corpuscularism, mechanism, organicism, hierarchism, systemism, textualism. ↑**Worldview**.

COSMOS The totality of existents. **Syn** ↑**universe**.

COUNTER-ENLIGHTENMENT The family of cultural movements, emerged over the past two centuries, that reject the peculiar values of the ↑**Enlightenment**, in particular reason and science. The first Counter-Enlightenment was Romanticism. Its main philosophers were Fichte, Schelling, Hegel, Herder, and Schopenhauer—all of them idealists and vehement enemies of science. The second Romantic wave was initiated by Nietzsche and continued by Dilthey, Rickert, Bergson, Vaihinger, the later William James, and Croce. The third wave was started by Husserl's ↑**phenomenology**, and followed by the ↑**existentialism** of Heidegger and Sartre. It has culminated in ↑**postmodernism**, particularly the antiscientific and antitechnological movements, and such schools as ↑**textualism**, poststructuralism, ↑**constructivism-relativism**, ethnomethodology, phenomenological sociology, critical theory, and feminist philosophy. All of these schools mistrust reason, are subjectivist and relativist, as well as obsessed with symbol and metaphor, and deny the possibility of progress.

COUNTEREXAMPLE Exception to a generalization. Example that falsifies a hypothesis or a theory. Example: the ↑**biosocial** disciplines constitute counterexamples to the idealist (in particular neo-Kantian and hermeneutic) thesis that the social studies are disjoint from the natural sciences and call for a special method, namely interpretation or ↑*Verstehen.* Warning: The popular phrase 'the exception that proves the rule' is an oxymoron, for counterexamples undermine or even falsify generalizations. In mathematics, a single counterexample suffices to falsify a hypothesis. This is why looking for counterexamples is a favorite method of mathematical proof. By contrast, in factual science counterexamples, if few, may undermine hypotheses without falsifying them. The reason is that the counterexamples themselves may be false.↑**Error.**

COUNTERFACTUAL a Logic and semantics A conditional statement containing what looks like (but is not) a factually false antecedent. **Syn** subjunctive conditional. Example: "If I had been in charge, that disaster would have been averted." Strictly speaking, the "antecedent" of this subjunctive is not such, because 'I had been in charge' is a phrase, not a sentence designating a proposition. Hence it cannot be tested for truth any more than 'a sweet smell'. Therefore it can be neither true nor false. Counterfactual sentences are therefore the stuff of fiction. (This is why they do not occur in the mathematical, scientific, or technological literatures.) Believers in the plurality of worlds think they can get around this difficulty by stipulating that 'If it were that A, then it would be that C' is true if C is true at the selected A-world. But since by hypothesis the "A-world" is imaginary, the truth in question is equally imaginary, that is, a matter of make-believe. Unsurprisingly, counterfactuals are useless to ↑**causal analysis.** ↑**Plurality of worlds. b Epistemology** By contrast to counterfactual statements, some counterfactual questions are heuristically valuable. In fact, some research projects are sparked by what-if questions such as "What would happen (or would have happened) if A, which is a B, were (or had been) a C instead?" For example, the economic historian R. W. Fogel asked "How would the modern United States have fared without railways?" He came up with the astounding if controversial answer that the United States would have attained roughly the same level of development had alternative means of transportation been used. ↑**Thought-experiment,** ↑**what-if question.**

COUNTERFACTUAL INFERENCE No such thing. Indeed, the ↑**counterfactual statements** do not designate conditional statements. Even if they did, they would entail nothing. In fact, nothing follows from the conjunction of "If p, then q" and "Not-p."

COUNTERINTUITIVE An idea that is or appears to be incompatible with an ingrained belief, in particular ordinary knowledge. All radically new ideas are counterintuitive at first. Moreover counterintuitiveness, when justified, is the mark of theoretical greatness. ↑**Plausibility.**

COURAGE, INTELLECTUAL A moral virtue required to tackle tough problems, to defend unpopular views, and to change one's views when they are shown to be false or barren.

COVERAGE The coverage or breadth of a construct is the collection of items for which it holds. In particular, the coverage of a predicate is its ↑**extension**, and that of a factual theory is the domain of facts for which it is (sufficiently) true. Example 1: In the biological universe of discourse, the extension of "hybrid" is the offspring of organisms belonging to different species. Example 2: The coverage of quantum electrodynamics is the collection of all known facts involving electromagnetic fields. Example 3: The coverage of existentialism is nil. The more a predicate covers, the poorer its content (the less it "says"). For example, "being" is both broader and weaker than "living being." Interestingly, this law of the "inverse relation" between extension and intension (content) may fail for theories. Thus, the theory of real numbers is both richer and broader than the theory of whole numbers, and electrodynamics has both a greater intension and a greater coverage than electrostatics.

CREATION The formation, spontaneous or guided, of something new. Examples: chemical combination, egg fertilization, invention, the formation of a new business firm. According to most religions, creativity is a divine prerogative. According to empiricism, humans can only put together or combine pre-existing elements, never fashion anything radically new. ↑**Emergentist materialism** holds that creativity is pervasive in nature and society. But, since it denies the supernatural, its creativism is noncreationist. The emergence of new ideas can be explained, at least in principle, as the ↑**self-assembly** of new systems of neurons.

CREDENCE Degree of credibility. ↑**Plausibility**, ↑**subjective probability**.

CRIME Serious infringement of a legal or moral norm. Crime comes in all sizes, from cribbing to genocide, and from hate propaganda to holy war. In an ideally just society, all and only moral crimes are legal crimes. In a real society some moral crimes, such as humiliating for no reason, and refraining from doing a good deed within one's reach, go unpunished. Crime and punishment are studied by ethics, the law, and criminology (a sociotechnology).

CRITERION A rule for identifying some property. Examples: truth tables for the truth value of compound propositions; convergence criteria for infinite series; empirical confirmation as a criterion of factual truth; outcome as a criterion of rule efficiency. Criteria may be based on definitions, laws, theories, or rules. Criteria are often mistaken for ↑**definitions**. For example, many ecologists state that the following defines "competition": "Two species compete when an increase in the density of one species leads to a decrease in the density of the other, and vice versa." But this is a criterion useful to form or test hypotheses about interspecific competition. Only the unveiling of a specific competition ↑**mechanism** can confirm the existence of competition.

CRITICAL THINKING Thinking characterized by clarity, precision, formal rigor (logical validity), and a careful examination of the presuppositions and the evidence relevant to the premises. Critical thinking is characteristic of mathematics, the "hard" sciences, and technology. It is less frequent in the "soft" sciences, the humanities, and theology. And it is abhorred by the postmodernists, who take pride in "weak thinking." Ant ↑magical thinking.

CRITICISM Analysis and evaluation sparked by flaws, real or apparent, of some kind. Criticism is a normal feature of research in all fields. Its role is to prompt improvement. But this function should not be exaggerated, for criticism is not creative: it can only weed out and stimulate further work. Indeed, before an item is subjected to critical analysis it must have been brought into existence. And, if found faulty, it should be repaired or replaced, instead of being protected by untestable ↑ad hoc hypotheses.

CROSS-DISCIPLINARY That trespasses disciplinary frontiers. **Syn** transdisciplinary. There are two kinds of cross-disciplinary approaches, investigations, or findings: ↑multidisciplinary and ↑interdisciplinary. The former boils down to the logical addition (∪) of two or more disciplines, whereas the latter amounts to their intersection (∩). For example, any serious social issue, such as poverty or war, calls for a multidisciplinary approach; cognitive neuroscience and socioeconomics are interdisciplines.

CRYPTO-CONTRADICTION A statement that, though contradictory, does not have the explicit form "*p* and not-*p*." Example: "I went tomorrow." This is a ↑**contradiction** because the grammar of the verb "to go" requires that the expression 'I went' be followed by an expression of the form 'at some time before now', whereas tomorrow comes after today.

CRYPTO-TAUTOLOGY A statement that looks factual but is actually ↑**tautological**. Example 1: "Here I am." By definition, "here" is where I am, so that the original proposition is actually "Where I am I am." However, the statement will convey information to someone who understands that "here" is taken to mean either the speaker's habitual place or his final destination. Example 2: "Water freezes at 0°C" is tautologous in being an implicit definition of "0°C." But, like every other definition, it does convey information to someone who did not know it before. Example 3: "Not everyone can be a free rider." This is a tautology because there is no rider without a mount. A first conclusion is that, contrary to what most textbooks assert, not every tautology involves logical connectives. Second, Informative ≠ Nontautological.

CUBISM, PHILOSOPHICAL The construction of formally rigorous but simplistic and utterly artificial theories or "languages." Philosophical cubism is exact but remote from science and technology.

CULT, PHILOSOPHICAL Uncritical adherence to a philosophical view. Examples: the Plato and Marx cults, the cult of common sense.

CULTURAL SCIENCES Humanities plus social studies. According to the ↑**hermeneutic**, "interpretive," or *Verstehen* school, those disciplines differ from the natural sciences with regard to both subject matter and method: the former in dealing with the spiritual, and the latter in using more intuition and empathy than reason, and in seeking understanding (↑*Verstehen*) rather than ↑**explanation**. Objections: (a) there are ↑**biosocial sciences**, such as psychology and demography; (b) the social sciences, no less than the natural ones, study concrete things rather than purely spiritual items; (c) the scientific method, rather than *Verstehen*, is used routinely in all the social sciences; (d) "interpretation" is another name for unchecked guessing; (e) the "interpretive" approach has been barren, particularly in accounting for large-scale social facts such as poverty, gender discrimination, war, and globalization. **Syn** ↑*Geisteswissenschaften* (sciences of the spirit), *sciences morales.*

CULTURALISM The name of two related but different theses. One is that ↑**culture** (in the strict or sociological sense) is the dominant "force" in society and history. The other is that individuals are nothing but products of their culture: a particular case of ↑**externalism**. The first thesis is falsified by the obvious importance of environmental, economic, and political events. The second cannot account for deviant behavior, in particular originality and rebelliousness.

CULTURE One of the three artificial (made) and concrete subsystems of every human society, along with the economy and the polity. It is characterized by such relations as those of inquiring, theorizing, myth-making, communicating, teaching, persuading, healing, and worshiping. The culture of an advanced society is composed of a number of subsystems, such as the professional communities, the publishing and entertainment industries, the school system, and the churches. This (sociological) characterization is at variance with the idealist conception of culture as a collection of disembodied objects, such as morality, art, and religion taken in themselves, i.e., regardless of the people who produce or consume epistemic, moral, artistic, or religious items. It is also different from the anthropological equation of culture and society— which makes it impossible to talk about the economy and the politics of culture.

CULTUROLOGY The study of ↑**cultures**. Examples: the sociology and history of art, philosophy, science, technology, and religion.

CYBERNETICS The study of systems endowed with control (negative feedback) devices, whether natural or artificial. Cybernetics is of interest to philosophy for the following reasons. First, it gives a naturalistic explanation of goal-directed behavior, which was earlier regarded as proof of spiritual forces. Second, negative feedback explains the stability (stationary states) of certain systems, whereas feedforward explains the onset of instability in others. Third, since it deals only with structural aspects, cybernetics is substrate-neutral: it applies to physical systems, organisms, organizations, and artifacts. However, the design, construction, or maintenance of particular cybernetic systems requires a knowledge of the behavior of the particular materials of which the systems are constituted.

DADAISM, PHILOSOPHICAL Preference for ↑**miniproblems**, and belief in simple and safe ultimates, as well as in the possibility of representing anything with a few simple strokes. **Syn** minimalism, ↑**simplism**.

DARWINISM The worldview or ideology sparked by ↑**evolutionary biology**. Its key tenets are that everything evolves in a gradual manner; that variation and selection (natural or social) are the main evolutionary mechanisms; that the fittest survive; and that teleology is an illusion created by the evolution of the unfit. ↑**Evolution**.

DAS WAHRE IST DAS GANZE The truth is the whole. Hegel's formula for ↑**holism**. This principle cannot be put into practice because the investigation of any whole proceeds by analysis. However, it is correct in implying that (a) every item is either a whole or a component of such: ↑**systemism**; and (b) any sectoral or highly specialized approach yields partial and imperfect knowledge that can be improved upon only by placing the item of interest into its context.

DASEIN Being-there. The trademark of existentialism. In some texts, *Dasein* = Real existence. In others, *Dasein* = Human existence. In still others, *Dasein* = Consciousness. The hermeneutic difficulty is compounded by the recurrent phrase "das Sein des Daseins," i.e., the being of being-there. Related terms not yet used by existentialists: *Hiersein* (Being-here), *Dortsein* (Being-over-there), *Irgendwosein* (Being-somewhere), and *Nirgendwosein* (Being-nowhere). Along with such spatial categories we may introduce their chronological counterparts: *Jetztsein* (Being-now), *Dannsein* (Being-then), *Irgendwannsein* (Being-sometime), and *Niemalssein* (Being-never). On the other hand, *Ursein* (primordial-Being), *Frühsein* (Being-early), *Frühersein* (Being-earlier), *Spätsein* (Being-late), and *Wiedersein* (Being-again) have no spatial partners. (This asymmetry may suggest an interesting indictment of Einstein's special relativity theory.) Finally, the chronotopic syntheses *Hierjetztsein* (Being-now-here), *Jetzthiersein* (Being-here-now), *Jetztdortsein* (Being-over-there-now), *Danndortsein* (Being-there-then), *Dannunsein* (Being-there-now), *Dortirgendwannsein* (Being-over-there-sometime), *Dortniemalssein* (Being-never-over-there), *Irgendwoirgendwannsein* (Being-somewhere-sometime), *Irgendwannirgendwosein* (Being-somewhere-sometime), and several others can easily be formed. Note how natural these combinations sound in German, and how clumsy their English counterparts sound. Which proves that German (when suitably macerated) is the ideal language for existentialism. A number of deep metaphysical questions involving these concepts can be framed. For example, '*Was ist der Sinn des Dawannseienden?*' (What is the

65

sense of Being-there-whenness?) *'Was ist das Sein des Nirgendsniemalsseins?* (What is the being of Being-never-nowhereness?) 'Are you there-then Hans?' and 'What will Grete find there-later?' A systematic exploration of this vast family of expressions might lead to a considerable extension of existentialism, particularly if related to such deep ontologico-semantic concepts as *Quatschsein* (being-fool's talk) and *Unsinn* (nonsense), and the corresponding profound questions 'What is the essence of *Quatschsein*?' and 'Why *Unsinn* rather than *Sinn*?' Caution: *Dasein* and its relatives should not be mistaken for *Daschein* (appearance-there), much less with *Daschwein* (pig-there).

DATA Plural of ↑**datum**.

DATAISM The radical empiricist doctrine according to which all genuine knowledge is either an empirical datum or an inductive generalization from data. Most experimental scientists profess dataism even if they seldom abide by it. Dataism influences the teaching of experimental science when it emphasizes technique at the expense of ideas, and meticulousness at the expense of understanding. ↑**Empiricism**.

DATUM a General philosophy Given, as opposed to constructed. Examples: sense data, newspaper information, instrument readings. Warning: data are not really given, but are constructed out of sensory inputs. And most of them are the products of active exploration: they are sought rather than given. **b Epistemology** Piece of empirical information. Examples: "You are reading a book," "This book weighs about one pound." Science and technology seek only certified empirical data. Such certification involves not only methodological rigor but also compatibility both with sound theories and with the philosophy inherent in scientific research. Thus reports on the Virgin's sightings and communication with the dead, even if in good faith, are not scientific data because they are at variance with the naturalist ontology of science.

DEATH a The termination of life. A state, not a thing. Hence all reifications of death, in particular its personifications, are mistaken. ↑**Afterlife**. **b Death of philosophy** It has become fashionable to hold that philosophy is not just sick, but finished once and for all. This view goes back to Comte and Wittgenstein. The former held that science supersedes philosophy, and the latter that philosophy is a linguistic disorder to be treated by linguistic therapy. However, scientific research involves a number of philosophical concepts (such as those of law and truth) and principles (such as those of the reality and knowability of the world) that no special science examines. And ↑**linguistic philosophy**—indifferent as it is to deep knowledge—refrains from tackling any important philosophical problems, as a consequence of which it has not come up with any philosophical theories (hypothetico-deductive systems). Whoever believes sincerely that philosophy is dead, and in particular that he is finished as a philosopher, has the moral duty to shut up. If on the other hand one disbelieves in the death of philosophy, or believes that the latter is in poor health but can still be saved, he should do something to cure it. And the only thing that can be done in good faith to contribute to the recovery of philosophy is to do some serious and interesting philosophizing. Whom should we believe: the gravedigger or the builder? The latter is more credible, because there are uncounted unsolved philosophical problems. Most entries in the present *Dic-*

tionary raise some problems. Hence the announcement of the death of philosophy has been premature. It is likely that there will be philosophical investigation as long as unsolved philosophical problems remain. And there will be such problems as long as some people engage in thinking about the most general features of reality and our knowledge and control of it. To write about the death of philosophy is an indication of impotence to tackle any of the many open philosophical problems. However, the alleged death seems to have become an industry. Yet this does not entail that philosophy is in good health: far from it, current philosophy exhibits serious symptoms of stagnation and even ↑**decadence**.

DEATH PENALTY A barbaric means of revenge and intimidation. It has no proven deterrence efficacy, and it is immoral for violating the rights to life and to redemption.

DEBATE Discussion among proponents of rival theses, methods, or proposals. Thought to have originated in ancient Greece jointly with civil liberties, political democracy, and courts of law. Essential to democracy. Frowned upon in social systems where cohesion or obedience to authority are paramount values. For a debate to be rational and fruitful, rather than an acrimonious and barren shouting match, its participants must agree beforehand to abide by certain rules: ↑**argument**, ↑**consensus**. In particular, scientific controversies are expected to be resolved only by rational debate involving the recourse to calculation or empirical data. The social constructivist-relativists claim, on the contrary, that truth is not involved in such controversies: that they are all terminated by either negotiation or force. The historical record shows that this has been the case only under ecclesiastical or political dictatorship, as in Galileo's trial and in the controversy between Lysenko and the geneticists under Stalinism. But of course these were not precisely purely scientific debates. And in any case truth claims were involved in them, and objective truth prevailed in the end.

DECADENCE a General concept The concept of decadence applies (refers) only to concrete complex things, such as molecules, organisms, and social systems. A concrete system may be said to be in decadence if it is in a process of disintegration or—in the case of artificial things such as machines and social organizations—if it no longer discharges its usual functions. **b Decadence of philosophy** Although there have never before been so many philosophy teachers, at the time of writing there is little radically new, interesting, and useful philosophizing going on in the world. In fact, most philosophers devote themselves to teaching, commenting on, or analyzing other philosophers' ideas, when not playing ingenious but inconsequential conceptual games. In short, the philosophical world community is presently in decadence. In fact, philosophy is suffering from the following ailments: (1) substitution of profession for vocation, and of occupation for passion; (2) confusion between original philosophizing and doing ↑**history of philosophy**; (3) mistaking obscurity for ↑**depth**; (4) obsession with language; (5) ↑**subjectivism**; (6) focusing on ↑**miniproblems**, ↑**pseudoproblems**, and *jeux d'esprit*; (7) ↑**formalism** without substance, and substance without form; (8) contempt for ↑**system**: preference for fragment and aphorism; (9) estrangement from the two intellectual engines of modern culture: science and technology; (10) weak interest in the most pressing social issues of our time—except as they provide an excuse for superficial essayism. Any one of the ten above-mentioned ailments should have sufficed to send philosophy to the emergency ward. All ten together have made it imperative to carry it to the intensive-care unit. The treatment is obvious: tackling hard and interesting problems whose solution is likely to advance knowledge; increased conceptual rigor and the concomitant clarity; feeding choice morsels of science and technology; and resumption of contacts with the best philosophical tradition. However, this diet will be insufficient if the patient does not realize how poorly it has been doing lately. In this case academic philosophy will die, and amateur philosophers will take over the torch. After all, neither of the founders of modern philosophy was a professor of philosophy.

DECENCY Prosocial behavior: the conjunction of temperance, honesty, truthfulness, loyalty, helpfulness, and compassion. Seemingly a cross-cultural invariant. Ant ↑**immoralism**. Decency is not to be confused with propriety, which is largely a matter of convention. A person's behavior can be perfectly decent even if it contravenes some of the norms of the recognized code of propriety—which may tolerate selfishness, cruelty, and zealotry. For example, an atheist and homosexual bohemian may be perfectly decent, whereas a devout and straight bloodsucker is not. By extension, a social order may be said to be decent if it promotes common decency. ↑**Good society**.

DECIDABLE / UNDECIDABLE ↑Decision.

DECISION a Metamathematics A formula is *decidable* in a theory if it can be either proved or refuted within the theory. Otherwise it is *undecidable*. A decision *procedure* for a given theory is a method for finding out whether any proposition in the theory can be proved within the theory. (Examples in logic: the truth-tables and the normal-form techniques.) A decision *problem* for a theory is the problem of finding out whether there is a decision procedure for the theorems of the theory. A theory is *decidable* if such a procedure exists; otherwise it is *undecidable*. The decidability of a theory is coextensive (though not cointensive) with its recursiveness. As it turns out, only a few theories are decidable. This negative result has dashed the ↑**formalist** foundationalist strategy but it has not affected mathematics. All it says is that in the vast majority of cases there is no uniform "mechanical" *method* of proof. A first consequence is that the proof of the vast majority of new theorems requires just as much ingenuity as their conjecturing. A second consequence is that, in general, it is not possible to program computers to prove theorems. Theorems, unlike mere corollaries, do not just drop from the axioms: typically, the latter must be enriched with auxiliary constructions and lemmas before they entail theorems. **b Psychology and action theory** The last stage in a process of deliberation aiming at taking action—or refraining from acting. ↑**Decision theory**.

DECISION THEORY The theory purporting to help weigh alternative decisions concerning actions. It underlies all ↑**rational-choice** theories, in particular ↑**game theory** and neoclassical microeconomics. Its key concepts are those of subjective ↑**probability** of an event, and the subjective ↑**utility** of the outcome of an action. Its central dogmas are that (a) every event can be assigned a probability; and (b) agents always act so as to maximize their expected utilities. These are indeed dogmas, because affairs under human control are rarely random, even if they are often under the cloud of uncertainty; because rational calculation is not the only factor entering decision making; and because experimental economists have found that we are loss-minimizers (risk averse) rather than gain maximizers.

DECONSTRUCTIONISM Variety of ↑**hermeneutics** derived from Hegel, Husserl, and Heidegger, and practiced by Jacques Derrida, Paul de Man, Harold Bloom, and other literary theorists. It holds that there is nothing outside texts; that language is prior to meaning; that authoritarianism may lurk behind even the most innocent-looking texts; and that such hidden threats must be "deconstructed" (unmasked, debunked). Characterized by wordplays, hence hardly translatable. Example: Derrida's musings about the alleged relations between *écrit* (writing), *écran* (screen), and *écrin* (coffin). A fad among literary critics posing as philosophers or social scientists. Not to be taken seriously except as a ↑**decadence** indicator.

DE DICTO / DE RE About words / about things. For instance, possibility can be conceptual (*de dicto*) or real (*de re*). Some expressions are ambiguous, in that they can be interpreted either way. For example, in ordinary language 'probable' can be interpreted as either ↑**plausible** (*de dicto*) or ↑**random** (*de re*).

DE GUSTIBUS NON EST DISPUTANDUM Taste is not debatable. The thesis of radical aesthetic ↑**relativism**. ↑**Taste**.

DE MORGAN'S LAWS The negation of a conjunction equals the disjunction of the negation of its conjuncts: $\neg(p \;\&\; q) = \neg p \vee \neg q$. The negation of a disjunction equals the conjunction of the negations: $\neg(p \vee q) = \neg p \;\&\; \neg q$. The analogs for sets are obtained by substituting complements for negations.

DEDUCTION Reasoning from premise(s) to conclusion(s), or "unpacking" the consequences of a set of assumptions. Some of these consequences, though "potentially contained" in the premises, are unknown at the time of asserting the latter. Hence they can be unexpected—one more proof that logic is not the study of the laws of thought. Deduction is the central theme of deductive ↑**logic**. Example 1: That a particular individual has a certain feature entails that some individuals have the same property: Fb $\vdash \exists x \, Fx$. Example 2: If one of the options of an alternative is false, then the remaining option is true: $p \vee q, \neg p \vdash q$. Unlike all other kinds of inference, deduction is ruled by strict universal rules of inference, such as ↑*modus ponens* and ↑*modus tollens*. It is also subject to axioms and theorems, such as the *deduction theorem*: For every set S of ↑**well-formed formulas**, and for any well-formed formulas p and q, if $S \cup \{p\} \vdash q$, then $S \vdash (p \Rightarrow q)$. A deduction is said to be *valid* if and only if it abides by such rules. Since there are several different systems of deductive logic, deductive validity is contextual. In other words, there are as many ↑**entailment** relations as logics. However, the logic underlying the overwhelming majority of theories in mathematics and factual science is ordinary (classical) logic.

DEFINABILITY A concept is said to be definable in a given context if it can be equated with a combination of concepts occurring in that context. The defining or basic concepts are called "primitive" relative to the given context. For example, in predicate logic "some" is definable in terms of "all" and "not," namely thus: Some = not-all-not. But one may also choose "some" and "not" as primitives or definers of "all." In particle mechanics, "mass" is primitive, whereas in continuum mechanics (which encompasses particle mechanics) it is defined in terms of "mass density." There appears to be only one absolutely undefinable concept, i.e., one that must be taken as basic or primitive in all contexts. This is the concept of identity. The reason is that ↑**definitions** are identities. Thus if one were to define "identical" as "not different," one would perpetrate the following nonsensical string of symbols: $== \neg \neq$.

DEFINITE DESCRIPTION The pointing to a unique object, such as "the logarithm of 1," "the president of the United States," and "the lowest price." A definite description may be analyzed as an incomplete function. More precisely, it may be conceptualized as the RHS of a formula of the form "$y = f(x)$." ↑**Description**.

DEFINITION Elucidation of a concept (or a sign) in terms of other concepts (or signs), as in "numerals are names of whole numbers." The elucidating concepts constitute the definiens, and the elucidated one the definiendum. There are two main kinds of definition: explicit and implicit. Explicit definitions are identities, often written in the form "A $=_{df}$ B," such as "Quanton $=_{df}$ Physical entity describable only in terms of quantum physics." In the philosophical literature, explicit definitions are usually construed as ↑**biconditionals**. This is a mistake, because the two sides of a biconditional need not have the same meaning; hence they are not always mutually substitutable. For example, although all mammals are hairy and conversely, the predicates "mammal" and "hairy" have different senses. Implicit definitions are propositions or sets of propositions where the definiendum does not occur separated from the definiens. Example: a standard definition of the implication (or if-then) relation $\Rightarrow$ is this: p $\Rightarrow$ q $=_{df} \neg p \vee q$. *Axiomatic* definitions are implicit definitions in terms of axiom systems. Example: Peano's five axioms define the concept of a natural number. *Recursive* definitions are implicit definitions where the definienda occur at least twice. Example: the addition of natural numbers can be defined recursively by the following equations: For any natural number m, $m+1 = m'$, $m+n' = (m+n)'$, where the primes designate the successor function.

DEFINITION, REAL Description. ↑**Real definition**.

DEISM Belief in a god, personal or impersonal, that once upon a time created the world but does not interfere with it any longer. Also called the absentee-landlord view of the deity. To be distinguished from ↑**theism**. Deism was most widespread in the eighteenth and nineteenth centuries. The American Founding Fathers were split into deists and agnostics.

DEMARCATION PROBLEM The problem of finding the precise border between science and nonscience. This problem presupposes the existence of such a border. This is a genuine problem with regard to pseudoscience and theology: unless a rigorous demarcation criterion is adopted, psychoanalysis will be sold as a science, and "creation science" will appear to be compatible with science. But the demarcation problem is a pseudoproblem with reference to philosophy and science, for these are not disjoint, as shown by the philosophical presuppositions of scientific research, such as those of the autonomous existence and knowability of the world. The problem is to adopt a demarcation criterion, or else a definition of "science," at once strict enough to disqualify a pseudoscience such as parapsychology, and broad enough to accommodate the emergent sciences with dubious credentials.

DEMATERIALIZATION Disappearance of matter. In particular disembodiment, as in death according to religious myths. The Information Revolution under way is often characterized as a dematerialization process, although it involves material transmitters, receivers, satellites, electromagnetic waves, and other bits of matter. **Syn** ↑**annihilation**.

DEMOCRACY The rule of the people, as first described twenty-five centuries ago by Pericles and Herodotus. A key concept in ↑**politology** and ↑**political philosophy**, and yet one that has as many meanings as political theories. The common core of all of them seems to be constituted by the ideas of ↑**freedom**, ↑**equality** (in some regard), civic duty, and self-governance (inclusive of open debate and free voting). Democracy can be biological (neither gender nor ethnic discrimination), economic (or equal opportunity to make a living and acquire wealth), political (liberty to elect and be elected for public office), legal (equality under the law), and cultural (free access to education and culture). Integral democracy may be defined as the conjunction of these four partial democracies. ↑**Liberty, equality, fraternity**.

DEMONSTRATION Proof that includes an explicit reference to all the inference rules involved in it. Such complete proofs are seldom given.

DENOTATION The relation(s) between a concept and its referent(s), as in "students are people whose main occupation is learning." There are two denotation relations: those of ↑**reference** and ↑**extension**. For instance, the concept of fairness refers to people, and its extension is the subset of the set of people who happen to be fair. Reference is one of the two components of ↑**meaning**.

DEONTIC Referring to duty or obligation.

DEONTIC LOGIC The theory aiming at elucidating and interrelating the concepts of obligation, prohibition, and permission, as in the rule that whatever is not forbidden is permitted. So far, no satisfactory system of deontic logic has been built. This is not surprising given that the bearers of the deontic operators "permitted" and its kin are propositions, whereas only actions are actually permissible or otherwise. It might be possible to build reasonable deontic logics with deontic operators acting on actions (and inactions), and including alternative postulates about the relation between basic permissions and obligations. Such deontic theory would straddle ↑**praxiology** and ↑**ethics**. But presumably the result would be a mere formalization of ethical and legal norms without changes in logic.

DEONTOLOGISM A duties-only ethics. Deontologism can be ↑**consequentialist** and religious, like the Christian and Moslem ethics, or nonconsequentialist and secular, like

Kant's. It fits in with authoritarian social orders. In a democracy, duties are supposed to be paired off to rights: ↑**Duty / right**.

DEPTH An object is deeper than another if the latter depends upon the former but not conversely. We must distinguish conceptual from ontological depth. **a Conceptual** A ↑**construct** is deeper than a second one if the latter depends upon the former but not conversely. In particular (a) in a ↑**definition**, the definiens is deeper than the definiendum; (b) in a ↑**theory**, the axioms are deeper than the theorems; (c) in a family of logically related theories, the reducing theories are deeper than the reduced theories. In general: the lower, the deeper. Caution 1: Because definability and derivability are contextual, so is conceptual depth. Caution 2: Obscurity must not be mistaken for depth. Caution 3: There is no conceptual bottom line, for in principle any construct can be replaced by a deeper one. This is in sharp contrast to ontological depth, which does have a floor. **b Ontological** A factual item lies deeper than another factual item if the latter depends upon the former but not conversely. In particular (a) a thing lies deeper than another if the former is a proper part (e.g., a component) of the latter; (b) a property lies deeper than another if the former determines the latter but not conversely; (c) an event or process lies deeper than another if the former causes the latter but not conversely.

DESCRIPTION a Logic and semantics Descriptions may be indefinite, as "a cat," or definite, as "the cat next door." Indefinite descriptions are unproblematic: "a cat" is just an arbitrary member of the set of cats. By contrast, definite descriptions are harder to crack. The standard definition is Bertrand Russell's: A definite description presupposes existence and indicates uniqueness. This analysis is unsatisfactory because of the ambiguity of the "existential" ↑**quantifier**. In the case of descriptions we are interested only in uniqueness, which can be expressed in several ways. A clear and simple way is this. Consider the functional formula "The price of x equals y," or "$P(x) = y$" for short. The LHS of this equality is the definite description "The price of x." In other words, the definite description results from truncating the function concerned, which in this case is P. But P may not be defined for some objects, such as planets and dreams, which are priceless till new notice. In this case one may speak of *improper* definite descriptions. Examples: "The emperor of America" and "The Creator." Only proper ↑**definite descriptions**, such as "my mother" and "the sine of 90^0," can be analyzed as truncated functions. **b Epistemology** Characterization of a concept or fact, as with "1 is the successor of 0," and "Schools are learning places." Mathematical descriptions can be complete. Not so descriptions of factual items: most of these are incomplete. True, the theoretical description of the state of a rather simple thing such as a hydrogen atom can be complete. But one cannot ascertain experimentally what state a particular atom is in until after it has jumped to another energy level. If a description of a fact includes the corresponding mechanism, it is an ↑**explanation** proper. Example: "The stock market fell when it was announced that the employment rate had risen, because a rise in demand could be expected and, with it, a period of demand inflation."

DESCRIPTIONISM The methodological prescription to restrict all studies to ↑**descrip-**

tion, refraining from seeking to analyze or explain. A component of both ↑**positivism** and ↑**phenomenology**. ↑**Black-boxism**, ↑**functionalism**. Descriptionism can be enriched and thus salvaged by requiring that the description include the pertinent ↑**mechanism**, for in this case it amounts to an ↑**explanation**. In other words, an explanation of a fact is a description of the fact together with a mention of the underlying mechanism. Example: A sun eclipse is the occultation of the Sun [description] caused by the interposition of the Moon [mechanism].

DESIDERATUM A goal that is considered valuable and attainable. Like ↑**value**, a desideratum may be objective, subjective, or both. And its attainment can be offset by undesired side effects. This is why desiderata must be weighed along with the means envisaged to attain them.

DESIGN The deliberate and intelligent sketching of an artificial thing or process, as in "aircraft design" and "the design of new materials." The hub of ↑**technology** and a key praxiological concept. Typically, the designer's task is to pose and solve an ↑**inverse problem**: Given a desired performance, imagine what could execute it.

DESIGN, ARGUMENT FROM The claim that the (alleged) perfection of nature is a clear sign of its having been designed by an intelligent deity. This claim, central to "natural" theology and creation "science," ignores the many natural imperfections, such as defective crystals, imploding stars, meteoritic impacts, floods and droughts, species extinctions, plagues, junk DNA, genetic diseases, bursting appendices, infected "wisdom" teeth, troublesome coccyxes, and much more. Besides, the argument cannot compete in explanatory power with the scientific theories of cosmic, molecular, biological, and social ↑**evolution**. However, many evolutionary biologists write carelessly about such and such an organ that has been "designed" by natural selection to perform such and such a function. And evolutionary psychologists even write about "optimal design" in the engineering sense.

DESIGNATION Relation between symbol and construct, as in "∅ designates the empty set." Such a relation is conventional, hence changeable at will.

DESIGNATOR Symbol that ↑**designates** a ↑**construct** or ↑**denotes** a ↑**thing**. There are two kinds of designator: proper ↑**names** (such as 'ℕ' for the set of natural numbers), and ↑**definite descriptions** (such as "your mother" and "the square root of 2"). Since designators are conventional, they are philosophically insignificant. What may be of philosophical interest are their designata. For example, whereas numbers are of mathematical and philosophical interest, numerals are of interest only to historians and typesetters. However, ↑**linguistic philosophers** set great store by designators.

DESTINY No such thing. ↑**Determinism**.

DETERMINACY / INDETERMINACY As used in physics and its philosophy, incorrect translation of the German original *scharf/unscharf* (sharp / blunt, clear-cut / fuzzy). ↑**Heisenberg's inequalities**, ↑**indeterminacy**.

DETERMINATION a Ontology Mode of becoming, as in "Causation, chance, and goal-seeking are modes of determination." **b Epistemology** The narrowing down of a universe of discourse. Alternatively, the calculation or measurement of the value of a property, or the inclusion of a thing into its natural kind or species.

DETERMINISM a Ontology The doctrine that everything happens either lawfully or by design. To put it negatively: there is neither ↑**accident** nor ↑**chance**. Traditional determinism admitted only causal, teleological (goal-directed), and divine determination. Contemporary scientific determinism is broader in some respects and narrower in others: it is identical with the ↑**lawfulness** principle together with the principle ↑**Ex nihilo nihil fit**. **b Causal determinism** Every ↑**event** has a ↑**cause**. Only partially true, because there are spontaneous processes, such as natural radioactive disintegration and neuron discharge, as well as probabilistic laws. **c Genetic determinism** We are what our genomes dictate. Only partially true, because environmental factors are as important as genetic endowment, and ↑**creativity** is undeniable. **d Cultural determinism** We are what society (in particular culture) makes us. This doctrine has a grain of truth, since we learn and act in society. But we are also partially shaped by our genetic endowment as well as by what we learn and do on our own initiative. **e Historical determinism** The course of history is predetermined: individuals and accidents can only accelerate or retard it. A component of the collectivist version of ↑**holism**. This view ignores the role of favorable and unfavorable environments, as well as that of inventiveness and initiative, neither of which is predictable.

DIAGNOSTIC, MEDICAL The task of guessing ("inferring") usually imperceptible pathological processes (causes) from observable signs or symptoms (effects). A typical ↑**inverse** problem, hence one that requires the framing and testing of ↑**hypotheses**. This suffices to indict the empiricist ↑**iatrophilosophy**.

DIALECTICAL MATERIALISM The philosophy of ↑**Marxism**. ↑**Dialectics**, c.

DIALECTICS a In ancient and medieval philosophy, synonymous with logic or the art of argumentation. In Hegelianism and Marxism, dialectics is sometimes regarded as a method, and at other times as a philosophy. The first construal is mistaken, because neither Hegel nor Marx nor their followers have proposed any method proper (or standardized procedure) smacking of dialectics. Dialectics is a philosophy and, more precisely, an ontology: see **c**. Dialectical epistemology and ethics are nonexistent. **b Dialectical logic** has been sold as a generalization of formal logic. The latter would be a sort of slow-motion approximation to the former: it would hold only for short stretches, whereas dialectical logic would cover processes in their entirety. For better or for worse, dialectical logic has remained at the stage of a project. In fact, no one has ever proposed any clear dialectical rules of formation or of inference. Moreover, the very idea of a dialectical logic seems to be a misunderstanding stemming from Hegel's identification of logic with ontology—an equation that makes sense only within an idealist system. **c Dialectical ontology** boils down to the three so-called laws of dialectics, stated by Hegel and reformulated by Engels and Lenin. These are: (1) every thing is a union of opposites; (2) every change originates in opposition (or "contradiction"); (3) quality and quantity change into one another. The elementary particles—the bricks that constitute the world—are counterexamples to the first "law." Every case of cooperation in nature or society ruins the second. The third "law" is unintelligible as it stands. However, it can be charitably reformulated thus: In every quantitative process, qualitative changes (may) occur and, once these occur, new modes of growth or decline set in. This is the one clear and true "dialectical law"; but it does not involve the concept of contradiction, which is the trademark of dialectics. Unsurprisingly for such a foggy doctrine, dialectics has never been formalized.

DICHOTOMOUS PREDICATE A ↑**predicate** or variable that can have only two values, such as alive and dead. Most unary ↑**predicates** are dichotomous or ↑**qualitative**, particularly during the first phase of a study. It is unknown whether there are irreducibly dichotomous properties other than ↑**existence**. Even the spin of an electrically charged particle in a magnetic field, though said to be either "up" or "down," actually performs a precession movement around the field.

DICHOTOMY Division of a whole or of a collection into two mutually disjoint and complementary parts. Examples: the ↑**mind / body**, ↑**reason / cause**, ↑**fact / value**, and ↑**nature / culture** dichotomies in idealist philosophies.

DICTUM DE OMNI, or UNIVERSAL INSTANTIATION What holds for all holds for any: $\forall x\, Fx \vdash Fy$.

DIFFERENCE Two objects are different if they are not identical—i.e., if they do not share all their properties. Identical items "are" one, not many. Hence, if there were no differences in the universe, it would consist of a single thing. And, being a single thing and always identical to itself, it would be changeless. But of course there is diversity and there is change. Things change because they differ from one another, whether in kind or because of their respective positions in space and time. For instance, gradients (in field potential, mass density, heat, etc.) are sources of forces, which in turn alter the mode of change (e.g., causing accelerations). So, the concepts of difference and change, though not ↑**cointensive**, are ↑**coextensive**. In short, difference makes all the difference. Regrettably, "difference" is a neglected category. Only extreme difference, namely ↑**opposition**, has drawn the attention of philosophers, particularly the defenders of ↑**dialectics**. But they often mistake mere difference for opposition—as when they hold that change is (ontologically) contradictory because it consists in the transformation of a thing or a property into its opposite.

DIGNITY Respect for self and others. Not to be confused with pomposity. **Ant** debasement. Dignity is a central value in any ↑**humanist** ethics. By contrast, fundamentalist religion and totalitarianism require blind obedience and therefore self-debasement. True, Christians regard human dignity as God-given, but also as limited by blind obedience to divine fiat. Historians know that, far from being a gift, human dignity has always been hard to win and keep. And anyone knows that it is next to impossible to uphold dignity on $1 a day or less—the income of one out of every three human beings.

DILEMMA Problem of choice between two mutually exclusive alternatives. Examples: the logical dilemma posed by two mutually contradictory propositions in a theory; the epistemological dilemma posed by two different hypotheses accounting for the same empirical data; the moral or legal dilemma raised by conflicting interests or norms. The concept of an epistemological dilemma can be generalized from propositions to sets of propositions, such as doctrines. But in this case there is more choice, because one may accept some parts of the contrasting views. For example, the rationalism-empiricism dilemma may be resolved by combining the moderate versions of the two epistemologies. This faces the student with a ↑**trilemma**. Actually, all moral dilemmas are trilemmas, because there are always three practical options: doing nothing, doing the right thing, and doing what is convenient. ↑**Aporia**, ↑**ratioempiricism**, scientific ↑**realism**.

DING AN SICH ↑Thing in itself.

DISCONTINUITY A break or jump in an otherwise continuous or smooth object or process. Biological and historical processes, though continuous in some respects, are punctuated by discontinuities, namely the emergence or submergence of properties. ↑**Continuum**, ↑**revolution, epistemic**.

DISCONTINUITY, FALLACY OF The claim that the present is totally different from the past; in particular, that scientific revolutions are total and have no roots.

DISCOVERY Unveiling of a previously unknown existing item. There are two kinds of discovery: conceptual and empirical. Example 1: The proof of a mathematical theorem is a discovery of the logical relation existing between the theorem and its premises. But both the former and the latter have to be invented (guessed) before their relation can be discovered. Example 2: The oncogenes were discovered. However, this discovery was the culmination of a process that started with the unorthodox hypothesis—an invention— that the cancers of some types might be caused by certain genes. There are no rules for making discoveries, and there is no reason to believe that everything will eventually be discovered. This has not prevented a number of philosophers from writing about a logic of discovery. ↑**Invention**.

DISENCHANTMENT OF THE WORLD The removal of supernatural and spiritual fictions from the worldview: the replacement of magical thinking with rationalism, naturalism, and secularism. A characteristic of modernity according to Max Weber, though with strong roots in ancient atomism and stoicism. By contrast, Romantic philosophy, postmodernism, and New Age are attempts at reenchanting the world.

DISJUNCTION The formal counterpart of the ordinary-knowledge "or." Alternative, as in "p or q," symbolized as "$p \vee q$." An inclusive disjunction is true if at least one of the disjuncts is true. Hence the *disjunctive syllogism*: $p \vee q, \neg p \vdash q$. By contrast, an exclusive disjunction is true if only one of the disjuncts is true: $(p \vee q) \& \neg (p \& q)$. Material things do not practice disjunction: there are neither disjunctive properties nor disjunctive facts. Disjunction, as in "either this or that will happen," is a mental process.

DISJUNCTIVE PROPERTY The disjunction of two properties, as in "people are animals or minerals." There are no such properties: the very idea of a disjunctive property arises from the confusion between properties, which individuals either possess or not, with ↑**attributes** or ↑**predicates**, concepts that need not have real counterparts. Thus, while it is trivially true that the present president of the United States is a person or a rock, there is no point in attributing to him the property "person or rock," if only because mineralogy cannot say anything nontrivial about him.

DISPOSITION Ability, potentiality, ↑**propensity**, or tendency for a thing to pass from one state to another. Examples: fragility, refractivity, polarizability, hereditability, learnability, benevolence. **Syn** ↑**potency**, real ↑**possibility**. The very idea of a dispositional property has been distrusted either because it resembles the powers of the medieval schoolmen, or because it would seem that one must wait for a disposition to be actualized before attributing it. However, a theoretical study of a thing may reveal some disposition of it—for example, to associate with other things, to grow, to decay, or to learn. Hence, talk of dispositions does not necessarily amount to invoking a ↑**black box**, let alone an obscure power. But of course any hypothesis about a disposition must be empirically testable, and it will become true or false only upon completion of the test, which will coincide with the actualization of the disposition. There are two kinds of disposition: causal and stochastic. A *causal* disposition is always actualized under certain circumstances. Examples: the propensity of eggs to crack when dropped onto the floor; the disposition of an unstable system to decay; the disposition of children to learn to speak and walk. A stochastic disposition is actualized only sometimes, with a (constant or variable) frequency. Example: the propensity of radioactive atoms to disintegrate. This second concept of disposition is exactified by ↑**probability**. The existence of two modes of propensity shows that the phrase 'the propensity interpretation of probability' is not a ↑**definite description**: that is, it does not suffice to specify the realistic interpretation of probability theory.

DISTRIBUTIVE LAW Any of several mathematical laws combining conjunction (or multiplication) with disjunction (or addition). Examples: "$p \,\&\, (q \lor r) = (p \,\&\, q) \lor (p \,\&\, r)$," "$p \lor (q \,\&\, r) = (p \lor q) \,\&\, (p \lor r)$," "$x(y+z) = xy + xz$." It has been claimed that ↑**quantum mechanics** violates distributivity. This claim is false, as shown by the fact that the logic underlying the mathematical formalism of that theory is the ordinary predicate calculus, which obeys distributivity.

DIVISIBILITY The property of an object of being decomposable or analyzable. **Ant** indivisibility. Examples of indivisibles: prime numbers and electrons. ↑**Elementary**. The question of divisibility has divided ontologists from ancient times on. Whereas the continuists taught the infinite divisibility of every existent, the ↑**atomists** postulated the existence of indivisibles. Contemporary physics assumes the existence of both continua (fields) and indivisibles (quanta). ↑**Atomism**, ↑**plenism**.

DOCTA IGNORANTIA Educated ignorance: acknowledgment of the limitations or of the conjectural nature of one's knowledge. This idea, traceable to Socrates, Augustine, and Cusa, is part of all the versions of ↑**skepticism**. **Ant** naive ignorance.

DOCTRINAIRE Attached to a ↑**doctrine** in an extreme and ↑**dogmatic** fashion. Examples: religious fundamentalisms, neoclassical microeconomics, Marxism, neoliberalism. **Ant** having a critical attitude or an ↑**open mind**.

DOCTRINE Collection of propositions taught as true in some school. Doctrines are less well organized than theories, and they do not necessarily enjoy empirical support. They can be secular or religious.

DOGMA A belief taken to be impregnable to argument and experience. Example: the so-called revealed truths of religion. Difference between dogma and tautology: tautologies are provable. Difference between dogma and postulate: postulates are testable by their consequences. If these are false, the postulates that entail them stand falsified. The expression 'central dogma of molecular biology' is mistaken, because it is a hypothesis—moreover, one that has been corrected.

DOGMATISM The adoption of ↑**dogmas** in a certain field. The ancient skeptics called 'dogmatists' all those who claimed to know something with certainty. Nowadays dogmatism is rampant not only in philosophy, religion, and politics, but also in some chapters of science, particularly in cosmology and economics.

DOT, DOT, DOT, or . . . Synonym of "etc." or abbreviation of "and so on, indefinitely." Not precise enough in formal discourse, which, to avoid ambiguity, requires an explicit name for the general term of the sequence or series in question. For example, the infinite series $S = 1 + 1/2 + (1/2)^2 + (1/2)^3 + . . .$ is best rewritten as $S = \sum_n (1/2)^n$.

DOUBLE NEGATION a Ordinary language Strong negation, as in "smoking is a no-no." Likewise, "yes-yes" is a strong assertion—except when uttered as "yeah, yeah" with a sarcastic tone. **b Logic** Law of both classical logic and set theory, whereby a second negation (or complement) cancels the first. Symbolized $\neg\neg p \Leftrightarrow p$ in ordinary logic. This is not a theorem in intuitionistic logic. And it is rejected by dialecticians, who interpret negation in an ontological manner, namely as superseding. **c Ontology** The dialectical "law" of double negation is not a law proper but Hegel's definition of a peculiar concept of negation, namely as the *Aufhebung* (supersession, overcoming, sublation) of the lower by the higher, or of the older by the newer. A quaint restatement of the myth of continual progress.

DOUBLE-TALK Duplicity, whether deliberate or unconscious, as in professing philosophical idealism while behaving like a materialist.

DOUBLE-TRUTH, DOCTRINE OF The view that on certain matters there can be two apparently opposite yet mutually compatible sets of truth, scientific and religious: that ↑**science** and ↑**religion** do not overlap, hence they can coexist peacefully. This medieval doctrine has been invoked to protect inquiry on dangerous subjects, such as the eternity of the world and the mortality of the soul. Stephen J. Gould revived the same doctrine under the name NOMA (for non-overlapping magisteria). However, this trick cannot bring about a truce in the age-long war between science and religion, because these collide head-on on a number of decisive points. For example, every religion asserts the existence of miracles, whereas scientists abide by the ↑**lawfulness** principle; prayer presupposes telepathic communication between worshiper and deity, but is discounted by experimental psychology; all religions assert that ↑**life** is mysterious, which defeats the purpose of biology; no religion admits that the mind is a collection of brain processes, as ↑**cognitive neuroscience** assumes and confirms; no religion encourages the scientific study of itself: the sociology of religion is part of science; and most religions consecrate certain texts, some of them called 'sacred scriptures', that every member of the faith is expected to believe and worship—a typically unscientific attitude. In short, both science and religion ask some of the same ↑**big questions**, but they handle them in diferent fashions and give mutually incompatible answers.

DOUBT The state of mind, or mental process, consisting in being unable or unwilling to assert or deny a proposition (or set of propositions), for ignoring whether it is true or false. Ant ↑**certainty**. Doubt is the trademark of ↑**skepticism**. However, whereas radical skeptics doubt everything, moderate skeptics doubt only in the face of incomplete or contradictory evidence. Moreover, doubt paralyzes the former but spurs the latter. Typically, scientists and technologists are moderate skeptics when on the job. But even they are occasionally either gullible or radically skeptic when straying to other fields.

DOWNWARD CAUSATION The alleged action of mental events on brain events, as in blushing as a consequence of feeling shame. The dualistic construal of a process that ↑**cognitive neuroscience** conceives of as an ordinary causal chain within the body. For instance: Behavior or recall of it → Evaluation of behavior (a cortical process) → Activation of a component of the limbic system (such as the amygdala) → Motor strip → Dilation of capillaries in the face.

DOXASTIC Concerning ↑**opinion** rather than well-grounded knowledge. Doxastic logic, the so-called logic of belief, is the unsuccessful attempt to study and regiment a priori what is empirical and inherently undisciplined if only because it is strongly atached to tradition and colored by emotion.

DRAWING CONCLUSIONS Extracting logical consequences from a set of premises. The science of drawing conclusions is deductive ↑**logic**. It is illegitimate to draw conclusions from facts, or even from propositions describing facts. Facts only raise the problem of guessing hypotheses capable of explaining them. ↑**Explanation**.

DUAL Complement. The pairs of concepts everything / nothing, unity / plurality, exactness / fuzziness, full / empty, love / hatred, cooperation / competition, trust / betrayal, and right / duty consist in a concept and its dual. The semantic characteristic of dual concepts is that neither makes sense without its dual. For example, a person can betray another only if the latter trusts the former. Caution: Duals are not opposites (or contradictories). For example, "nothing" is the dual of "everything" but not its opposite; that of "love" is "hatred," but its negation is "hatred or indifference"; and the negation of "greater than" is "smaller or equal." In mathematics there are several duality laws, or rather metalaws. For example, the exchange of the ∪ and ∩ operations in any lattice yields another lattice: its dual. Incidentally, this is a ↑**metatheorem**.

DUALISM a Ontological The view that the world is composed of things of two kinds: material and ideal, worldly and otherworldly, profane and sacred, or good and bad. A particular case of ↑**pluralism**. Ontological dualism is part and parcel of all religions and of most idealist philosophies. Psychoneural dualism is at variance with cogitive neuroscience, which postulates that mental processes constitute a subset of brain processes. ↑**Mind-body problem. b Economic-cultural** The view that human society as composed of a material (or economic) and an ideal (or cultural) layer. A view shared by both historical idealists and historical materialists. The difference between them is that, whereas idealists hold the primacy of culture, historical materialists claim the converse. According to systemic materialism, all the subsystems of a society—in particular its economy and its culture—are material because they are composed of concrete things (people and their artifacts); and moreover they interact rather than some being agents and others patients. ↑**BEPC** schema, ↑**culture. c Methodological** The convention that, for analytical purposes, ideas can be treated as self-existing, in particular separately from brains and societies. This convention is indispensable to analyze and evaluate ideas of any kind. It is systematically violated by the externalist sociologists of knowledge.

DUHEM THESIS No hypothesis can be checked in isolation. For example, checking a chemical hypothesis involves assuming the mechanical and electromagnetic hypotheses involved in the construction and operation of the measuring instruments utilized in the test. ↑**Hypothetico-deductive method.**

DUHEM-QUINE THESIS Scientific hypotheses and theories are not unambiguously determined by the relevant empirical evidence. That is, one and the same set of data is compatible with alternative hypotheses or theories. This thesis applies to stray hypotheses better than to theories (hypothetico-deductive systems), since these can be checked against data of different kinds, as well as against adjoining theories. ↑**Underdetermination.**

DUTY / RIGHT A duty is an obligation sanctioned by a social group, whereas a right is a permission granted by a social group. Duties and rights can be moral, legal, or political (inclusive "or"), local or universal. They constitute the poles of the ↑**moral** sphere, as well as of ethics and social philosophy. A duties-only morality imposes sacrifices without rewards, whereas a rights-only morality enshrines privilege. Both are unfair and incompatible with a sustainable social order. The latter calls for a morality where rights imply duties and conversely. For example, the right to vote implies the duty to vote responsibly and regularly. And the duty to provide for one's children implies the right to earn the wherewithall to discharge that duty. ↑**Agathonism,** ↑**obligation, prohibition, permission,** ↑**right / duty.**

DYNAMICISM ↑**Processualism.**

E = mc² The theorem in relativistic mechanics that relates the energy and the mass of a particle. It holds only for entities endowed with mass, not for photons. The occurrence of c, the speed of light in vacuum, shows that relativistic mechanics cannot be understood apart from electrodynamics. Although one of the most famous physical laws, it is also one of the most misunderstood. The most common mistake is to regard it as expressing the conversion of matter into energy and conversely. This is mistaken because energy and mass are properties, not things. Indeed, every energy value is the energy *of* some thing or other; the same holds for mass.

ECLECTICISM Combination of disparate views or schools of thought. There are two kinds of eclecticism: mosaic (or inconsistent) and systemic (or consistent). *Mosaic eclecticism* is a jumble or juxtaposition of views with no regard for internal consistency. Example: the belief system of a religious scientist. *Systemic eclecticism* blends in a consistent way components drawn from different sources. Examples: ↑**ratioempiricism** and ↑**systemism**.

ECONOMICS a Science The branch of social science that studies such economic systems as firms, industries, markets, and entire economies. Distinguishable from the other social sciences but inseparable from them, as shown by the prosperity of economic sociology, socioeconomics, economics and law, and economic history. **b Philosophy of** The branch of the philosophy of science that seeks to elucidate the most general and problematic concepts of economics, and evaluate its most basic and problematic principles and methods. Sample of problematics: Conceptual and empirical status of utility; examination of the principle of the maximization of expected utility; nature of the micro-macro connection; existence of economic laws; relations with other sciences; and scientific and moral foundation of economic policies.

ECONOMISM The attempt to explain all political and cultural facts in terms of economic interests. Syn economic imperialism. Two varieties: Marxist and ↑**rational-choice theory**. An increasingly popular research strategy, but one that fails to account for cooperation, moral constraints, ideological commitment, disinterested curiosity, heterodoxy, and even such economic facts as business cycles, inflation, and stagflation. ↑**Marxism,** ↑**rational-choice theory**.

EFFICACY An event or process is efficacious (or effective) if it brings about the expected or desired result. In the domain of human action, "efficacy" is a praxiological concept definable as the degree of success of an action, or rate of attained goals. **Syn** effectiveness, success. **Ant** wastefulness. Efficacy is not to be confused with ↑**efficiency**.

EFFICIENCY An event or process is efficient if it brings about the desired outcome at low cost. The standard measure of efficiency is the output / input ratio, where "output" is defined as valuable outcome. Efficiency is not the same as ↑**efficacy**. First, because the concept of input (or work) does not occur in the definiens of that of efficacy. Second, because some courses of action are effective but inefficient (wasteful).

EGALITARIANISM The doctrine that all persons have the same rights, as well as the same duties commensurate with their abilities. Narrow version: legal, or isonomy (equality before the law). Broad version: biological, economic, political (in particular legal), and cultural. **Syn** Integral ↑**democracy**. Radical economic egalitarianism = income equality. Moderate or qualified economic egalitarianism = equal minimal income plus merit increase proportional to social value of work. ↑**Communism, socialism**.

EGOCENTRIC PARTICULAR A construct or symbol relative to a particular person. Examples: I, mine, here, now. ↑**Indexical, here, now**.

EGOISM The pursuit of gain or happiness at the expense of everything and everyone else. Two varieties of egoism can be distinguished: rational and irrational. The rational egoist ponders the possible consequences of his acts, whereas the irrationalist (or ↑**hedonist**) seeks only instant gratification. The former will do good if it advances his own interests, whereas the latter will do good only if it feels good. Both varieties of egoism are immoral, since morality is about others.

EIDETIC Essential, where "essences" are understood as self-existing ideas. **Ant** ↑**factual**. At one time Husserl, the founder of ↑**phenomenology**, described his own philosophy as eidetic science.

ELEMENTARY Indivisible, individual, basic, atomic. Examples: electrons, alphabet letters, points, prime numbers, primitive concepts. Some of the things we now regard as elementary may, on closer investigation, turn out to be composite.

ELUCIDATION Clarification. Much philosophizing consists necessarily in elucidating concepts and theses. Elucidation is achieved through exemplification, analysis, definition, reduction, or ↑**theorification**. The most important concepts are those that serve to define others, whence they are undefinable or primitive. The best way of elucidating a primitive concept is to incorporate it as a primitive into a theory. For example, the concept of logical necessity has been elucidated by rendering it the central concept of ordinary logic: ↑**entailment**. Likewise the concept of electromagnetic field, another primitive, has been elucidated by electrodynamics. **Syn** explication, not to be confused with ↑**explanation**.

EMBODIMENT Materialization of an idea. In objective-idealist philosophy, such as

Plato's, all concrete things and processes are embodiments of self-existing ideas. In particular, brain processes would embody the self, soul, or mind. This is at best an untestable hypothesis, because there is no way of finding out the alleged original blueprint. According to ↑materialism, only actions, artifacts, and artificial processes can be said to embody ideas. Thus, a computer may be said to embody ideas generated by its designer and user—not so a brain, for it is only in part made by the subject. The frequent occurrence of the expression 'embodiment of the mind' in computationist psychology is a Platonic relic. ↑Mind-body problem.

EMERGENCE a Static concept A property of a ↑system is emergent if it is not possessed by any component of the system. Examples: equilibrium, synergy, synchrony, being alive (an emergent property of cells), perceiving (an emergent property of certain systems of neurons), and social structure (a property of all social systems). Emergent properties can be local (like clustering) or global (like stability). Formal definition: P is an emergent property $=_{df} \exists x \, \forall y \, (Px \, \& \, y < x \Rightarrow \neg \, Py)$, where < stands for the ↑part/whole relation. **b Dynamic concept** According to the assumption that all systems are formed through the (natural or artificial) assembly of their components, emergence is typical of both individual development (or ontogeny) and ↑history (in particular ↑evolution). Examples: speech emerges in children around the first year of life, and it is likely to have emerged with the birth of Homo sapiens sapiens about 100,000 years ago. The concepts of emergence should not be confused with the fuzzy concept of ↑supervenience. And they should not be dismissed just because holists cherish them, particularly since they regard emergence as unanalyzable. The main point of a scientific study of a system is to try and explain its systemic (or emergent) properties in terms of either the interactions of its parts, or of its history. Emergence is beyond the ken of ↑holism as well as of ↑individualism. Only ↑systemism does it justice.

EMERGENT A newly arisen system characterized by new properties. Examples: organisms of new species, neuronal systems that think new ideas, and social inventions. The dual of ↑resultant. ↑Emergence.

EMERGENTISM The family of ontologies that emphasizes the idea of ↑emergence. The idealist version of emergentism postulates an uppermost level composed of disembodied minds (or spirits), both human and divine. By contrast, ↑emergentist materialism regards the mind as a collection of brain processes. ↑Mind-body problem.

EMERGENTIST MATERIALISM The version of ↑emergentism that holds that, although all real existents are ↑material, they are grouped into different ↑levels. To be distinguished from ↑physicalism, mechanism, and vulgar (or eliminative) materialism.

EMOTION A spontaneous mental process in the limbic system that can, however, be stemmed and occasionally even triggered by reason. Emotion colors perception, valuation, and action. Guilt, embarrassment, shame, empathy, and sympathy are called moral emotions, because they often elicit prosocial behavior. They are studied empirically by developmental and social psychologists. Emotion has raised a number of scientifico-philosophical problems, such as "Is it true that, as Hume taught, reason is but a tool of emotion?"; "Do animals other than people feel moral emotions, as Darwin believed?"; "Are moral emotions innate or learned?"; "Is it possible and legitimate to detach valuation from emotion?"; "Should education try to suppress emotions or rather refine and control them, particularly anger and fearfulness?"; and "Are moral rules mere expressions of emotions, as the emotivists hold?" ↑**Emotivism**.

EMOTIVISM The thesis, advanced by David Hume and adopted by ↑**logical positivism**, that all value judgments and moral rules are just expressions of emotions, and thus beyond both rational analysis and empirical justification. An irrationalist view opposed to axiological and ethical ↑**cognitivism** and ↑**realism**. Developmental psychology has shown that valuation depends largely upon experience and education.

EMPIRICAL Item inherent in or derived from experience. Sometimes identified with ↑**"factual**," as in the expression 'empirical science'. This identification is mistaken in a ↑**realist** philosophy because experiences constitute only a minute subset of the set of facts.

EMPIRICAL SUPPORT The collection of observational or experimental data that ↑**confirm** a hypothesis or theory, or ↑**a method** or ↑**norm**. According to ↑**falsificationism**, data may undermine but not support. This view is at variance with scientific and technological practice. Indeed, although scientists and technologists look for ↑**counterexamples**, they also seek empirical support. After all, they are more builders than destroyers: they are after truth and efficiency. However, falsificationism and empiricism notwithstanding, hypotheses, theories, methods, and plans do not live by data alone. They are also expected to jibe with other items of knowledge, in the same field of inquiry as well as in other disciplines. In particular, scientific hypotheses and theories are expected to be compatible with the bulk of antecedent knowledge, and even with certain philosophical principles, such as that there are no properties and changes in themselves, i.e., independent of things. ↑**Consistency b**.

EMPIRICISM a Epistemology Traditional empiricism is the family of philosophies according to which experience is the only source of knowledge. Most modern empiricists make an exception for logic and mathematics, which they admit as a priori. **b Ontology** The view that the world consists of experiences. The methodological implication, drawn by Ernst Mach, is that all the sciences are reducible to psychology. This is obviously false, because psychology uses some physics, whereas physics makes no use of psychology. It follows that the premise too is false. To be sure, there is no factual knowledge without experience. But science and technology go beyond experience when hypothesizing, theorizing, and designing scientific experiments and technological tests. Examples: the concepts of force field, DNA, efficiency, and globalization are transempirical. Like rationalism, empiricism is only half-true. The ticket is ↑**ratioempiricism**, in particular ↑**scientific realism**.

EMPTY a Logic A logical truth (↑**tautology**) is factually and empirically empty in that it describes no facts. **b Semantics** An expression devoid of sense (such as "the being of existence"), precise reference (such as the variables in a logical formula), or truth value (like the untestable propositions). **c Ethics** A moral exhortation so vague that it does not help making any decisions, such as "Do the right thing."

END Last state of a process. Recipe for a trendy book: start its title with "The end of."

END / MEANS ↑Means / end.

ENERGETISM The monistic ontology according to which all things consist of ↑**energy**. Untenable because energy is a ↑**property** of material things, not an entity. Energetism was put forward by Wilhelm Ostwald at the end of the nineteenth century as an alternative to both materialism and idealism, and it was endorsed by the positivists. Its contemporary heir is ↑**informationism**, which involves the same mistake, namely detaching a property from its bearer.

ENERGY a Property The extent to which a concrete thing can or does change. Hence coextensive with "changeability." The most universal property of real things, even more so than location in spacetime. Hence a possible definiens of "material": For all x: (x is material $=_{df} x$ has energy). The total energy of a closed system is constant: principle of energy conservation. Caution 1: Energy is a property, not a thing; hence it does not exist by itself on a par with matter. ↑$E = mc^2$. Caution 2: Having zero energy is not the same as having no energy: ↑**zero**. Thus, it seems that the positive rest and kinetic energies of the universe balance exactly the negative potential energy of gravitational attraction. **b Predicate** The most general measure of actual or potential change. There are different kinds of energy: potential and kinetic, elastic and thermal, electromagnetic and nuclear, etc. Energy is represented by different predicates in different theories: by functions in some and by operators in others. This is a reason for not confusing ↑**predicates** with the ↑**properties** they represent. It is also a reason for regarding the concept of energy as ontological as well as scientific.

ENGINEERING The branch of ↑**technology** concerned with the design and test of artificial systems of all kinds, from microchips, prostheses, and domestic appliances to mines, dams, chemical reactors, artificial satellites, robots, and algorithms. Historically the first branch of ↑**technology** to become scientific—whence the popular confusion of technology with engineering. Main branches: civil, mechanical, electrical, chemical, nuclear, biological, and epistemic (in particular ↑**artificial intelligence** and robotics).

ENGINEERING, PHILOSOPHY OF The philosophy of ↑**engineering** tackles such problems as the nature of machines and machine design; the analysis of the inverse problem of inventing a mechanism likely to accomplish the desired function; and moral problems raised by new labor-saving devices bound to eliminate jobs, and macroengineering projects likely to affect the natural or social environment. The contribution of ↑**humanism** to engineering is to view human beings—in particular workers, users, and potential victims—as the most important factors in engineering projects. Shorter: humanist engineering is systemic rather than sectoral.

ENIGMA Unsolved or insoluble problem. Said by radical skeptics of such ontological problems as those of the beginning of the universe, the essence of matter, the origin of life, the nature of mind, and the origins of thought and language. Scientific realists prefer to talk of problems that have so far not been solved, or that are unlikely to be ever solved due to the destruction of the required data.

ENLIGHTENED a In accordance with reason, aiming at the scientific understanding of facts, or at the use of social science in social reform. Examples: ↑**secular humanism**, ↑**Enlightenment. Ant** ↑**obscurantist. b** In Buddhism, Hinduism, and some varieties of mysticism, 'enlightened' means having found the truth or the right path through revelation, insight, or ascesis, not inquiry or experience.

ENLIGHTENMENT The eighteenth-century cultural movement that promoted secularism, free inquiry, reason, science, human rights, liberty, equality, solidarity, and the pursuit of happiness. Some of the best-known Enlightenment philosophers were Hume, Voltaire, Diderot, d'Holbach, Helvétius, Cabanis, Condorcet, and Bentham. Rousseau was ambivalent: whereas his social philosophy was progressive, his preference for feeling over reason and his hostility to science made him, along with Vico, the first Romantic. Kant too was ambiguous: his ↑**categorical imperative** was humanist, but his subjective idealism opened the door to the ↑**Counter-Enlightenment**.

ENTAILMENT The relation between the premises and the conclusion of a proof or valid argument. **Syn** deducibility. Definition: p entails q, or $p \vdash q$ for short, if "$p \Rightarrow q$" is a logical truth (↑**tautology**). Caution 1: Since there are different logical theories, the preceding must be understood as relativized to some logical calculus. Caution 2: In the preceding no restriction concerning truth is placed on the premise or antecedent p. This is why $\vdash$, the turnstile, is called the relation of *syntactic* entailment. The use of $\vdash$ allows for maximal freedom in exploring the consequences of a premise. The relation of semantic entailment is far more restrictive: p entails q *semantically* if, when p is true, p implies q, and q is true as well. Standard symbol: $\vDash$.

ENTHYMEME Argument with one or more tacit premises. Example: "I think, therefore I am" hides the premise "All thinking beings exist."

ENTIA NON SUNT MULTIPLICANDA PRAETER NECESSITATEM Entities are not to be multiplied needlessly. Ockham's maxim. A useful warning against the tendency to introduce unnecessary fictions. Often misunderstood as preference for simplicity even at the price of depth or truth. ↑**Simplism**.

ENTITY Real or concrete ↑**thing**, actual or possible.

ENTROPY There are two unrelated technical concepts of entropy: thermodynamical and informational. Although neither of them is relevant to philosophy, the word 'entropy' is a favorite with pop philosophers.

ENVIRONMENTAL ETHICS Ethics applied to problems involving actions likely to degrade the environment. Sample of problems: Does anyone have the moral right to alter the environment in ways likely to cause more harm than good? Do we have the right to keep depleting nonrenewable resources? What can we do to minimize the destructive effects of individual and collective actions? What principles of environmental ethics should be incorporated into the legal codes and the practice of resource management?

ENVIRONMENTALISM ↑Externalism.

EPIMENIDES ↑Liar paradox.

EPIPHENOMENALISM The philosophy of ↑**mind** according to which the mental is an ↑**epiphenomenon** of the physical, or an emanation of the brain, and thus incapable of modifying the latter. A variety of both vulgar materialism and psychoneural dualism. ↑**Mind-body problem**.

EPIPHENOMENON Concomitant and secondary fact that does not react back on the source event. Examples: one's shadow and the noise made by a car. ↑**Epiphenomenalism**.

EPISTEMIC Having to do with knowledge, as in "proving and measuring are epistemic activities."

EPISTEMOLOGY The study of cognition and knowledge. Hopeful **syn** theory of knowledge. **a Scientific** cognitive psychology: the investigation of cognitive processes from perception to concept formation, conjecturing, and inferring. When it takes the brain and society into account, cognitive psychology may be said to naturalize and socialize epistemology. ↑**Cognitive neuroscience**. **b Philosophical** The study of cognitive processes— particularly inquiry— and their product (knowledge) in general terms. Sample of problematics: relations between knowledge, truth, and belief; commonalities and differences between ordinary, scientific, and technological knowledge; role(s) and limits of induction; philosophical stimuli and inhibitors of research; social matrix of cognition; relations between epistemology, semantics, and the social sciences of knowledge; relations between theology and science; merits and flaws of the various epistemological schools. The investigation of some epistemological problems requires advanced mathematical, scientific, or technological knowledge. Examples: Is all knowledge local, or is some cross-cultural? Is objective truth attainable? Are internalism and externalism mutually exclusive or complementary? What are mathematical objects and how do they exist? Which interpretation of probability is correct? How can mathematics, which is a priori, play any role in factual science? How are theories operationalized, i.e., readied for confrontation with empirical data? Are rival theories mutually "incommensurable" (incomparable)? Does quantum mechanics entail the downfall of realism? Can psychology unveil any mechanisms without resorting to neuroscience? and Can social science be reduced to biology (or to psychology)?

EPISTEMOLOGY, GENETIC The scientific study of the way children acquire knowledge. A chapter of both developmental and cognitive psychology, sometimes claimed to replace philosophical ↑**epistemology**. Actually the two disciplines are mutually complementary. The former helps criticize apriorism, in particular the ↑**innate ideas** hypothesis, whereas philosophical epistemology can help asking questions and forming hypotheses in developmental psychology.

EPOCHÉ The discarding of the concrete, external, and accidental, to focus on the ideal, internal, and essential. **Syn** bracketing out, phenomenological reduction. Phenomenologists recommend such suspension of any assumptions about real things, and reliance on introspection instead, as the way to grasp their essences. This is why Husserl described ↑**phenomenology** as the science of essences. Unsurprisingly, no phenomenologist has ever discovered the ↑**essence** of anything, whereas scientists have discovered uncounted essential properties by studying the external world instead of pretending that it is not there.

EQUALITY a Logic and mathematics In mathematics equality is taken to be the same as identity. The latter is a reflexive, symmetric, and transitive relation, such that identical objects, such as 5 and 2 + 3, are interchangeable. Outside mathematics this identification can be misleading. For example, the '=' in "The number of known planets = 9" does not stand for identity but for a weaker relation, which may be called equality. This is so for two reasons. Firstly, if the statement in question were one of identity, then its two sides could be exchanged, to yield "9 = The number of known planets." But this is not a proper definition of the number 9—which it should be if, following Peano, we take ↑**definitions** to be identities. Secondly, the LHS of the above equality contains predicates absent from its RHS, hence they cannot mean the same. Moreover, the two sides do not even have the same logical form, since the LHS of the original statement is a definite description, whereas 9 is an individual. Like identity, equality is reflexive. But, unlike identity, equality is not necessarily symmetric or transitive. If '≡' is consistently used to designate identity, then equality may be designated by '='. Another possibility is to keep '=' for identity, and use ':=', called the *assignment operator* in some programming languages, to designate equality. In plain language, equality may be called 'contingent identity', and identity 'universal equality'. **b Social philosophy** Social equality is a component of the democratic credo: ↑**Liberty, equality, fraternity**. It can be construed as either legal, political, cultural, economic, or integral. Legal equality, or isonomy, is equality before the law. Although entrenched in most constitutions, it is violated whenever money buys influence or expert legal advice. Political equality is the right of all citizens to elect public officials and run for public office. It can be corrupted not only by dictatorial measures but also by large campaign contributions. Cultural equality is equal access to education, and equal opportunity to enjoy the cultural resources. Again, it can be severely limited by poverty and discrimination. Economic equality can be conceived in several ways, such as equality of opportunity to get jobs, and equal share in the total wealth. Finally, integral equality is at the same time legal, political, cultural, and economic. ↑**Democracy**.

EQUIVALENCE a Logical Two formulas are logically equivalent to one another if each implies the other and, a fortiori, if they entail one another. Examples: All tautologies are mutually equivalent; "3 = 2 +1" is equivalent to "2 = 3 - 1." **b Semantical** Two predicates or propositions are semantically equivalent if they "say the same thing," i.e., if they have the same intension or content, even though they may have different logical forms. For example, in a materialist ontology, "x is material" is semantically equivalent to "x is changeable." Semantical equivalence is not the same as logical equivalence. For example, with reference to plane Euclidean triangles, the predicates "equilateral" and "equiangular" are logically equivalent (coextensive), but the intensions or contents of these predicates are obviously different. **c Linguistic** Two linguistic expressions are equivalent if they have the same meaning, i.e., if they "stand for the same idea." **Syn ↑synonymous. d Pragmatic** Two intentions, plans, or actions are practically equivalent if they have the same outcome, even though they differ in the means envisaged or employed. ↑**Means / end**, ↑**functional equivalence**.

EQUIVALENCE CLASS A class resulting from the partition of a broader class by an ↑**equivalence relation**. For example, if individuals a and b possess a common property P, such as age, we say that they are *equivalent with respect to P*, even though they may differ in all other respects. Standard symbol: $a \sim_P b$. All such individuals constitute an *equivalence class* under P. The great scientific and philosophical importance of equivalence relations and classes lies in their joining diversity with similarity, thus reducing heterogeneity and facilitating the discovery of pattern in the midst of a mess. And the old objection to the possibility of social science due to the diversity of individuals is met by recalling that different items can be lumped together on the basis of a suitable equivalence relation. Thus equivalence classes overcome the ↑**lumper / splitter** dichotomy.

EQUIVALENCE RELATION A reflexive, symmetric, and transitive relation. Examples: parallelism, congruence, logical equivalence, coextensiveness, synonymy. Standard symbol: $\sim$. An equivalence relation induces the partition of an arbitrary collection into ↑**equivalence classes**. Notation: $P = S/\sim$. Example: the equivalence relation of same sex splits the class H of humans into three mutually disjoint, complementary classes: M, F, and I (for intersex). This splitting or partition is indicated thus: $H/\sim = \{M, F, I\}$. These three classes are pairwise disjoint, that is, their pairwise intersections are empty.

EROTETIC Having to do with ↑**problems** or ↑**questions**.

EROTETIC LOGIC The investigation of the logical form, content, and context of problems. Consider, for example, the problem "Who did that?" It presupposes the existence of an agent; it is generated by the propositional function "x is the agent," where x is the unknown to be uncovered; and it induces a solution of the form "b did that," where 'b' names a definite person or her artificial proxy. In other words, the problem is "Which is the x such that x is the agent," or $(?x)Ax$ for short. The generator of this question is Ax; the presupposition is $Ex\,Ax$, where E designates the ↑**existence predicate**; and the solution is Ab. Logically, then, we have the following sequence: Presupposition $Ex\,Ax \rightarrow$ generator $Ax \rightarrow$ problem $(?x)Ax \rightarrow$ solution Ab. In this case the unknown is an individual variable. In other cases, the unknown is one or more predicates, as in "What are the properties of b?" A problem is *well formed* if it satisfies the following formation rules: (1) The generator contains as many variables as unknowns;

(2) as many question marks as variables are prefixed to the generator; (3) every elementary problem has either of the following forms: $(?x)(\ldots x \ldots)$, and $(?P)(\ldots P \ldots)$, where x is the individual variable occurring in the generator $(\ldots x \ldots)$, and P is the predicate variable occurring in the generator $(\ldots P \ldots)$; (4) every nonelementary problem is a generalization or combination of elementary problems. A problem is *well conceived* if none of its presuppositions is unclear or manifestly false. A problem is *well formulated* if it is well formed and well conceived. Which suggests the last rule: Every problem shall be well formulated. ↑**Problem, inverse problem, pseudoproblem.**

ERROR a Epistemic Departure from truth. The extreme form of error is falsity. Unlike practical errors, which may be fatal, epistemic errors are corrigible if detected. ↑**Meliorism.** The occurrence of epistemic errors and their corrigibility is a powerful argument for ↑**realism** and against ↑**constructivism**, since error is discrepancy between knowledge and reality. There are as many kinds of error as there are types of inquiry: logical, computational, in classing, measuring, etc. And they come in all sizes. The worst of all errors are the wrong choice of problem and of approach. These two errors are frequent in philosophy, and even more so in theology. Example 1: Asking 'Why is there something rather than nothing?' is a serious error because it presupposes the theological idea that, were it not for God's will, there would be nothing. Example 2: Believing that philosophy is only a matter of syntax, whence knowledge of a language and of logic is enough to philosophize, is erroneous because most philosophizing, whether in ontology, epistemology, or ethics, involves some substantive knowledge. Example 3: Believing that empirical questions, such as that of the nature of mind, can be tackled a priori, is a serious error because psychology, the science of mind, is advancing at a quick pace. **b Experimental** There are two kinds of experimental error: systematic (flaw in design) and random. Whereas the former can be eliminated by redesigning the experimental setup, random errors can never be fully eliminated, because they originate in intrinsic fluctuations in the instruments, the mensurandum, or both. Experimental and computational errors are studied by the mathematical theory of errors—ignored by nearly all the philosophers who have written about truth and error, ↑**Measurement. c Statistical** Errors of two types can be made in evaluating a ↑**null hypothesis.** A *type I error* consists in rejecting a true null hypothesis. A *type II error* consists in failing to reject a false null hypothesis. The former error has more serious practical consequences than the second. For example, it is worse to claim that a certain drug is effective when it is not, than to claim that it is ineffective when it really is effective. In the first case the patients treated with the drug will get worse (barring the placebo effect), whereas in the second they will not get better. **d Moral** An action is *morally* erroneous (or wrong) relative to a given moral code if it infringes any of the norms of this code. An action is *absolutely* morally erroneous (or wrong) if its intention is to harm an innocent party or to damage a public good, even if it does not attain its goal. **e Practical** An action is practically erroneous if its outcome is significantly different from its goal. When both goal and outcome concern a given quantitative variable, the practical error equals the absolute value of the difference between the goal value and the actual value that the variable has attained. A ↑**control** (or negative feedback) device measures such difference and corrects it automatically by modifying the input.

ESOTERIC a Any doctrine reserved to the members of a closed society, such as the Pythagorean brotherhood. **b** Any view or practice at variance with the best science. Examples: the classical "occult sciences," cabala, theosophy, and New Age.

ESPRIT DE FINESSE / ESPRIT DE GÉOMÉTRIE Pascal's opposition between intuition and rigorous reasoning, ↑**subtlety** and ↑**exactness**. Although this difference is real, the opposition is not, since intuitions can often be formalized, and the exercise of rigor builds up intuition or insight.

ESSE EST PERCIPERE VEL PERCIPI To be is to perceive or be perceived—by man or God. Central principle of George Berkeley's subjective ↑**idealism** and ↑**immaterialism**. Long regarded to be false, if unfalsified. Yet we all take for granted the existence of plenty of imperceptible things, such as the center of the Earth and other people's mental processes. Still, Berkeley's principle was revived by the positivists J. S. Mill, R. Avenarius, E. Mach, R. Carnap, N. Goodman, and B. Russell for a while. Moreover it is inherent in the ↑**Copenhagen interpretation** of quantum mechanics, according to which the microphysical entities come into existence only upon being observed. If this were true, there would be no observers, since these are composed of microphysical entities, the vast majority of which are never observed.

ESSENCE The essence of an object is the set of properties that make it belong to its kind. In other words, an essential property, in contrast to an ↑**accidental** one, is a property without which the object in question would not exist as such. For example, the essence of an atom is its atomic number, that is, the number of protons in its nucleus. (By contrast, the number of its electrons is partly contingent upon its environment. In particular, all atoms can be temporarily stripped of their electrons; and some of them can capture extra electrons.) The more complex a system, the more numerous its essential properties. Think of the properties that characterize the cells of all species and human beings across cultures. In ordinary knowledge the difference between essential and accidental properties is often doubtful. Not so in science, where two alternative but mutually compatible definitions are possible. According to one of them, a property of things of a kind is essential if it occurs in a law of such things. According to the other, laws are essential, and circumstances accidental. Either definition can be used as a criterion for telling the essential from the accidental.

ESSENTIAL A necessary condition for something to exist or to be acceptable. Examples: water is essential to life, consistency to theories, and feasibility to rational plans. ↑**Essence**.

ESSENTIALISM a Ontological There are two essentialist theses. One of them is that every object has essential (or root) properties upon which all the others depend. This view, opposed by nominalists and positivists alike, is taken for granted in mathematics, science, and technology. Thus, the essence of a plane triangle is that it has three sides. All its remaining properties—e.g., that of having three angles, and that the sum of these equals two right angles—derive from that one. Likewise, the essence of a hydrogen atom is that its nucleus has a single proton. And the essence of a modern industrial plant is that it mass-produces artifacts with the help of technology. The second essentialist thesis is that essence (in the Platonic sense of self-existing idea) precedes existence. This thesis makes sense only in Plato's ontology. Neither it nor its dual ("Existence precedes essence") make sense in a materialist ontology, where essences are properties, not things, hence they coexist (and cease to exist) along with the things that possess them. **b Nomological** The thesis that the laws of a thing are part of its essence. For instance, the laws of motion and the so-called constitutive equations are essential to the concept of a body. By contrast, the constraints (such as the surface on which a body is constrained to move) are situational (↑**contingent** or ↑**accidental**). Likewise the initial and boundary conditions are accidental rather than essential, because their changes do not alter the nature of the body. Caution: Some biologists confuse essentialism with typologism, or thinking in terms of ↑**ideal types**, or even archetypes (ideal prototypes).

ETERNITY a Theology Intemporal, outside time. **b Science and ontology** Indefinite duration, without beginning or end. One of the oldest problems of ↑**cosmology** is to ascertain whether the universe is eternal or has had a beginning and will have an end. Modern physics, of which physical cosmology is only a chapter, points to the eternity of the universe, if only because of the many conservation laws.↑**Big Bang. c Epistemology** The questions whether there are eternal questions or eternal verities have occupied many thinkers. Radical skeptics deny that there are any. Others assert that some problems have disappeared for good, because they have been solved or have been shown to be ill-conceived.

ETHICS The study of ↑**morals. a Scientific** The branch of social psychology, anthropology, sociology, and history that studies the emergence, maintenance, decline, and reform of moral norms. **b Philosophical** The branch of philosophy that analyzes moral concepts (such as those of goodness, fairness, and moral truth) and moral precepts (such as that of reciprocity). ↑**Metaethics.** Ethics, ↑**praxiology**, and ↑**political philosophy** may be regarded as ↑**technologies** because their ultimate aim is to guide behavior. ↑**Bioethics**, ↑**nomoethics**, ↑**technoethics**.

ETHOS The system of values and norms of a social group. Example: the ethos of the scientific community.

EULER-VENN DIAGRAM The representation of classes as circles on a plane. The sum of two classes is represented by the entire region covered by the corresponding circles; their product by the region common to the corresponding circles; and their symmetric difference by the entire region covered by the two circles except for their intersection. Venn diagrams constitute a valuable didactic prop. **Syn** Venn diagram.

EVENT A change in a single step, such as a quantum jump (if indeed there is such). Definable as the ordered pair e = <initial state, final state>. Two events are consecutive if the end of one coincides with the start of the other. This order of successive states is mapped into a temporal order. Unlike ↑**processes**, events are usually regarded as taking no time. However, it is doubtful that there are instantaneous or point events, since even ↑**quantum jumps**, such as the emission of photons, can be analyzed as continuous though extremely swift processes. The concept of an event is basic or primitive in Whitehead's processual metaphysics. This is mistaken because the concept of an event presupposes that of state, which in turn presupposes that of property of a thing. In other words, in a consistent and science-oriented ontology the concept of event is derived, not basic (primitive). In relativistic physics, the term 'event' is often a synonym of point in ↑**space-time**; and in ↑**probability** theory the word often designates an arbitrary set in the family of subsets on which a probability function is defined. Both uses are misleading because neither involves change.

EVIDENCE An empirical datum constitutes a piece of evidence relevant to a hypothesis or theory if it may either support or undermine it. A necessary condition for a datum to count as an evidence for or against a hypothesis is that both datum and hypothesis be ↑**coreferential**. This condition disqualifies scientific data as evidence for supernatural and paranormal conjectures. For example, since nobody knows what God's fingerprints are, or even whether He has fingers, nothing can be regarded as bearing His fingerprints. That is, science cannot be invoked to support the creationist hypothesis, let alone natural theology. Evidence comes in degrees: strong, weak, inconclusive. Thus, a datum that confirms a theoretical prediction constitutes strong evidence for the latter. The reason is that, according to the theory, nothing else could have produced the datum in question. For instance, the bending of the trajectory of a celestial body is evidence for the hypothesis that a force is acting upon it (by Newton's second law). By contrast, the circumstantial evidence used in ordinary life, the law, and the historical disciplines is far weaker. The reason is that our knowledge of the situation is so scant that the datum in question might have been produced differently. For instance, having walked around barefoot and with long hair, as well as having invented a new religion, are only pieces of circumstantial evidence for the hypothesis that Jesus was Californian.

EVIDENT In no need of justification. Rationalists deny the existence of self-evident truths. And when they propose axioms or rules, they justify them either by higher-level principles or by their consequences. They admit, of course, that some ideas look obvious to some pople, but add that what looks obvious to the expert may look counterintuitive to the lay person. Unlike objective truth and efficiency, self-evidence is a psychological category.

EVIL Morally bad. Some supernaturalist worldviews regard evil as a thing. In a worldly ontology 'evil' is an adjective, not a noun: it only admits evil thoughts, intentions, and actions. Evil poses a serious problem to any monotheistic theology. It cannot exist if God is omnipotent—but the empirical evidence for the ocurrence of evil is overwhelming. And if there is evil, but it is all man-made, then God is either powerless to prevent it or the ultimate source of all evil, since we are supposed to be His creatures.

EVOLUTION History punctuated by the emergence and submergence of things of different kinds. (Hence the concept of evolution is a special case of that of history.) Examples: the evolution of chemical elements and molecules; the history of life from the first self-assembly of cells out of abiotic material; human history. Evolution is not to be confused with (individual) development or life history. Nowadays not even the Catholic Church disputes the occurrence of biological evolution. What it does dispute is the naturalist (materialist) account of evolution, in particular the scientific hypothesis that mental abilities have evolved along with anatomical and physiological features and without any divine intervention. ↑**Evolutionary psychology.**

EVOLUTIONARY EPISTEMOLOGY The attempt to understand the history of knowledge in evolutionary terms. Actually, it adopts Spencer's rather than Darwin's evolutionary ideas, in particular that of the survival of the fittest. The evolution of ideas would be a process of trial and error, whereby the "unfit" (false) ideas are eliminated. The biological analogy is misleading because scientific and technological hypotheses, far from occurring blindly and randomly like the genic mutations, are crafted in the light of the background knowledge. Moreover, alternative hypotheses, far from being equivalent, are unequally ↑**plausible.** Nor are they received equally by the society of the day. For example, the biological view of the mind is still being resisted by most psychologists and philosophers—not to mention theologians. In short, evolutionary epistemology does not seem to be able to evolve.

EVOLUTIONARY PSYCHOLOGY The unborn science of the evolution of cognitive abilities and strategies. So far it has been a speculative exercise, and moreover one inspired by the ↑**adaptationist** misreading of biological evolution. In this way anything can be "proved" to have evolved naturally as a response to environmental challenges. Thus, mysticism would be just as adaptive as rationality; likewise myth and science, music and rock, and so on. However, unlike ↑**evolutionary epistemology**, which is just a metaphor, evolutionary psychology does have a future, namely the same as the evolutionary aspect of ↑**cognitive psychology**, which is welded to neuroscience.

EVOLUTIONISM The ontological doctrine that every realm of fact is subject to ↑**evolution.** An extension of Darwinism to all the factual sciences. Being a philosophical principle, it is not to be confused with evolutionary ↑**biology**, a standard component of contemporary biology. Evolutionism transformed radically all the natural and social sciences, by enjoining researchers to regard everything as subject not just to change but also, possibly, to speciation and species extinction. It also had a decisive influence upon philosophy by killing the last remnants of static ontologies and epistemologies. Because it suggested that no institution is eternal, it encouraged reformist and revolutionary social ideologies. And, being misinterpreted by Spencer as stating the survival and superiority of the (physiologically) fittest, evolutionism also encouraged eugenics and such regressive creeds as racism and fascism.

EX FALSO QUODLIBET SEQUITUR Falsity implies anything. Proof: if $p \Rightarrow q$ is true, and p is false, then arbitrary q is true because $p \Rightarrow q =_{df} \neg p \vee q$. Moral: Falsity is bad not only in itself but also because it generates arbitrarily many propositions, true or false, germane or irrelevant.

EX NIHILO NIHIL FIT Nothing comes out of nothing and nothing goes into nothing. In positive terms: Everything emerges from some preexisting thing, and is transformed into something else. This principle, due to Epicurus and Lucretius, is the oldest and most general statement of the principle of conservation of matter. Its translations into the vernacular are the sayings "You can't get something for nothing" and "There is no free lunch." The principle does not hold in mathematics, as shown by these counterexamples: $0^0 = 1$, and $\{\emptyset\} \neq \emptyset$, where $\emptyset$ designates the empty set. This is not surprising, since mathematics deals with fictions and does not abide by any laws of nature. The principle is also said to be violated by quantum cosmology, which would assert the origin *ex nihilo* (but not by design) of the universe. However, this is not true: that theory postulates that before the Big Bang there was the so-called vacuum field, with zero average intensity but a positive vacuum energy density. In any event, this theory is highly speculative.

EXACT An idea (concept, proposition, problem, or norm) is said to be exact if it has a definite logical or mathematical form. **Syn** precise, rigorous. An argument is exact, precise, or rigorous if it is logically valid, i.e., satisfies some logical calculus. A construct that fails to be exact will be said to be *inexact, imprecise,* or *fuzzy.* For example, "1 mm long" is exact, whereas "short" is inexact. However, the predicate "short" can be exactified by transforming it from unary to binary, namely thus: "shorter than." Caution: Exactness must not be mistaken for symbolization. The main merit of mathematical logic is not that it is symbolic, but that it is exact. Symbols are valuable only if they stand for reasonably precise ideas. This is the case with the overwhelming majority of the concepts occurring in mathematics and in the mathematical theories in science and technology. By contrast, many of the key concepts occurring in the social sciences and humanities are inexact. "Exact" is the ↑**dual** of "intuitive." However, in the course of the research process, the one may get transformed into the other. Indeed, what began as an intuitive idea may get exactified; and in turn familiarity with exact ideas may lead to further intuitions, which in turn may be exactified, and so on. In other words, the ↑**elucidation** process looks like this: Intuition 1 → Exactification 1 → Intuition 2 → Exactification 2 → . . . . Consequently, the views that there are absolutely basic intuitions and ultimate exactifications are false. From the above definitions it is clear that exactness involves neither content nor truth. The semantic autonomy of exactness makes it possible to attempt to exactify some ↑**theological** ideas, to which one may attribute content (↑**intension** or ↑**sense**) but neither real reference nor truth. For example, the concept of omnipotence can be defined thus: "*x* is omnipotent $=_{df}$ for any event *y*, *x* can cause *y*." In a naturalist ontology this definition would be immediately followed by the postulate that there are no omnipotent beings. At first sight this postulate renders the definition pointless. On second thought it does not, for once in a while we need to be reminded that natural beings are finite, in the sense that they can wield only limited powers. (Actually theologians are bound to contradict themselves when attributing omnipotence to God, for they will not admit that God can contradict himself or win every battle with the Devil.) Of course, our particular definition of "omnipotence" may be unacceptable to theologians, in involving the ontological notions of event, real possibility, and causation, and thus rendering theology dependent upon a naturalist ontology. But this poses no logical problem, for the defining concepts can and, in fact, have been defined in exact terms. The problem for the exact theologian is to find an exact (explicit or implicit) definition of "omnipotence" different from the above—which is only a matter of ingenuity. What holds for theology holds, a fortiori, for philosophy. ↑**Exact philosophy.**

EXACT PHILOSOPHY Philosophy built with the help of formal tools such as mathematical logic, set theory, and abstract algebra. The advantages of exact philosophy are precision and the facilitation of systematization and deduction. In turn, these features minimize the risks of biased textual interpretation and unending debate. However, exactness is pointless without substance. It does not pay to use heavy formal artillery to tackle ↑**miniproblems.**

EXACTIFICATION The transformation of an imprecise or intuitive idea into an exact one. Example 1: The subject-predicate relation, mysterious in Aristotelian logic, can be analyzed thus: "*b* is a *P*" is the value of the function *P* at *b*, that is, *Pb*. The old and fuzzy concept of copula, "is," has been absorbed in the ↑**predicate**, which in turn has been conceived of as a function from individuals to propositions. Example 2: The aura of mystery around ↑**emergence** evaporates once this definition is adopted: "An emergent property is a property of a system as a whole, such that none of its components possess it." Example 3: ↑**Operational definitions** turn out to be indicators or criteria, as in "litmus paper is an acidity indicator." Example 4: The ↑**value** of an item is the degree to which it satisfies a need, and the disvalue of an item is the degree to which it generates a need. Caution: Since it is easier to exactify simple ideas than complex ones, exactification involves a risk, namely that of trivialization. In other words, if exactification is given absolute priority, then relevance, depth, or even truth are likely to be underrated. Beware ↑**hollow exactness.**

EXACTNESS, HOLLOW In their enthusiasm for exactness, some philosophers have constructed a number of exact but hollow systems, i.e., logical or mathematical theories that solve no interesting philosophical problems. For example, the earliest systems of ↑**modal logic** were invented in hopes of elucidating the notions of logical necessity and real possibility. But they failed to accomplish either task. By contrast, mathematical logicians have succeeded in exactifying the former without the help of modal concepts. As for the concept of real ↑**possibility** used in science and technology, it can be elucidated only in terms of the notions of law and circumstance, without the help of the concept of logical possibility. In short, modal logic has turned out to be as useless as exact. Further exact philosophical oddities, such as ↑**possible worlds** semantics and ontology (offshoots of modal logic), seem to have run their course. In all of these cases the process has been: Intuitive idea → exact idea → abuse or decontextualization of the exact idea → wrong idea. This degenerative process can be nipped in the bud by enforcing the rules to be proposed in the next entry.

EXACTNESS, POWER AND LIMITS OF Exactness has several advantages over fuzziness. Its psychological advantage is intelligibility—to those willing to learn what it takes. Example: The fog surrounding the concept of mind lifts upon defining "mind" as the collection of specific functions (or processes) of the plastic regions of the brain. The logical virtue of exact ideas is that they satisfy the laws of a ready-made theory, namely, mathematical logic. (To be sure, fuzzy predicates, and the resulting propositions, are regimented by ↑**fuzzy logic**. But this theory consecrates fuzziness instead of shrinking it.) In turn, subjection to mathematical logic expedites the settling of controversies. The methodological advantages of exactness are the facilitation of systemicity and the enhancement of testability. Indeed, the more precise a concept, the easier it is to link it to other concepts; and the more precise a hypothesis, the more demanding the tests for it.

EXACTNESS, PRINCIPLES ON (1) Any inexact but reasonably intelligible idea can be exactified. (2) Given any exact idea, it is possible to construct an even more exact and powerful one. (3) Always prefer the more exact of two roughly equivalent ideas. (4) The best conceptual analysis is synthesis, i.e., the embedding into a theory. (5) The importance of an idea is proportional to the number of ideas that it can be related to in an exact manner. (6) Do not expect a single exact concept, proposition, or theory to solve all your problems. (7) A good idea, even if somewhat fuzzy, is preferable to an exact but pointless or false idea. (8) Do not use exactness to bully or to fool. (9) Do not pursue exactness at the expense of substance. (10) Do not crow over any exactification, for eventually it may be shown to fall short of even higher exactness standards. The first two maxims are irrefutable. Like axioms, definitions, rules, and artifacts, they can only be vindicated by their usefulness. Rules 3 to 5 have some heuristic power. Rules 6 and 7 are designed to discourage purely academic games. The function of rule 8 is to help uncover useless symbolism. Rule 9 helps deflate correct but pointless mathematical formalisms. And rule 10 discourages triumphalism.

EXCEPTION ↑**Counterexample**.

EXCLUDED MIDDLE For every proposition p, p or not-p. A logical truth or ↑**tautology** in ordinary (or classical) logic. (This is not a theorem in intuitionistic logic. However, its negation is false in it.) The principle has been widely misunderstood as imposing dichotomies or binary partitions, as in "black or white," "good or bad," and "capitalist or socialist." This is a mistake, because the principle refers to propositions, not to concrete things: it just splits every set of propositions into assertions and their denials. Hence it does not prevent the partition of other collections into as many (equivalence) classes as needed. For instance, the principle is indifferent to the existence of organometallic compounds, hybrid species, mixed economies, and people who are good and bad by halves.

EXISTENCE Hamlet got it right: Existence is the mother of all questions. It is, indeed, the most important property anything can possess or lose. However, existence can be conceptual or material. An object exists conceptually (or ideally) if it belongs in some conceptual body (↑**doctrine** or ↑**theory**). For example, numbers exist in number theory. By contrast, an object exists materially (or really) iff it is changeable. ↑**Existence predicate**, **matter**.

EXISTENCE CRITERIA Mathematical existence is assumed, proved, or exemplified. By contrast, the material existence of anything other than the universe as a whole may be challenged unless firmly established. The simplest existence ↑**criterion** for a concrete object is observability. But this criterion is fallible, for one may be seeing a mirage. A more demanding and therefore more trustworthy criterion is experimental: a thing exists only if it reacts to some controlled stimulus. However, even this criterion may fail unless one can foresee, with the help of some empirically corroborated hypothesis, the kind of reaction to the stimuli in question. In short, the most rigorous way of ascertaining concrete existence is experiment combined with theory. In mundane matters simpler criteria are available, such as " To be is to have a driver's license," " To be is to have a home page," and " To be is to be on a T-shirt."

EXISTENCE PREDICATE The received view is that ↑**existence** is not a predicate but a quantifier, namely the so-called ↑**existential quantifier** ∃. This is indeed so in mathematics, where there are as many objects as mathematicians care to invent. But the view in question is false outside mathematics, because the existence of real (natural, social, or artificial) things is not merely a matter of fiat. So much so that a claim to the real existence of anything but the universe calls for empirical operations. ↑**Existence criteria**. An exact existence predicate can be defined as follows. Let U be an arbitrary but well-defined universe of discourse, such as a collection defined by an exact predicate. Call χ_U the characteristic function of U. (That is, $\chi_U(x) = 1$ if x belongs to U, and 0 otherwise.) We stipulate that "$\chi_U(x) = 1$" is the same as " $E_U x$," where the latter is read "x exists in U." In other words, the (contextual or relative) existence predicate is the function $E_U : U \rightarrow \mathbb{P}$, where $\mathbb{P}$ is the set of all existential propositions, such that $E_U x = [\chi_U(x) = 1]$. If U is a collection C of conceptual items, such as numbers, E_C indicates conceptual existence. And if U is a collection M of material items, such as organisms, E_M indicates material existence. These predicates can be combined with the "existential" (some) quantifier. Examples: "There are some gods," or $\exists x (Gx \& E_C x)$; "Some objects exist really," or $\exists x (Ox \& E_M x)$. Note that, because the characteristic function χ_U is a dichotomic (two-valued) function, the existence predicate E_U is a dichotomic predicate: an object either exists or it does not. The intermediate degrees of existence invented by some theologians are ill-conceived fictions. ↑**Commitment, ontological**.

EXISTENCE PROOF OR DISPROOF If an object is conceptual, the proof or disproof of its existence can be as conclusive as any proof. ↑**Existence theorem**. If material, the "proof" will be far weaker, as it will involve fallible empirical evidence for the belonging of the object in question in the relevant kind. Moreover, in this case the borders of the kind in question may be somewhat fuzzy, so that the belonging of a given (concrete) object to such kind may be open to doubt. What holds for proofs of conceptual existence also holds, mutatis mutandis, for nonexistence. (Example: it can be proved that there is no single real number closest to a given real number.) The case of the nonexistence of a hypothesized material thing or property is quite different. Obviously, there can be no empirical evidence for such hypothesis. Consequently, an empiricist will hold that one cannot prove empirical nonexistence. However, scientists often make correct claims of nonexistence on theoretical grounds. For example, a biologist can prove that a one-meter-tall mosquito cannot exist, for its legs would not support it—unless of course it looked like a pony, in which case it would not be a mosquito. Likewise a physiological psychologist will deny the possibility of psychokinesis on the strength of the law of conservation of energy. He will also deny the possibility of an afterlife on the strength of the psychoneural ↑**identity hypothesis**.

EXISTENCE THEOREM A theorem asserting the existence of at least one conceptual object with certain properties—e.g., a number that solves a given equation. An existence theorem need not identify that whose existence it asserts: it may be just a possibility proof. It may be like a black box that rattles when shaken: the noise only tells us that the box is not empty. But if we are curious we will try and pry the box open. Likewise, an existence theorem guarantees that, if we set out to identify the object in question, we will end up by constructing it. Thus, Euclid's theorem that there are infinitely many prime numbers assures us that, given the largest known prime number, there exists an even larger one—though it does not tell us how to compute it. This theorem underlies the computer program that allows one to find prime numbers. It does so by "brute force," that is, by trial and error. Intuitionist mathematicians and empiricist philosophers mistrust existence theorems: they demand that all mathematical objects be explicitly exhibited, that is, constructed. For instance, they reject statements of the form "There exists a function with such and such properties," unless the function be fully specified. This is why intuitionist set theory does not contain the ↑**axiom of choice**, and intuitionist analysis does not contain the intermediate value (or Rolle) theorem.

EXISTENT Really existing thing, in contradistinction to both possibility and idea, in particular fiction. **Syn** ↑**actual** thing. Science, technology, and ontology study not only existents but also (really) possible things. ↑**Possibility**.

EXISTENTIAL QUANTIFIER The prefix $\exists$ in the formula $\exists x\, Px$ may be regarded either as a primitive (undefined) or as defined in terms of the universal ↑**quantifier** $\forall$, namely thus: $\exists x\, Px =_{df} \neg \forall x \neg Px$. If P denotes a property of an element x of a given set, then "$\exists x\, Px$" is interpreted either as "There exists at least one individual with property P" or "Some individuals are Ps." The symbol '$\exists x$' is called the *existential quantifier*. This name is correct in mathematics but misleading elsewhere, because existence can be either conceptual or material. ↑**Existence predicate**, ↑**existential statement**.

EXISTENTIAL STATEMENT Assertion of the existence of objects of some kind, whether conceptual or material. Existential statements are of two kinds: those starting with the ↑**existential quantifier**, and those starting with the ↑**existence predicate**. A statement of either kind can be a premise, as when one assumes that the set of objects about which one is to talk is nonempty; or it can be an ↑**existence theorem**. Example 1: The hypothesis that Jesus Christ existed, i.e., was a historical character, can be admitted only on faith, because there are no archaeological or historical documents to support it. But of course such documents may yet be discovered. Example 2: The hypothesis of the existence of gravitational waves, which have yet to be detected, is usually admitted because, far from being a stray conjecture, it is a theorem in Einstein's theory of gravitation, which has been amply confirmed in dozens of cases. But of course their existence may yet be disproved. Positivists and others have claimed that all existential hypotheses are metaphysical, hence nonscientific in their view of science. Scientists think otherwise. Example 1: The existence of elements heavier than 92 was first hypothesized and vigorously debated, and finally confirmed by artificially making them. Example 2: The assumption that a ↑**quanton** exists in a given region R of space is expressed thus: the state function of the quanton does not vanish everywhere and at all times in R. Example 3: Any paleontologist or archaeologist who digs in a given site is guided by some indication that there may be interesting remains there.

EXISTENTIALISM A hodgepodge of enigmatic utterances about being and nothingness, human existence and ↑*Dasein*, temporality and death, the "worldliness of the world," and "the speech of language." One of its main theses is that "existence precedes essence"—a sentence that may have been meaningful in medieval metaphysics. Another is that "the word is the abode of being." A third, that philosophizing should be centered in the living subject instead of trying to picture the world. A fourth characteristic of existentialism is its irrationalism and consequent denunciation of logic. Existentialists are utterly uninterested in epistemology, ethics, and the philosophical problems raised by modern science and technology—to both of which they are inimical. Existentialism is a ↑**pseudophilosophy**, and one of the greatest swindles of any kind and of all times. It was adumbrated by Søren Kierkegaard and Miguel de Unamuno, neither of whom had any philosophical pretensions. (Kierkegaard was a theologian, moralist, and journalist, whereas Unamuno was a writer and literary critic.) It was turned into an academic industry by Martin Heidegger, the star pupil of Edmund Husserl and a Nazi activist. Heidegger's enigmatic sentences fall into two categories: intelligible but either false or platitudinous, and unintelligible. Being mostly obscure, they have no clear significations, whence their purported translations are fraudulent. Sample: "*Das Dasein ist in seiner Vertrautheit mit der Bedeutsamkeit die ontische Bedingung der Möglichkeit der Entdeckbarkeit von Seidendem, das in der Seinsart der Bewandtnis (Zuhandenheit) in einer Welt begegnet und sich so in seinem An-sich-bekunden kann* [original emphasis]." ↑**Gobbledygook**, ↑**translatability**.

EXPERIENCE Perception or action. A brain or a neuromuscular ↑**process**, not a ↑**thing** or a ↑**property**. The source of all knowledge according to radical empiricism. Experimental psychology shows that there are no pure experiences: that all experience is colored by beliefs and expectations. Whence the primacy and purity of experience are illusory. However, this does not entail that all observation is ↑**theory-laden** in the strict sense of ↑**theory**. Indeed, everyday experience, though not totally preconceptual, involves no theories proper (hypothetico-deductive systems). Only scientific observations, particularly precision measurements, are designed and interpreted in the light of hypotheses or theories.

EXPERIENTIAL Related to ↑**experience**. A subconcept of ↑**empirical**. Not to be mistaken for ↑**experimental**, which involves designed and monitored controls. Feelings, sensations, perceptions, and actions are experiential processes.

EXPERIMENT a Factual science and technology Deliberate alteration of some features of a concrete object in order to find out how it affects other features or other things. Examples: a laboratory test of a scientific hypothesis, and a trial of a new drug. ↑**Method, experimental**, ↑**observation**. Experiment is more powerful than observation because it involves a precise control of some variables and thus enables one to check for causal relations among their changes. Experiment performs three functions: finding new data, suggesting relations among them (or lack thereof), and testing hypotheses. **b Mathematics** The use of computers to try out hypotheses, models, or algorithms.

EXPLANATION Explanation is an epistemic operation bearing on facts. To explain a fact (state or change of state of a concrete thing) consists in showing how it happens. Example: sundown is explained in terms of the Earth's spin. Caution: Before rushing to explain a fact we must make reasonably sure that it is such rather than artifact or illusion. This involves describing it as carefully as possible and checking the accuracy of the description by empirical means, such as observation, measurement, or experiment. Thus, explanation is preceded by description and test. Explanation has three aspects: logical, ontological, and epistemological. The *logic* of explanation exhibits explanation as a deductive argument involving regularities (e.g., laws) and circumstances (e.g., initial conditions). The ontology of explanation points to a hypothesized mechanism (causal, random, teleological, etc.). And the *epistemology* of explanation concerns the relation between the known or familiar and the new or unfamiliar. Like magical and religious explanation, the typical scientific explanation invokes unfamiliar entities or properties—but, unlike the former, the latter are ↑**scrutable**. Besides, contrary to ordinary-knowledge and magical explanation, scientific explanation involves laws and well-certified facts. Two kinds of scientific explanation must be distinguished: weak or subsumptive, and strong or mechanismic. *Subsumptive* explanation is subsumption of particulars under universals. It has the form: Law(s) & Circumstances ⊢— Explanandum (fact to be explained). Here the laws can be purely descriptive, such as concomitance statements and rate equations. Example: Bob's mortality is (weakly) explained by the datum that he is human, and the generalization that all humans are mortal. (I.e., $\forall x\,(Hx \Rightarrow Mx)$, $Hb \vdash\!— Mb$.) This is how the majority of philosophers have understood explanation since J. S. Mill. Mechanismic or strong explanation is mechanism disclosure. It has the same logical form as subsumption, but the law(s) involved in it describe ↑**mechanisms**, such as those of assembly, collision, diffusion, competition, and cooperation. For example, human mortality is (strongly) explained in terms of a number of concurrent mechanisms: oxidation, DNA damage, wear and tear, loss of immunity due to the action of the glucocorticoids generated during stressful episodes, accidents, etc. Mechanismic explanation subsumes subsumption.

EXPLANATORY POWER The power of a hypothesis or theory to explain the facts it refers to. It may be analyzed as the product of ↑**coverage** (or degree of confirmation) and ↑**depth** (number of levels involved). A hypothesis that claims to explain everything is just as worthless as one that explains nothing.

EXPLICATION Clarification or ↑**elucidation** through definition, analysis, or exemplification. Not to be confused with ↑**explanation**.

EXPLICIT / IMPLICIT Syn stated / unstated. Examples: explicit and implicit ↑**definitions**, assumptions and ↑**presuppositions**, declarative and ↑**tacit knowledge** or knowhow.

EXTENSION A property of ↑**predicates** (attributes), such as "cohesive." The extension of a predicate is its coverage. This is the set of individuals, or n-tuples of individuals, that satisfy the predicate, i.e., for which the predicate holds (true). The extension of a unary predicate P defined on a domain A, is $\mathcal{E}(P) = \{x \in A \mid Px\}$. That of a binary predicate Q defined on the ↑**cartesian product** $A \times B$ is $\mathcal{E}(Q) = \{<x,y> \in A \times B \mid Qxy\}$. The generalization to an n-ary predicate is obvious. A predicate has an empty extension if it applies to (holds for) nothing. For example, the extension of the predicates "true & false," "scholar & infallible," and "omnipotent" is $\varnothing$. Extension must not be confused with reference class. A psychologist who rejects the notion of soul for having no real counterpart refers to the soul while regarding it as pure invention. And a physicist (or chemist or biologist) who surmises the existence of an object that has not yet been found assigns the defining predicate(s) a nonempty reference class even while admitting that, so far, the corresponding extension is empty. This extension fills up as specimens of the hypothesized entity are discovered; and it empties as such items disappear. For example, since dodos became extinct, the extension of "dodo" has become empty. The main differences between the extension and the reference class of a predicate are these. Firstly, whereas the notion of extension presupposes that of truth, that of reference class does not. Secondly, whereas the extension of an n-ary predicate is a set of n-tuples, the corresponding reference class is a set of individuals. Thirdly, whereas the extension function is sensitive to negation and the remaining logical connectives, the reference function is not. For example, the extension of "not wet" is the complement of that of "wet," whereas the reference class of both predicates is the same, namely the entire collection of medium-size material things. ↑**Reference**.

EXTENSIONALISM The semantic thesis that all concepts must be characterized exclusively by their ↑**extension**. In particular, all binary relations, and a fortiori all functions, are to be defined as sets of ordered pairs. This thesis fails already for the concept of identity, which is not defined as a set of ordered pairs. It also fails for the central concept of set theory, namely the ↑**membership relation** $\in$, which is not analyzable as a set of ordered pairs. It fails for all continuous functions as well, since no complete tables for these can be given. And it fails for the predicates representing properties of real things. For example, "temperature" and "entropy" have the same extension, namely the collection of all macrophysical things, but they have different contents (senses, intensions), hence different ↑**meanings**.

EXTERNAL WORLD The world outside a subject's (or knower's) mind or skin. **Ant** internal world, **subjective experience**. There is a single universe, but there are as many external worlds as animals, in particular knowers. The juxtaposition or physical sum of these subject-centered worlds equals the (unique) ↑**world**, or reality. Objectivists affirm, whereas subjectivists deny, the autonomous existence of the external world. Whether or not the existence of the external world can be proved is an open problem. But it is a purely academic one because all normal people, especially factual scientists, take the external world for granted. If they did not, they would neither explore it nor seek protection from it, and they would attempt neither to understand it nor to change it. Thus, the thesis of the autonomous (subject-independent) existence of the external world is much more important than any well-confirmed hypothesis: it is a presupposition of all cognition and all action.

EXTERNALISM The ontological view that whatever happens to a thing is an effect of the external stimuli impinging on it. Example: ↑**causalism**. In particular, every piece of human behavior would be a response to some stimulus. This was the gist of the defunct S-R (stimulus-response or behaviorist) psychology, and it is the main thesis of the externalist (or sociologistic) studies of science, which shift the focus of cognition from knowers to society. Externalism fails for all the known things. Not even electrons, though presumably simple, are the passive toys of their environment: the effect of the latter depends on their velocity and spin; and once set in motion, they continue moving until absorbed. Still, the externalists can be helpful in drawing the attention to external factors overlooked by the internalists. This is particularly so in the case of the history of ideas. However, radical externalism must be avoided because it does not explain the genesis of ideas and it leads to ↑**relativism**.

EXTRA Prefix that indicates that the item in question is not included in a given domain. For example, anything that is not an expression in some language is extralinguistic; thus, tables, unlike 'tables', are extralinguistic.

EXTRASENSORY Events that can allegedly be perceived though neither through the senses nor through a physical medium. Psychics and ↑**parapsychologists** claim that telepathy is extrasensory—whence the expression 'ESP', short for 'extrasensory perception'. No rigorous experiment has ever established the reality of ESP. Moreover, science makes no room for signals that carry no energy, let alone for detectors activated by such alleged signals.

FACT Actual or possible occurrence in the real world. The states of a concrete thing and its changes of state are facts. Example: rainfall (a process) and the resulting wet ground (a state). Caution 1: All ↑**phenomena** (appearances to some observer) are facts, but the converse is false. Caution 2: "Fact" should not be confused with "↑**truth**," the way it often is in ordinary language. Thus falling bodies have always been accelerated, but Galileo was the first to state the true proposition that freely falling bodies are accelerated. Caution 3: Nor should "fact" be mistaken for "datum": a ↑**datum** is a report on one or more facts. When we ask someone to "give us the facts," we do not want the facts themselves, but some data about them. Caution 4: The facts investigated by science are often called 'scientific facts'. This expression is equivocal because it suggests that all the facts in question are scientific creations, while in truth only some of them are—namely those produced in experiments. ↑**Constructivism**.

FACT / VALUE A key distinction in value theory, ethics, and social science. "Most women are oppressed" is a factual statement, whereas "The oppression of women is unfair" is a value judgment. The distinction and separation between fact and value is condoned by nearly all value theories and moral philosophies. It is so important that it deserves a special name: *axiological apartheid*. To be sure, value judgments—in particular moral maxims—do not follow logically from factual statements. However, the fact / value gap is not an abyss, for we cross it every time we succeed in altering facts to adapt them to our norms. Moreover, not all value statements are subjective: some can be justified. For example, not only is extreme social inequality bad for the poor: it also endangers the security of the rich, and it hampers the growth of the market. In sum, facts and values are distinct but not separate.

FACTUAL Referring to fact(s), whether or not in experience, as in "factual truth" and "factual science." Not to be mistaken for either "empirical" or "true," since a factual statement may refer to facts inaccessible to sense experience, or it may be false. In the perspective of scientific ↑**realism**, the collection of experiences is a small subset of the collection of facts, namely those in which some knower is involved.

FAD, PHILOSOPHICAL A philosophical view enjoying a short period of popularity, without leaving anything valuable. Examples: existentialism, hermeneutics, critical theory, and deconstructionism; modal logic, doxastic logic, and many-worlds ontology and semantics.

FAIRNESS Equity; impartiality; balance of rights and duties. Closely related to, if not identical with, distributive (or social) ↑**justice**.

FAITH Blind trust, groundless belief. Faith is not to be confused with trust, e.g., in one's friends, the solvency of a firm, or the power of reason. Every trust has some ground or other, and it weakens with negative experiences. Faith, on the other hand, is hardly pregnable to experience, because it is blind.

FALLACY Logical mistake. **Syn** paralogism. Example: the fallacy of affirming the consequent, i.e., of concluding p from $p \Rightarrow q$ and q. (The correct inference is: From p, and $p \Rightarrow q$, conclude q.) Other popular fallacies are the arguments ad hominem and from authority, the inference of causation from correlation, and the gambler's fallacy. However, some fallacies are heuristically fertile. For example, the fallacy of affirming the consequent is involved in every true inductive generalization, and some inferences of causation from correlation prove to be correct.

FALLIBILISM Syn ↑**skepticism**. Two varieties: radical and moderate. Radical fallibilism (or extreme skepticism) holds that all knowledge may turn out to be false. *Moderate* fallibilism tempers fallibilism with ↑**meliorism**. *Radical* fallibilism is a self-destructive view, whereas *moderate* fallibilism is inherent in science and technology, neither of which doubts the existence of atoms or neurons.

FALSE Untrue. Falsity, like truth, can only be predicated of propositions, not of facts, concepts, or rules. Hence the common phrases 'false fact', 'false friend', and 'false rule' are incorrect; they should be replaced with 'imaginary fact', 'disloyal friend', and 'ineffective rule'. ↑**Truth**.

FALSIFIABILITY A proposition is falsifiable if there is or could be anything that renders it false. Otherwise it is *unfalsifiable*. Example: "There are live micro-organisms under the earth's crust" is falsifiable, whereas "There are worlds other than ours and disconnected from ours" is not. To check whether or not a proposition is false, the latter must be falsifiable to begin with, i.e., it must be neither a ↑**tautology** (logical truth), nor elusive (for containing vague concepts), nor protected by an ↑**ad hoc hypothesis** which is itself unfalsifiable. For example, "p or not-p" is empirically unfalsifiable because it holds true whether or not the fact described by p comes to pass. "Something will happen to you" too is unfalsifiable, though for a different reason: because it is so vague that whatever happens to you confirms it. And "Every male harbors an Oedipus complex" is unfalsifiable in the context of psychoanalysis, where it is always accompanied by the repression hypothesis—an hoc hypothesis in bad faith. Outside that context it is vulnerable and, in fact, it has been falsified—which, incidentally, shows that falsifiability is contextual. Falsifiability is the ↑**dual** of ↑**confirmability**. Indeed, "p falsifies q" is the same as "p corroborates not-q." Hence, the falsificationist thesis that only negative results count is false. Worse, it is destructive, because it suggests converting nurseries into slaughterhouses. ↑**Falsificationism**.

FALSIFICATION Showing that a hypothesis or theory is false. Usually called ↑**refutation**.

FALSIFICATIONISM The thesis that scientific hypotheses and theories must be falsifiable but cannot be proved true. Advanced by C. S. Peirce and H. Poincaré, and worked out by K. R. Popper. ↑**Falsifiability**. The reason given looks straightforward. First it is (wrongly) assumed that all scientific hypotheses are conditional, i.e., of the form "If p, then q." (This condition excludes "existential" hypotheses, i.e., conjectures starting with "Some" or "There are," which are declared "metaphysical.") Now, if p implies q, and q is confirmed, nothing follows validly about the worth of p, i.e., confirmation is indecisive. By contrast, if q turns out to be false, by modus tollens p proves to be false as well. Although this argument is valid, it does not prove that we should disregard confirmation. Indeed, it is common practice in science and technology, no less than in everyday life, to look for favorable examples, not only for counterexamples or unfavorable cases. The reason is that we cherish truth, either for its own sake or for being the basis of practical efficiency. And a proposition can only be declared true (to some degree and for the time being) if it enjoys substantial (direct or indirect) empirical support. Certainly, a single exception or counterexample may carry more weight than ten positive instances. But sometimes a counterexample can be isolated and accounted for as an observation or computation error. (Common case: the outliers in an experimental plot.) Or else it can be accommodated by a slight modification of the hypothesis or by the conjunction of the hypothesis with an ↑**ad hoc hypothesis** of the bona fide type. The falsificationist strategy, *Conjecture-test-discard or at best diagnose "so far unscathed,"* is therefore simplistic, hence unrealistic. Moreover, it involves a severe devaluation of factual truth and consequently it encourages radical ↑**skepticism**. Science and technology care for confirmation as well as for falsification. Besides, they put up with ↑**partial truths**, in particular approximate results. Now, since truth comes in degrees, so does falsification (or refutation). For instance, the popular opinion that Newtonian mechanics has been refuted is false since it is an excellent approximation for medium-size bodies moving at low speeds.

FAMILY RESEMBLANCE Two or more constructs have a family resemblance if their ↑**senses** (or their ↑**intensions**) overlap appreciably. Examples: the pairs of concepts true-correct, circle-closed figure, monkey-man, and kindergarten-university.

FASCISM The most antiegalitarian, oppressive, and aggressive social doctrine and practice in history. Ant ↑**socialism**. Fascism contains two philosophies, one for the leadership and the other for the masses. The former practices ruthless individualism, rationalism, and utilitarianism while preaching holism, irrationalism (in particular intuitionism), and deontologism to the masses. However, these two philosophies share ↑**relativism** and ↑**pragmatism**, in particular ↑**vitalism**.

FATALISM The doctrine that everything is preordained, so there is nothing we can do to shape the future, in particular to avoid disaster. Two versions: secular and religious. The former equals ↑**determinism**. Koranic fatalism and Calvinistic ↑**predestination** are two versions of religious fatalism. Neither secular nor religious fatalism is consistent with either science or our common experience that we can shape our own "destinies" to some extent, particularly if we are willing to assume responsibility for the consequences of our actions.

FATE Predetermination. Invoked by the wicked to justify their evil-doings, and by the weak to excuse their failures. Only the strong and the lucky disbelieve in fate, for they try to shape their own to some extent.

FEAR A strong emotion that inhibits original philosophizing. Some philosophers have espoused irrationalism from fear of science, nominalism from fear of idealism, idealism from fear of either religion or Marxism, holism from fear of individualism, individualism from fear of holism, and so on.

FEASIBILITY The ability to bring to fruition an intention or plan. Feasibility can be physical, technical, economic, or moral. Physical feasibility is consistency with the known ↑**laws** of nature. Technical feasibility is compatibility with the present state of ↑**technology**. Economic feasibility is affordability or cost-effectiveness. And moral feasibility is consistency with the ↑**morality** that is taken for granted. Since natural science, technology, and morals are variable, feasibility judgments are subject to revision.

FEMINIST PHILOSOPHY An academic industry that claims that most if not all mathematical, scientific, and technological ideas and practices are only tools of male domination. In particular, it regards logic, quantitation, and the experimental method as "phallocentric." This industry thrives in the soft fields, both as an excuse for intellectual sloppiness and as a primitive reaction to male sexism. It offers no "feminist" alternatives to standard mathematics, chemistry, electric engineering, or even philosophy. Nor can it offer any, because all such disciplines are universal, hence asexual. ↑**Universalizability**. Feminist philosophy must not be confused with feminist politics. Feminist militants are amply justified in fighting gender-discriminatory ideologies and practices. But to do so effectively they must avail themselves of the very means that feminist philosophers reject, namely reason, science, and technology. What next? Queer philosophy? Wheelchair philosophy? Other-abled philosophy? Patriotic philosophy?

FEMINIST SCIENCE The unborn science made by women without relying on "phallocentric" science, and using instead their allegedly unique qualities, such as intuition, ability to grasp the whole, empathy, and nurturing disposition. No such science is possible because, by definition, scientific research consists of such gender-neutral operations as conjecturing, reasoning, controlled observation, and criticism. What is true is that gender discrimination is still common in scientific communities. The claim of "feminist scientists" can only reinforce such prejudice.

FICKLENESS, PHILOSOPHICAL The repeated changing of philosophical views from one paper or book to the next. Fickleness may come from superficiality, lack of system and program, or weak commitment to truth. And it must not be confused with readiness to alter beliefs in the face of adverse evidence or arguments.

FICTION Anything at variance with facts. Examples: pure mathematics, theology, science fiction, nonrepresentational plastic arts, and the deliberate idealizations used in science, technology, and the humanities—such as frictionless wheels, perfect competition, Hobbes's "state of nature,"John Rawls's "original position under a veil of ignorance," and Saul Kripke's "possible worlds." Fictiveness comes in degrees, from mere simplification to wild fantasy. Unlike the latter, the former can be relaxed if found too unrealistic. A fiction can then be more or less realistic. It can also be proposed in either good or bad faith. ↑**Ideal type**.

FICTIONAL DISCOURSE A discourse that takes or feigns to take ↑**fictions** for realities. Examples: science fiction, general equilibrium economic theory, and many-worlds metaphysics. Serious literary and philosophical criticism is nonfictional even when it is about fictional discourse.

FICTION(AL)ISM a Epistemological The thesis that all of our ideas about the world are fictions: that none of them is even partially true. Examples: the claim of Plato (in the *Timaeus*), F. Nietzsche, and H. Vaihinger that nothing that can be said about nature can be true: that all is fiction. Another example is Milton Friedman's influential thesis that the premises of an argument in economic theory need not be true: that only their consequences matter. An obvious objection is that the whole point of checking the conclusions of an argument is to evaluate its premises. Another is that a false premise entails anything, whether true or false, relevant or irrelevant: ↑*ex falso quodlibet sequitur*. **b Mathematical** The thesis that the mathematical objects, such as sets, functions, and numbers, are fictions on the same ontological footing as the characters of artistic fiction: that they have no existence except as ideas in the brains of those who think about them. Mathematical fictionism comes in two versions: radical and moderate. Radical mathematical fictionism is indistinguishable from radical conventionalism. It is clearly false, because assumptions and their logical consequences are clearly distinguished from conventions such as definitions, formation rules, and notational proposals. *Moderate* mathematical fictionism is the thesis that mathematical objects are just as fictitious as cartoon characters but, by contrast with the latter, are disciplined—that is, subject to logic—systemic and, when not assumed, required to be proved.

FIDEISM The variety of ↑**irrationalism** according to which faith (in particular divine revelation) is superior to both reason and experience, whence these ought to be subordinated to faith. Fideism is common to all theologies.

FINALISM ↑**Teleology**.

FINITISM The view that ↑**infinities** are either impossible or dispensable, whether in ideas or in reality. Finitism is a component of ↑**nominalism** and radical ↑**empiricism**. It comes in two strengths: strong and moderate. *Strong* finitism rejects all kinds of infinity, whereas *moderate* finitism admits potential infinity while rejecting actual infinity. Both versions reject set theory and thus fail to account for modern mathematics. And neither is related to Hilbert's finitary viewpoint, which concerns only mathematical proofs and is closely related to mathematical ↑**constructivism**. Ant ↑**infinitism**.

FLATUS VOCIS Meaningless sound. According to ↑**nominalism**, every class term (e.g., 'humankind') is a *flatus vocis*.

FOLK PSYCHOLOGY The body of psychological knowledge garnered and used in everyday life. The starting point of scientific psychology, which refines much of it while writing off the rest—particularly its psychoanalytic constituents.

FOLLY, PHILOSOPHICAL Smart but extravagant idea, cast in seemingly technical jargon, that would earn any layperson admission into a psychiatric ward. Examples: the theses that material things are but the shadows of ideas; that everything is a unity of opposites; that all worlds, whether actual or imaginary, are on a par; that to grasp the essence of things we must begin by pretending that they do not exist; that the knower constructs the world as he perceives it; that proteins, stars, and things are social constructions. A folly is not to be confused with a mistake. Whereas mistakes can be corrected, particularly if they hold a grain of truth, follies cannot be taken seriously because they are utterly at variance with science. For example, idealism is a folly because ideas, far from existing by themselves, are brain processes. By contrast, empiricism is not a folly but an exaggeration, because experience is, in fact, one of the sources and tests of ideas of certain kinds.

FOOTNOTE The mark of scholarship—at least according to the definition of a scholar as someone engaged in transporting bones between intellectual cemeteries. (Hence the expression 'buried in a footnote'.) The better a modern scholar, the larger the footnotes / text ratio in his writings. If this ratio is 0, we have to do with either a nonscholar, a premodern scholar, or an original thinker; 1/2 is an indicator of average scholarhip; 1 indicates solid scholarship; and greater than 1 proves excellent scholarship. The eminent scholar will footnote footnotes, and so on—as much as the printer will bear.

FORBIDDEN KNOWLEDGE Knowledge whose possession might harm self or others. Examples: Knowledge of a human embryo's sex (for in many countries it induces the abortion of females); of one's exact time of death (for in the case of weak persons it would lead them to despair or apathy); or of the assembly of homemade bombs. The very existence of taboo knowledge poses theoretical (in particular philosophical) and practical (in particular political) problems. Thus, if we submit that there is forbidden knowledge we must exhibit a specimen of it, which entails that we have got it, so that we have violated the taboo. Moreover, if we subscribe to the taboo, we commit ourselves to stopping the search for what it forbids, and thus we enforce or condone cultural censorship. In a democratic society nobody should exert such power, except on himself. Thus, I have no right to prevent others from seeking knowledge I regard as forbidden. But, if I am a loyal member of a given social system (e.g., a government), I have no right to divulge classified knowledge, whose possession may benefit the system's enemies. And I must be able to exercise my right to refrain from acquiring knowledge the possession of which might unnecessarily upset me, such as the exact time of death of any of my close relatives or friends. Physicians often refrain from communicating such knowledge. This case is being debated in ↑**bioethics**.

FORCE a Physics Whatever may or does change the state of motion of a piece of ↑**matter**. **Syn** cause. **b Metaphorically** Anything assumed to account for change. Example 1: Natural selection is often called a force, while actually it is an evolutionary ↑**mechanism**. Example 2: The state, organized religion, technological innovation, advertising, class warfare, and nationalism are often called social forces. Some of them are better described as systems, and others as mechanisms of social change.

FORM a Logic The logical form of a *proposition* is found by analyzing it into subject(s) and predicate(s) with the help of some logical calculus. Since there are many alternative logical calculi, the logical form of a proposition is a mutual property of it and the calculus concerned. Example in first-order predicate calculus: the form of "All thinkers are alive" is: $\forall x(Tx \Rightarrow Lx)$. Example in second-order predicate calculus: the form of "There are no stray (unrelated) ideas" is: $\forall x\,[Ix \Rightarrow \exists y\,\exists R\,(Iy\;\&\;Rxy)]$. The logical form of an *argument* boils down to the inference rule(s) involved in it. And, as regards its logical form, a *theory* is—regardless of its content—a hypothetico-deductive system. The logical calculi (theories) concern only logical forms: they are indifferent to content or reference. The same holds for the theories of sets, categories, abstract algebra, and general topology. In contradistinction, Euclidean geometry and the infinitesimal calculus have definite (mathematical) contents in addition to precise forms. **b Mathematics and science** In geometry and physics, Form = Shape. Quantum mechanics suggests that elementary "particles" have no shape of their own. Shape emerges gradually as the elementary particles assemble into atoms and these into molecules. Developmental biology, in particular embryology, investigates the morphogenetic processes, in particular the mechanisms underlying the changes of shape of the various organs.

FORMAL/FACTUAL DICHOTOMY The splitting of propositions into formal (independent of any facts) and factual (true or false depending on the facts they refer to). An alternative to the simplistic ↑**analytic / synthetic** dichotomy:

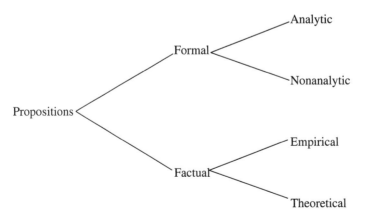

FORMAL LOGIC All logic proper, from Aristotle on, is formal, that is, valid regardless of content. ↑**Logic**, ↑**form**.

FORMALISM a Mathematical formalism of a theory The mathematical formalism of a theory is the collection of mathematical ideas included in the theory. For example, the mathematical formalism of classical mechanics includes the infinitesimal calculus, which in turn includes the predicate calculus. Two different theories may have the same formalism; but, being different, they must differ in organization, interpretation, or both. **b Formalist philosophy of mathematics** The view that mathematics is a system of signs or inscriptions, such as numerals, that do not stand for anything except perhaps other symbols. Formalism, upheld by D. Hilbert, is the ↑**nominalist** philosophy of mathematics. It is also the philosophy of mathematics that computers would hold if they could philosophize. In fact, computers do not need to "know" what, if anything, the symbols they handle mean: they only need to "know" how to operate on them. ↑**Chinese room argument**. **c Formalist philosophy of science** The view that science is the "form" of facts or the "logic" of processes—e.g., that life, mind, and evolution are essentially algorithmic, i.e., guided by formal rules toward preestablished goals. This view is triply flawed: (a) neither nature nor society are substance-free (or substrate-neutral); (b)↑**accidents** are unavoidable, and while some of them frustrate potentialities, others offer opportunities for new developments; and (c) development, ↑**evolution**, and most thought processes are not targeted but open-ended. **d Philosophical formalism** The view that to philosophize is nothing but to unveil the logical structure of concepts, propositions, and theories. ↑**Syntax**, ↑**hollow exactness**, ↑**panlogism**.

FORMALIZATION a Science Mathematization: transformation of ordinary-language expressions into mathematical formulas or models. Not to be mistaken for symbolization, which is only an ingredient of formalization. Symbolization and formalization coincide only if all the symbols are mathematically well-defined. **b Metamathematics** Mathematization plus explicit mention of all the rules of formation of the formulas and the inference rules.

FORMULA ↑**Sentence**, open as "x is a P" or closed as "Some x are Ps." ↑**Wff**.

FOUNDATION a Epistemology The source, root, or basis of knowledge. Although every research project starts from some body of knowledge which it does not question, some such presuppositions may be questioned in different projects. So, there are foundations but they are not necessarily final. **b Logic** The foundations of a theory consist of two layers: the presupposed theories, and the specific axioms (postulates) of the theory. Hence *foundational research* consists in axiomatization or criticism of presuppositions or explicit axioms. ↑**Axiomatics**. **c Foundations of mathematics** The foundation of a mathematical theory is constituted by one or more formal theories. For example, the foundation of a set theory is made up of the underlying logic plus a system of postulates defining (implicitly) the concepts of set, set membership, and the like. All mathematical theories, with the sole exception of first-order predicate logic, have foundations. Mathematics may be conceived of as a tree or network of theories rooted in first-order ↑**logic** and either ↑**set** theory or ↑**category** theory. Correspondingly, foundational research in mathematics consists in organizing a body of mathematical knowledge and placing it in the network of mathematical theories. **d Foundations of science** Every factual theory has foundations constituted by postulates or theories of three kinds: philosophical, mathematical, and specific. For example, the foundations of quantum mechanics consists of large areas of classical mathematics (such as abstract algebra and analysis), which in turn are based on ordinary predicate logic; philosophical principles such as that of lawfulness; and specific postulates such as the Schrödinger equation together with the ↑semantic assumptions that endow the mathematical formalism with a physical content.

FOUNDATIONALISM The epistemological view that all factual knowledge is anchored to a firm basis or ultimate ↑foundation. Varieties: ↑intuitionism (intuitive insight), ↑rationalism (logic), and ↑empiricism (experiential basis). Foundationalism may be traced back to the confusion between psychological or historical root or source, and conceptual foundation. Thus the historical root of geometry was land surveying, but any ↑geometry has a purely conceptual foundation, which includes logic. According to ↑scientific realism, there are no ultimate foundations of knowledge of matters of fact, for sometimes research starts from observation, at other times from theory, and at still other times from combining hypotheses with data, or from questioning philosophical presuppositions. It is only when a body of knowledge has been transformed into a theory (hypothetico-deductive system) that one can raise the problem of its logical organization or foundation. ↑Axiomatics.

FRAGMENTARY / SYSTEMATIC The work of some writers, such as Lichtenberg, Nietzsche, and the second Wittgenstein, is a collection of disjoint opinions and aphorisms: they are fragmentarians. By contrast, that of a few others, notably Aristotle and Hegel, is systematic: all their principles hold together. Fragmentarians avoid theories and sustained arguments, hence they do not investigate deep problems in any depth. Furthermore, their pronouncements, being brief and dogmatic, are eminently quotable but lend themselves to alternative interpretations.

FRAME OF REFERENCE A macrophysical system with precise spatial and temporal features, such as a solid body equipped with a clock, used to measure or calculate positions and times. All positions and times are relative to some reference frame. The same holds for motion: no movement is absolute, that is, frame-independent. On the other hand, any qualitative changes that may result from motion, such as chemical combination, egg fertilization, and the assembly of a social system, are absolute. Reference frames are not to be confused with observers, all the more so since most reference frames are uninhabitable. Hence the true proposition "Positions, lengths, periods, velocities, and energies are frame-dependent" should not be confused with the false claim that such physical properties are observer-dependent. This confusion is a root of the subjectivist interpretation of relativistic physics. ↑Relativity principle.

FRAMEWORK Generic theory, such as general systems theory and the theory of evolution, that serves as a scaffolding for investigating a problem or building a specific theory. Frameworks are fruitful or barren, but they can be neither true nor false, because they cannot be put to the test without being enriched with assumptions specifying the peculiar features of concrete individuals.

FRAMEWORK, CONCEPTUAL A polysemous term designating a set of basic ↑**assumptions**, an ↑**approach**, or a ↑**point of view**. Whereas ↑**relativists** regard frameworks as straitjackets, ↑**realists** use them as springboards.

FREE LOGIC Any predicate calculus that allows for "nondenoting" terms, such as "unicorn." It is argued that the standard predicate calculus requires all individuals (both constants and variables) to have a denotation in all models (or examples). However, this condition would place undesirable restrictions upon ordinary language, where one may wish to talk about unicorns and other fictions. Still, it may be countered that this reasoning presupposes the ontological interpretation of the "existential" quantifier. Hence the need for free logics disappears if '$\exists xFx$' is interpreted as "Some individuals are Fs," not as "There are Fs." ↑**Existence predicate, nondenoting**.

FREE-WHEELING Out of logical or empirical control. Examples: Hegelianism, phenomenology, existentialism, surrealism, and postmodernism.

FREE WILL The ability to make decisions and implement them without or despite coercion, and on the basis of deliberation rather than in automatic response to external stimuli. The matter of free will is still hotly contested. During the heyday of behaviorism the admission of free will was considered a mark of nonscientificity, for if everything we do is an adaptive (rewarding) response to external stimuli, then there is nothing we can do spontaneously, let alone against the current. Nowadays, cognitive neuroscientists tend to admit the possibility of free will as an inner-directed (that is, not stimulus-bound) process occurring in the prefrontal cortex, the "executive office" of the brain. Being presumably a lawful process, it does not violate ↑**determinism**: it only violates ↑**causalism**. Hence the problem has become a scientifico-philosophical one—which is one more illustration that philosophy and science are not disjoint, and that they should stimulate and check each other: ↑**demarcation problem**.

FREEDOM Ability to think or act despite external constraints. **Syn** liberty. Two main kinds of freedom: negative and positive. *Negative* freedom: thing *a* is free *from* thing *b* if *b* does not act upon *a*. *Positive* freedom: thing *a* is free *to* perform action *b* if it has the means to do *b*. Either can be good or bad. The most interesting philosophico-scientific problem about freedom is whether it can be total (↑**voluntarism**), impossible (↑**externalism**), or partial. It seems likely that there are choice experiences of all three kinds. Indeed, there are both inner and outer determinants of choice, and we can usually alter both to some extent. In metaphorical terms: we can choose from a given menu, choose the menu, or write the menu. Different social orders and different social systems allow for different kinds and degrees of freedom. For example, secular universities grant academic freedom. However, like every other freedom, academic freedom is constrained by responsibility and, in particular, by the duty to search for truths and teach them regardless of consequences, as well as by the duty to tolerate alternative ways of reaching similar goals. Elsewhere, the freedom to investigate and teach is limited to themes that do not challenge the ruling ideology, such as the habits of cheetahs and the grammar of the verb 'to see'. But of course freedom is multidimensional: not only cultural but also economic and political. When conceived of in this broad fashion, freedom is seen to be possible only among equals, since concentration of power of any kind restricts the freedom of the powerless. It is only when construed in a narrow way, as free enterprise, that freedom threatens equality.

FREGE'S CONFUSION The great logician Gottlob Frege's conflation of ↑**reference** and ↑**truth value**. ↑**Predicate**.

FREQUENCY The frequency of events of a certain type is the number of times they occur in a collection or during a time interval. The *relative* frequency of events of a kind equals that number divided by the total number of items in the collection of reference or over a given time. And the *long-run* frequency of such events is the value that the relative frequency approaches (irregularly) in the long term (or for a large sample of the total population). Frequency must not be mistaken for ↑**probability**. (In particular, the definition of probability as long-run frequency is mathematically incorrect: see below.) Yet the two concepts are related: frequencies are probability indicators. The evidence pertinent to a probabilistic model often consists, particularly in the less advanced sciences, in long-run relative frequencies. This suggests the belief that probabilities can be defined or at least interpreted in terms of long-run relative frequencies. But this belief is mistaken, as even a cursory glance at any modern probability textbook will show. For one thing, regular and repetitive events, such as the sounding of the alarm clocks of employees and the departure of scheduled Japanese trains, have constant frequencies alien to chance. For another, even if according to a true model the probability of events of some kind is constant, the corresponding frequency will be observed to fluctuate lawlessly around the probability. True, the amplitude of this fluctuation decreases with the number of events (or the sample size) until the discrepancy vanishes for all practical purposes. But this process is irregular: it fits no laws. Thirdly, probabilities are theoretical, whereas frequencies are empirical (observed or measured). So much so that, unlike probabilities, frequencies depend not only on the sample size (relative to the total population) but also on the sampling method—which can be more or less satisfactory but never perfect. In short, some frequencies are probability indicators. When this is the case one tests the probabilistic model concerned by enriching it with an indicator hypothesis of the form "The numerical value of the probability is roughly equal to the long-run relative frequency." But, again, this does not authorize equating the two. In short, Frequency ≠ Probability.

FUNCTION a Logic Propositional function: a formula with one or more free variables, such as "x is young" and "x loves y." A propositional function is transformed into a proposition or statement when preceded by one or more quantifiers, as in "Everyone loves someone," or $\forall x \exists y (x$ loves $y)$. **b Mathematics** A many-to-one or one-to-one correspondence between two sets, symbolized as $f : A \rightarrow B$. A is called the *domain*, and B the *range* of the function. Either or both can be the ↑**cartesian product** of two or more sets. Example 1: The age function maps the collection of systems (in particular organisms) into the positive real numbers. Hence $A(s) = t$. Example 2: The power function is a map of the real line into itself, such that $y = x^{\alpha}$, where α is a real number. Example 3: Velocity is a function from triples <physical thing, reference frame, unit> into triples of real numbers (the velocity components). A *partial* function is defined only for a subset of its domain. For example, the truth valuation function, that maps propositions into truth values, is not defined for undecidable or untested propositions. ↑Truth-gap theory. c Ontology The functions of a concrete thing are what the thing does, i.e., the collection of processes that occur in it. The specific function of a thing of a given kind is what it, and no thing of any other kind, performs. For example, cognition is the specific function of the cerebral cortex. d Science In the sciences, particularly in biology, the term 'function' designates several different, though related, concepts. Among them two basic concepts help define the others. The first concept is that of internal activity of a system. Example: one of the specific internal activities of the heart is the performance of rhythmic contractions. The second concept is that of external activity or role of a subsystem of a larger system. Example: the role of the heart is blood pumping. None of these two concepts involves the notions of value or usefulness. In addition to those two concepts, biologists and social scientists use those of aptation (survival value), adaptation (survival value as a result of selection), and goal. Hence the ambiguity of the terms ↑functional account and ↑functionalism. e Technology Function = Use or purpose, as in "the function of computers is to help solve well-posed problems of the computational kind."

FUNCTIONAL ACCOUNT An account in terms of functions or roles rather than underlying mechanisms. It describes what things do, not how they do it. Example 1: Catalysts accelerate chemical reactions or even make them possible. Example 2: Experiences, if recalled at all, are first stored in short-term memory, then in long-term memory. Example 3: The mind (or the brain) has a language-acquisition device. A functional account is all the user of an artifact needs to operate it. The repairman and, with all the more reason, the designer, need to know also how the artifact works. Likewise, the first stage of a scientific discovery or invention may be purely functional or descriptive. But if an ↑explanation proper is desired, a search for the (usually unobservable) ↑mechanisms is called for, particularly when the function concerned can be implemented by different mechanisms, as are the cases with locomotion and learning.

FUNCTIONAL EQUIVALENCE Two systems are said to be functionally equivalent with respect to a given property if they share this property. Thus, birds, gliders, propeller planes, and jet aircraft are all equivalent in that they can fly. Neither ornithologists nor aeronautical engineers have found much use for this superficial observation. However, this is all functionalists are interested in: they do not care that the flying mechanisms are utterly different, because to them matter does not count. ↑Functional account, functionalism.

FUNCTIONALISM The thesis that only ↑functional accounts are required in all cases. This thesis is popular among experimental molecular biologists, cognitive psychologists of the information-processing persuasion, and idealist philosophers of mind. Functionalism is an obstacle to scientific and technological research, for it discourages the unveiling of ↑mechanisms. In physics it inspired action-at-a-distance theories. In chemistry it led to the characterization of a catalyzer as a substance that accelerates a chemical reaction, or even makes it possible, by its mere presence. Consider, e.g., the synthesis of a molecule AB from atoms A and B. In some cases, if As and Bs come to-

gether, nothing happens. But if a catalyzer C is added, a reaction occurs, and C reappears unscathed among the reaction products:
$$A + B + C \rightarrow AB + C.$$
This equation describes correctly the net effect of the intervention of Cs, but it explains nothing. Worse, it suggests that catalyzers are uncanny and unexplainable. In modern chemistry the above single reaction is analyzed in two steps:
$$A + C \rightarrow AC$$
$$AC + B \rightarrow AB + C,$$
where AC is a short-lived intermediate compound. In turn, these two reactions can be explained at a deeper level with the help of physical chemistry (activation energy). At an even deeper level they can be explained, at least in principle, with the help of quantum chemistry (inelastic scattering of the reactants). In molecular biology, functionalism has led to the sketchy description of protein synthesis as "RNA acts as a template for the synthesis of proteins out of amino acids." In psychology, functionalism suggests accounts of the information-processing (in particular computational) type. In social science, it invites accounting for the existence of a social system or an institution in terms of its (real or imaginary) advantages, regardless of its origin and structure, as well as for the social forces in operation. Functionalism is both a first step and a dead end: it must be completed with the search for deep ↑**mechanisms**.

FUNDAMENTALISM Uncritical adherence to a doctrine, whether secular or religious. Syn ↑**dogmatism**.

FUNDAMENTUM DIVISIONIS Principle of division: the criterion used to split a collection into mutually disjoint (nonoverlapping) classes. It is important to make it explicit because different fundamenta induce different partitions. ↑**Classification**.

FUTURE The collection of all the events that will happen from now on. Since "now" keeps moving forward, the future keeps changing. Besides, since every "now" is relative to some reference frame or other, there are as many futures as mutually nonequivalent frames.

FUTURE GENERATIONS The selfish individual, intent on short-term gratification, disregards the welfare of future generations. By contrast, a humanist ethics, such as ↑**agathonism**, enjoins us to take them into account. This is a principle of any humanist ↑**environmental ethics**.

FUZZY Syn vague. **Ant** ↑**exact**. Examples: "some," "long," "old." A property of some concepts, hence of the propositions containing them. A predicate is vague if its connotation or sense is imprecise, as a consequence of which its extension, too, is blurred. Shorter: fuzzy predicates allow for borderliners. Logic does not hold for vague concepts. For example, in many cases one can say truly of a man that he is at once bald and not bald. Indication of context may restrict the vagueness of a concept. For example, "old," in the phrase "old people," nowadays and in the industrialized world denotes people over eighty. Vagueness is detrimental to testability. Thus the psychoanalytic hypotheses that contain the vague concepts of id, superego, trauma, psychic energy, and the like are hardly testable—which is of course why they can be upheld regardless of empirical data. ↑**Testability**. Two interesting philosophical problems about vagueness are whether every fuzzy concept can be exactified, and whether degrees of vagueness can be rendered exact. The first problem is insoluble, because success in exactifying any inexact concepts is no guarantee that some intuitive concepts still to be invented will not resist all taming attempts. However, the problem gives rise to a methodological injunction: "Try to exactify all useful concepts." As for the second problem, it seems to be open. ↑**Exactness**.

FUZZY LOGIC The calculus of fuzzy (vague) predicates and their extensions. The motivation is to describe sloppy thinking. This aim is in stark contrast with the ideal of ↑**logic** as the organon of correct thinking, which enjoins us to remove imprecision instead of sweeping it under a formal rug. Its effect is similar to that of the psychoanalyst who reassures his client by telling her that we are all abnormal, instead of doing something to improve her condition. Fuzzy ideas should be exactified as far as possible, and dispensed with or at least handled with care if they are unexactifiable. Fuzzy logic, though useless in theoretical disciplines, is being used in the design of certain artifacts.

FUZZY SET A collection whose membership is imprecise, but where membership in a fuzzy set is precisely graded. Fuzzy mathematics, once in fashion, has not produced any sensational results and is currently in decline. By contrast, fuzzy talk of fuzzy sets, catastrophe, chaos, and fractals is still popular.

GAIA HYPOTHESIS The hypothesis that the Earth is a living and self-regulating organism. A holistic and organicist conjecture. A modern version of the ancient Mother Nature myth, and part of the New Age belief system. The hypothesis is irrefutable because the subsistence of our planet after a major cataclysm can be interpreted as proof of its self-healing power. And when its final demise comes, as it will in a couple billion years, nobody will be around to say, "I told you the hypothesis is false!"

GAME THEORY A mathematical theory sometimes used in social studies and evolutionary biology. In the social applications it deals with two or more agents engaged in a "game," or social transaction, from which they are bound to gain or lose something. The most popular games are the Prisoner's Dilemma and the Game of Chicken (or Brinkmanship). The theory is widely believed to capture the competitive and cooperative sides of social action. The central concept of the theory is that of payoff matrix, which exhibits the expected gains or losses (positive or negative utilities) of the participants in a game resulting from their actions. Whereas the mathematical theory is exact, its social applications are not, because they involve invented utilities. Indeed, in the social applications the entries of the payoff matrix are set so as to obtain the desired results, such as proving that the best strategy is "defection" (disloyal competition)—or else cooperation. Because of their ad hoc nature, game-theoretic models in social studies neither explain nor predict any social processes. But, because they involve some symbols, they give an impression of scientific rigor. Ironically, game theory, unhelpful in social studies, has found legitimate use in the study of evolutionarily stable "strategies." Here it is legitimate because the probabilities and values concerned are objective and measurable. Indeed, the former concern random genic changes; and utility is set equal to Darwinian fitness (offspring size).

***GEISTESWISSENSCHAFTEN* (SCIENCES OF THE SPIRIT)** ↑Cultural sciences.

GENERAL / PARTICULAR A general predicate or statement is one that holds in more than one case. A general statement starts with either "some," "most," or "all." In the third case the statement is called 'universal' (in the given set).

GENERALIST / SPECIALIST A generalist is someone who has studied a little bit of everything, and in the end knows nothing well in particular. By contrast, a specialist is someone who has studied a single subject, and as a consequence does not even know his own subject, because every item of knowledge is related to other components of the whole system. The good scholar or scientist—like the good chef, manager, clinician, or orchestra conductor—is an expert in one field or craft, and knowledgeable in many. Like a mouse, he can explore the details of a terrain; and, like an owl, he can also soar to get a view of the landscape—mice and all. He is capable of learning new subjects as needed, as well as of placing every particular subject in a wide context and a long-term perspective. He is thus open to multiple inputs and capable of multiple outputs. In sum, the best expert is the specialist turned generalist. This holds in all fields of thought and action, particularly in philosophy. ↑**Glocal.**

GENERALIZATION / INSTANTIATION To generalize is to go from particulars to generalities; instantiation is the inverse process. Both operations are typical of advanced thinking, which seeks patterns underneath particulars, and treats the latter as examples of generalizations. ↑**Nomothetic / idiographic.**

GENETIC FALLACY The discrediting of an idea because of its humble origin or because it was first proposed by an unsavory character. Example 1: Attacking egalitarianism, solidarity, and internationalism because they were first proposed by the early Christians, and much later on by the socialists. Example 2: Praising capitalism because it was born together with rationality and democracy. Ideas should be judged on their own merits, not on the merits or demerits of their origins, sources, defenders, or detractors. With regard to ideas, test certificates can be valid, whereas birth certificates are not.

GENETICISM Genetic ↑**determinism.**

GEOMETRY a General concept The study of ↑**spaces**—topological, projective, cartesian, metric, physical, etc. For example, metric geometries study metric spaces. In turn, a metric space is a set together with a distance function defined on it. **b Mathematical and physical geometries.** A mathematical geometry studies a conceptual or ideal space, such as an n-dimensional ↑**state space**, or the three-dimensional Euclidean space. There are as many conceptual spaces as mathematicians care to invent. The properties of such spaces are mathematical and independent of the features of the real world—except of course that they are human creations. On the other hand, there is a single physical space, because the world is one. A physical geometry studies physical space, i.e., the basic structure of the collection of all material entities. Whereas the elements of a conceptual space are concepts, such as dimensionless points and lines without width, those of physical space are things, such as particles and light rays. A physical geometry is built by assigning a physical interpretation to the basic concepts of a conceptual geometry. For example, a physical line is a light ray. **c General relativity** This theory, i.e., Einstein's theory of gravitation, has highlighted the difference between conceptual and physical geometry. It has done this by showing that the metric of a region of space where there is a strong gravitational field is influenced by the latter. More precisely, the deviation of the real metric from the flat Euclidean one depends on the distribution of matter (including fields other than the gravitational field). This deviation (or space curvature) vanishes when the mass density and the field energy density approach zero. **d Philosophical geometry** The family of theories purporting to answer the question 'What is physical space: is it rooted in physical things (realism) or in the subject's intuition or experience (subjectivism)?' A philosophical geometry should then solve the geometrical questions that lie beyond the reach of physical geometries, such as whether there would be any space left if all matter disappeared, or if no sentient organisms were left. A materialist and realist philosophical geometry will answer the first question in the negative, and the second in the affirmative. To be scientific in addition to being philosophical, the theory should be consistent with the most accurate physical theories we have, in particular general relativity and quantum physics. One such possible philosophical geometry revolves around the concepts of interposition and separation between any two different changing things. However, in a philosophical geometry the concept of separation, though ↑**exact**, must be qualitative. One candidate is this: the separation between two things is the set of things that interpose between the given things. Finally, the set of things, together with the separation function, may be called the thing space. So, real (or physical) space turns out to be the basic structure of the collection of things.

GESTALT Polysemous German word that designates form, configuration, structure, whole, or ↑**system. a Ontology** A Gestalt quality is a systemic or ↑**emergent** property, such as the structure of a crystal or the cohesiveness of a social system. **b Psychology** The main tenet of Gestalt psychology is that the perception of the whole precedes that of its parts. It was hailed by antianalytical philosophers as having killed psychological ↑**associationism** and gravely injured the analytic method. While later experimental psychologists have replicated some of the important findings of the Gestalt psychologists, they have also falsified their main hypothesis. Indeed, they have shown that perceptual synthesis comes at the end of a process that starts with sensory analysis. For example, the shape, texture, color, and movement of a moving body are perceived separately by different regions of the visual cortex, and the binding of these various features is performed at the end.

GIVEN a Ontology Self-existing, belonging to the external world. **b Logic** Assumed. **c Epistemology** Empirical data. Actually, the most interesting data are sought rather than given. Think, e.g., of atomic weights, stress indicators, and social inequality measures.

GLOBAL A wide-embracing view or viewpoint. Philosophers are natural globalizers. Ant local. ↑**Glocal.**

GLOCAL A piece of research or action that, though special or local, is embedded in a global or systemic perspective. Example: the environmentalist slogan, "Act locally, think globally." ↑**Generalist / specialist.**

GLOSSOCENTRISM The view that language is everything or at least the center or root of everything. Examples: the hermeneutic (or textualist) view that "social facts are texts or like texts"; Heidegger's dictum "The word is the abode of Being"; Peter Winch's claim that social science is reducible to linguistic philosophy; Richard Rorty's thesis that to investigate is to converse; Jacques Derrida's thesis that "there is nothing outside the text"; and Bruno Latour's opinion that laboratory work consists in making inscriptions. Consequently any theory of knowledge, and even any theory of the world, would depend on some theory of language. For better or for worse, there have been plenty of epistemologies and ontologies before the first theories of language were formulated. Moreover, it may be argued that linguistics, like every other science, has philosophical presuppositions and assumes the existence of extralinguistic items such as speakers and linguistic communities. Syn ↑linguistic imperialism. ↑Language, ↑hermeneutics, ↑textualism, ↑linguistic turn.

GLUE FORMULA Formula containing concepts belonging to different research fields and making their merger possible. Example: "The divergence of economic interests is a major source of political strife" helps bridge economics and political science. ↑Interdiscipline.

GNOSIOLOGY ↑Epistemology.

GNOSOPHOBIA Hatred of or allergy to learning. Religious fanatics, existentialists, phenomenologists, ordinary-language philosophers, and postmodernists are gnosophobic, for they refuse to learn anything about mathematics, science, and technology. ↑Ignorance.

GOAL The final state of a system under the control of a higher vertebrate. In the case of humans, goals are first imagined or conceived, then pursued or shunned. Therefore, to attribute goal-seeking behavior to unintelligent things such as cells, organizations, or societies is a mark of anhropocentrism. What is usually called the goal (or mission) of a social system, such as a business firm or a school, is the goal its organizers have in mind when setting it up or managing it. Goals are not always achieved. To facilitate their attainment it is necessary to devise systems with feedback mechanisms, for these regulate the input as a function of the discrepancy between the state achieved and the goal envisaged. ↑Cybernetics.

GOBBLEDYGOOK, PSEUDOPHILOSOPHICAL Unintelligible and wordy jargon that passes for profound philosophy. ↑Babble, ↑existentialism.

GOD Any of the superhuman and supernatural persons invented by some religions. Some gods are fancied to be material and perceptible, others neither; some are postulated to be immortal or even eternal, others not; some are imagined to be omnipotent and omniscient, others not; some are helpful and merciful, others are unhelpful and cruel; some are loners, others have families and courts. The possibility of the existence of deities poses interesting philosophical problems, such as those of the kind of evidence for or against religious belief, the range of human freedom, the ultimate source of good and evil, and the possibility of free will and responsibility. For example, if God is omnipotent, then humans can have no free will, and they sin only by proxy, hence they should not be punished. If on the other hand humans have free will, then they can sin, and thus God, their creator, is indifferent to human suffering, or even perverse.

GOD, PROOFS OF EXISTENCE The question of the possibility of a proof of the existence of a god depends crucially on the concepts of proof and of deity. Every reputable theologian knows that a purely logical proof is impossible because every proof starts from some premises, which in this case would have to be assumptions containing already some concept of God. He also knows that, before setting out to render theism or deism plausible, he must define "God," i.e., list the essential properties he attributes the deity—e.g., existence, omnipotence, ubiquity, omniscience, immateriality, and eternity. He may claim that certain features of the world, such as lawfulness, the "wisdom of the body," and the alleged immateriality of the mind, suggest that the world was created by a deity. But he is likely to admit this to be a postulate that cannot be justified empirically, and that it can only be believed by someone who has been given a special gift (grace). In short, belief in some God or other is ultimately a matter of faith, not reason, much less experience.

GOD, PROOFS OF NONEXISTENCE There are as many concepts of deities as religious denominations. These can be partitioned into two large classes: those which affirm, and those which deny, the active participation of (some) deity in world affairs. Those who believe in an aloof deity—the absentee landlord of the deists—need not worry about the imperfections of the world, such as the facts that most of the biospecies that ever lived have become extinct, or that humans are subject to sickness, violence, poverty, and ignorance. But, because they recognize no link between the world and the deity, they cannot expect to find any traces of it in things. Hence their belief, precisely for being well sheltered, is groundless and so a matter of pure faith. Consequently, it is incompatible with a scientific worldview. By contrast, those who believe that their deity continues to play an active role in world affairs, presumably do so because they see tracks of the deity, particularly miracles. Now, whoever accepts, if only provisionally, the findings of science, will refuse to believe in miracles, and will regard all facts as either natural or social or a combination of facts of both kinds. In fact, no scientific theory or experiment involves the hypothesis of the existence of a deity. Moreover, every scientific theory and every experiment presupposes (assumes tacitly) the *nonexistence* of any deities capable of interfering with the world, in particular with telescopes, meters, and the like. So much so that, if anything goes wrong with either, the theorist, the experimentalist, or the lab technician will be blamed—not some deity. The only gambit the believer could try is to claim that the deity is so clever that he covers his every track: that he (or his aids) are behind every event, though in a secret manner. This conspiracy (or Almighty Company) alternative is rationally tenable. But, being untestable, it provides no evidence, and so no comfort to the believer. In short, if science holds, then there are no gods. By contraposition, if there are gods, then science fails. A choice between belief and disbelief is therefore logically and morally mandatory. However, belief in god(s) is compatible with science as long as no ↑**big questions** are tackled.

GÖDEL'S INCOMPLETENESS THEOREM Any consistent theory including a fragment of arithmetic is incomplete. That is, such a theory contains at least one statement that is true but not provable in the theory. Though a capital ↑**metamathematical** result, it is of little interest to working mathematicians. By contrast, it fascinates philosophers, perhaps because it was initially misinterpreted as exhibiting a radical limitation of reason, while in fact it only proves the limitation of any given formalism including a fragment of number theory. ↑**Axiomatics**.

GOLDEN RULE The most famous of moral maxims. It comes in at least two versions. The *positive* or Christian version is: "Do to others what you wish others did to you." The *negative* or Confucian is: "Never do to others what you would not like them to do to you." In either version it is generally regarded as the basic principle entailing all the needed prescriptions and proscriptions. However, neither of the two versions covers all possible cases, for what one wishes done to oneself (e.g., surgery) may not be agreeable to others, or conversely. Besides, the rules concern wishes of self and others rather than needs, and they overlook aspirations. The ↑**agathonist** maxim "Enjoy life and help live" does not have these flaws and it is easier to state, understand, and apply.

GOOD a Value theory Whatever has the desirable properties—e.g., does what it is expected to do, promotes well-being, or gives pleasure. The word can be used either as a noun (as in "clean air is a public good") or as an adjective (as in "strive to do good deeds"). Contrary to the claim of the axiological intuitionists, such as G. E. Moore, the predicate "good" is seldom treated as a simple and therefore unanalyzable quality. Instead, it is usually analyzable as a conjunction of predicates. For example, a good person is someone who refrains from causing needless suffering and is willing to help others. ↑**Naturalistic fallacy. b Ethics** Some moral philosophies enjoin us to pursue the good for self or others. Most of them posit also a single best thing or ↑*summum bonum.* ↑**Value,** ↑**value theory,** ↑**agathonism.**

GOOD LIFE The lifestyle chacterized by health, cheerfulness, usefulness, love of self and others, honesty, dignity, and devotion to a worthy cause.

GOOD REASON FOR ACTING A rationalist will take a course of action only if he has good reasons for doing so. Such good reasons will include the evaluation of the costs (material and moral) of the means, and the possible benefits and bad side effects (on self and others) of the outcome. But they will also involve constraints such as social conventions and legal norms. Although ↑**decision theory** is widely assumed to be the theory of rational action, it does not even include the general concept of a good reason.

GOOD SOCIETY A society that ensures the ↑**welfare** and ↑**decency** of the vast majority of its components.

GOODWILL Disposition to do good. A character trait and a moral ↑**virtue.** Goodwill, along with empathy, fairness, and a willingness to assume the risks inherent in any action, is necessary for the implementation of any humanist morality and any democratic program.

GRADUALISM The thesis that all change is gradual or continuous: that there are no leaps in motion, development, or evolution. **Ant** ↑**saltationism.** Actually there are examples of both continuity and discontinuity. For example, light propagates in a continuous manner until absorbed; chemical reactions are continuous processes until the reaction products are formed; new ideas emerge suddenly as culminations of periods of preparation; and biological evolution is continuous in some regards (e.g., inheritance of some characters) but discontinuous in others (e.g., mutations and environmental catastrophes). In short, truth lies in a combination of gradualism with saltationism.

GRAIN OF TRUTH ↑**Partial truth.**

GRAPH A set of dots (nodes) joined by lines (edges). Graphs are widely used to visualize ordered sets, lattices, theories, social networks, and other ↑**systems**, whether mathematical or concrete. The objects of study of graph theory.

GRAY AREA Any ill-defined set of vague concepts or uncertain beliefs. It is a programmatic hypothesis of ↑**exact philosophy** that analysis, formalization, and theory can eliminate any gray area.

GREAT MEN THEORY OF HISTORY The philosophy of history according to which only heroes and villains count in history. The elitist version of social ↑**individualism**. Practiced by Suetonius and praised by T. Carlyle, M. Weber, and B. Mussolini among others. Fun to read but not very instructive. It is inadequate because (a) to place the great man in context and thus explain his impact, it must borrow global social data, such as the economic and political conditions prevailing at the individual's times; (b) it ignores the preexisting social networks in which the individual is embedded, as well as the lives of the ordinary people the great men lead or prey on; (c) it does not study social transformations, such as those brought about by climate change, mass migration, invasion, conquest, war, technological innovation, and ideological strife; and (d) although it rightly stresses the importance of exceptional individuals, it overlooks the possibility that, under different circumstances, the same persons might have passed unnoticed.

GRUE PARADOX An academic miniproblem bound to irritate any scientist. Suppose that emeralds could afford to stay green until a certain future date T, turning blue thereafter. If this were the case, we might called them 'grue' or 'bleen'. Can there be such emeralds? According to empiricism, yes, because, until the year T, the same body of empirical evidence supports the alternative generalizations

H1 All emeralds are green.
H2 All emeralds are grue.

This "paradox of confirmation" made quite a stir among philosophers when N. Goodman first proposed it. But of course crystallographers never took notice of it, because they know that emeralds cannot change color spontaneously and overnight, anymore than lions can metamorphose into gazelles. The reason is that the color of emeralds is determined by their chemical composition. And, if the latter changes, then the crystal ceases being an emerald. The inference is as follows.

For all x, x is an emerald if and only if x has composition C.
For all x, if x has composition C, then x looks green under white light.
∴ For all x, if x is an emerald, then x looks green under white light.

The conclusion, initially an empirical generalization, has been derived from higher-level (and deeper) hypotheses. Hence it has more than just the empirical support constituted by uncounted but often wrong observations of emeralds. Moral 1: Empirical generalizations are not typical of science. Moral 2: Empirical evidence is not all there is to science. Moral 3: The grue paradox is a ↑**pseudoproblem**. ↑**Paradox**.

GUESS Conjecture. A guess can be wild or educated. Wild if groundless, and educated if consistent with a body of knowledge. Educated guesses are usually called ↑**hypotheses**. Scientific research consists largely in framing, exactifying, and testing educated guesses. Wild guesses belong in fiction. However, according to radical (or absolute) ↑**skepticism**, every item of knowledge is a wild guess—except of course for this statement. And radical empiricism bans guesses altogether.

GUILT / SHAME a Social psychology and ethics Emotions learned in the course of socialization, and without which morals might not emerge. **b Political philosophy** Although only individuals can be guilty of their own wrong actions, guilt by association and collective guilt figure prominently in authoritarian societies. Examples of such moral and legal abominations are the execution of randomly chosen hostages, and the bombing of civilian populations.

H The most dangerous letter in the German language.

HAIRSPLITTING Analysis pushed to an unnecessary extreme. A favorite with theologians and with philosophers without long-term research projects.

HAPPINESS a Psychology State of mind of the person who believes to have met all her needs and desires. Largely a delusion. **Syn** the village idiot's state. By contrast, the pursuit of bounded happiness is really possible; and it is morally permissible as long as it does not infringe on other people's basic rights. **b Ethics** The ↑*summum bonum* of ↑**hedonism** and ↑**utilitarianism**. The latter's top moral maxim is "The greatest happiness of the greatest number," coined by Helvétius, copied by Priestley, and adopted by Bentham. For better or for worse, there are two reasons why this principle cannot be implemented. The first is that we do not know yet how to ↑**quantitate** happiness. The second difficulty is more serious. Assume that happiness has been successfully quantitated, and imagine the total happiness pie to be divided into n equal parts (number of people). Every person is assigned a slice that spans the angle h (quantity of happiness). Any partition of the pie is constrained by the total angle, 2π. That is, $nh \leq 2\pi$. Obviously, maximizing n entails minimizing h, and conversely. Hence, no distribution can comply with the utilitarian maxim.

HAZARD, MORAL The risk of unwittingly encroaching on someone's rights or frustrating someone's legitimate aspirations. A risk inherent in all social actions, whence the latter should not be assessed solely in terms of their expected utility.

HEDONISM The pursuit of pleasure with disregard for the welfare of others. A variant of ↑**egoism**. Caution: anhedonism, or the avoidance of pleasure, is a pathological condition. ↑**Agathonism** moderates hedonism by requiring that the welfare of others be not only respected but also promoted.

HEISENBERG'S INEQUALITIES Formulas of quantum mechanics asserting that the variance (scatter around the average) of the position of an electron, or any other ↑**quanton**, is inversely related to the spread of its velocity. Corollary: as the spread in position shrinks, the spread in velocity expands, and conversely. The formula is deduced rigorously from some of the axioms of the theory, with no reference to measurement operations. Hence it should hold everywhere, not only in laboratory settings. However, it has often been misinterpreted in terms of the disturbances caused by the measuring apparatus, or even by the knower. It has also been misinterpreted in terms of the experimenter's uncertainty concerning the exact location and the exact velocity of the thing measured—hence the popular misnomer 'uncertainty principle'. This interpretation is incorrect for two reasons. First, physics is not about mental states such as ↑**uncertainty.** Second, the said interpretation presupposes that electrons and the like have always an exact position and an exact velocity, as if they were classical mass points, only we cannot know them accurately. But quantum mechanics makes no such assumption: it does not postulate that electrons and the like are pointlike and that all their properties have sharp values at all times. In this theory, talk of particles (or of waves) is analogical and therefore often misleading. Once these confusions are clarified, Heisenberg's inequalities lose interest for epistemology, except as an example of the distortions of scientific findings that a false philosophy can bring about. However, they retain interest for ontology, as a reminder that the bricks that constitute the universe are shapeless, hence indescribable in geometric terms. This suffices to dash Descartes's program of describing everything physical in terms of figures and movements.

HEMPEL'S PARADOX ↑**Raven's paradox.**

HERE Location in relation to a given ↑**reference frame.** Since there is any number of reference frames, there are also uncounted 'heres'. That is, location is relative, though not necessarily subjective. When the reference frame is a subject, 'here' is said to be an ↑**egocentric particular,** along with 'there', 'now', and 'later'. In ↑**quantum mechanics,** precise or pointlike location is exceptional.

HERMENEUTICS a General Text interpretation. **b Philosophy** The idealist doctrine that social facts (and perhaps natural ones as well) are symbols or texts to be interpreted rather than described and explained objectively. ↑*Verstehen.* Philosophical hermeneutics opposes the scientific study of society; it is particularly contemptuous of social statistics and mathematical modeling. And, because it regards everything social as spiritual, it underrates the environmental, biological, and economic factors, and refuses to tackle macrosocial facts, such as poverty and war. Hermeneutics thus constitutes an obstacle to the search for truths about society, hence to the grounding of social policies.

HEROISM, MORAL The defense of unpopular worldviews, just but banned causes, or the public interest, at the risk of liberty or even life, and without expectation of material gains. The civil-rights activists under authoritarian regimes, advocates of secularism in church-dominated societies, and environmental activists and whistle-blowing engineers who denounce activities against the public welfare are among the moral heroes of our time.

HEURISTIC Nonalgorithmic aid in problem finding and problem solving. Examples: finding a few cases of As being Bs suggests that all As are Bs; an analogy between two problems suggests using the same method to investigate both; what-for questions trigger research into biological or social functions. Heuristic devices belong in the scaffolding of a construction, and they must be discarded after use. Their role is strictly midwifery.

HIERARCHISM The view of the cosmos in the image of a stratified society: as a ladder from lower to higher beings. This model is a sort of inverted evolutionary worldview, for it assumes that the ladder is static, and that the higher beings originate and dominate the lower ones, hence they have not evolved from the lower ones. This cosmology was rather popular throughout the Middle Ages. It was later transmogrified into present-day ideas about the ↑**level** structure of the world current among biologists and ↑**emergentist materialists**.

HIERARCHY A collection ordered by a relation of domination, as in "military hierarchy." Not to be confused with ↑**level** structure, for the relation involved in the latter is that of emergence, not domination.

HINDCAST Retrodiction, projection to the past, as in "Darwin hindcast the existence of our hominid ancestors."

HISTORICAL MATERIALISM The Marxist philosophy of history. According to it, the main engines of history are changes in the mode of production and class struggles. This hypothesis has been extremely fruitful, particularly in deflating historical idealism. And it has been confirmed in many cases, but falsified in as many others. For instance, modern society is indeed largely a product of the Industrial Revolution, but it is also a product of modern science, technology, and philosophy, as well as of the political enfranchisement of increasing sectors of the population. The valid kernel of historical materialism has fructified in the French *Annales* historical school, which is both materialist and systemic.

HISTORICISM a Biology The idea that, since nothing in biology makes sense except in an evolutionary perspective, evolutionary biology precedes all the other branches of biology. This requirement cannot be met, if only because species and speciation diagnostics are based on genetics, organismic biology, and ecology, which in turn are enriched when seen in the light of evolution. **b Social studies** The view that nothing in society can be understood unless placed in historical perspective, hence history is prior to all the other social sciences. Historicism corrects ahistorical views, such as the popular dogma that human nature is constant and boils down to the quest for maximal profit. But it is open to the objection that before we inquire into the history of something, we must have some idea, however rough, of what that something is. The questions "What is it?" and "How did it evolve?" are mutually complementary. Any correct response to one of them helps investigate the other—a case of ↑**virtuous circle**.

HISTORIOGRAPHY The study of history. It is the oldest and most rigorous of all the social sciences. Idealists conflate historiography and history: according to them historians make (or at least relive) history rather than narrating and explaining it. Therefore, the very concept of objective historiographic truth does not make sense to them. Historiography would then be a branch of literature.

HISTORY a Ontology The history of a concrete entity x over some period T is the ordered sequence of its states over T, i.e., $h_T(x) = < s(x,t) \mid t \in T>$. **b Biology** The *life his-*

tory of an individual organism is its history from conception to death. Evolution is the history of biopopulations and their constituents from the origin of life on, insofar as they involve the emergence and extinction of species. **c Of philosophy** The retrieval, rethinking, evaluation, and placing in context of the thought of philosophers from antiquity to the present. As with all retrievals, this one is bound to be partial and to be cast and recast in contemporary terms. Hence this task is unlikely to ever be finished: There can be no definitive histories of philosophy—or of anything else. Every generation views its precursors in the light of new findings and from a new perspective. But not all perspectives are equally adequate and fruitful. For example, it is wrong to pass the pre-Socratics for protoexistentialists just because they were rather enigmatic, or Aristotle for a precursor of Wittgenstein just because both were interested in words. The history of philosophy is the story of the emergence, submergence, and reemergence of philosophical problems, as well as of the attempts to solve them. Some such problems have actually been ↑**pseudoproblems**, and many of the solutions proposed to them have been wrong if not nonsensical. Hence the history of philosophy is an aspect of the history of human folly as well as of human ingenuity. A "whig" history of philosophy, i.e., one restricted to listing successes, would be rather slender. Partly for this reason, not all historians of philosophy are scrupulous custodians of the truth. Some of them have a vested interest in falsity, nonsense, or occultation. This is why philosophy students seldom learn about Aristotle's ambiguity about the soul, Descartes's materialist cosmology, the materialists of the French Enlightenment, Kant's agnosticism, or Mill's socialism. The history of philosophy is fun to read and necessary for philosophizing, but secondary to original philosophizing. Without fish there would no fishermen, let alone fish-mongers. The task of the historian of philosophy is to catch, dissect, and distribute fish, not to cook them to his own taste. Doing good history of philosophy involves not only familiarity with philosophy but also mastering the special skills of the historian—and not being allergic to archival dust. Ironically, the highest standards of philosophical scholarship are found in the two extremes of the philosophical spectrum: logic and the history of philosophy. The modern standards of logical rigor were set by mathematicians, and those of historical accuracy by historians. The regions lying between those two extremes, i.e., the properly philosophical fields, are characteristically lax in standards. To sum up, the history of philosophy is necessary, but it should not be allowed to displace philosophy.

HOBBESIANISM Thomas Hobbes's thesis that all humans are selfish and ruthless, and permanently at war with one another—unless they are held in check by a ruthless sovereign. A particular case of both ↑**agonism** and ↑**individualism**.

HOLISM a Ontological Holism is the view that the ↑**whole** is more important than the part, as in Hegel's famous dictum "The truth is the whole." Ant ↑**atomism, individualism**. Holism comes in two strengths: radical and moderate. *Radical* version: The whole determines its parts, and the knowledge of the latter is unnecessary to understand the totality. Examples: the views that the parts of an organism are subordinated to the whole, that individual action is totally determined by the social structure, and that persons are to serve institutions, not the other way round. Taken literally, the thesis is absurd, because the whole exists only by virtue of its parts and their interconnections. A charitable interpretation is that the behavior of an item is now constrained, now stimulated, by its presence in a whole—which is what ↑**systemism** teaches. *Moderate version*: "The whole is more that the sum of its parts." This is a notoriously fuzzy view, both in containing the undefined notion of "sum" and in being negative. Still, it may be charitably interpreted as the thesis that wholes have ↑**emergent** properties, that is, properties that their components lack. Ontological holism is one of the earliest cosmologies. Nowadays it has few defenders outside the social studies, where there is still some talk about "collective memories," the "will of the people," and "social welfare." This holistic contamination is obvious in the assumption that social agents interact through the market rather than face-to-face. This quaint symbiosis of holism and individualism passed off as individualism may be called ↑**individholism. b Epistemological** The epistemological component of holism is ↑**intuitionism**, according to which we can grasp a whole only as such and by instant insight rather than laborious conceptual or empirical analysis. But in fact only analysis can show that a thing is complex, and only a study of the bonds among its parts can explain what holds them together. **c Methodological** The thesis that wholes must be studied and understood on their own level rather than in terms of their parts. Methodological holism rejects ↑**analysis** and, a fortiori, ↑**reduction**. But analysis is inherent in all of the sciences and technologies because it is only by distinguishing the components of a whole and guessing or discovering their bonds that we can explain what holds it together, what threatens or promises to break it down, or how we might improve on it. Think, e.g., of atomic physics and management science. ↑**Individualism,**↑**systemism. d Semantical** The view that the ↑**meaning** of any symbol is determined by the totality of human knowledge. Since this whole is inaccessible to any individual, no sign would have a clear-cut meaning. But this is obviously false in the case of exact theories. Hence semantic holism is false. Worse, it is obscurantist, for it condemns us to ignorance. What is true is that meaning is contextual, hence the elucidation of the meaning of a construct requires placing it in its context, such as a theory. For example, the meaning of "predicate" is elucidated by the axioms of first-order predicate logic.

HOMO ŒCONOMICUS The human being intent on maximizing his expected gains regardless of the harm he may cause others. **Syn** rational egoist. The referent of mainstream economics and ↑**economic imperialism**, or the annexation of all social studies to neoclassical microeconomics. A fiction best approximated by sociopaths and pirates. ↑**Egoism**.

HONESTY Uprightness, sincerity, commitment to truth. A capital ↑**virtue** impossible to practice if truth or goodness are denied.

HUMAN NATURE The bundle of properties that characterize human kind vis à vis the other animal species. There are as many characterizations of human nature as anthropological schools, and most of them focus on a single feature. Let the following formulas suffice: *homo faber, homo œconomicus, homo ethicus, zoon politikon* (Aristotle), *homo sapiens, homo loquens, homo symbolicus* (Ernst Cassirer), *homo ludens* (Johan Huizinga), *homo aleator* (gambler), *self-interpreting animal* (Charles Taylor), *structure-making animal* (Claude Lévi-Strauss), *homo mechanicus* (La Mettrie and computationist cognitive psychology)—and, of course, the being graced by an immaterial and immortal soul. A less one-sided characterization might be this one: Having twenty-three chromosomes, bipedalism, brain and behavioral plasticity, curiosity, adventurousness, abstraction, generalization, language, sociality, compassion and cruelty, work, competitiveness and cooperativity—and constituting a branch of the primate genealogical tree. The great apes share most of those traits to some extent. Genetic determinism (in particular sociobiology) holds human nature to be unalterable for being wholly determined by the "genetic blueprint" or "gene machine." However, cellular and developmental biology have shown that genes are not enough; and history and anthropology have shown that human nature is partly made (artificial), hence plastic and historically variable in some respects. Man is the encyclopedic and self-made social animal. ↑**Nature/nurture**. The very notion of human nature has been cast aside in favor of the sociologistic (in particular Marxist) view that the essence of humanness consists in sociality. This view ignores biology and ethology. The study of human nature is unlikely ever to be completed, and it behooves all the disciplines and interdisciplines dealing with man: human biology, the biosocial sciences, and the social sciences.

HUMAN RIGHT A right that a moral or legal code, such as the UN Universal Charter of Human Rights, bestows on all human beings, alive or to be born. According to ↑**humanism**, in particular ↑**agathonism**, human rights are the same as basic rights. These are the rights a person must exercise to survive and help live in her society. Examples: the rights to live and love, work and learn, associate, worship or not to worship, and participate in the governance of the commonwealth. Since all such rights are modern acquisitions, they are anything but natural, notwithstanding the ↑**natural law doctrine**.

HUMANISM A broad secular worldview and progressive social philosophy. It rejects beliefs in the supernatural and invites the critical examination of all beliefs; advocates moral codes and political programs that emphasize free inquiry, human rights, and welfare; and promotes the separation of church from state. Humanist ethics asserts that morals are not God-given but man-made, and that a person's greatest obligation is not to imaginary deities but to his fellow human beings. Secular humanism has often been regarded as a purely negative doctrine that boils down to the denial of the supernatural. This is not so, as any fair sampling of the humanist literature will show. Indeed, secular humanism is a positive worldview composed of five main theses. *Cosmological*: Whatever exists is either natural or a product of human manual or mental work. *Epistemological*: It is possible and desirable to find out the truth about the world and ourselves with the sole help of experience, reason, imagination, criticism, and action. *Moral*: We should seek survival in this world, the only real one, through work rather than prayer, and we should enjoy living, as well as trying to help others live instead of damning them. *Social*: Liberty, equality, and solidarity. *Political*: While defending the ↑**freedom** from and to religious worship and political allegiance, we should work for the attainment or maintenance of a secular state and a fully democratic social order. However, not all humanists assign the same value to all five components. Typically, whereas some of them stress the intellectual components, others emphasize the social ones. Which is just as well, for it is proof that, far from being a sect or party, secular humanism is a wide umbrella covering social activists as well as free-thinkers.

HUMANITIES A variegated and ill-defined research field lying between literature and science. Main contemporary components: philosophy, the study of languages, classics, religious studies, history of ideas, history of art, and history of science and technology. ↑**Psychology** and the ↑**social sciences** used to be included in the humanities. Some disciplines, such as history, linguistics, and culturology, straddle the science / humanities divide. And all of the humanities can use some ↑**mathematics** (in particular logic) as well as the ↑**scientific method**.

HUMANITY The species *Homo sapiens sapiens*. The central concern of ↑**humanism** in contradistinction to religions as well as to secular ideologies that promote the special interests of ethnic or social groups.

HUME'S PROBLEM Do inductive generalizations warrant forecasts? For example, does the fact that the Sun has "risen" every morning until now guarantee that it will rise tomorrow? Hume's correct reply was in the negative. But he was wrong in claiming that this holds for all predictions. Indeed, the predictions made with the help of scientific ↑**laws** are reliable. For instance, theoretical astronomy has proved the stability of the solar system, which allows us to forecast that the Sun will "rise" tomorrow. However, theoretical astrophysics has also predicted that the Sun will eventually implode, as a consequence of which there will only be a finite, albeit huge, number of tomorrows.

HYPOTHESES NON FINGO I do not feign hypotheses. A claim of Newton's in his *Principia*. He claimed that his axioms were "inferred by general induction from phenomena," and so quite different from the groundless hypotheses of Descartes and Leibniz. Actually, Newton did not proceed inductively: his axioms were counterintuitive and could not be directly checked; they contained the nonempirical notion of mass; and they were organized into the earliest ↑**hypothetico-deductive system** in factual science.

HYPOTHESIS Educated guess. A statement that embraces more than the data that suggest or confirm it. All the empirical generalizations and law-statements, even the well-confirmed ones, are hypotheses. Thus, human knowledge is largely hypothetical. However, not all hypotheses are equally plausible: whereas some are proffered as tentative, others are regarded as very close to total truth, and still others as final: ↑**plausibility**. Examples of definitive truths that started out as tentative hypotheses: "The universe has evolved," "There are force fields," "RNA takes part in protein synthesis," and "Individual decision making is located in the prefrontal cortex."

HYPOTHETICAL Conjectural, conditional, unproved. ↑**Hypothesis**.

HYPOTHETICO-DEDUCTIVE a System A system of propositions held together by the relation ⇒ of implication and rules of inference. Example: the propositions p and $p ⇒ q$, and the ↑***modus ponens*** rule. The latter permits the detachment of the consequence q. This deduction is the ↑**emergent** property of the system: that which neither of its components p and $p \Rightarrow q$ has. **Syn** ↑**theory. b Method** The procedure whereby a ↑**hypothesis** is subjected to empirical tests. Let H designate a hypothesis, S a subsidiary (or auxiliary) assumption (such as an ↑**indicator hypothesis** or a simplification), and D a datum, which jointly imply an observable consequence O. That is, H & S & $D \Rightarrow O$. If O is found to obtain, H is said to be ↑**confirmed**. By contrast, if O fails repeatedly to obtain, the antecedent is falsified. But, since this antecedent is the conjunction of (at least) three propositions, namely H, S, and D, either of them may be blamed. When this is the case, each must be reexamined separately: the observations leading to D must be replicated, the subsidiary assumptions S must be varied, or H must be altered. ↑**Duhem thesis**. **c System** ↑**theory**.

I The name that the self-conscious actor, speaker, or writer gives himself, as in "I am reading this book." **Syn** me, ego, self. Idealists distinguish between themselves and their bodies, as in "the self and its brain." Materialists regard the self as a brain state: that of self-consciousness. This can be conceived of as the state of a part of the brain while it monitors what another part of the brain is feeling or thinking. ↑**Consciousness, mind, mind-body problem.**

IATROPHILOSOPHY The philosophy of ↑**medicine**: the study of the ontological, epistemological, and moral problems raised by biomedical research, medical practice, and public health care. Examples: What is the nature of disease: process or thing, material or spiritual, individual or social? What kind of problem is that of medical diagnosis: direct or inverse? What is the logic of medical diagnosis: inductive, deductive, or neither? Should the Hippocratic oath be updated to make room for risky invasive procedures or assisted suicide? Can health-care policymaking (a sociotechnology) learn anything from social science? What distinguishes scientific medicine from medical quackery?

IDEA An umbrella term that designates a percept, an image, a concept, a proposition, a classification, a doctrine, a theory, or whatever else can be thought. Because of such generality, it is hard to conceive that there could be a single precise theory of ideas of all kinds.

IDEAEFICATION The construal of concrete things or processes as ideas, in the manner of Plato and Hegel. The dual of ↑**reification.** Contemporary examples: the identification of a solid body with the set representing it; of a basket of goods with the vector representing it; and of a social mechanism with a theoretical model of it.

IDEAL a General Ambiguous term designating both the nonmaterial and the perfect. Examples: numbers are ideal objects; ideal knowledge would be complete; ideal conduct would be blameless; ideal surfaces are frictionless; ideal markets are fully competitive. **b Social philosophy** Desirable social goal, "the fairness and equity ideals." Every social ↑**ideology** and every political platform contains a set of social ideals.

IDEAL TYPE Idealized model of a thing or process. ↑**Idealization.** It is formed by focusing on features regarded as salient or typical, and consequently disregarding others thought to be secondary though, on closer inspection, they may turn out to be important. ↑**Typology.**

IDEALISM The family of philosophies that asserts the primacy of ideas or even their independent existence. **Syn** ↑**immaterialism**. There are two main varieties: objective and subjective. *Objective* idealism maintains that ideas exist by themselves and that we only "grasp" or discover them. Examples: Plato, Leibniz, Hegel, Bolzano, Dilthey, Frege. *Subjective* idealism holds that only ideas in the mind's subject exist: that there is no autonomous external world. Examples: one of Descartes's two masks, Berkeley, Kant, Fichte, Mach, Cassirer, Collingwood, and most of the members of the ↑**constructivist** sociology of knowledge. Neither version of idealism is countenanced by science or technology: these take the external world for granted: this is why they explore or modify it. Caution: The mere assertion that ideas matter does not qualify as idealist. Most materialists and realists admit the existence and importance of ideas; they only deny their self-existence.

IDEALIST An adherent of ↑**idealism**. Not to be confused with 'idealistic' or driven by geneous ideals.

IDEALIZATION In ordinary language, the overlooking of imperfections, as in "People in love tend to idealize the objects of their love." In science and technology, the deliberate schematization or simplification of a real object in the process of its conceptual representation. **Syn** Stylization.

IDEATION The mental (or brain) process consisting in having ideas, i.e., in perceiving, imagining, conceiving, relating, analyzing, criticizing, synthesizing, etc. Presumably, ideation is the specific function of the plastic part of the brain, i.e., of the neuronal systems held together by changing ("soft-wired") connections.

IDENTITY a General concept The concept of identity is not explicitly definable in any theory. In particular, it cannot be defined as a set of ordered pairs, as required by ↑**extensionalism**. One reason is that "=" is part of every definition, since—as Peano noted—definitions are nothing but identities. ("= = Definiens" is not a wff.) But "=" can be defined axiomatically, e.g., by $\forall x \, (x = x)$ plus the conditions of reflexivity, symmetry, and transitivity. Besides, "=" satisfies Leibniz's "law" or rather postulate of *identity of indiscernibles*: If two objects are identical, then they have exactly the same properties. (I.e., for any individuals x and y, and every relevant predicate F: If $x = y$, then: if Fx then Fy, and conversely.) Although this formula (in second-order logic) is usually regarded as a definition, it cannot be such, for the reason given above. Leibniz's formula is ordinarily taken as asserting not only the identity of indiscernibles (when read from left to right) but also the *indiscernibility of identicals* (when read in the opposite direction). However, the concept of discernibility is epistemological, not logical. Indeed, discernibility is relative to analytical tool or observation technique. If two objects are identical, then they are indiscernible, but the converse is false. Leibniz's "law" may also be read as the assertion that, if "two" objects are identical, then "they" are one, though perhaps with different names in different contexts or circumstances. This sounds puzzling, but it is natural in mathematics and science, where one may start by examining two objects that are prima facie different, only to conclude that they are the same. Example: all equiangular triangles are also equilateral, and conversely. Sometimes one meets objects so similar to each other that one (mistakenly) calls them "identical," while the weaker concepts of ↑**equality** and ↑**equivalence** are in order. A familiar example is that of "identical copies" of a document or a merchandise. The facts that they are at different places, and that they can be counted, shows that they are not strictly identical. A closer examination, e.g., through a microscope, would show further differences. Another familiar case is that of "identical" (or monozygotic) twins. Even if they have "the same" genome (or rather two nearly identical copies of a genome), they are born with certain differences (e.g., in fingerprints) and they develop further differences, particularly if they grow up in different environments. The case of "identical" particles, such as a cloud of electrons in a chunk of metal, is prima facie more difficult because such entities have far fewer properties. Still, according to Pauli's exclusion principle, no two electrons in such a cloud can be in exactly the same quantum state. This principle holds for electrons and other particles with half-integral spin, but it fails for all others (bosons). In principle, any number of bosons can be in the same quantum state; moreover, they can clump into a "Bose condensate." Yet, since they can be counted, they cannot be strictly identical. What is true is that nothing changes if they trade positions: they are interchangeable. One may thus speak of *functional* identity by contrast to strict identity. **b Personal identity** The continuity of a person's life. A person's state at any given time surely differs from his state at some other time: there is no strict identity between different stages in a life history. However, we may attribute them to "the same" person if our definition of a person involves the person's history, or at least his past—as it should since what we are now is, at least in part, a result of what we have experienced since conception. **c Identity hypothesis** The philosophico-scientific hypothesis that mental states are brain states. This hypothesis (usually called 'theory') underlies the neurophysiological approach to the study of behavior, emotion, cognition, and volition. ↑**Mind-body problem**.

IDEOLOGY A system of factual statements and value judgments that inspires some social movement or social policy. An ideology can be religious or secular; and it can be comprehensive, like Thomism and Marxism; sociopolitical, like liberalism and socialism; or cultural, such as cultural nationalism and multiculturalism. The received idea is that all ideological statements are false and tools of some special interest group, hence without a future in a technological society. However, it is hard to imagine how any action in defense of the public good could be prompted without some ideology. Nor is it hard to imagine a scientific ideology, i.e., one whose factual statements are scientifically justified value judgments. Examples of statements at once scientific and ideological: "Poverty is individually degrading and socially destabilizing, hence it should be eradicated," and "Free inquiry is necessary for the advancement of culture and the improvement of welfare, hence it should be protected and promoted."

IDIOGRAPHIC / NOMOTHETIC Idiographic = singular or descriptive. Nomothetic = Generalizing or accounting in terms of laws. According to the ↑**hermeneutic** school, whereas the natural sciences are nomothetic, the social studies are idiographic. But granting the singular / general distinction does not entail that a discipline must be either singularizing or generalizing. Thus, every natural science accounts for individual facts in terms of both pattern and circumstance. And every social science assumes or seeks pattern beneath individual facts. Thus, the shrinking of the industrial workforce is explained by the generalization that all technological advancement eliminates manufacturing jobs through increasing productivity. ↑**Generalization / instantiation**.

IF Suggesting a condition. ↑**Implication**. Big if = A conditional whose antecedent is implausible.

IF-THEN ↑**Implication**.

IFF Abbreviation of "if and only if." Thus, "A iff B" is the same as "A ⇔ B." Iffy = Doubtful prospect, event unlikely to come to pass because the necessary and sufficient conditions for its occurrence are met rarely if ever.

IGNORABIMUS We shall always ignore. A radical skeptical slogan concerning such problems as the size of the universe, the interior of stars, the nature of life and mind, the existence of God, and other matters is *Ignoramus et ignorabimus* (We ignore and shall always ignore). This maxim may have retarded scientific research, but it has failed to stop curious people from challenging it successfully again and again.

IGNORANCE Lack of knowledge. Everyone knows something but ignores most of what is known. Ignorance can be involuntary or voluntary. Involuntary ignorance, when realized, is a challenge to exploration and invention. Willful ignorance is the common lot of the dogmatists, the narrow-minded, and the hyperspecialized. For instance, the philosopher of mind who refuses to learn some contemporary (in particular physiological) psychology exhibits willful ignorance; likewise the philosopher of language uninterested in linguistics; the philosopher of science ignorant of science, and so forth. The systematic rejection of all new knowledge may be called ↑**gnosophobia**.

IGNORANCE, SPECIFIED A prerequisite of research in any field, from crime detection to mathematics, is to admit that one ignores something worth knowing. For such admission and evaluation to be fertile it must be specific, not generic: it must describe, as precisely as possible, what it is that we do not know and should investigate—e.g., the detailed mechanism of protein synthesis or the emergence of a new abstract idea. Caution: Such specification is unavoidably sketchy precisely because the item to be investigated is largely unknown. This is why ↑**invention** cannot be entrusted to computers.

IMAGINATION The psychological power without which no new ideas are crafted in art, the humanities, mathematics, science, or technology. Imagination is suspect to dogmatism because it can lead to heresy; and to empiricism because, in going beyond experience, it may produce groundless speculation. The only difference between artistic imagination, on the one hand, and mathematical, scientific, technological, or humanist imagination, on the other, is that the former is not constrained by considerations of truth, consistency, or efficiency.

IMMANENT / TRANSCENDENTAL Intrinsic / extrinsic, this-worldly / other-worldly, self-sufficient / other-governed. A pair of vague concepts important in theology, the philosophy of religion, and idealism, in particular Kantianism. Example 1: God is immanent (pantheism), transcendental (theism), or neither (atheism). Example 2: The laws of nature are immanent (materialism), transcendental (idealism), or neither (subjectivism). ↑**Transcendental**.

IMMATERIALISM Any philosophy that denies the existence of autonomously existing ↑**material things**. Immaterialism can be idealist (e.g., Leibniz's) or empiricist (e.g., Berkeley's). It is an obsolete doctrine in view of the fact that all of the factual sciences and technologies only study material entities. However, Berkeley's view, that things are bundles of qualities, is still held by some philosophers. But it is untenable. Indeed, every quality (or property) is a feature of some object or other, material or ideal. A mathematical analysis of properties makes this clear: ↑**predicate**. Moreover, the idea that things are bundles of properties leads to nonsense. Indeed, if an object were identical with the set of its properties, then neither of these could be predicated of the object. That is, if $b = \{P_1, P_2, \ldots, P_n\}$, then $P_1 b = P_1 \{P_1, P_2, \ldots, Pn\}$, which is an ill-formed formula.

IMMORAL The opposite of ↑**moral**, as in 'revenge is immoral'. The question whether immorality is absolute (or cross-cultural) or relative (or culture-bound) is at once philosophical and scientific (in particular anthropological and historical).

IMMORALISM Opposition to the norms shared by all the moral codes, and that make up common ↑**decency**.

IMMORTALITY Everlasting life. Three kinds of immortality may be distinguished: corporeal, spiritual, and vicarious. Corporeal immortality is impossible: all organisms age and eventually become disabled to the point of being unable to undergo all the physiological processes that characterize ↑**life**. (In principle there could be continual regeneration and self-repair. But an impregnable armor against lethal external inputs would drastically restrict freedom and communication, to say the least.) Spiritual immortality, postulated by some religions, is likewise impossible, because all of the spiritual (or mental) functions are brain functions: no living brain, no mind. Vicarious or indirect immortality can be achieved through offspring, for a part of every person's genome passes on to his descendants. But it gets progressively "diluted" down the generations, so that vicarious biological immortality is hardly significant. On the other hand, every individual makes his mark through his actions, good or evil, because every action, however humble, alters the person's environment. Immortality through works won't satisfy that character of Woody Allen's who wanted to become immortal "through not dying." But it is the best we can reasonably hope for.

IMPARTIALITY Equidistance, detachment, dispassionateness. A virtue in matters of knowledge and justice, where the overriding concerns are truth and the right, respectively. For example, the judge is expected to be impartial between conflicting private interests, and the scientist is expected to be equidistant between rival theories as long as the available evidence favors neither of them. But impartiality is a vice with regard to moral problems, where the upright person is expected to take the part of the good and the right instead of staying "beyond good and evil" (as Nietzsche preached). For example, the anthropologist will study cannibalism, widow-burning, and slavery in an objective way, even while exposing and condemning them for their cruelty and divisiveness. And the policymaker cannot help taking part for or against the downtrodden; however, for his policies to be effective they must be based on impartial social studies as well as on moral principles.

IMPERATIVE a General Command or instruction, as in 'Thou shalt not perpetrate existentialism'. **b Logic** Since imperatives are neither true nor false, they would seem to call for a logic of their own. However, the project of building a logic of imperatives has foundered. Anyhow such logic, even if it were possible, is unnecessary, for every imperative can be translated into at least one declarative. For example, 'Come!' can be translated into 'I beg you to come', 'I order you to come', 'You are told to come', or even 'If you are good, you will come', 'If you do not wish to displease me, you will come', etc. Such translations are actually so many analyses exhibiting the particular circumstances of the issuance of the command. Hence they have truth values and they can be rationally argued about. **c Ethics** Kant's widely misunderstood ⭡**categorical imperative** is a metaethical maxim.

IMPERFECTION Deviation from the ideal type, norm, or statistical mode. Material examples: ionized atoms, mutants, eccentrics, markets off equilibrium, democracies. Conceptual examples: ill-defined concepts, ill-posed problems, partially true hypotheses or theories, inconsistent theories. **Ant** ⭡**perfection**. Everyone agrees that everything human is imperfect, and some believe that some imperfections can be corrected. But the equally popular thesis, that every imperfection is undesirable, is false. Indeed, whereas some imperfections are defects or liabilities, others are not. For example, academic excellence, a deviance from mediocrity, is a liability in an environment that punishes excellence. Imperfect DNA replication is a source of biodiversity and the raw material for selection, hence biological evolution. Social deviance of some kind is a source of social change and a challenge that, if met, may be beneficial. Hence, aiming for the perfect society—one fitting an a priori final blueprint—is not only unrealistic but also counterproductive, for perfection involves stagnation. The aim should be the progressive society, one fitting a sequence of increasingly improved blueprints.

IMPERIALISM a Linguistic The thesis that language is central. It comes in two versions. Ontological or radical linguistic imperialism claims that every object is a linguistic expression. Epistemological or moderate linguistic imperialism holds that linguistic (in particular syntactical) analysis precedes every other study. **Syn** ⭡**glossocentrism**. ⭡**Hermeneutics**. **b Logical** The view that logic is not only necessary but also sufficient to handle all philosophical problems. **Syn** ⭡**panlogism**. This strategy has four possible roots: (a) the belief that form is all-important, or at least far more important than content; (b) Platonism, or the idea that the world is made of ideas or crude copies of them; (c) unwillingness to study anything requiring more than pencil and paper; and (d) ignorance, arrogance, or both. ⭡**Hollow exactness**. **c Economic** The view that all social sciences should be modeled on economics, in particular neoclassical microeconomics. The root of this thesis is the belief that all human beings, regardless of place and time, are selfish utility maximizers. This movement has been spreading like wildfire throughout the social sciences since about 1970. It has had important consequences: the reduction of the multiplicity of human motivations to gain maximization; the indiscriminate use of mostly undefined ↑**utility** functions and inscrutable subjective ↑**probabilities**; a proliferation of simplistic ↑**rational-choice models** of social facts; the focusing on individuals at the expense of social systems; and the persistent overlooking of work and the time variable.

IMPLICATION A logical connective in all the systems of deductive logic, as in "If it is philosophical, then it is general." Standard symbols: ⇒, ⊃, →. Standard implicit definitions of this connective in classical logic: $p \Rightarrow q =_{df} \neg p \vee q$, $p \Rightarrow q =_{df} \neg(p \,\&\, \neg q)$. Implication should not be confused with the far stronger relation ⊢ of ↑**entailment** (or deducibility). If p ⊢ q, then p ⇒ q, but not conversely. (Hence a standard method to prove a conditional p ⇒ q is to prove that q follows from p.) To detach or separate or assert q from p ⇒ q, we must assert p separately and add the ↑***modus ponens*** inference rule. The controversial concept of strict (or necessary) implication, introduced by modal logicians, has been replaced with that of ↑**entailment**.

IMPONDERABLE A property is imponderable if it can be neither quantitated nor measured. The paragons of imponderabilia are existence and beauty. Logic and mathematics are full of imponderabilia, such as the logical concepts of negation and disjunction, the set-theoretic concepts of membership and inclusion, and the metalogical ones of consistency and completeness. By contrast, a presupposition of natural science is that all the properties of natural objects, except for existence, are quantitative even if they have so far resisted ↑**quantitation**. This is not a presupposition of the social studies and technologies, which teem with qualitative concepts, such as those of justice, political stability, product quality, and management style. However, it would be dogmatic to rule out the possibility of quantitating these concepts.

IMPORT The import of a context in a given context equals the set of constructs it entails in that context. Dual: ↑**purport**. The union of import and purport equals ↑**sense**.

IMPOSSIBLE Not possible. Impossibilia can be conceptual or factual. Self-contradictions, such as "round and square," are conceptual impossibilities. Imaginable events that, if they occurred, would escape some laws of nature, are factually impossible. Examples: the unscrambling of eggs, resuscitation, and psychokinesis. Most conceptual impossibilities can easily be diagnosed and eliminated. On the other hand, the discovery of a factual impossibility may be the outcome of a long-drawn research, as were the cases with the impossibility of spontaneous generation of multicellular organisms, and building a perpetual-motion machine.

IN PRINCIPLE Possible in theory but not in practice, at least for now. For example, in (wrong) principle one could go on counting indefinitely. ↑**Impossible**.

INACTION The absence of action. The highest virtue according to Taoism—a moral philosophy suitable only for crippled rentiers. A much-underrated type of behavior, inaction is bad only when action is called for. Inaction is good when a beneficial process is best left alone because intervention might deviate or even stop its course. Inaction is also desirable when we have no solid grounds to intervene in a rational way with some likelihood of success. However, the concept of inaction is absent from most ↑**action** theories.

INCOMMENSURABLE Incomparable. Example: moral and aesthetic values. The fashionable relativistic view that rival scientific theories are incommensurable is false: they are rival precisely because they are comparable, and one of them is likely to fit the evidence, or a contiguous theory, better than the other. ↑**Revolution, epistemic,** ↑**rival views.**

INCOMPLETE SYMBOL ↑**Syncategorematic.**

INCONSISTENCY The opposite of ↑**consistency.** A set of propositions is *internally* inconsistent if it contains at least one pair of mutually contradictory propositions. And it is *externally* inconsistent if it contradicts the bulk of the background knowledge. Inconsistency is always to be avoided or remedied in the search for truth. Hence ↑**paraconsistent logic,** which allows for inconsistency, is at best an ingenious toy.

INDEPENDENCE Two or more *concepts* are mutually independent if neither is definable in terms of the other. Examples: "probability" and "frequency"; "truth" and "knowledge"; "force" and "mass." Two or more *propositions* are mutually independent if neither is deducible from any of the others. Examples: p and $p \Rightarrow q$; $1 > 0$ and $1 - 1 = 0$; "I know p" and "p is true." A desideratum for axiomatic systems is that their basic concepts (primitives) and basic assumptions (postulates) be mutually independent. Whereas in mathematics independence is mainly a matter of conceptual economy, in factual science it has occasionally philosophical significance. For example, Mach claimed to have disproved materialism by "defining" mass in terms of acceleration (as if this were not a property of material bodies). An application of Padoa's independence test (belonging in model theory) proves that the concepts of mass and force are mutually independent in particle mechanics, which refutes Mach's argument.

INDETERMINACY a Ontology A state or event is indeterminate if it is not bound to occur, as a consequence of which it is not predictable, except perhaps in a probabilistic manner. **b Physics** A physical property is said to be indeterminate (or indefinite) if it has a distribution of values rather than sharp values. The measure of the indeterminacy of a physical magnitude is its variance. ↑**Heisenberg's** inequalities.

INDETERMINISM a Ontology *Radical* = There are no laws. *Moderate* = There are noncausal (e.g., probabilistic) laws. **b Ethics** The thesis that humans are capable of ↑**free will**. A misnomer for, if the will can be freely exerted, it is surely by virtue of certain neuropsychological laws as well as of certain social circumstances.

INDEXICAL What holds only at a certain place or time or for a particular individual. Ex-

.

amples: "I feel cold right now." **Syn** contextual. Related: ↑**egocentric particular.** ↑**Relativism** holds that all statements should be regarded as indexical—except of course this injunction.

INDICATOR Symptom or sign: observable property or event regarded as a manifestation of an unobservable property or event. Examples: the deviation of a magnetic needle in a vacuum indicates the presence of either a magnetic field or an electric current; fever may indicate infection or overheating; and GDP is an indicator of national wealth or economic activity. Indicators can be empirical or supported by theories. In the former case they are ambiguous; thus, blushing can indicate embarrassment, shame, anger, or physical exertion; choice indicates either evaluation or acquisitive power; and IQ may indicate either information or intelligence. The theoretical indicators are more reliable than the empirical ones, because the underlying theory exhibits the mechanism whereby the observable indicates the unobserved, and thus shows that nothing else could have caused the observed event. To minimize ambiguity it is advisable to use a battery of independent indicators. **Syn** proxy. ↑**Indicator hypothesis.**

INDICATOR HYPOTHESIS A hypothesis relating an unobservable property to an ↑**indicator** of it. **Syn** ↑**operational definition.** Example: any functional relation of the form "$U = f(O)$," where O is a measurable variable and U the corresponding unobservable variable, as in "temperature = constant × height of thermometric column," and "Intensity of economic activity = Gross Domestic Product."

INDIVIDHOLISM A philosophy of social science. The combination of (methodological) ↑**individualism** with (ontological) ↑**holism** that focuses on individuals acting within wholes and in circumstances that are taken as wholes, i.e., are not analyzed in individualistic terms. Examples: situational "logic" and ↑**rational-choice** models treating the market as an unanalyzed whole. Individholism combines the objectionable features of individualism (or atomism) and holism (or functionalism). Ironically, individholists claim to be radical individualists even while postulating such unanalyzed wholes as the objective mind (Dilthey) or ↑**world 3** (K. R. Popper).

INDIVIDUAL Indivisible in a given context or level, though perhaps not in another. **Ant** collection. Individuals can be constructs or concrete things. Examples: the elements of a set, and systems such as persons and societies. The individual/set distinction is contextual. Thus the members of a family of sets are sets. The component/system distinction is contextual too. Thus families, firms, and other social systems are individuals in society at large: they are analyzable but not decomposable.

INDIVIDUALISM a Ontological Every object is either an individual or a collection of individuals. This thesis is a component of ↑**nominalism. Syn** ↑**atomism. Ant** ↑**collectivism,** ↑**holism,** ↑**organicism.** Ontological individualism is falsified by the very existence of wholes with properties of their own: ↑**systems.** For instance, a body of water is not an aggregate of H_2O molecules, an organism is not a collection of cells, and a machine is different from the set of its parts. Nevertheless, individualism is often a useful antidote to holism, and it is still very influential in all the branches of learning. It has inspired the following doctrines, all of which come in two strengths, radical and moderate. **b Logico-linguistic** The view that all ↑**constructs** are built out of suitable units. In particular, relations would be *n*-tuples of individuals: ↑**extensionalism**. Objection: classes, propositions, arguments, etc., have (emergent) properties that none of their components possess. And the relations of ↑**identity** and **membership**, central in ↑**set theory**, are not definable as sets of ordered pairs. **c Semantic** The meaning of a conceptual or linguistic whole, such as a sentence or the proposition it designates, is a function of the meanings of its parts. However, the function in question has never been defined. Besides, some meaningful expressions, such as "It did so," can be constructed from ↑**syncategorematic** terms. And some meaningless sentences, such as "Mother cooked drunken ships," are constituted by meaningful terms. **d Epistemological** The view that the knower is necessary and sufficient to get things known: that to inquire he does not need to be embedded in a social network. This thesis has been falsified by social psychology and the sociology of knowledge. For example, scientists learn from one another; they are motivated by the desire for peer recognition as well as by curiosity; and they are stimulated or inhibited by governments. **e Methodological** The thesis that the study of the individual components of a whole is both necessary and sufficient to account for the behavior of the totality. ↑**Reductionism**. The ground of methodological individualism is ontological individualism. It avoids the fictitious totalities of holism, but it overlooks social systems and their structure. **f Axiological** Only individuals evaluate (true), and all values are individual (false). Individualism ignores social values such as solidarity, justice, social cohesion, good governance, and peace. **g Praxiological** All action is individual and independent of social structure. Objections: all individual actions, whether prosocial or antisocial, are restricted by social structure; and some actions are concerted and, to be successful, they require compromises on the part of the actors. **h Moral** Any moral code or ethical doctrine centered on the respect for individual rights and aspirations. It proposes, in particular, that individuals be evaluated and treated exclusively on the strength of their particular merits rather than on their membership in some group. **Ant** ↑**communitarianism**, racism. In its radical version, moral individualism promotes self-interest above everything else. Consequently it minimizes or even writes off duties—which disqualifies it as a moral philosophy. ↑**Agathonism** combines concern for the individual with social responsibility. **i Historical** History is made exclusively by individuals. Elitist version: the ↑**great men theory of history**. Democratic version: all rational decision makers are historical agents. Flaws: overrating of isolated individuals, and neglect of natural environment, tradition, and social networks. **j Political** Individual liberty is the maximal value. **Syn** ↑**libertarianism**. Most obvious flaw: liberty is possible only among equals.

INDIVIDUATION The procedure whereby an object is distinguished from all other objects: indication of its peculiarities. Usually Leibniz's definition (or rather criterion) of ↑**identity** does the job since, according to it, two objects are not identical if they differ in at least one property. This criterion might be thought to fail for photons and other bosons, which are said to be indistinguishable. Actually they are distinguishable but interchangeable. ↑**Identity**.

INDUCTION a Ordinary Generalization from either particulars or empirical generaliza-tions. Example: "Higher learning does not flourish in rural societies." Without induction there would be no general knowedge, whether ordinary or specialized. But advanced sci-ence and technology start off where induction ceases to work, for both involve hy-potheses that exceed observation. Indeed, all the high-level scientific and technological ↑**hypotheses** and ↑**theories** contain predicates that do not occur in the relevant data. Ex-ample: "Social cohesion favors political stability" involves the unobservables "cohe-sion" and "stability." ↑**Inductive logic,** ↑**hypothetico-deductive method. b Scientific** In science and technology, induction occurs at two important junctions: in testing hy-potheses and in generalizing from sample to population. Indeed, the "conclusion" that a body of empirical evidence confirms or infirms some of the testable consequences of a given theory is an inductive hypothesis. The second occurrence of induction is in the form of statistical inference from observations conducted on the members of a small sample to the total population from which it has been extracted. Both kinds of induction differ from ordinary induction in at least two important respects. First, probability con-siderations are involved, particularly in estimating the likelihood that a certain result could happen by chance. Second, samples are not found, but are carefully constructed with the help of sampling methods. The philosophical upshot is that it is just as mistaken to underrate statistical induction as it is to overrate ordinary induction. **c Mathematical** A principle and method of mathematical proof applicable to denumerable sets of propo-sitions: Any property that holds for zero and for the successor of any number having that property is a property of all (natural) numbers. Whereas ordinary induction is dicey, in depending on content or substance, mathematical (or arithmetical) induction is rigorous, in being purely formal. The principle of mathematical induction can be proved.

INDUCTIVE LOGIC The attempt to justify inductive leaps and inferences by assigning probabilities to hypotheses and data. This, the flagship of logical ↑**positivism**, sank for several reasons, among them the following. First, inductive inferences are inherently unruly because they depend on content rather than form: sometimes they succeed, but at other times they don't. Second, it makes no sense to attribute ↑**probabilities** to propositions, except arbitrarily. In particular, it makes no sense to assign them prior subjective probabilities, that is, credibilities before performing empirical tests. The most we can do is to pronounce them ↑**plausible** or implausible. Third, even if prob-ability assignments made sense, there would be no guarantee that the rival hypothe-ses that are being considered are mutually exclusive and jointly exhaustive, so that the sum of all the probabilities equals unity. Indeed, someone might come up with further candidates. In any event, there is not a single historical case where inductive logic has been used: it is just an academic toy.

INDUCTIVE METHOD Any technique for obtaining a low-level generalization from a set of data. The most common and useful techniques of this kind are the curve-fitting (or interpolation) methods. These yield polynomials that join experimental dots. However, such polynomials rarely coincide with the true law statements, for most of these in-volve predicates that do not occur in the empirical data. For instance, the elementary law of the pendulum, which does not have the polynomial form, can only be inferred from the basic law of motion.

INDUCTIVISM The thesis that all generalizations are or must be gotten by ↑**induction**, as in the case of "All mammals are hairy." Inductivism is an integral part of ↑**empiricism**. None of the principles of modern science is an inductive generalization: all of them are hypotheses containing concepts that do not occur in the relevant data. Example 1: The energy of the photon that an atom emits when decaying from one energy-level to a lower one equals the difference in energy between those levels. Example 2: Biological evolution is an outcome of genic variation and natural selection. Example 3: Economic inequalities, as measured by the Gini index, are greatest in the less-developed countries.

INDUSTRY, ACADEMIC Sustained intellectual effort to produce irrelevant publications. Discourse on pseudoproblems or miniproblems, often originating in elementary misunderstandings, that only serves the purpose of getting academic promotion. Examples: ↑**Bayesianism**, ↑**doxastic logic**, many-worlds semantics, general ↑**measurement theory**, ↑**quantum logic**.

INEFFABLE Inexpressible, that nobody can state in any language. Said of mystic experiences. The rationalist view is that ineffability is an indicator of conceptual confusion.

INERTIA The property of concrete things, of continuing to change even after the external force that triggered their change ceased to act. Examples: mechanical and thermal inertia, the propagation of light, and the social inertia of large organizations. Inertia is a special kind of ↑**self-determination**, and as such a counterexample of ↑**externalism**.

INFERENCE Reasoning from premises to conclusion. There are two kinds of inference: ↑**deductive** and seductive, or logical and nonlogical respectively. Only deductive inferences are rigorous (logically valid). Seductive inference can be ↑**analogical** or ↑**inductive**. Neither proves anything because neither is subject to strict rules: there are no such things as analogical logic and ↑**inductive logic**—except in the imagination of some philosophers. But, of course, occasionally analogies and inductions do suggest true generalizations. This is particularly the case with statistical inductions, or "inferences" from samples to populations, because there are methods to estimate the confidence with which such leaps can be made.

INFINITE REGRESS The logical fallacy consisting in requiring that every assertion requires a separate foundation or justification.

INFINITISM The view that there are conceptual and real infinities. ↑**Infinity**. Ant ↑**finitism**. Modern mathematics and science endorse infinitism: they study infinite sets and infinite series, as well as continuous things, such as fields, that exist at every point in some spatial region. Indeed, such region, even if finite in volume, is composed of a nondenumerable infinity of points.

INFINITY a Mathematics There are several kinds of infinity. To begin with, infinity can be either ↑**potential** (like a quantity or a collection that grows without bounds) or ↑**ac-**

tual (like the set of all the points inside a ball). The symbol of potential infinity is ∞, as in "$(n/n +1) \to 1$ as $n \to \infty$." Actual infinities come in infinitely many sizes. The smallest of them are the denumerable (countable) sets, such as those of the natural numbers—that is, $\mathbb{N} = \{0, 1, 2, \ldots\}$—their negatives, doubles, squares, and ratios. All the infinite denumerable sets have the same numerosity or cardinality, called $\aleph_0$ (aleph-zero). This is the first infinite cardinal, or transfinite number. The higher-order infinities, or transfinite numbers, can be constructed by first forming the power set of N, and then the succesive power sets of the resulting sets. (The power set 2^S of a set S is the family of all the subsets of S. If the cardinality of S is C, then that of its power set 2^S is 2^C.) The cardinality of any power set is greater than that of the given set: this is Cantor's theorem. This teorem guarantees the (ideal) existence of an unending "hierarchy" (ladder) of transfinite numbers. Next to $\aleph_0$, the most commonly used cardinal is $\aleph$, the cardinality of the ↑**continuum** (such as the set of real numbers, the lines, the surfaces, and the higher-dimensional spaces). Moreover, there is an arithmetic of cardinals that has a superficial resemblance with ordinary arithmetic. For example, $1 + 2 + \ldots + n + \ldots = \aleph_0$; $\aleph_0 + \aleph_0 = \aleph_0$; $\aleph_0 \cdot \aleph_0 = \aleph_0$; $\aleph + \aleph_0 = \aleph$, and $\aleph_0 \cdot \aleph = \aleph$. The mathematical ↑**intuitionists** reject transfinite arithmetic. On the other hand, the ↑**Platonists** not only admit it, but believe in the actual existence of the infinite (but denumerable) totality of transfinite numbers. By contrast, ↑**fictionism** and scientific ↑**realism** admit the transfinite numbers on a par with the other mathematical fictions, such as the number one and the infinite straight line. And, along with the Platonists, they regard the invention of set theory as one of the great triumphs of disinterested inquiry, and proof of the superiority of abstract thought over empirical groping.↑**Continuum hypothesis. b Science** Only two concepts of infinity occur in factual science: potential infinity (∞), and the cardinality of the real line ($\aleph$). However, it is tacitly postulated that no magnitude referring to a finite part of the universe can take on (positive or negative) infinite values. In other words, a function representing a property of a real thing is not defined at a singularity. For example, infinite densities and prices are to be avoided.

INFORMATION a Engineering Information theory deals with the transmission of electromagnetic signals along wires or through space. It is particularly concerned with the fidelity of transmission, hence with ways of minimizing the effects of noise (random perturbations) on the transmission channels. Contrary to popular belief, information theory is utterly unconcerned with meaning. For example, the amount of information of the message 'I love you' is exactly the same as that of 'I hate you'. The reason is that the relation between signal and meaning is conventional. So, it takes different messages to transmit the same idea in different languages. **b Science** The word 'information', if not the concept, has spilled over from engineering, contaminating first biology (in particular genetics), then biochemistry (and through it molecular biology), psychology, sociology, and more. One reason for such rapid expansion is that, in each case, the word 'information' was tacitly assigned a different signification. For example, in genetics "information" is identical with DNA structure (or order of the constituent nucleotides). Moreover, because it concerns individual molecular sequences, it is unrelated to the information in bulk dealt with in communications engineering. In neuroscience, an "information flow" is nothing but a signal propagating along a nerve—but it is definitely not a signal that carries a message such as an instruction, because neurons cannot understand anything. Besides, whether a signal will activate the target neuron will depend on the state of the receptors on the latter's membrane. In psychology, the expression 'information processing' designates any mental process whose mechanism is unknown. In fact, it may be argued that the entire information-processing cognitive psychology is essentially the old mentalistic psychology translated into smart Informationese. As for the computationist version of information-processing psychology, there is no question but that it is exact, since it contains mathematical models. The questions are (a) whether it is pertinent and fertile; (b) whether, by extending the domain of applicability of the concept of computation even to motor behavior, emotion, and perception, it does not confuse fact with model; and (c) whether, by detaching cognition from motivation and affect, it does not impoverish and fragment psychology. However, you ain't seen nuthin yet. Some sociologists have claimed that all social events boil down to information flows. Once again an exact idea, taken out of context (in this case telecommunications engineering), has led to grotesque confusions. **c Semantics** Several attempts have been made to elucidate the concept of meaning in terms of that of information. They were all bound to fail for two reasons. First, because, as noted in **a** above, the quantity and the content of information are unrelated. Second, because meaning is unrelated to the concept of objective probability that occurs in the statistical information theory.

INFORMATIONISM The view that information is the stuff the world is made of. In John A. Wheeler's words, "its from bits." This view is being proposed as an alternative to ↑**materialism**—just like ↑**energetism** a century earlier. It is mistaken, for information requires an information system, an artificial device capable of coding, sending, and decoding physical or chemical signals. And such a device is composed of coder, sender, channel, receiver, and decoder, all of which are material. So, it is "bits from its."

INNATE IDEA Idea we are born with, not learned. The hypothesis of innate ideas has been held by, among others, Socrates, Leibniz, and Chomsky. It explains why people in different cultures and at different times occasionally come up with the same ideas. But it does not explain why these are rare occurrences; why most of the ideas we learn nowadays at school were unknown only a couple of centuries ago; or why it is so hard to invent radically new ideas. Worse, the hypothesis is incompatible with genetics and developmental biology and psychology. Indeed, genes are not complex enough to encode ideas, and the newly born human brain is so underdeveloped that it cannot think. The hypothesis was initially wedded to the ↑**universal grammar** hypothesis, and it is a constituent of ↑**evolutionary psychology**.

INPUT-OUTPUT MODEL The simplest model of a system is a box with inputs and outputs, and total disregard for the mechanisms that may be hidden in the box and activated by the inputs. A simple formalization of this model is a function that maps the inputs onto the outputs. Hence the equivalence between input-output and functional models. Classical examples of such models are the behaviorist learning theories and the Leontief matrix representation of an economy. ↑**Mechanism**.

INQUIRY Search for knowledge. The trademark of science and the humanities, by contrast to pseudoscience and religion. ↑**Research**.

INSIGHT The ability to grasp important features that are usually overlooked. Near synonyms: ↑**intuition**, penetration, perspicacity.

INSOLUBLE A problem can be insoluble either in principle or in practice. Some mathematical problems have been proved to be insoluble (or unsolvable). ↑**Undecidable proposition**. In factual science and technology, a problem is regarded as insoluble in principle on the strength of well-corroborated laws. For example, it is impossible to construct a perpetual motion machine, because it would violate the principle of conservation of energy. Other problems are insoluble in practice because of a temporary lack of the requisite means. For example, no gravitational waves have been detected to date, because they carry so little energy that they require extremely sensitive detectors.

INSTANT a Time instant Point in time; point of the real line representing time; value of a time coordinate. Like time intervals, time instants are not absolute but relative to the reference frame. **b Instant philosophy** A philosophy so poor that it can be learned and discussed in a very short time, or else seemingly so comprehensive that it has ready-made answers to all problems.

INSTANTIATION a Logic Exemplification, as in "the principle of universal instantiation": What holds for all holds for an arbitrarily selected individual. The dual of generalization. **b Ontology** Realization, materialization, or embodiment of an idea, as in the fashionable ↑**computationist** dogma that computer programs and other algorithms can be "instantiated" either in machines or in brains. This usage is incorrect, because 'instance' is synonymous with 'example', not with 'realization'. A frank use of the Platonic idiom 'embodiment' would be preferable.

INSTITUTIONALISM The philosophy of social science according to which institutions precede and shape individual agency. It comes in two strengths: radical (or classical) and moderate (or new). The former is a form of ↑**holism**, whereas the latter is close to ↑**systemism**. Both are rivals of ↑**rational-choice theory**.

INSTRUMENTALISM The view that scientific hypotheses and theories are only handy calculation devices or useful tools for action, rather than true or false representations of reality. If this were the case, the choice between two alternative hypotheses or theories would be either unnecessary or only a matter of either convention or expediency. The ancient astronomer Ptolemy and Cardinal Bellarmino (Galileo's accuser) upheld instrumentalist views concerning the heliocentric and the geocentric planetary models. ↑**Positivists** and ↑**pragmatists**, too, are instrumentalists. Hence they are unable to account for the fact that checking for truth and attempting to improve the accuracy of models are normal occupations of ordinary people and scientists.

INTEGRITY, MORAL Consistent honesty. Hard to maintain under a government that demands ideological allegiance.

INTELLECTUALISM a Ontology The thesis that everything is, or is reducible to, ideas, either in themselves or in someone's mind. Plato, Descartes, Leibniz, Wolff, and Hegel were ontological intellectualists. **Syn** ↑**idealism. Ant** ↑**materialism. b Epistemology** Radical intellectualism is the doctrine that reason is the only source of knowledge, valuation, and action. **Syn** radical ↑**rationalism.** Moderate rationalism holds that reason is an indispensable component of high-level cognition, valuation, and action. But it acknowledges the roles of experience, passion, and interests, and it admits that the intellect, far from being fixed, evolves both in individual development and in human history. ↑**Ratioempiricism, scientific realism. Ant** ↑**anti-intellectualism.**

INTELLIGIBILITY The ability to understand something. A joint property of object and subject, and moreover one dependent upon the state of the art in question. Such questions as whether nature, mind, or society are intelligible are ill-stated. They provoke the question: "Intelligible to whom and by what means?"

INTENSION What a predicate "says": its sense. Example: the intension of "triangle" is "plane figure composed of three intersecting straight line segments." The complement of ↑**extension** or ↑**coverage.** A semantical concept not to be confused with either the psychological concept of intention or the obscure notion of ↑**intentionality.** Nor should "intensional" be defined as nonextensional. The intension of a predicate may be defined as a function from predicates to predicates satisfying the following axioms: (1) the intension of a conjunction equals the union of the intensions of the predicates; and (2) the intension of the negate of a predicate equals the complement of the intension of the predicate in the given universe of discourse. For example, the intension of "woman" equals the union of the intensions of "female" and "human"; and the intension of "bachelor" equals the complement of the intension of "married" in the universe of human males. These axioms entail, among others, the theorem that the intension of a disjunction equals the intersection of the intensions of the disjuncts. That is, disjunction weakens, just as conjunction strengthens. It also turns out that tautologies are intensionally void, whence they add nothing when conjoined with a nontautologous predicate. The relation between intension and extension is this: The greater the intension of a predicate, the smaller its extension, and conversely. That is, the more conditions are imposed, the smaller the set of the objects that satisfy them. Intension is a sort of poor relative of ↑**sense**: whereas the latter is definable only for a hypthetico-deductive system, intension can be determined in an open flabby context with the help of definitions and descriptions.

INTENTION The mental (or brain) process consisting in envisaging an action with a definite goal. Cognitive neuroscience has found that the organ of intention is located in the prefrontal cortex. The occurrence of an intention in a primate can be detected by electrodes inserted in that part of the brain.

INTENTIONALITY ↑**Reference** to objects in the external world.This usage is misleading because it confuses a semantic category with a psychological one. According to Franz Brentano, (semantic) intentionality is the peculiarity of the mental in contrast to matter. This opinion is not shared by ↑**cognitive neuroscience.** ↑**Mind-body problem.**

Semantic intentionality (reference) is best regarded as a component of ↑**meaning**, which in turn is a property of ↑**constructs** and their symbols.

INTERACTION Two concrete things interact if each of them acts upon the other. Neither properties nor ideas taken in themselves can interact: they can only be related. Mechanical interactions satisfy the principle of the equality of action and reaction. This principle is not valid in electrodynamics, biology, or social science. All these fields study actions that are not accompanied or followed by equal reactions, such as light absorption, chemical combination, infection, and conquest.

INTERACTIONISM a Ontology The "block universe" view, that every thing interacts with everything else, hence nothing can be known independently of the rest. **Syn** ↑**holism**. This thesis is only half-true, because the great majority of interactions weaken with distance and are not equally strong. This makes it possible to isolate things or to regard them as isolated for practical purposes, studying them separately from the rest of the universe. **b Philosophy of mind** The vulgar opinion that mind and body interact. The concept of interaction between material entities has been defined in a number of cases (e.g., mechanical, gravitational, electric, social, etc.). By contrast, the notion of mind-body interaction has not been defined. Moreover, there is no reason to expect that it will ever be defined, because science studies only material objects (though of course with the help of ideas). Hence, to assert that mind and brain interact amounts to asserting that mind and brain blah-blah. What can be characterized in rather precise terms are the interactions between bodily systems that perform mental functions and others which do not, as is the case with cerebral cortex-endocrine interactions.

INTERDISCIPLINARITY PRINCIPLE Given any scientific discipline, there is an ↑**interdiscipline** that links it to another scientific discipline. This methodological maxim invites trespassing disciplinary frontiers. And it is fertile, if unfalsifiable. Besides, it helps distinguish science from ↑**pseudoscience**, which is typically isolated.

INTERDISCIPLINE A hybrid or merger of two disciplines. Examples: biochemistry, neuropsychology, social psychology, epidemiology, and economic sociology. D_{12} is the *interdiscipline* comprised between the disciplines D_1 and D_2 if (a) D_{12} has a nonempty reference class equal to the intersection of the reference classes of D_1 and D_2; (b) D_{12} contains technical (or specific) concepts taken from both D_1 and D_2; and (c) there is a nonempty set of ↑**glue formulas** which combine concepts belonging to both D_1 and D_2. These formulas are either hypotheses, definitions, or indicators. Example from bioeconomics: "A renewable resource is exploited rationally if its renewal rate is greater than its harvesting rate." From neuropsychology: "Speech is the specific activity of the Wernicke and Broca areas." Interdisciplinarity is far more common, though much less studied, than ↑**reduction**.

INTERNALISM The approach that focuses on the composition and structure of systems while neglecting their environment. **Ant** ↑**externalism**. Obviously, the more fruitful approach combines internalism with externalism.

INTERPOLATION a Logic With suitable restrictions, if $A \Rightarrow B$, then there is a proposition C such that $A \Rightarrow C$ and $C \Rightarrow B$. **b Mathematics and science** There are interpolation problems and interpolation techniques. The most common interpolation problem is this: Given the values of a continuous function at two given points, find its value at an intermediate point. An interpolation technique is a rule that solves problems of this form: Given $n + 1$ points on a plane, find the nth degree polynomial that joins them. The interpolation techniques are widely used in curve fitting, that is, in finding empirical (inductive) generalizations. ↑**Induction b.**

INTERPRETATION a Semantics An operation performed on symbols or concepts. In the first case, *Int* (symbol) = concept, as in "Let n stand for an arbitrary integer." In the second case, *Int* (concept) = fact, as in "$Pr(e)$ is the probability of event e." This interpretation is *literal*. By contrast, the interpretation of the same mathematical concept as the degree of certainty of a person in his belief that e will happen, is *adventitious*, for no person is explicitly named in "$Pr(e)$." In mathematics and science, all interpretations are literal, if not always explicit. In inexact philosophy, interpretation is the more arbitrary, the more obscure the text. Witness the multiple interpretations of Kant, Hegel, and Marx—not to mention the postmodern oracles. In art and theology, *allegorical* interpretations are common. For instance, theologians have interpreted the Song of Songs not as an erotic poem but as an allegory of God's love for either Israel or the Virgin Mary. The dual of interpretration is deinterpretation or ↑**abstraction. b Hermeneutic school of social studies** The "interpretation" (or *Verstehen*, or comprehension) of a human action is said to uncover its "meaning." Actually, to "interpret" an action is to conjecture its intention, purpose, or aim. That is, hermeneutic interpretation = hypothesis. The difference between hermeneutic "interpretation" and scientific hypothesis is that the former is rather arbitrary, whereas the latter is expected to be empirically testable. And, being arbitrary, the hermeneutic "interpretation" calls for the authority of the interpreter, whereas the scientific hypothesis is subject to objective tests and rational debate. **c Jurisprudence** In all legal systems, the judge is expected to "interpret" the law when judging a case. But such "interpretation" has nothing to do with hermeneutics. What it means is that the judge either (a) reduces the imprecision (ambiguity or vagueness) of a law, such as a constitutional precept; or (b) "applies" the general law to the particular case in the light of the available evidence and its solidity, much as the scientist "applies" a hypothesis to account for a fact. What makes legal interpretation much more delicate than scientific explanation is that the judge must reduce the deliberate imprecision of the law, as when it states that a certain crime is to be punished by a fine or a prison term comprised between certain bounds; that at other times he must reckon with imponderables, such as the litigants' backgrounds, antecedents, or even demeanors; and that at all times his decision is bound to affect the lives of the parties, a thought that is likely to affect the verdict itself—a sort of feedback loop. In common law, when facing hard cases the courts are also expected to fill the gaps in the legal codes, though always respecting the constitution and the general legal principles (such as "No crime without law"). All such discretionary powers may render judicial verdicts somewhat subjective and occasionally even unjust. But they also make room for legal progress. No such dangers and opportunities lurk behind the interpretation of a literary text or a scientific formula.

INTERSUBJECTIVITY A proposition is said to be *intersubjective* in a given social group if everyone in the group upholds it, or at least understands it. Obviously, intersubjectivity is no substitute for objective truth, since many people may share the same superstition or be under the same delusion. Consensus in a professional community is at best a fallible truth ↑**indicator**. The procedures for checking intersubjectivity are sociological, not methodological. This suffices to indict ↑**hermeneutics**, ↑**phenomenology**, social ↑**constructivism**, ethnomethodology, and all the other schools that reject objectivity in favor of intersubjectivity.

INTUITION The ability to understand or produce new ideas instantly and without prior rational elaboration. **Syn** ↑**insight**, vision. Thus 'intuitive' is opposed to 'rational' and in particular to 'exact' and 'formal'. However, the intuitive and the formal are only the extremes of a wide gamut. Moreover, intuitions never come out of the blue, but culminate processes of learning and search. And, if promising, they can often be exactified. This shows that intuition is often only the first stage in a process of concept formation. Moreover, the practice of reason strengthens intuition: the experienced scholar develops an intuitive "feel"—though never an infallible one.

INTUITIONISM a Mathematical A strategy in the foundation of mathematics. When first proposed, mathematical intuitionism was inspired by Kantian intuitionism and it was very restrictive, as a consequence of which it failed to reconstruct large tracts of mathematics. Nowadays it is more open. Most mathematical intuitionists demand only that all proofs be ↑**constructive** (rather than, say, by contradiction), and refuse to use the ↑**axiom of choice**. **b Philosophical** A variety of ↑**irrationalism**: the view according to which intuition is superior to both experience and reason. The importance of these two in science and technology, as well as in ordinary knowledge and praxis, suffices to refute irrationalism—which is not to deny the importance of ↑**intuitions** of various kinds.

INTUITIVE Preanalytic, that can be grasped immediately. Experience has shown that intuitability depends not only on the subject matter but also on the knower: what is intuitive to the master may be counterintuitive to the apprentice. So much so that in science counterintuitiveness is the trademark of originality and depth.

INVENTION The ↑**creation** of a new idea: approach, concept, hypothesis, or theory; design, plan, musical score, painting, or what-have-you. Nonexamples: natural things, empirical data, and computations. Some inventions, such as those of the microscope, telescope, particle-accelerator, and computer program, have made it possible to make new discoveries. Invention is not a rule-directed epistemic operation. This has not prevented many a philosopher from writing about the logic of invention. ↑**Discovery**.

INVERSE Polysemous term. In logic, the inverse of a binary relation R is the relation R^{-1} such that $R^{-1}xy = Ryx$. Examples: "to be loved" is the inverse of "loved"; > is the inverse of <. In set theory, the inverse (complement) of a set is the set such that its union with the given set equals the universe of discourse, whereas their intersection is empty. In algebra, the inverse of the element of a set is the element such that, joined (concatenated) with it equals the unit element e: x^{-1} o $x = e$. In analysis, the inverse of a function f of one variable x is the function f^{-1} such that $f^{-1} f(x) = x$; examples: the logarithm is the inverse of the exponential, and $\sin^{-1}$ (or arc sin) is the inverse of sin. ↑**Inverse problem**.

INVERSE PROBLEM The inverse of a problem is the problem of finding the premises of a given conclusion or the cause of a given effect. Examples: given the roots of an algebraic equation, find the latter; given a set of propositions, guess the axioms that entail them; given the output of a system, find its input; given the X-ray diffraction-pattern of a crystal, find the latter's structure; given the behavior of a person, guess her intentions. The great majority of inverse problems have multiple solutions if any: they are not well-posed problems, and there are no uniform rules to tackle them. This makes inverse problems in mathematics, science, and engineering so intriguing and exciting. But it also makes the task of the ↑**hermeneutic** (or "interpretive") social student next to impossible. Indeed, the task of "interpreting" the behavior of others—that is, of guessing their intentions and circumstances—is an inverse problem in an underdeveloped discipline. Even worse: if he comes up with a plausible guess, the hermeneuticist will not put it to the test, because he rejects the scientific method—or because the individuals in questions are not accessible. ↑**Interpretation b**.

INVISIBLE HAND The name Adam Smith gave to the largely unknown control mechanisms of the market that, ideally, result in equilibrium (supply = demand). Natural selection has been called the invisible hand of the evolutionary process, that at first sight looks goal-directed.

IRRATIONALISM The family of doctrines that deny or demean the power of reason and propose to replace it with religious illumination (↑**mysticism**), feeling (↑**emotivism**), intuition (↑**intuitionism**), will (↑**voluntarism**), action (↑**pragmatism**), raw experience (radical ↑**empiricism**), or something else. A radical and persistent irrationalist does not argue for his fuzzy views, and he offers no rational arguments against those of his opponents. He just makes assertions or denials: he is irrational. Heidegger is perhaps the best-known persistent (though not consistent) irrationalist. When he attempts to argue he fails, as when he first defines truth as the essence of freedom, and then freedom as the essence of truth. Irrationalism is a component of the ↑**Counter-Enlightenment** movement, but it was not absent from the origins of modernity. The seventeenth-century berating of scholasticism as a philosophy of words and abstract ideas had an unwitting irrationalist component. So had the criticisms of pure reason offered by Hume and Kant, though in some regards they were members of the Enlightenment. Marx and Engels regarded themselves as heirs to the Enlightenment, but they shared some of Hegel's irrationalism, particularly that inherent in ↑**dialectics**. And, though so clear that it attracts the lazy, Wittgenstein's writings have four irrationalist features: the cult of ordinary language, pragmatism, dogmatism, and the thesis that there are no philosophical problems.

IRREVERSIBILITY Irreversible processes are those that cannot be fully undone or that require an extra expenditure of energy to be reversed. Examples: the transformation of mechanical or electromagnetic energy into heat; aging; biological evolution; historical processes. Irreversibility falsifies the myth of eternal recurrence. History cannot be rewound: it can only be rewritten. Irreversibility is often, mistakenly, referred to as the ↑**arrow of time**.

IS In traditional logic, "is" was called "the copula." It was regarded as a pivotal yet enigmatic logical concept: it was said to "glue" the predicate to the subject, as in "Bob *is* happy." In modern (mathematical) logic, "'is'" is tacitly regarded as a ↑**syncategorematic** term. Indeed, "is" and its cognates ("are," "were," etc.) come together with predicates, as in "is happy." In other words, whereas in traditional logic a proposition such as "Bob is happy" was analyzed into three irreducible concepts, in modern logic it is analyzed into two: the subject "Bob" and the unary ↑**predicate** "is happy." However, even though predicates can be exact, the word 'is' is ambiguous. Indeed, it is the ordinary-language equivalent of the following distinct logical concepts: (a) *identity*, as in "$a = b$"; (b) *predication* or attribution, as in "a is an (or has the property) F"; (c) *membership*, as in "a is a member of the set S"; (d) *inclusion*, as in "Humans are primates." Only logical analysis can finesse the coarseness of ordinary language. Which is just one of the many counterexamples to Pascal's dichotomy ↑*esprit de finesse / esprit de géométrie*. Nowadays both coincide—the ordinary-language philosophers notwithstanding.

IS / OUGHT ↑**Fact / Value**.

ISOMORPHISM a Mathematics One-to-one mapping between two sets, that preserves operations. Two isomorphic sets have essentially the same structure. Example: the isomorphism between sets and propositions, that maps unions into disjunctions, intersections into conjunctions, and complements into negations. Let O and O' be two operations defined on the sets S and S' respectively. Call c the result of a binary operation O on the elements a and b of the set S, and a', b', and c' the corresponding elements of S'. The correspondence between S and S' is isomorphic if c' is the result of the operation O' on a' and b'. If any two ↑**models** (interpretations) of an abstract theory are isomorphic, the theory is said to be *categorical*. This is a rare property. b **Epistemology** The word 'isomorphism' is often misused with reference to social and physical processes, as well as when true scientific theories are said to be isomorphic to their referents. These are howlers, because neither things nor their changes are sets: only their corresponding theoretical models can be sets.

ISSUE Practical problem, as in "the issue of gender discrimination." In everyday life we tackle issues; scientists investigate problems; and technologists study problems raised by issues.

ITERATION Repeated application of an operation or rule. Mathematical examples: x^n, $\partial^n/\partial x^n$. Biological example: repeated cell division. Social example: reproduction of social behavior.

IUSNATURALISM ↑**Natural law doctrine**.

JOURNALISM Journalism is of interest to philosophers because, if honest, it practices at least three philosophical principles: it is systemic (in placing events and texts in their context); it is realist (in seeking the truth); and it upholds universal values such as human rights. Whether honest journalism will sell is another matter.

JUDGMENT A polysemous term. In one sense it denotes the mental process of making an assertion or thinking of a proposition. In another it denotes the ability to make realistic appraisals of matters of fact, as in "he is intelligent but has no judgment." A third signification of 'judgment' is ↑**intuition**, or the ability to recognize at a glance that something is correct or incorrect, right or wrong, promising or futile, and so on.

JUMPING TO CONCLUSIONS Guessing, conjecturing, hypothesizing. Frowned upon by ↑**dataists**, but objectionable only if not followed by an attempt to check the "conclusion" (guess) for truth.

JUNK, PHILOSOPHICAL Plain nonsense, obvious falsity, or platitude presented in philosophical garb. It comes in two varieties: inoffensive, or lint, and offensive, or poison. For example, musings about the meaning of life are lint, whereas irrationalism is toxic. At the time of writing, the lint industry is in decline, whereas the poison industry is thriving. Philosophical junk is produced by amateurs as well as by academics. Unlike the latter, the former work for the love of it, and often defray the cost of having their stuff published by vanity presses.

JURISPRUDENCE The theory and practice of positive law. It may be regarded either as a craft or as a ↑**social technology** in close touch with the social sciences. It gives rise to legal philosophy. ↑**Law d.**

JUST WAR Oxymoron. All war is unjust to its victims. ↑**War.**

JUSTICE A polysemous term with three main meanings: distributive, retributive, and positive. *Distributive* justice refers to the equitable distribution of rights and duties, benefits and burdens. **Syn** social justice. *Retributive* justice refers to the correction of antisocial behavior. Formerly it was effected through revenge: a tooth for a tooth, and all that, as in the Old Testament. Scientific criminologists recommend addressing the social roots of crime (poverty and the concomitant anomie and ignorance), and treating criminals as people in need of reeducation and rehabilitation, as well as of control to prevent them from harming others. This change in perspective owes much to the decline of religion and authoritarianism, the concomitant rise of humanism and social science, and the victory of utilitarianism over deontologism. *Positive* justice is the justice defined by the law of the land—which may or may not cohere with any principles of fairness or distributive justice. Legal ↑**positivists** equate justice with positive law.

JUSTIFICATION a General Providing a ground or reason for a construct or an action, as in "Axioms are justified by their consequences," "She was justified in complaining about sex discrimination," and "Doubting this result is justifiable given the sloppy way in which it was obtained." The concept is relational: A justifies B, where A is a body of knowledge or norms. **b Logical** Proving that an argument is valid (logically correct). **c Semantical** Procedure whereby a proposition is shown to be meaningful in a given context. **d Methodological** Showing that a method or technique is likely to deliver what it purports to. **e Epistemological** An attempt to show that a proposition is true or at least plausible in relation to a body of knowledge. Not only assertion but also doubt may have to be justified. **f Ethical** Procedure showing that a policy, plan, or course of action abides by certain moral principles. **g Technological** Showing that a course of action is feasible, effective, convenient, or moral.

JUSTIFICATIONISM The methodological principle that every scientific or technological hypothesis and every method should be justified by reference to evidence and theory.

JUXTAPOSITION The association of items, as in their being placed next to each other. The ontic counterpart of conjunction. Examples: physical addition, and the concatenation of letters to form words. Juxtaposition may or may not ensue in qualitative novelty. It may be conceptualized as a binary and associative operation $\oplus$ on a set S, so that $<S, \oplus>$ constitutes a semigroup. This allows one to symbolize such expressions as "The total population of two countries equals the sum of their partial populations" as $P(a \oplus b) = P(a) + P(b)$.

KINEMATIC / DYNAMIC A kinematic account of change is purely descriptive, whereas a dynamic account points to change mechanism(s). Examples: rate equations and equations of motion respectively.

KNOWABLE / UNKNOWABLE Irrationalism and radical skepticism deny the possibility of knowledge. But as a matter of fact even the supporters of such antiphilosophies know lots of things. Indeed, we all know something, and moreover human knowledge has been on the increase over the past half millennium. Yet, no one can ever get to know everything: some items are unknowable in principle (hence forever), others in practice (hence only for the time being). Among the former are all the events that cannot be linked to us with light signals, and all those past events that have left no traces. As for the practical limitations, suffice it to mention the inaccuracy of measurement instruments, the limited capacity of computation devices, the restricted research funds, and the artificial constraints imposed by antiscientific ideologies and philosophies.

KNOWER Person who attempts to know or succeeds in knowing something. Syn ↑**subject**, inquirer. One of the three terms of the epistemic relation: "Individual a, in circumstance (or with means) b, studies object c." Since knowers are the producers and bearers of knowledge, there can be no knowledge, and a fortiori no epistemology proper, without knowing subjects. Indeed, the expression "x is known" is impersonal only in that it omits to indicate who knows x. Actually the expression in question is short for "there is at least one animal y who knows x." Consequently the idealist principle of the autonomy of the "world" of ideas (such as Plato's, Dilthey's, or Popper's) is sheer fantasy. As such it can only obstruct the advancement of our knowledge about knowledge.

KNOWLEDGE The outcome of a cognitive process, such as perception, experiment, postulation, or deduction. Warning: for something to qualify as knowledge it is sufficient but not necessary that it be true. True knowledge is a special case of knowledge: much of our knowledge is conjectural and only half-true. Two kinds of knowledge must be distinguished: *know-how* (or tacit, by acquaintance, or instrumental) and *know-that* (or explicit, by description, or declarative). I know how to ride a bike, but ignore the complicated mechanisms (both mechanical and neuromuscular) of this action. I am intimately acquainted with myself, but I do not know myself thoroughly.

LANGUAGE a Concept System of ↑**signs** serving to ↑**communicate** and think. Whether natural (historical), artificial (designed), or mixed, a language is made up of conventional signs. Since every sign must be elucidated in terms of other symbols, stray signs are nonsignificant. Therefore, when in doubt about the signification of a sign, we place it in some context: we attempt to discover or conjecture the system of signs from which it may have been drawn. We always do so when trying to desambiguate an ambiguous expression. This procedure highlights the systemic nature of language. **b Definition** A language L is a system of conventional signs such that

Composition of L = the vocabulary of L;
Environment of L = the collection of extralinguistic items referred to by expressions   in L;
Structure of L = the grammar of L; *Mechanism* of L = ∅.

Note that the mechanism that makes L "work," namely communication, is missing in the above, whereas it occurs in the definition of a ↑**semiotic system**—which, unlike a language, is a concrete system including speakers. As for grammar, it is construed here in the broad sense, that is, as composed of syntax, semantics, and phonology. The syntax of L plus the logical relations among the concepts designated by the signs of L constitute the internal ↑**structure** (or endostructure) of L. (The former is a linguistic category, while the latter is logical, and thus independent of the particular linguistic wrapping.) And the exostructure of L is the collection of relations that bind the signs of L with the (natural and social) world, in particular the speaker and his interlocutor. The relations of designation, denotation (or reference), speaking, and hearing belong in the exostructure of a language: they relate signs to concepts and concrete things. The exostructure of a language is the bridge between the language and the world. It is what makes language a means of communication. **c Language and logic** Language and logic are related in two ways. First, logic is a tool for the conceptual analysis and cleansing of ordinary-language expressions, as well as of grammars and linguistic theories. For example, logic tells us that the prefix 'anti' is not equivalent to negation. Thus, 'anti-anti-Arab' is not the same as either 'Arab' or 'pro-Arab': double 'anti' does not amount to double negation. The reason is that, whereas negation is a unary operation, 'anti' is a binary relation that denotes an attitude or action. (A is anti-B = A opposes B.) The logical analysis of linguistic expressions has shown that the ordinary languages are imprecise and even logically defective. For example, the billboard announcing "We repair all kinds of shoes" is logically wrong, because shoemakers can repair only individual shoes: Kinds are concepts, hence they cannot be repaired with awl and hammer. A correct announcement would be "We repair shoes of all kinds." (This is a point against Platonism.) As for the grammar-logic connection, logical analysis shows that— *pace* Noam Chomsky—grammars are not theories, and this for three reasons. First, like all rules, those of grammar are conventional, hence neither true nor false; consequently they are neither confirmable nor falsifiable, the way law statements are. Second, the grammatical rules of transformation—of, e.g., a passive into an active voice— are not inference rules, because they are not required to conserve truth values. Third, unlike logic, most grammars are permissive: they turn a blind eye to exceptions, particularly of the phonological kind. Usage is master in matters of grammar, consistency in matters of logic. However, logic (inclusive of set theory) is not only a theory and a tool. It may also function as the most universal of languages, particularly as a technical language for mathematics, science, technology, and exact philosophy. For instance, the mathematical expression "$y = sin\ x$" is just an instance of Pxy, an expression in first order predicate logic. One may use the vocabulary of logic without invoking any logical laws. For example, in defining the ↑**extension** of a predicate one employs only a bit of logical notation, leaving logic the task of defining (implicitly) the notions of predicate, identity, set, and set membership. Likewise, one makes tacit use of the logical concept of set inclusion when saying that humans are animals—or, expressed in the "formal" mode, that the extension of the concept "human" is included in that of "animal." But, although a logical calculus can be used as a language, it is not true that it is just a language: it is a theory, whereas languages are nothing of the sort. First, unlike theories, languages make no assumptions: they are noncommittal. They are just neutral skeletons to be fleshed out. This is why we can assert and deny anything, true or false, in any language. Second, languages contain no rules of inference, although the latter must always be couched in some language or other. In short, every logic is both a theory and a language. The rationale for the mistaken characterization of logic as nothing but a language has a philosophical root, namely ↑**nominalism**. Nominalists are against concepts and propositions, for believing that talk of concepts is Platonic, whereas talk of signs and sounds looks physicalist. But this is mistaken: signs are not symbols unless they symbolize something, which something can be a concept. For example, @ is not yet a standard road sign, and $ is not a standard mathematical symbol. By contrast, numerals—whether roman, arabic, or others—designate numbers. The former are linguistic items, the latter conceptual ones. Moreover, all sign-concept pairings are conventional. This holds not only for the word-concept relation but also for the sentence-proposition pairing: these, too, are conventional relations between signs and constructs. Nominalism, then, fails even to account for names—in particular its own. **d Language and the world** As defined in **b** above, languages—unlike individual inscriptions—are not real, concrete, or material systems. What are real are language users and the social systems (linguistic communities) they constitute. (If preferred, ↑**semiotic systems** are the real things.) Consequently, languages do not evolve by themselves. Hence there are no linguistic evolutionary forces. Whoever is interested in the dynamics of language change must look at ↑**communication systems**, in particular linguistic communities. For instance, to understand the emergence of the modern European languages we must reconstruct the slow westward movement of the shepherds and farmers who, between five and ten millennia ago, took with them a few

Indo-European languages. **e Language as picture of the world** The young Wittgenstein held that language pictures the world. Or, as Russell put it, every "atom" of meaning matches a simple ("atomic") fact in the real world. A related view is that of the linguists Sapir and Whorf, who claimed that every ordinary language constrains thought and moreover is committed to some worldview. (The corollary is clear: Study language and you'll know the world—or at least the way the speakers view the world and their own behavior.) These views are versions of naive ↑realism. ↑Reflection theory of knowledge. They ignore the fact that all linguistic expressions, including the descriptions of matters of fact, are symbolic, hence studded with conventions. They also overlook the fact that ordinary language is insufficient to describe most of the facts studied by scientists and technologists. Despite these obvious objections, at one time the picture view of language gained popularity among anthropologists. In particular, some of them reported that certain modern Amerindian languages lack a word for time and do not tense verbs. The inference was that those peoples ignore change. Eventually it was shown that, even when the vocabulary of a native language fails to contain a word for time, its speakers have no difficulty conveying information about becoming. (On the other hand, Buddha and the Eleatic philosophers, who denied the reality of change, spoke languages that did contain words for time and becoming.) Apparently only philosophers still cite the Wittgenstein and Sapir-Whorf hypotheses. **f Language and social structure** The ↑**structure** of a society is the collection of social relations that hold in it. Since human social relations are mediated by communication, linguistic communication (but not language as an abstract object) is included in the social structure. This helps explain the linguistic differences among different social groups, in particular occupational groups and social classes. Sociolinguists study these differences. For example, it is well known that the "correct" accent is the one prevailing in the upper classes, and that an "incorrect" accent can be a serious obstacle to upward social mobility.

LANGUAGE-GAME Use of language. According to Wittgenstein, asking questions, answering them, issuing orders, greeting, guessing, solving problems, insulting, and joking are so many language-games. To understand a linguistic expression requires playing a language-game, and thus finding out how it functions in the language, rather than trying to find its meaning: a typically ↑**functionalist** view. Wittgenstein's recipe may work in elementary school, and even there with the proviso that the pupils have a rough idea of the meanings involved. But it fails utterly in mathematics, science, technology, and the humanities: here one engages in research, not just talk, and one finds meanings not by talking but by uncovering and analyzing the ideas expressed by linguistic expressions. For example, the expression 'power elite' is defined in political sociology, not in the "language games" played by citizens when engaging in political small-talk.

LANGUAGE LEVEL The language in which we speak about another language is said to be a *metalanguage* of the latter. Example: The sentence 'English is an unruly language' belongs to a metalanguage of English; and the sentence 'The previous sentence is true' belongs to a meta-metalanguage of English. In general, a language L_n of level n is a language that refers to components of a lower level language L_{n-1}. For any given language L_n there is an unlimited number of higher-level languages $L_{n+1}, L_{n+2},...$ However, there is seldom need for more than a second-level language. ↑**Language level,** ↑**liar paradox,** ↑**metalanguage,** ↑**object language / metalanguage.**

LATENT / MANIFEST a Ontology Potential/actual, as in adaptability / adaptation. **b Epistemology** Unobservable / observable, as in economic activity / GDP, and other hidden variable / indicator relations.

LAW a Philosophy of science and technology Universal pattern. Four different meanings of the term 'law' should be distinguished. (1) Law_1 or stable objective pattern: a regularity in nature or society. Such patterns cannot be instantiated because they are the referents of the laws of the next kind. (2) Law_2 or law-statement: a conceptualization of a law_1. Examples: the law of diminishing returns. (3) Law_3 or nomopragmatic statement: a rule based on one or more $laws_2$. Example: In the long run, decrease in fertility is best achieved through rise in the standard of living. (4) Law_4 or meta-law-statement: a condition that a set of $laws_2$ satisfies or ought to satisfy. Example: the laws of relativistic mechanics are covariant (do not change) under a Lorentz transformation. ↑**Metanomological statement. b Pattern-statement distinction** The distinction between objective patterns and their conceptualizations matches the scientific practice of trying increasingly accurate representations of those patterns. It is just a particular case of the distinction between ↑**property** and ↑**predicate.** (Moreover, a law-statement may be regarded as centered on a predicate. Thus "For all x : If x is F, then x is G," can be formalized as follows: $\forall x \, Lx$, with $Lx = (Fx \Rightarrow Gx)$.) Typically, subjective ↑**idealism** admits neither of these kinds of law, whereas objective idealism conflates them; ↑**empiricism** admits only certain law-statements, namely empirical generalizations; and ↑**pragmatism** admits only $laws_3$. Most if not all of the law-statements in the emergent sciences are empirical generalizations. Some of these are the precursors of law-statements in the strict sense, which are typical of the advanced sciences. In these, a law-statement is an empirically confirmed hypothesis belonging to some theory (hypothetico-deductive system). Typically, law-statements contain predicates representing properties that are not directly accessible to experience, such as "mass" and "acceleration" in Newton's second law. **c Structural and constitutive law-statements** Whereas some law-statements are assumed to hold (be true) for whole genera, others are specific or stuff-dependent. For example, the general mechanical laws of motion are supposed to be true of all bodies—solid, liquid, or gaseous. These may be called *structural* laws. On the other hand, the laws peculiar to things of a given species, such as rigid bodies (or semiconductors, superconductors, plastics, plasmas, or what-have-you) are called *constitutive equations.* They represent the constitution of the things concerned, i.e., the particular kind of stuff they are "made" of. Thus, chemistry has comparatively few structural equations (such as those of chemical kinetics) but millions of constitutive equations (one per chemical reaction).

LAW, PHILOSOPHY OF The discipline that tackles such problems as the nature of positive law; the relations between the law and the various branches of philosophy, in particular logic, epistemology, ontology, and ethics; the relations between law and the social sciences, in particular sociology, economics, and history; and the virtues and flaws of the various legal philosophies, such as natural law, legal positivism, contractualism, utilitarianism, and legal realism. The *natural law* school is mistaken because legal norms are made. However, natural law rhetoric has occasionally been used to denounce privilege or oppression as unnatural. ↑**Natural law**. The main thesis of *legal positivism* is that all legal systems are just and legitimate: might is right. This thesis enshrines political conservatism and even totalitarianism. Hence it cannot account for, let alone justify, legal reform. Nor can it countenance the right of the courts to question laws on moral grounds. *Contractualism* is close to legal positivism in that it posits that all contracts, however unfair, are legitimate and must be enforced. It shares with legal positivism the unrealistic thesis of the moral neutrality of the law. *Legal utilitarianism* has all the virtues and defects of philosophical ↑**utilitarianism**. Hence its ambivalence: it has promoted progressive penal reform but, at the same time, it has defended economic privilege because of its sophistic principle that altruism is nothing but enlightened egoism. Finally, *legal realism* regards the law as a tool of both social control and social reform. It also regards ↑**jurisprudence** as a body of knowledge that benefits from a close contact with all the social sciences. If jurisprudence is regarded as a ↑**sociotechnology**, then the philosophy of law, or legal philosophy, becomes a branch of the ↑**philosophy of technology**. **Syn** legal philosophy.

LAWFULNESS, PRINCIPLE OF The hypothesis that all facts are lawful. This ontological hypothesis underpins scientific research. Besides, it undermines belief in ↑**miracles**.

LEGAL PHILOSOPHY ↑Philosophy of law.

LEGITIMACY a Ethics According to ↑**agathonism**, an action is morally legitimate if it does not prevent anyone from satisfying their basic needs. **b Political philosophy** A government or governmental action is politically legitimate if it complies with the pre-existing laws of the land, however monstrous these may be. And it is morally legimate if such laws do not prevent anyone from exercising their ↑**human rights**.

LEVEL Polysemous term, hence one to be used together with an adjective. In ontology, an *integrative* level, or level of *organization* of reality, is a collection of material (concrete) entities that share certain properties and laws. The simplest hypotheses about integrative levels are that (a) reality (the collection of all real objects) is composed of five major levels: physical, chemical, biological, social, and technical; (b) the entities in any supraphysical level are composed of entities belonging to lower levels; and (c) the higher levels (or rather the individuals belonging in them) have emerged in the course of time through either the association or the development of individuals of lower levels. We have not added a mental level, because in a materialist ontology minds are not things but collections of brain processes. Note also that any given level may be analyzed into as many sublevels as needed. For example, the physical and social levels may be divided into micro-, meso-, macro-, and megalevels.

LEVEL STRUCTURE The set of ↑**levels** together with the order relation of level precedence (or its dual, level emergence), or $\mathcal{L} = < L, < >$. The level precedence relation <

can be defined as follows: For any level L_n, $L_n < L_{n+1} =_{df} \forall \sigma [\sigma \in L_{n+1} \Rightarrow C(\sigma) \in L_n]$, where $C(\sigma)$ stands for the composition of system σ. To be distinguished from the hierarchical ↑**chain of being**, because levels are ordered by precedence, not by domination, let alone by closeness to the Creator.

LIAR PARADOX An instance of the class of self-referring expressions. The sentence *I am lying* is said to be paradoxical because its truth value seems to oscillate between T and F. Indeed, if I am actually lying, then I am telling the truth; and if I am telling the truth, then I am actually lying. The standard dissolution of the paradox consists in distinguishing between what is being said (in a language) and the valuation (in the ↑**metalanguage**) of what is being said. This accords with the way we treat confessions about lying in real life. Indeed, even when admitting that we lied before, we never say, except in jest, that what we are now stating is a lie. That is, in real life we distinguish a statement made at a previous time from the ↑**metastatement** about the truth value of that statement. However, there is an even simpler dissolution of the paradox. This consists in deciding that, because the sentence 'I am lying' cannot possibly acquire a definite truth value, it fails to designate a proposition. Hence it should be banished— and the writing of any further papers about it should be discouraged. A mathematical analog is the oscillating infinite "series": 1-1+1- . . . This is not a series proper because it adds up to 1, 0, or -1, according to the ways its terms are grouped using associativity.

LIBERTARIANISM The moral and political doctrine according to which liberty is the supreme good. Syn ↑**egoism**. According to it, the individual ought to enjoy unrestricted freedom to choose and to become and do what he wants, regardless of the needs and desires of other people. All the enemies of the state, whether on the left or on the right, are libertarians.

LIBERTY ↑Freedom.

LIBERTY, EQUALITY, FRATERNITY The slogan of the 1789 French Revolution, and still the core of any democratic social philosophy.

LIE The deliberate utterance of a falsity. Not to be confused with involuntary ↑**error**.

LIE, VITAL A lie told to prevent people from rebelling. Justified by Plato, as well as by Nietzsche, William James, and other vitalists. **Syn** royal lie.

LIFE The central concept of the life sciences. There are four main views on the nature of living beings or organisms: vitalism, mechanism (or physico-chemism), machinism, and organicism (or biosystemism). ↑**Vitalism** defines "life" in terms of some immaterial entity, such as "vital impulse," together with the alleged goal-striving tendency. ↑**Mechanism** claims that the predicate "is alive" is definable in physicochemical terms: that organisms are merely very complex physicochemical systems. ↑**Machinism** conceives of organisms as being machinelike: designed, programmed, and goal-directed. Organicism (or biosystemism) regards life as an emergent property of some extremely complex systems whose remote ancestors, about four billion years ago, were abiotic. Vitalism has been utterly discredited because it is barren, and because the alleged immaterial entelechy is inaccessible to observation and calculation. Mechanism is still popular, particularly since the birth of molecular biology, but it fails to account for some of the peculiarities of living beings. In particular, it does not explain why, on the whole, metabolic processes in the organism "serve" it rather than being either indifferent or self-serving. Nor does mechanism explain the emergence of self-cleaning and self-repairing mechanisms: a nonliving chemical system might accumulate reaction-inhibiting chemicals that would eventually bring some or even all of its reactions to a halt. Machinism, fathered by Descartes and widespread since then, is nowadays popular with the computer science crowd, who refer to computer simulations of particular features of life processes as ↑**artificial life**. Ironically, machinism shares with vitalism the teleology involved in the notions of design and computation. Only biosystemism recognizes life as an emergent level rooted in the chemical level, as well as the molecular-biological account of the self-assembly of biosystems from chemical precursors, and the theory of evolution by genic changes and natural selection. ↑**Emergence**, ↑**emergentist materialism**, ↑**systemism**.

LIKELIHOOD Events can be said to be more or less likely (or unlikely) to happen. Chance events are absolutely likely or unlikely to some degree or other: their likelihood equals their probability. Nonchance events are said to be likely if they occur frequently, unlikely otherwise. Their likelihood equals their relative frequency. In both cases, a fair amount of knowledge is required to quantitate the likelihood of events of some kind. For instance, a woman who walks in New York by night and unaccompanied is likely to be held up. How likely? We do not know and may never find out. The police get to know only the reported cases; and if the police beat were perfect, such cases would be very unlikely. Still, the police may come up with a lower bound of the frequency of events of the kind in question. Even so, we would not be justified in holding that the *probability* of being mugged is such and such, because events of this kind are anything but random: they are planned, and sometimes they can be avoided. The ordinary concept of likelihood is basically qualitative. However, with the help of statistics we may be able to rank events according to their likelihood. For example, it is more likely for a graduate student to choose a safe dissertation topic than an interesting one. Caution: Do not confuse the likelihood of facts with the ↑**plausibility** of hypotheses. There are plausible hypotheses about unlikely facts (such as the collision of a neutrino with an atom), and implausible guesses about likely facts (such as the next downturn in the business cycle).

LIMITS TO KNOWLEDGE There are two kinds of limit to the advancement of knowledge: natural and social. The natural limits are restricted curiosity, inaccessibility of data, and scarcity of the knowledge items necessary to make further progress. For instance, we cannot know everything that happened in the past—nor would we care to. The social limits are philosophical prejudice, censorship, and lack of support for research. For example, idealism and irrationalism have obstructed scientific research, particularly in psychology and social studies. And the pragmatism inherent in short-sighted politics restricts the funding of basic research almost everywhere. Moral: If you wish to promote the advancement of knowledge, start by adopting a philosophy friendly to it.

LINEAR SYSTEM A ↑**system** that satisfies the principle of superposition, according to which the total effect or output equals the sum of the several causes or inputs taken separately. Consequently, a small change in the input has a correspondingly small effect. In particular, more of the same will result in more of the same. By contrast, in a nonlinear system a small change in the input is likely to produce a huge change in the output. The systems accounted for by most of mechanics, electrodynamics, and quantum mechanics are linear. By contrast, chemical, biological, and social systems are likely to be basically nonlinear, because the inputs to them are likely to interact in such a way that ↑**emergents**, rather than resultants, will ensue. ↑**Chaos theory** deals with nonlinear systems.

LINGUISTIC PHILOSOPHY Philosophical analysis done with the sole help of common sense and ordinary language. ↑**Ordinary-language philosophy**, ↑**analytic philosophy**. Though often called 'philosophy of language', linguistic philosophy is not a serious philosophy of language because it ignores linguistics. Yet it is sometimes offered as a kind of linguistics, for legislating on the "grammar" of words, i.e., the rules for the proper use of words. Examples: perception cannot be a process because we say 'I see x', not 'I am seeing x'; bodies cannot possibly think, because in ordinary parlance 'body' is synonymous with 'corpse'. The name 'analytic philosophy' for the collection of simplistic ruminations of this kind is misleading because it is restricted to common sense and ordinary knowledge and makes no use of the analytic tools par excellence, that is, formal logic and mathematics. 'Prescientific linguistic semianalysis' would be more appropriate. This harsh evaluation of commonsensical analysis of daily life and ordinary language does not imply its rejection. Linguistic philosophy is an excellent literary exercise and a good preamble to philosophy, in being a "philosophy without tears" (Bertrand Russell). It has also been known to be an effective antidote to obscurantist intoxication. Hence it has a legitimate place in preuniversity teaching. But it is not a philosophy proper because it is not in love with knowledge and it does not build anything: it resembles more a demolition team than a construction crew. ↑**Puzzle**, ↑**sawdust philosophy**.

LINGUISTIC TURN The shift from serious ontological, epistemological, and ethical problematics to the view that everything turns around words, or even is an assemblage of words. ↑**Glossocentrism**, ↑**hermeneutics**, ↑**linguistic philosophy**. A version of ↑**idealism**. It crumbles upon realizing that any question about the syntactic, semantic, phonological, or stylistic properties of molecules, emotions, or business transactions is ridiculous.

LINGUISTICS a General The scientific study of speech and ↑**language**. It may be divided into general linguistics, the study of the grammars and phonologies of the various natural (or historical) languages, psycholinguistics, sociolinguistics, historical linguistics, and neurolinguistics. Only the first of these branches is purely theoretical: the other subfields involve empirical research, and the last four mentioned are ↑**interdisciplines**. Thus, unlike its predecessor, philology, modern linguistics is a cross-disciplinary field. General linguistics belongs in the humanities, but historical linguistics straddles linguistics, history, and nowadays even the genetics of human populations.

Comparative linguistics belongs in anthropology and history as much as in the humanities. Sociolinguistics lies at the intersection of linguistics and sociology. Neurolinguistics is a part of neuroscience as much as of linguistics. In particular, aphasiology is every bit as interesting to linguists as to neurologists. And psycholinguistics is cultivated by psychologists centrally interested in speech, as well as by linguists and educators interested in the relations between speech on the one hand, and cognition and emotion on the other, as well as in language learning and unlearning. **b Linguistic generalization** If the maturity of a science is measured by the number of generalizations it handles, it must be admitted that linguistics is still a fledgling science. To be sure, every original grammarian discovers some patterns, but these are likely to be conventional rules (prescriptions) rather than laws. Which suggests a possible reason for the paucity of linguistic laws: namely, the real difficulty in distinguishing them from grammatical (syntactic, semantic, or phonological) rules. Another reason is the underdevelopment of mathematical linguistics, whose main goal is precisely to find linguistic laws. Whether linguistics will mature any further depends very much upon the philosophy of science adopted by linguists. Empiricists, bent as they are on gathering data, may at most come up with a few empirical generalizations. And rationalists, who are given to a priori fantasizing, may invent some generalizations but are unlikely to discover any genuine laws. Only ↑**scientific realism** can guide the fruitful search for linguistic laws. This is so because, by definition, a scientific ↑**law** (or law-statement) is not only an empirically confirmed generalization but also a member of some theory or theoretical model. Which brings us to the next topic. **c Linguistic explanation** Because of the paucity of known linguistic laws, the explanatory power of linguistics is restricted. Now, a law-statement can belong to either of two kinds: ↑**mechanismic** (i.e., referring to some mechanism) or nonmechanismic. A mechanismic law-statement is expected to explain why something is, or is not, the case by showing what makes the thing concerned tick. For example, we may try to explain the introduction of neologisms into a given language in terms of either of three major social mechanisms: conquest, migration, and autogenous structural change. Conquest by a people speaking a different language has either or both of these effects on the natives' speech: enrichment or impoverishment. For instance, the Norman conquest introduced a large number of French and Latin expressions into medieval English. But it also, fortunately, simplified somewhat the syntax—e.g., by depriving the overwhelming majority of nouns of gender. Immigrants import their language, some snippets of which spread throughout the new country if they serve a useful purpose, or are just found amusing by some of the natives. Examples: 'frappé', 'adagio', and 'chutzpah'. Moreover, whole new languages, from pidgins to créoles, emerge from the encounter of different languages or dialects. As for autogenous social change, it involves the emergence of new items whose description requires new linguistic expressions. And some of these are indispensable newly minted or adopted expressions, such as 'marketing', 'transistor', and 'networking'. Other neologisms are invented in special social groups to shield their activities from the indiscretion of outsiders. Still others are invented by parvenus eager to imitate their "betters." And so on and so forth. All such explanations of linguistic change, if speculative, are explanations in terms of ↑**mechanisms**—and, of course, mechanisms exist only in concrete objects, such as speakers and linguistic communities. This is why grammars have no explanatory power. Indeed, grammars, like mathematical ideas, are abstract objects, not concrete ones: they are contemplated *sub specie aeternitatis*. Now, nothing ever happens in or to abstract objects. Hence, no ↑**explanation** in theoretical linguistics, understood as the study of grammars in themselves, can be of the mechanismic type. At most it can be of the subsumptive kind. In other words, theoretical linguistics is necessarily descriptive rather than explanatory. By contrast, mechanismic explanations should be possible in all the branches of linguistics that study speech rather than language in itself: neurolinguistics, psycholinguistics, sociolinguistics, and historical linguistics. For example, neurolinguists have sketched mechanismic explanations of some speech anomalies, such as stammering, dyslexia, and the inability to utter words of certain types. To be sure, most such explanations are tentative. But at least the hypotheses they depend upon are empirically testable. As for languages in themselves, some of their features might be explained if they are regarded as ideal types representing actual or possible speech. This is in fact how some linguistic regularities have been discovered. **d Linguistic community** A group of people that, regardless of political frontiers, share a language and therefore also some of the traditions attached to it. The object of study of sociolinguists, who are interested in language not as an abstract object but as a means of ↑**communication**. Moreover, they may not confine their interest to language proper, but may also be interested in other means of communication, such as body language. In other words, sociolinguists deal with ↑**semiotic systems** embedded in social systems. If preferred, they study the uses that flesh-and-bone people make of language. The study of a linguistic community over time is expected to yield not only descriptions and rules but also laws and explanations of linguistic changes. Now, an ↑**explanation** proper (unlike a mere subsumption under a generalization) invokes a ↑**mechanism**: see **c** above. In the case of linguistic changes, the mechanism is psychosocial: even if started by an individual, a change becomes a linguistic change only when spread throughout an entire culture or at least subculture. And presumably it is socially condoned for being generally regarded (rightly or wrongly) as convenient. For example, the sound /t/ is slowly being replaced by /d/ in American English, modern Greek, and other languages, perhaps because of ease of delivery and thus communication. By contrast, the subjunctive is disappearing from English, perhaps because of the increasing permissiveness and the massification of culture, both of which impoverish language in some respects while enriching it in others. In addition to such spontaneous changes there are, from time to time, linguistic decrees such as those issued by governments or academies. A clear example is the linguistic "cleansing" of the German language conducted by the Nazi regime—which banned all the non-Germanic words, such as 'Adresse' and 'Telephon'. The point in recalling this episode is to emphasize the idea that languages do not evolve by themselves. Hence the patterns of language evolution must be sought in linguistic communities.

LITERATURE The art of writing primarily for the sake of aesthetic pleasure. Literature, like ↑**art** in general, has been an object of philosophizing. The philosophy of literature deals with such questions as the nature of style, the form-content relation, and the difference between poetry and prose. However, the philosophy of literature has yet to make its mark. What is certain is that (a) genuine philosophy is a type of knowledge, whereas literature need not convey any knowledge; (b) rhetorical devices, in particular ↑**metaphors**, which at best play a heuristic role in science and philosophy, are essential to literature, particularly poetry; (c) emotion and style are central to literature but peripheral to philosophy; and (d) only a few important philosophers have been superb writers: Plato, Galileo, Berkeley, Hume, Diderot, Bergson, and Russell.

LITTERBUG, PHILOSOPHICAL Anyone with a sure flair for detecting and savoring pseudophilosophical garbage.

LOGIC a General The organon of valid (correct) reasoning: the theory of ↑**deduction**. Logic is formal, that is, independent of content and therefore of truth. Hence it condones formally valid arguments regardless of the truth of premises, just as it indicts invalid reasoning from true premises. Abidance by logic is therefore necessary though insufficient for rational discourse. **Syn** mathematical logic. **b Classical logic** The field of mathematics, originated in philosophy, whose basis is the first-order predicate logic with identity, and which asserts the ↑**excluded middle** and the ↑**double negation** principles. It is the logical theory that underlies most of mathematics and all of factual science and technology. **c Intuitionistic logic** The logical theory that asserts neither the excluded middle nor the double negation principles. These strictures have controversial philosophical motivations. Because of them, proofs in intuitionistic logic are far more involved than in classical logic. **d Deviant logic** Any logic that is neither classical nor intuitionistic. There are dozens of deviant logics, most of them invented by philosophers: ↑**deontic**, ↑**fuzzy**, ↑**many-valued**, ↑**modal**, ↑**paraconsistent**, ↑**relevance**, ↑**quantum**, ↑**tense**, and others. None of these has helped to solve any philosophical, mathematical, or scientific problems. For example, quantum logic has not helped prove a single theorem in quantum theory. The legitimate uses of deviant logics are: (a) to show that one may reason validly in alternative ways; (b) to falsify the belief that logic studies the psychological laws of thought; and (c) to show that exactness is desirable but insufficient for the advancement of knowledge. **e Philosophical logic** The application of logic to semantical, epistemological, ontological, or ethical problems. A part of ↑**exact philosophy** prone to ↑**hollow exactness**.

LOGIC, APPLIED The application of mathematical logic (inclusive of set theory) to the elucidation of ordinary-language expressions and philosophical concepts and theses, in order to better understand and discuss them.

LOGICAL POSITIVISM The twentieth-century phase of ↑**positivism**. **Syn** Logical empiricism, neopositivism. Main tenets: philosophy is syntax; unrequited love of science; experience is the root of all nonmathematical knowledge; every proposition is either tautological or empirical; mathematics is formal; antimetaphysics; phenomenalism; verification theory of meaning; operationism; emotivist axiology and ethics; behaviorist psychology. Most influential authors: M. Schlick, O. Neurath, H. Reichenbach, R. Carnap, B. Russell (for a while), P. Frank, K. Menger, J. Kraft, V. Kraft, H. Feigl, F. Ayer, C. G. Hempel, W. v. O. Quine. No living logical positivist has recently been sighted.

LOGICISM The strategy in the foundations of mathematics that attempts to reduce (by way of definitions) all mathematical concepts to logical ones. This program proved not to be viable. In particular, the central concept of set theory, that of membership, is not definable in logical terms. The failure of logicism is parallel to the fate of radical ↑**reduction** attempts in other fields.

LUCK Good luck = Unexpected opportunity. Equivalent 1: Good match of the individual and his circumstances. Equivalent 2: Being at the right place at the right time. Lucky person = Some one who remembers only his lucky strikes. Bad luck = Adverse circumstance. Equivalent 1: Mismatch between goal and circumstance. Equivalent 2: Being at the wrong place at the wrong time. Unlucky person = Someone who remembers only his unlucky strikes. A total ignoramus is neither lucky nor unlucky, for he is incapable of expecting anything, hence of finding anything unexpected. An omniscient being could be neither lucky nor unlucky either, because he would expect everything. There is nothing irrational or superstitious about the idea of luck. It occurs in evolutionary biology, often referred to as ↑**contingency** (or nonbiological accident, such as continental drift). A lucky organism is one that is born in circumstances that favor its survival; a lucky species (or rather biopopulation) is one that emerges in circumstances that favor its survival and radiation. Similar considerations apply in history, politics, and management. However, imputing every failure to bad luck is silly, dishonest, or both. Moreover, it really gives bad luck, because it predisposes the subject to failure, and thus saps his resolve to go ahead.

LUDDITE, PHILOSOPHICAL Opposed in principle to the use of modern conceptual tools (mathematical logic, formal semantics, and mathematics) in philosophy. Examples: Hegelians, intuitionists, Wittgensteinians, hermeneuticists, phenomenologists, existentialists, and postmodernists.

LUMPER / SPLITTER Philosophers have been classed into lumpers, or synthesizers (or system-builders), and splitters, or analyzers. However, a good synthesis, in particular a theory, facilitates analysis; and an adequate analysis may point the way to a theory. For example, the predicate calculus is a tool of logical analysis; and in turn the analysis of complex predicates, such as "descends from," motivated and guided the construction of the predicate calculus. Again, molecular biology, an eminently analytical discipline, is helping understand the functioning of cells, organs, and organisms. And evolutionary biology, a synthetic discipline, acts as a searchlight in the rest of biology.

MACHINE Artifact capable of doing work of some kind. Being ↑**artifacts**, machines are designed and operated according to explicit ↑**rules**. Hence, only human beings or their proxies are capable of designing, constructing, or operating them. And, since they work to rule, machines can have neither initiative nor creativity—let alone feelings, moral sensibility, or leadership skills. Therefore, the fear that they may eventually take over the world is unfounded. So is the hope that the study of computers will explain how the mind works. ↑**Computationism**, ↑**computer worship**, ↑**machinism**.

MACHINISM The view that all things, or at least organisms and brains, are ↑**machine**-like, that is, are designed and operate according to rules or ↑**algorithms**. Accordingly biology and psychology would be branches of engineering. The so-called ↑**Artificial Life** project, as well as the computationist approach to cognitive psychology, are instances of machinism. ↑**Computationism**. Both claim that matter does not matter to life and mind: that these are "substrate-neutral." Consequently the understanding of life and mind would not require the search for ↑**laws** of nature, all of which are properties of matter of some kind or other. Thus machinism combines the worst features of ↑**mechanism** and ↑**idealism**.

MACRO / MICRO Entities can be grouped, as to size, into microthings and macrothings. Examples: molecules and bodies, persons and social systems. It is often possible to distinguish more than one microlevel and more than one macrolevel. Moreover, what is regarded as micro in a given context may be treated as macro in another. Caution: a peculiarity of ↑**quantons** is that, unless bound together, they spread until they occupy all the available space. Besides, there are macrophysical quantons, such as black bodies and superconducting rings. Hence, the quanton / classon distinction does not coincide with the micro / macro one. The latter is particularly crucial in social science, where it helps explain otherwise puzzling connections. For example, the stock market drops every time the unemployment rate drops. The accepted explanation is this:

Macrolevel	Rise in employment	→	Drop in stock market prices
↓			↑
Microlevel	Rise in consumption	→	Fear of inflation

MAGICAL THINKING Thinking about the world in terms of entities or forces that can

170

be conjured up or controlled by incantations, spells, or rites rather than by work done in the light of technology. Examples: the animistic, ancient Chinese, Christian, and ↑**New Age** worldviews and practices. Paragons: sacrifice, prayer, cursing, and rubbing Aladdin's magic lamp.

MAGNITUDE A particular kind of predicate or attribute: a numerical function representing a ↑**property** of a concrete entity. **Syn** quantity. Examples: distance, electric charge, metabolic rate, age, birth rate, population density, and inflation rate. Most variables in scientific theories are magnitudes, which are functions. For example, mass is a function of the form $M : B \times F \times U_M \rightarrow \mathbb{R}^+$, where B denotes the set of bodies, F that of reference frames, U_M that of mass units (g, Kg, etc.), $\mathbb{R}^+$ that of the nonnegative real numbers, and $\times$ the ↑**cartesian product**. A particular value of M for a body b, relative to a reference frame f, and reckoned or measured in the unit u, will be $M(b, f, u) = m$. This number m is the value that occurs, e.g., in the formula for the linear momentum: $p = mv$. In general, a magnitude M is a function of the form $M : A \times B \times \ldots \times N \times E^3 \times T \times U_M \rightarrow \mathbb{C}^n$, where $A, B, \ldots, N$ denote kinds of things, E^3 and T space and time respectively, U_M is the set of all conceivable M-units, and $\mathbb{C}^n$ the set of n-tuples of complex numbers. In quantum physics many of the variables, such as momentum, energy, and spin, are operators. However, they help define magnitudes proper, namely, the corresponding densities, functions of the form $\psi^* A_{op} \psi$, where ψ is the state function. Typically, magnitudes have dimensions—not to be confused with units. The basic dimensions of physical magnitudes are L (for length), T (for time), and M (for mass). Thus the dimension of a force is MLT^{-2}. By contrast, relative expansion and other ratios are dimensionless. Magnitudes are related to ↑**predicates** in the following way. Let $M : D \rightarrow N$ be a magnitude with domain D and codomain N, a set of numbers or n-tuples of numbers of some type. The predicate associated with M is $\mathcal{M}: D \times N \rightarrow S$, where S is the set of statements containing M. For example, let M designate the mass function, and $M(b, f, u) = m$, as above. The corresponding value of the associated predicate is the statement $\mathcal{M}(b, f, u, m)$, short for "the mass of b, relative to reference frame f and in mass unit u, is m."

MANAGEMENT, PHILOSOPHY OF The emerging ontology, epistemology, praxiology, and ethics of management. Some typical problems: nature of the firm; elucidation of the concepts of policy, plan, and rule; identification and test of management rules; management "science" as a social technology; influence of ideology on management practices; moral problems raised by management.

MANY-VALUED LOGIC A family of logical calculi including more than two truth values. Originally, the main rationale for introducing three-valued logic was the consideration of propositions that have not yet been assigned a truth value, e.g., because they refer to future events such as the outcome of tomorrow's sea battle. Such propositions are usually assigned either the value "indeterminate" or the value 1/2. An objection against the entire enterprise is that ↑**logic** is not concerned with assigning truth values to atomic (simple) propositions, any more than the probability calculus is expected to assign values to the elementary probabilities. Hence the propositions that have not yet been evaluated do not call for a special logic. It is enough to regard truth valuation as a partial function defined on a proper subset of the set of all propositions. As a matter of fact, this is what we do whenever we suspend judgment. ↑**Truth-gap theory**. It has been claimed that many-valued logics exactify the fuzzy notion of partial truth, which must be attributed to such propositions as "The value of π is 3," and "The Earth is spherical." It does not, because ordinary (two-valued) logic suffices for scientific and technological reasonings with partial truths. This is so because logic studies deduction regardless of truth and falsity: it is alethically neutral. Hence, a useful theory of partial truths will retain ordinary logic. ↑**Truth, partial**.

MAPPING a Mathematics A many-to-one or one-to-one correspondence between two complex mathematical objects, such as sets, algebras, or spaces. The first set is called the domain, and the second the codomain of the map. **Syn** ↑**function, morphism. b Science and technology** The conceptual representation of a domain of facts. In ↑**cognitive neuroscience**, "mapping the mind on to the brain" means localizing the mental functions in the brain, as when anxiety is localized in the amygdala and disgust in the insula.

MARXISM An extremely influential mixed bag made up of largely obsolete social science, philosophy, and ideology. Marxist philosophy consists of dialectical and historical materialism. The former is an ontology, and the latter its application to the study of society. ↑**Dialectics**, whether materialist or idealist, is extremely imprecise, and it has more exceptions than examples. By contrast, ↑**historical materialism** has a sound and fruitful if narrow kernel. ↑**Imperialism, economic**. It is high time someone were to find out what can be salvaged from the intellectual and political shipwreck of Marxism.

MATERIAL ENTITY The traditional concept is that of a passive thing, incapable of changing by itself. **Syn** concrete thing. This view was falsified by Newton's discovery of ↑**inertia**. The modern concept is that of an object capable of changing. Thus, to be (material) is to become. All physical things are material, but the converse is false for, in addition to physical things, there are chemical, biological, social, and technical ones. Likewise, possessing a mass is sufficient but not necessary for being material: gravitational and electromagnetic fields are material but massless. Besides, since otherwise empty space is filled with the fluctuating electromagnetic zero field, space itself may be regarded as being material. ↑**Vacuum**.

MATERIALISM, PHILOSOPHICAL The family of ontological doctrines according to which reality is composed exclusively of ↑**material** or concrete things. Unrelated to moral materialism, or greed and the pursuit of pleasure. **Ant** ↑**idealism**. Main variants: physicalist and emergentist. Physicalism (or *vulgar materialism*, or *mechanism*, or *eliminative materialism*, or *reductive materialism*) is the view that every existent is a physical thing, hence one ultimately describable in purely physical terms. The mere existence of sciences which, like biology, psychology, and sociology, study supraphysical properties, suffices to dispose of this early phase of materialism. By contrast, *emergentist materialism* holds that all existents are material or concrete but, far from belonging to a single ↑**level**, are grouped into several levels of organization: physical, chemical, biological, social, technological, and semiotic. The members of every level above the physical one are systems endowed with peculiar properties that ↑**emerge** from the interactions of the systems' components, or between these and environmental items. ↑**Emergentism**. **Syn** ↑**reism**.

MATHEMATICAL PHILOSOPHY ↑**Exact philosophy**. Not to be confused, as it often is, with the philosophy of mathematics. ↑**Mathematics, philosophy of**.

MATHEMATICS Maximally clear, abstract, and general thinking. The science of form and pattern in themselves, i.e., regardless of possible content, interpretation, or application. According to this definition, mathematics includes ↑**logic**. The ancient definition of mathematics as "the science of figure and number" became obsolete in the seventeenth century, with the birth of the infinitesimal calculus, and even more so in the nineteenth, with the emergence of such nonquantitative mathematical fields as topology, abstract algebra, and set theory. These are particularly valuable in ↑**exact philosophy**.

MATHEMATICS, PHILOSOPHY OF The philosophical study of mathematical research and its products. Examples of its problematics: Nature of mathematical objects and mathematical truth; relation between invention and discovery in mathematical research; roles of intuition and reason, as well as of examples and heuristics, in mathematical research; physical interpretations of geometry and probability; relations between pure and applied mathematics. There are five main philosophies of mathematics: Platonism, nominalism, intuitionism, empiricism, and fictionism. As regards the nature of mathematical objects, Platonists hold that they are self-existing, ideal, and eternal; nominalists, that they are inscriptions; intuitionists, that they are mental constructions; empiricists, that they are mental experiences; and fictionists, that they are fictions. Concerning the mode of introduction of mathematical objects, Platonists and empiricists claim that they are discovered; nominalists, that they are conventional; intuitionists, that they are invented; and fictionists, that some are invented whereas others are discovered. With regard to meaning, Platonists assert that their meaning consists in noncontradiction; nominalists, that they have none; intuitionists, that they are meaningful to the extent that they can be related to positive integers; empiricists, that they refer to experience; and fictionists, that both their senses and referents are conceptual. About mathematical truth, Platonists and fictionists hold that it is formal; nominalists, that it is conventional; intuitionists, that it is reducible to numerical computation; and empiricists, that it is empirical. Concerning mathematical knowledge, Platonists and fictionists hold that it is a priori and conceptual; nominalists, that there is no such thing; intuitionists, that it is a priori and intuitive; and empiricists, that it is empirical. The main views about mathematical activity are that it is strictly hypothetico-deductive (Platonism); that it consists in the formal manipulation of symbols (nominalism); that it is both intuitive and rational (intuitionism); that it proceeds by ordinary induction (empiricism); and that it proceeds through invention and discovery, abstraction and generalization, trial and error and formal manipulation, analogy and induction (ordinary as well as mathematical), postulation and deduction (fictionism).

MATTER The collection of all actual or possible ↑**material entities**. That is, $\mathcal{M} = \{x \mid Mx\}$, where M = is material = is changeable. Since $\mathcal{M}$ is a collection, matter is conceptual, not material: only individual objects can be material. By contrast, any system composed of material entities, from society to the universe, is material. Warning: matter ≠ mass. Indeed, mass is a property of only some material things, such as protons and electrons; photons and gravitons are assumed to be massless. ↑**E = mc²**.

MEANING a Semantics Meaning is a peculiarity of constructs, or of the symbols that designate them. It can be equated with ↑**reference** (denotation), ↑**sense** (connotation), or the two taken together. Reference is insufficient to determine meaning because every concrete thing has different properties, conceptualized as so many predicates. For example, both "metabolism" and "divisibility" apply to cells but they are obviously different. Nor is sense sufficient: we must always know what objects we are talking about, not just what we say about them. Therefore we stipulate that, in general, the meaning of a construct c is its sense together with its reference, or $\mathcal{M}(c) = <S(c), \mathcal{R}(c)>$. For example, the definite description "That book" refers to the book that is being pointed to; and its sense is "A bloc of printed pages bound together." **b Social science** In ordinary language, 'meaning' can signify almost anything, as in 'the meaning of experience', 'the meaning of life', and 'the meaning of history'. The question of the meaning of life is a pseudoproblem, because what is really being asked is "What is the purpose or life?" or "What do we live for? Pleasure, service, or both? For the greater glory of God, for the state, or for our own sake?" and so on. In the social studies inspired by W. Dilthey and M. Weber, as well as in German and English, 'meaning' is used to designate purpose or goal. Thus 'He meant well' signifies "He had a good intention." The confusion between the ordinary language and the semantic concepts of meaning has led to viewing social actions as linguistic facts, and social science as ↑**hermeneutics**. This view has been a potent obstacle to the transformation of social studies from literature into science. ↑*Verstehen*.

MEANS / END The distinctive property of deliberate action is that it seeks to attain definite ends (goals, aims) through definite means. And a characteristic of the means / end pair is its permutability: what is now a means may become a goal, and vice-versa, as in the cases of learning / livelihood and liberty / political action. And yet, whereas some philosophies see only means, others see only goals. ↑**Formalism**, ↑**methodism**, and ↑**contractualism** exemplify the former, whereas ↑**pragmatism** and ↑**utilitarianism** instantiate the latter. In particular, the maxim "The end justifies the means" is pragmatist and utilitarian. ↑**Agathonism** demands that both means and ends be evaluated morally as well as practically.

MEASURE a Mathematics A property of sets studied by measure theory, a branch of pure mathematics. It deals with lengths, areas, and the like, and it underlies the probability calculus. Not to be confused with ↑**measurement**. Nor does it make sense to define "measure" as "the dialectical unity and interaction of quality and quantity" (Hegel). **b Methodology** Ambiguous term that designates either a ↑**magnitude** or an ↑**indicator**. Examples: mass is a measure of both inertia and quantity of matter; participation is a measure of social cohesion; and church attendance is a measure (indicator) of either religious fervor or the wish to appear respectable.

MEASUREMENT a General The empirical procedure whereby a value of a quantitative property is determined. Measurement can be direct or indirect (i.e., via some theoretical formula). Often several alternative methods to measure the same variable are available. Any such method can only be justified by a ↑**measurement theory** tailored to it. **b Measurement error** There are no perfect measurements. Errors of two kinds are bound to occur in nearly any precision measurement: systematic and accidental (or random).The former are flaws in experimental design—typically the overlooking or underrating of some variable(s). By contrast, accidental errors are due to small random changes during the course of the experiment in the measuring device, the object measured, or both. Accidental errors distribute randomly: that is, every one of them is paired off to a definite probability. Typically, though not always, they distribute on Gauss's bell-shaped error curve: most of them bunch around the average, and there are few very small and very large ones. This is the reason behind the convention that the true value equals the average value. The size of the entire set of accidental errors is measured by the mean standard deviation (or dispersion, or scatter). The calculation of this statistic involves the differences between the individual measured values and their average. A standard account of a run of measurements of a magnitude M has the form: $M = m \pm \sigma$, where m designates the average and σ the mean standard deviation around the mean. Both m and σ depend not only on M but also on the design and execution of the measurement.

MEASUREMENT THEORY A theory of the measurement of a particular magnitude with a particular method. Every particular measurement method calls for a specific measurement theory, and every such theory involves specific law-statements. Think, e.g., of the different theories describing alternative methods for measuring masses, e.g., with a scale of some type, or with the mass spectrometer. Therefore no general theories of measurement can be true: they are just academic industries. They originated in the confusion between measurement, an empirical operation, with the mathematical concept of ↑**measure** of a set (e.g., length of a line). And they are so remote from scientific practice that they do not contain the concepts of dimension (such as LT^{-1} in the case of velocity) and unit (e.g., $cm\ s^{-1}$ in the same case).

MECHANISM a Process Whatever process makes a complex thing work. Example 1: The mechanical or electrodynamic "works" of a watch. Example 2: The neural mechanism of learning and creation, thought to be the self-assembly of new systems of neurons from previously uncommitted ones. Example 3: In social life, cooperation is a coordination mechanism. Example 4: Voting is a participation mechanism. Example 5: Morality is a social coexistence and control mechanism. A *mechanismic* or *strong* ↑**explanation** involves the disclosure of the mechanism(s) in a system. These are represented in the law-statement(s) occurring among the premises of the explanatory argument. **b Worldview** The worldview according to which the universe is clocklike. Consequently, cosmology would equal mechanics—Descartes's speculative fluid dynamics, or Newton's more realistic particle mechanics. Mechanism was the first scientific worldview. It generalized the most advanced science of its day, and it directed researchers to investigate the mechanical properties of all things visible. By the same token, it turned people away from the holistic and hierarchical worldview prevailing earlier. In particular, Descartes and others regarded the animal body as merely a complicated machine driven by a pump—the heart. Only the soul was spared, and this not always. Mechanism comes in two versions: secular and religious. *Secular* mechanism holds that the cosmos is a self-existing and self-regulating mechanism—a sort of self-rewinding eternal clock. By contrast, *religious* mechanism assumes a Watchmaker. Descartes's cosmic clock was perfect, as befits God's creation, so it was in no need of a Repairman. Having created matter and endowed it with dynamical laws, the Cartesian God need not busy Himself any longer with the physical universe and could devote all His attention to spiritual matters. By contrast, the Newtonian cosmos was dissipative: there was friction among the wheels of the celestial machine. Hence God had to give it a push from time to time to keep it going. From its inception in the seventeenth-century Scientific Revolution till mid-nineteenth century, secular mechanism stimulated a prodigious scientific and technological production. It began to decline with the birth of field physics and thermodynamics and the rise of evolutionary biology. By the beginning of the twentieth century it was quite dead. We now understand that mechanics is only one of the chapters of physics. We also realize that relativistic mechanics makes no sense apart from electrodynamics, and that quantum "mechanics" is not quite mechanical, for it does not describe corpuscles with definite shapes and precise trajectories. In sum, mechanism had its glorious day. Four centuries ago it showed the way to the scientific exploration of the physical world. Indeed, it taught that the right approach to the study of reality is to try to decompose it into basic constituents behaving according to laws that can be represented by mathematical formulas capable of being tested in the laboratory or the field. Thus, though not explicitly, mechanism called for a synthesis of rationalism and empiricism (↑**ratioempiricism**). And its successes and failures show that worldview and science may interact. ↑**Materialism**, ↑**minimalism**.

MECHANISMIC MODEL A model of a system that, unlike a ↑**black-box model**, includes the ↑**mechanism**(s) mediating between inputs and outputs. Examples: field-theoretic models (unlike action at a distance models), neurophysiological models of cognitive processes, psychological and economic models of social processes.

MEDICINE The applied science and technology of health care. It is composed of four different but intersecting and interacting spheres: biomedical research, or human biology; therapy, or the design of treatments—a branch of biotechnology; social medicine (descriptive and normative epidemiology); and medical praxis. All four raise a number of philosophical problems. ↑**Iatrophilosophy**.

MEDICINE, PHILOSOPHY OF ↑**Iatrophilosophy**.

MELIORISM a Epistemology The thesis that error can be detected and corrected. The complement of ↑**fallibilism**. A ↑**scientific philosophy** is at once fallibilist and meliorist. **b Social and political philosophy** The family of ideologies holding that the individual and society can be perfected. Main examples: classical liberalism and left-wing ideologies.

MEMBERSHIP RELATION The binary relation ∈ between an individual and a set, as in 0 ∈ {0,1}, and Aristotle ∈ Humankind. A basic (undefined) concept in set theory. A counterexample to the ↑**extensionalist** thesis that all relations are sets of ordered pairs (or, in general, n-tuples). If ∈ were so definable, "$x ∈ y$" could be restated as "$<x,y>$ ∈ ∈," a meaningless string of signs.

MENTAL Occurring in the mind. Nonexistent according to radical ↑**behaviorism**, and a particular neurophysiological process according to ↑**materialism**. If the latter is admitted, the expression "It's only in your mind" should be replaced with "It's no less than in your brain." ↑**Mind-body problem**.

MENTALESE The language of thought, that is, thought stripped of linguistic accoutrements—hence no language at all.

MENTALISM ↑**Subjective idealism**. Not to be mistaken for the assertion that there are mental processes, for these can be construed in either a mentalist or a materialist way.

MENTION / USE ↑**Use / mention**.

MEREOLOGY The chapter of ontology that deals with the part-whole relation and the "sum" or physical juxtaposition of individuals. Classical mereology is an extremely complicated theory using an idiosyncratic symbolism, and yielding only elucidations of the above-mentioned notions with the sole help of first-order logic. Using the slightly more powerful tool of semigroup theory, the whole of mereology can be compressed into a handful of sentences: ↑**Part-whole**, ↑**model theory**. Mereology may be regarded as a tiny fraction of ↑**systems theory**, all the more so since it does not involve the concepts of property and of change.

MERGER OF DISCIPLINES The hybridization of two previously disjoint disciplines, to constitute an ↑**interdiscipline**, such as analytic geometry, electrodynamics, psychophysics, cognitive neuroscience, sociolinguistics, and political sociology. Such fusion is effected by introducing hypotheses that combine key concepts of one of them with key concepts of the other(s). Example 1: Analytic geometry synthesizes geometry with algebra through the points-numbers correspondence. Example 2: The synthetic theory of evolution joins evolutionary theory with genetics via glue formulas such as "Phenotypic variations are the result of genic changes." Example 3: Cognitive neuroscience synthesizes neuroscience with psychology through the glue formula "Every mental process is a brain process." ↑**Glue formula**, ↑**interdiscipline**.

MESO Intermediate in size or degree of complexity between micro and macro, as in "DNA molecules are mesoscopic objects," and "corporations are mesoeconomic systems." The understanding or management of such entities calls for the ↑**merger** of theories of the micro and the macro types. ↑**Macro-micro**.

METAETHICS Discourse about ethical concepts, maxims, and theories. Examples: analysis of the general concepts of right and duty, of the relations between ethics and technology, and of the utility of utilitarianism. Between circa 1900 and the rise of bioethics and environmental ethics in the 1970s, the bulk of ethical writings was metaethical.

METALANGUAGE A language that refers to another language, called ‘↑object language’. For example, any assertion about a theory is metatheoretical and thus couched in a language that is one rung above the language of the theory. A language, such as English, can be used to talk about itself. ↑**Use-mention**.

METALOGIC The ↑**metatheory** of ↑**logic**, a part of ↑**metamathematics**. It investigates the problematics of inference rules, decision, proof, consistency, independence, and the logical relations among theories. Examples: Padoa's technique for finding out whether the concepts in a set are mutually independent; Gödel's incompleteness theorem; and Tarski's theory of theories.

METAMATHEMATICS The family of mathematical theories about ↑**mathematics** as a whole. Its nucleus is proof theory. Once the preserve of logicians, metamathematics is nowadays cultivated by theoretical computer scientists as well, interested as they are in proofs, computations, programs, and algorithms, which is one more example of the unpredictable practical spinoffs of basic research.

METANOMOLOGICAL STATEMENT a Mathematics and science A statement about one or more ↑**law-statements**. For example, the duality principle for sets ordered by the relations $\geq$ and $\leq$: "The converse of a partially ordered set is a partially ordered set." ↑**Metatheorem**. Some metanomological statements are heuristic, regulative, or methodological, whereas others are rigorous theorems. For example, the metastatement that the basic laws of physics should be Lorentz (or else generally) covariant is of the first kind. It is a condition that guides and limits the choice of physical law-statements. By contrast, the metastatement that Maxwell's field equations are Lorentz covariant is a theorem. So is the CPT (charge-parity-time reversal) theorem in quantum field theory. **b Philosophy** A broad principle concerning law-statements. Examples: "Laws are constant relations among properties," "All facts are lawful, none is lawless or miraculous," and "The laws of the higher integrative levels have emerged from those of the lower levels."

METAPHILOSOPHY Philosophy of philosophy. Examples: the rules for philosophizing, as well as the definitions of and value judgments on philosophy, are metaphilosophical statements. Example: "Philosophical research should keep close to mathematics, science, and technology." A peculiarity of metaphilosophy is that it is not systematic: there are no theories about philosophy. Another peculiarity of metaphilosophy is that it is part of philosophy. In this regard metaphilosophy is similar to metalogic and metamathematics. In this respect all three metadisciplines are in sharp contrast to others. For example, metahistory, or the philosophy of history, is part of philosophy, not history.

METAPHOR Figure of speech suggesting an ↑**analogy**. Examples: 'the fabric of society' (social structure), 'the circulation of elites' (revolution), 'the meaning of action' (the aim of action). Peculiar to poetry, archaic thinking, political discourse under tyranny, postmodern musings, and new research lines. A once-influential view is that scientific theories are metaphors rather than literal descriptions of facts. This view is false because (a) metaphors can be replaced with literal expressions; and (b) whereas scientific theories are testable for truth, metaphors can at best be suggestive, at worst confusing. In science metaphors are tolerable to handle facts of a new and puzzling kind, in the expectation that they will be transitory disguises of ignorance. For example, it is expected that talk of trancription, translation, and edition in genetics will eventually be replaced with literal descriptions of the underlying chemical mechanisms.

METAPHYSICS a Common sense Pompous nonsense, talk of the supernatural, untestable fantasy. For example, according to Heidegger in his famous *Sein und Zeit,* "Phänomenologie sagt dann: ἀποφαῖνεσθαι τὰ αἰνομένα: Das was sich zeigt, so wie es sich von ihm selbt her zeigt, vom ihm selbst her sehen lassen." One of several possible translations: "Phenomenology then says: [. . .] to make a thing's appearance from the thing's own point of view in precisely the way the thing shows itself from its own perspective." **b Philosophy** The philosophical discipline that deals with the most pervasive features of reality, and possibly also with the objects imagined by theologians and by philosophers out of touch with reality. Metaphysics got a bad name in the nineteenth century for several unrelated reasons: for its close association with theology in the past; for having been practiced by such enigmatic and unscientific writers as Hegel; for having been denounced by the latter as being limited to fixed categories; and for being imprecise and disjoint from science. For these reasons sober metaphysics is often called ↑**ontology**. Moreover, *scientific metaphysics,* i.e., metaphysics consistent with science, are logically possible, as Charles Peirce first claimed. For example, it is possible and advantageous to look into metaphysical concepts (such as those of space, chance, and mind) and metaphysical hypotheses (such as those of lawfulness and psychoneural identity) in the light of contemporary science and mathematics.

METAPROBLEM A problem about one or more problems. E.g., "Is that an open problem?" "Is that open problem worth being investigated?" "Is that problem soluble with the help of this theory?" "What are the necessary and sufficient conditions for problems of that kind to be soluble?" "How does one check the proposed solutions to problems of that kind?" and "How are direct and inverse problems related?"

METARULE A ↑**rule** about one or more rules. Examples: Kant's ↑**categorical imperative**, and the legal principle that bans laws with a retroactive effect.

METASCIENCE The research field composed of the philosophy, sociology, and history of ↑**science**.

METATECHNOLOGY The research field composed of the philosophy, sociology, and history of ↑**technology**.

METATHEOREM A theorem about one or more theorems. Example: in a Boolean algebra, the operations of multiplication and addition are mutually dual.

METATHEORY a Strictly speaking, a metatheory is a theory about one or more theories, where 'theory' is taken in the strict sense of hypothetico-deductive system. Thus metalogic and metamathematics are collections of metatheories. And Bell's famous theorems in quantum physics belong to a theory about the set of all possible hidden variables theories, hence they are metatheorems included in a metatheory. **b** Loosely speaking, 'metatheory' designates any comment on, or criticism of, a body of theoretical knowledge. This is the sense in which the word is used in social science and its philosophy. For example, any philosophical or methodological remarks on sociological or linguistic theory pass for metatheories.

METHOD a A well-specified repeatable procedure for doing something: an ordered sequence of goal-directed operations. Every branch of mathematics, science, and technology has its own special methods: for computing, sampling, making preparations, observing, measuring, etc. In addition, all the sciences use the ↑**scientific method**, and some of them employ the ↑**experimental method** as well. **b Experimental method** The planned setting up of a device to make observations or measurements on individuals of definite kinds, distributed more or less evenly among two groups: the experimental group, where the stimulus is present, and the control group, where it is not. **c Scientific method** The sequence: Survey of a body of knowledge → Choice of problem in this body of knowledge → Problem formulation or reformulation → Application or invention of an approach for handling the problem → Tentative solution (hypothesis, theory, experimental design, measuring instrument, etc.) → Checking the tentative solution → Evaluating the tentative solution in the light of both test and background knowledge → Revision or repetition of any of the previous steps → Estimation of impact on background knowledge → Final evaluation (until new notice). Whereas the experimental method can be used only in the factual sciences and technologies, the scientific method can be employed in all intellectual pursuits. This is the thesis of ↑**scientism**.

METHODICS The collection of methods employed in a research field. Not to be confused with ↑**methodology**.

METHODISM, PHILOSOPHICAL The worship of method. **Syn** methodolatry. That is, the belief that all one needs to make inventions and discoveries is the right method: that no substantive knowledge is required to this end. As an exaggerate reaction against this view, it is sometimes claimed that scientific research involves no method. ↑**Scientific method**.

METHODOLOGY The study of ↑**methods**. The normative branch of ↑**epistemology**; a knowledge technology. Often confused with 'method', as in 'the methodology used in the present research'.

MIDDLE RANGE A ↑**hypothesis** or ↑**theory** is said to be of the middle range if it is neither very narrow or specific nor very broad or generic. Example: a hypothesis concerning the causes of crime of a given type in a given society, rather than either (a) the causes of holdups in Central Park after sundown; or (b) the causes of crimes of all kinds in any society. Robert K. Merton stressed that it is important to multiply hypotheses and theories whose range is comprised between that of a narrow empirical regularity and a "grand" or all-encompassing theory. The reason is that the former tend to be shallow, whereas the latter may be imprecise and therefore hardly testable. In the advanced sciences, theories of the middle range are crafted by enriching well-tried general theories with special (subsidiary) assumptions. (Example: the dynamical theory of a particular asteroid.) By contrast, in the emerging sciences, where data and untested commonsense assumptions are abundant, whereas sound general theories are rare, the middle-range theories are usually built from scratch on the basis of one or more empirical generalizations. The resulting special theories may be called bound and free theoretical models respectively. ↑**Model b.**

MIGHT MAKES RIGHT The powers that be stipulate what is legally (and perhaps also epistemically and morally) right. The slogan of ↑**legal positivism**.

MIND The collection of possible mental states and processes, whether affective, cognitive, or volitional, in humans and other higher vertebrates. Sciences of mind = Psychology and cognitive neuroscience. Philosophy of mind = Philosophical reflection upon the nature of the mental and its relations to the brain. This branch of philosophy studies the ontological and epistemological problems raised by the nature of the mental and its knowledge. Most philosophers still conduct this study a priori, that is, without using the sciences of mind. Hence the idealist fantasy that the mind exists above the brain. ↑**Mind-body problem.**

MIND-BODY DUALISM The thesis that mind and body are different substances. Example: ↑**computationism**, according to which the mind is a sofware detachable from the brain hardware. ↑**Mind-body problem.**

MIND-BODY PROBLEM a Statement This problem boils down to the questions 'What is mind and how is it related to the body?' A capital ancient problem in theology, philosophy, science, medicine, and engineering. **b Main views** There are two main broad views on the nature of ↑**mind** and its relation to ↑**matter**: monism and dualism. Psychoneural monists assert the unity of mind and body (or brain), and dualists their separateness. However, each of these views is a family composed of at least six different doctrines. Here are the six main *monistic* views. M1 *Idealism (spiritualism)*: Everything is mental. M2 *Neutral monism* or *double aspect doctrine*: The mental and the physical are two manifestations of an unknowable neutral substance. M3 *Eliminative materialism*: Nothing is mental. M4 *Machinism*: Mental events are brain events, and the brain is machinelike. M5 *Physicalism or reductionist materialism*: Mental events are physical or physicochemical. M6 *Emergentist materialism*: Mental processes constitute a subset of neurophysiological processes in brains of higher vertebrates that emerged in the course of evolution. The six main *dualistic* views are: D1 *Autonomism*: The mental and the physical are unrelated. D2 *Psychophysical parallelism*: Every mental event is accompanied by a synchronous but otherwise unrelated neural event. D3 *Epiphenomenalism*: The mental is caused by the physical. D4 *Computationism*: The mind is a collection of programs (or algorithms) that can be embodied ("instantiated") in either brains or machines. D5 *Animism*: though immaterial, mental events can cause neural or physical changes. D6 *Interactionism*: Mental events cause or are caused by neural or physical ones, the brain being only the tool or "material basis" of the mind. Every one of these twelve solutions is part of some philosophical school. But of course this does not entail that only philosophers are competent to handle the problem. On the contrary, when confusion reigns in a philosophical field, it may be the chance for scientists to step in and establish some order. c **Scientific evaluation of the monistic philosophies of mind** M1 (idealism) entails that all the sciences are reducible to mentalistic psychology. This thesis is manifestly false, if only because psychologists are not equipped to investigate electromagnetic fields, chemical reactions, cell division, or even social systems, except insofar as they affect mental processes. As for M2, or neutral monism, it is not a scientific doctrine because it postulates that the neutral substance cannot be investigated, and because it does not explain how that unknowable substance can now appear as physical, now as mental. Eliminative materialism (M3) is at variance with the fact that psychologists happen to investigate mental processes and have even discovered some regularities concerning affect, memory, learning, inference, dreaming, and other kinds of mental phenomena. Machinism (D4) underrates the environment and denies neural plasticity and the concomitant creativity. Physicalist or reductionist materialism (M5) is too simple to be true: it makes no room for the emergent properties of nervous tissue (such as lateral inhibition, spontaneous neuron discharge, and the self-assembly of neuron systems), or even for the peculiarities of organisms vis-à-vis physical or chemical systems. The elimination of the first five monistic views leaves us with M6, or emergentist materialism. This holds that mental functions are brain processes that emerge in the course of individual development, and that have arisen in the course of evolution. (More precisely, every mental function is a process occurring in some brain subsystem. Hence, if the latter alters in any way, so does the function it discharges.) This view is attractive for being no less than the philosophy underlying neuropsychology (or cognitive neuroscience, as it is now called). Indeed, the goals of this discipline are precisely (a) to identify the neural processes that perform known psychological functions; (b) to discover the possible psychological functions of certain neural systems, hoping to uncover new mental phenomena; (c) to explain the mental in terms of such mechanisms as long-term potentiation, dendritic sprouting and pruning, and changes in the concentrations of neurotransmitters; and (d) to supply psychiatry with some of the knowledge required to treat mental disorders, helping design and test neuroleptic drugs. Even a quick perusal of the recent scientific literature should convince anyone that this enterprise is highly successful, not only in terms of findings but also for having opened up a huge mine of scientific, medical, and other intriguing problems likely to be tackled in the coming decades. Suffice it to recall the following ones: At what point in evolution did ideation begin? At what stage in human development does reasoning start? Which are the smallest neuron assemblies (psychons) capable of performing mental functions? Where and how do the outputs of the various visual systems (those perceiving shape, color, texture, and motion) become bound into percepts? Which subsystem of the human brain can perform mathematical computations? How do emotions affect reasoning? How do mental processes affect the immune system? Which are the mechanisms of the actions of drugs on the various mental processes? How might depression be cured (not just treated)? How might the progression of Alzheimer's disease be slowed down? Could live prostheses replace damaged parts of the human brain? (Artificial prostheses implanted in brains and connected to artificial arms are already enabling quadraplegics to perform some tasks.) **d Scientific evaluation of the dualistic philosophies of mind** Notwithstanding the achievements and heuristic power of emergentist materialism, we have yet to examine its dualist rivals, to which we now turn. Autonomism, or D1, is too far-fetched to be believable: Even folk psychology knows of psychosomatic effects, such as the increase in morbidity caused by grief, as well as of the mental deficits caused by some brain injuries. Psychophysical parallelism, or D2, is too vague to qualify as a scientific hypothesis: it does not specify what makes the mental peculiar, or what the synchronization mechanism could be. In fact, it is so vague that it may be regarded as being confirmable by any data about the "correlation" of the mental and the physiological. Still, given its popularity, we shall take a closer look at it below. D3, or epiphenomenalism, leaves the mental unexplained, and it involves the obscure notion of one of the two "entities" acting upon the other. The notion of action is clear for concrete things such as photons, cells, and whole organisms, because in these cases we can often describe their states and changes of state, as well as the mechanisms of such changes. For example, we understand—at least in principle—what it is for a center of the will, located in the prefrontal cortex, to act upon the motor strip; or for organs of emotion, belonging to the limbic system, to act upon the immune system. But the idea of something material acting upon, or even secreting, an immaterial entity, or conversely, is obscure. Moreover, such hypothesis is experimentally untestable, because laboratory tools can only alter or measure properties of concrete things such as people. Computationism or D4 has the same defect as machinism (M4): it makes no room for emotion and creativity. Besides, it is wedded to the Platonic notion of embodiment. What holds for epiphenomenalism also holds for animism or D5, as well as for interactionism or D6. Indeed, these views also adopt the vulgar concept of mind, and they do not bother to elucidate the even fuzzier idea that the mind can act on the brain or conversely. In sum, all the six varieties of psychoneural dualism share several fatal flaws. First, dualism takes the mental for granted instead of explaining its emergence and submergence; in particular, it writes off the problem of accounting for its emergence in the course of evolution and of individual development. Second, it hinders research into the neural mechanisms that drive mental processes, as well as into the interactions between such processes and muscular, visceral, endocrine, and immune processes. Third, and consequently, dualism hinders the interaction and advancement of psychiatry, psychosomatic medicine, and clinical psychology. In short, psychoneural dualism is worse than barren: it is an obstacle to the advancement of science, medicine, and philosophy. **e Comprehensive evaluation of the dualistic views** To assess the merits of any doctrine we need definite criteria. We adopt the following: intelligibility, internal consistency, systemicity, literalness, testability, empirical evidence, external consistency, originality, heuristic power, and philosophical soundness: ↑**B test**. Let us check which of the twelve philosophies of mind discussed above comes closest to satisfying these ten criteria. Let us start with psychoneural dualism. All of its six varieties fail to clarify the very notion of mind, which they take from either religion or folk psychology. Epiphenomenalism, animism, and interactionism are afflicted with an additional obscurity, namely the notion of action of matter on mind or conversely, which is left undefined; and computationism involves the unclear notion of embodiment. Because of such unclarities, neither of these views can be said to be internally consistent. Nor do they satisfy the systemicity condition: indeed, no dualistic hypothetico-deductive system is known. Furthermore, most dualists think in metaphors. Thus, parallelists use the metaphor of the two independent synchronized clocks; computationists think in terms of computers; animists are fond of the Platonic proportion: Mind is to matter what the pilot is to the ship; and psychoanalysts use several physical and anthropomorphic metaphors. But the worst defect of dualism is that, strictly speaking, it is untestable by scientific means. Indeed, if the mind is immaterial, then, unlike the minding brain, it is inaccessible to electrodes, lancets, drugs, and other tools. Moreover, epiphenomenalism, animism, and interactionism are at odds with physics, for they violate the conservation laws. (Epiphenomenalism involves energy loss, whereas animism and interactionism involve energy gain out of nothing material.) Far from being novel, dualism is as old as religion and idealist philosophy. It is not heuristically powerful either: it suggests no new experiments and no new conjectures. Finally, dualism is not philosophically sound, for it posits ghostly entities. In sum, dualism fails to pass at least eight out of the ten scientificity tests listed above. **f Comprehensive evaluation of the monistic views** All the monistic views, except for neutral monism, are reasonably clear, consistent, systemic, literal, and testable. But only emergentist materialism seems to possess the five additional virtues. In fact, it enjoys empirical support—namely all of the findings of cognitive neuroscience; it is consistent with what is known in psychology and neuroscience; though not brand new, it is far newer than its rivals; it is heuristically powerful, since it underlies an entire research project, namely that of psychobiology; and it is philosophically sound in being ↑realist and ↑naturalist. Interestingly, although emergentist materialism postulates that the mind is a set of brain functions, it does not claim that neuroscience suffices to explain subjective experience. Rather, it suggests that, because brains are sensitive to social stimuli, mental processes are strongly influenced by the social context. This implies that cognitive neuroscience must be supplemented by social psychology and even merged with it. In technical jargon, emergentist materialism is ontologically reductionist because it posits the identity of mental states and brain states; but in epistemological matters it fosters the merger of psychology and sociology with neuroscience rather than the full reduction of the former to the latter. It thus promotes the vigorous interaction of all the branches of psychology, as well as with philosophy. ↑**Interdiscipline**, ↑**merger**, ↑**mind**, ↑**reduction**.

MINIMALISM, PHILOSOPHICAL a Ontology The doctrine that all existents are simple individuals or collections of basic entities of a few kinds, and that qualitative novelty (emergence) is illusory. Examples: ↑**nominalism**, ↑**physicalism** (in particular ↑**mechanism**), and the Berkeley-Mach-Carnap thesis that the world is an aggregate of sensations. **b Epistemology** The doctrine that every idea is either simple or a combination of simples. Examples: psychological associationism, and Mach's principle of thought economy. ↑**Dadaism, philosophical**.

MINIPROBLEM A problem whose solution makes hardly any difference except to prospects for academic promotion. Examples: finding out what so-and-so actually meant, the logic of quotation marks, tense logic, Hempel's ↑**confirmation paradox**, Goodman's ↑**grue**, and Newcomb's problem.

MIRACLE An event that eludes all laws, known and unknown, in being performed by a supernatural being or with the help of one such. Miracles are impossible according to the ↑**lawfulness principle**, which underlies factual science and technology. Hence the methodological rule: If a fact looks miraculous, investigate it until disclosing the underlying natural or social mechanism. For example, look for hidden devices in weeping or bleeding statues of saints, and for little-known physiological processes in miraculous healings and the feats of yogis.

MIRROR Knowledge and language have been said (metaphorically) to mirror reality, or to be isomorphic to it. ↑**Reflection theory of knowledge**.

MODAL LOGIC Any theory that attempts to exactify, interrelate, and regiment the concepts of ↑**possibility** (◊) and ↑**necessity** (definable as ¬◊¬). Modal logic was originally expected to solve two problems with one stroke: the logical problem of necessary logical consequence (in contrast with mere implication), and the ontological problem of real possibility. It failed to solve the former problem, which was eventually solved by ordinary mathematical logic and model theory: ↑**entailment**. Modal logic also failed to solve the second or ontological problem, and this for five reasons. First, it is an a priori theory purporting to deal with a feature of reality, and is thus doomed to failure from the start. Second, modal logic concerns propositions, whereas real possibility is a property of things. Third, it is unrelated to the theories of probability and of random processes, which quantitate one kind of real possibility. Fourth, it makes no contact with the concept of natural law, which is indispensable to decide whether a conceivable fact is really possible. (Indeed, in the sciences a fact is deemed to be really possible if and only if it is lawful.) Fifth, it is ridden with unresolved controversy concerning Byzantine problems, such as whether or not possibility implies necessarily possibility, and whether necessity implies necessarily necessity. For these reasons science has no use for any of the 256 possible systems of ↑**modal logic**. These are just exercises in ↑**hollow exactness**: games with fake diamonds (◊) in paper boxes (□). Hence the claim that modal logic is a central part of philosophy, or even the foundation of mathematics, is extravagant. However, some systems of modal logic have found unexpected applications in computer science, much as the tools of alchemists proved to be useful in the chemical laboratory.

MODALITY The property of something being possible, necessary, or impossible. A construct is (conceptually) possible if it is not inconsistent. A fact is (really) possible if it is compatible with the pertinent laws. The study of real possibility, in contrast with mere logical possibility, is an ordinary business of science and technology. It can be argued that the real modalities are derivative rather than basic or primitive. Example 1: "Thing x may be found at y" amounts to "x is at y & a careful search for x will find it at y." Example 2: "Fact x will necessarily occur" is equivalent to "x is lawful & the circumstance required for the occurrence of x will be present." ↑**Possibility**, ↑**modal logic**.

MODEL a Visual A visual or iconic model of an unobservable thing or process is a visual analogy of it. Examples: lines of force models of electromagnetic fields; the Bohr model of atoms; and the Feynman diagrams of electrodynamic processes. In the nineteenth century some eminent physicists got involved in a spirited controversy over the role of such models. Typically, the realists defended them whereas the positivists and conventionalists attacked them. Nowadays it is generally admitted that, whereas some such models (e.g., Bohr's) are rough representations of real things, others (e.g., Feynman's) are just analogs or even mere mnemonic devices. **b Model-theoretic** A *model*, in the model-theoretic sense of the word, is an example (or "realization," as it used to be said) of an abstract theory (or formalized language). For example, the propositional calculus is a model or example of Boolean algebra. ↑**Interpretation**, ↑**model theory**. **b Scientific and technological** A *theoretical model* in science or technology is a special theory of some factual domain. Examples: models of the helium atom, cell proliferation, and of a manufacturing firm. Although such models are unrelated to those studied by model theory, a whole philosophy of science is based on their confusion: ↑**Models muddle**. There are two kinds of theoretical model: bound and free. A *bound model* results from enriching a general theory (such as classical mechanics or general equilibrium theory) with specific assumptions. Examples: models of the simple pendulum and of the capital market. By contrast, a *free model* is built from scratch. Examples: models of a business firm and of the diffusion of an invention. Most theoretical (or mathematical) models in biology, the social sciences, and technologies are free. This indicates either that these disciplines are still theoretically backward, or that generality is hard to come by in them.

MODEL THEORY The branch of logic that investigates the possible ↑**interpretations** or examples of abstract (uninterpreted) theories, such as the theories of sets, groups, and lattices, none of which is committed to a particular interpretation, not even within mathematics. To get a feel for it, consider semigroup theory, one of the simplest of all theories and one of the most useful in ↑**exact philosophy**. A *semigroup* can be defined axiomatically as follows: A semigroup is an arbitrary set S together with an ↑**associative** operation o (concatenation) between any two members of S: $G_{1/2} = < S, o >$. Semigroup theory can be complicated (enriched) in many ways: i.e., one can construct a very large number of abstract semigroups by adding assumptions, such as that S contains an identity element, and that every element of S has an inverse—in which case the semigroup becomes a group. There is an unlimited number of objects that satisfy the above definition—i.e., an indefinite number of ↑**models** of a semigroup. One of the simplest is constituted by the natural numbers $\mathbb{N}$ together with the arithmetic addition operation, i.e., $\mathcal{M}_1 = < \mathbb{N}, + >$. Indeed, for any three nonnegative whole numbers x, y, and z, $x + (y + z) = (x + y) + z$. In other words, from the viewpoint of abstract algebra, $\mathcal{M}_1$ results from $G_{1/2}$ by adding the ↑**assumptions**: $Int (S) = \mathbb{N}$ and $Int (o) = +$. An alternative model is produced by interpreting S as the set $\mathbb{Z}$ of integers and o as multiplication. I.e., $\mathcal{M}_2 = < \mathbb{Z}, \times >$. (Of course, the addition and multiplication of whole numbers came historically much earlier, and they only provide two familiar examples or models of the abstract semigroup formalism.) A third model of a semigroup is obtained by interpreting S as the set of all the sentences of a language, and o as sentence concatenation. A fourth, by interpreting S as the collection of all concrete things (or substantial individuals), and o as physical addition (or juxtaposition). This latter interpretation allows one to define the ↑**part-whole** relation in an exact fashion. Concerned as it is with abstract mathematical theories and their interpretations, not with modeling facts, model theory is irrelevant to the ↑**metatheory** of theoretical models. ↑**Models muddle**.

MODELS MUDDLE The confusion between 'model' in the model-theoretic sense and in the epistemological sense is the source of an entire philosophy of science, namely the "structuralist" or "semantic" view of theories. ↑**Model b, c**. Another confusion to be avoided is the view that theoretical models are just ↑**analogies** or ↑**metaphors**. Actually these play at best a heuristic role in constructing and teaching theoretical models, as was the case with the partial analogy between electric current and fluid flow. At worse they can obstruct theoretical work, as has been the case with the particle and wave analogies in quantum physics, communications engineering metaphors in psychology, and biological metaphors in social studies.

MODERATE / RADICAL Many, perhaps all, philosophical doctrines come in two versions: moderate (mitigated) and radical (extreme). For example, skepticism, empiricism, rationalism, materialism, idealism, reductionism. There is no reason to be either moderate or radical in the choice between moderation and radicalism, for the adequate choice depends on the nature of the case. Thus, whereas in biology moderate ↑**reductionism** is advisable, full-blown ↑**evolutionism** is always mandatory.

MODULAR A complex thing whose constituents are units that can be altered or even removed independently of one another. **Syn** nonsystemic. Examples: Lego blocks, data, and opinions. The brain is modular, in the weak sense that it is a supersystem constituted by systems with different specific functions. However, the mind is not modular: it is not constituted by mutually independent faculties, in the manner of a Swiss Army knife. Although the mental functions are localized in different brain regions, all of these systems are linked more or less strongly to one another. As a consequence, the mind is unitary. For example, smell is linked to vision, and both are tied to memory, expectation, and emotion.

MODUS NOLENS The praxiological inference rule: For any action *A* and its corresponding outcome *B*,

> If *A*, then *B*.
> *B* is undesirable.
> : : Avoid *A* or abstain from doing *A*,

where : : stands for the somewhat imprecise concept of practical inference. ↑**Praxiology**, ↑*modus volens*.

MODUS PONENS A basic rule of inference in the propositional calculus: For any propositions *p* and *q*: $p \Rightarrow q, p \vdash q$. Also called 'rule of detachment' because it allows one to detach the consequent *q* of a conditional provided its antecedent *p* is asserted. ↑*Modus tollens*.

MODUS TOLLENS A derived rule of inference in propositional logic: For any propositions p and q: $p \Rightarrow q$, $\neg q \mathrel{|\!\!-} \neg p$. Derived from ↑*modus ponens* upon replacing p with $\neg q$, and q with $\neg p$.

MODUS VOLENS The praxiological inference rule: For any action A and its corresponding outcome B,

If A, then B.
B is desirable.
: : Seek or do A.

↑**Praxiology**, ↑*modus nolens*.

MONISM The family of ontological views asserting that the world consists of entities of a single kind, or "is made of a single stuff." Main kinds of monism: ↑**materialism** and ↑**idealism**. Minor monisms: radical ↑**empiricism**, ↑**energetism**, ↑**informationism**, ↑**neutral monism**, ↑**panlogicism**, ↑**panpsychism**, radical ↑**pragmatism**.

MORAL Attitude, proposal, or action fitting a moral code. On any humanistic morality, such as ↑**agathonism**, whatever concerns other people's welfare and our responsibility to them qualifies as moral (or immoral). Accordingly, moral problems and precepts refer to actions that may harm or benefit others. On such moralities, cheating, disloyalty, gender and racial discrimination, revenge, torture, and murder on all scales—from assassination to genocide and war—are immoral. ↑**Morality**, ↑**ethics**.

MORALISM The thesis that our actions should be ruled by moral norms. **Ant** immoralism.

MORALITY System of moral precepts. **Syn** morals, moral code. To be viable, a moral code must be constraining (negative) in some regards and enabling (or positive) in others. That is, it must balance burdens with rewards. Typically, religious moralities postpone rewards and punishments to the afterlife, whereas humanist moralities seek or face them in life. In every social group there is a dominant moral code—though one that is sometimes violated by some individuals. More often than not, the various moral codes in a society overlap partially. Any society where such overlap is small is unstable. ↑**Ethics** may be defined as the study of moral problems, precepts, and codes.

MOTION Change of place. The simplest kind of change, for it involves no qualitative novelty. However, motion may lead to ↑**qualitative** change, as when two atoms approach one another and combine into a molecule, or when several people converge on a place and constitute a social system. In other words, quantitative change may render qualitative transformation possible.

MOTIVE The desire or need, emotion or reason, that impels a deliberate action. A central concept in psychology, social science, ethics, and praxiology. To understand a motive for an action we must relate it to its known or guessed goal or purpose, as in "A's motivation for doing B was C."

MULTIDISCIPLINARY That joins two or more disciplines without coalescing them. For example, the adequate study of science is multidisciplinary—philosophical, psychological, sociological, and historical—whereas that of development, whether biological or social, is interdisciplinary. ↑**Interdisciplinary**.

MUMBO JUMBO Nonsense paraded as deep wisdom. Example: "The essence of truth is freedom" (Heidegger).

MYSTERY a Religion Allegedly insoluble problem defying scientific research and even rational discussion. **b Science** Unsolved problem. ↑**Scientism** admits that there are unsolved problems and even insoluble ones for lack of information or instruments, but denies that there are mysteries. The finding that a mathematical or scientific problem is unsolvable or insoluble, respectively, is a result of scientific research, whereas mysteries are supposed to be accepted without further ado.

MYSTICISM Belief in the instant union of the soul with the deity or some secular surrogate of it, such as nature. The resulting knowledge, though ineffable (incommunicable), would be superior to any other. **Syn** incomprehensible, untestable, weird. Mystics claim to have deep insights and to enjoy ecstasy, neither of which they can describe or discuss in rational terms. Mysticism has inspired (or disguised) some beautiful poetry and much impenetrable theology and pseudophilosophy. It is also standard ↑**New Age** fare.

MYTH A story or view known to be false, even if originally invented in good faith to account for something. Examples: the myths of the origin of the world and of morality, the immateriality of the mind, the superiority of certain races, and the universal benefits of either communist dictatorship or unfettered capitalism. Cosmology, psychology, and the social studies are the last refuges of mythology. Enemies of democracy, from Plato and Nietzsche to Mussolini and Hitler, have held that common men, the components of "the herd," need myths or "noble lies" to live by. Humanists promote the scientific, hence nonmythical, study of myths both old and new, to remove obstacles to research as well as to defend democracy.

NAIVE Unexamined, uncritical. Examples: naive set theory (which was shown to contain some paradoxes); naive ontology, which fills the world with fantastic beings, such as ideas in themselves; naive ↑**realism** (which takes sense data at their face value); and naive morals (which abides by received moral norms).

NAME A conventional linguistic label attached to an object and serving to identify it. Names are tags that facilitate identification. There are proper names, such as 'Aristotle'; class names, such as 'humankind'; and ↑**definite descriptions**, such as 'the president of the United States'. Naming may be analyzed as a function from a set of objects into a set of names. In the natural languages this function is a many-to-one relation between objects and nouns (since some nouns are polysemous). In an artificial language naming is usually a partial function, that is, a mapping from a subset of objects to a set of symbols. Indeed, not all the members of a continuum, such as the real line, can be named. So a paradox arises: An infinite totality can be named, as in the case of the real line ℝ, but nearly all of its members remain unnamed. (Incidentally, this is a fatal blow to ↑**nominalism**, according to which there are names but not concepts.) Names are conventional: there is no logical or physical necessity about any name-named relation. As Shakespeare noted, there is nothing in a name: What really matters is the nominatum. Because names are arbitrary tags, they have no logical status: they are neither predicates nor sets. Therefore it is mistaken to look for the meaning of names in general: Only a few proper names, such as Baker, Lemaître, and Schneider, used to mean something in the beginning.

NATIONALISM The ↑**ideology** according to which the nation should have precedence over everything else, even human rights, justice, and truth. **Ant** internationalism. The ontology, axiology, and moral philosophy of nationalism are ↑**holistic**. However, nationalism is not monolithic: it can be defensive or aggressive. And in each of these modes it can be territorial, biological (or ethnic), economic, political, or cultural—or a combination of two or more of these variants. ↑**Communitarianism**.

NATIVISM The hypothesis that all biological and psychological traits are inborn, and that experience can at best trigger, hone, or blunt them. In particular, according to nativism we cannot learn radically new concepts. Nativism flies in the face of the whole of genetics, developmental biology, and developmental psychology. ↑**Innate ideas**.

NATURAL / ARTIFICIAL Natural things, unlike artificial or made things, come into existence and change independently of humans. Humans themselves are partly natural and partly artificial, for they make themselves both biologically and socially. Hence the severe limitation of ↑**naturalism** in the narrow sense. ↑**Materialism** does not have this defect.

NATURAL KIND A collection that, far from being arbitrary, is defined by a property or a law. Examples: all the living beings constitute the class (natural kind) of organisms; all the entities composed of people bound by social relations constitute the class (natural kind) of social systems. Nominalists, conventionalists, and subjectivists (in particular phenomenalists) reject the very idea of a natural kind. Hence they cannot account for the periodic table, the transmutation of chemical elements, or biological speciation.

NATURAL LANGUAGE Any of the thousands of historically evolved languages used in daily life. Actually all these languages are just as artificial as the technical languages crafted by mathematicians, scientists, technologists, and other specialists. ↑**Ordinary language**.

NATURAL LAW DOCTRINE The view that morality and the law are natural rather than artificial. There are two main versions: secular and religious. The former view, held by Rousseau, is that man is born good, but is rendered evil by society. The religious variant is the view that divine will is embodied in the natural order of things, which man-made laws ought to match. But, given that all behavior norms are made, and thus subject to social constraints and historical change, the very concept of natural law is a contradiction in terms. Not surprisingly, sometimes the doctrine has been used to justify injustice, and at other times to fight it; sometimes to argue for the unity of humankind, and at other times to deny such unity in the name of race, class, or religion.

NATURAL SCIENCE / SOCIAL SCIENCE DICHOTOMY The idealist (in particular neo-Kantian, hermeneutic, and phenomenological) thesis that the social sciences have nothing in common with the natural ones. Falsified by the mere existence of such biosocial sciences as demography, geography, psychology, anthropology, and linguistics.

NATURAL SELECTION The process whereby the organisms of a given variety outnumber those of other varieties, due to their greater fertility and adaptedness, and thus prevail in the long run. Along with genic variation, natural selection is one of the two most important mechanisms of biological ↑**evolution**. The process is roughly this: Random genic variation → Accidental aptedness (aption) → Natural selection → Adaptation. Sudden and drastic environmental changes are likely to decimate or even wipe out a population of the best-adapted organisms. In the case of gregarious animals, in particular humans, natural selection intertwines with social selection on the basis of economic and political power.

NATURALISM The ontology centered on the thesis that the world consists exclusively of natural entities. By implication, the rejection of all claims about the reality of autonomous ideas and supernatural objects such as ghosts and deities. Naturalism coincides with ↑**materialism** concerning the objects studied by physics, chemistry, and biology. But it is too restrictive with regard to social life and technology, for the first is largely artifactual and the second totally artificial. Indeed, although human beings are animals, they happen to create artificial things, such as rules and utensils, which in turn condition their own lives. Materialism *lato sensu* includes such artifacts. Materialism also encompasses the conceptual artifacts, such as logic and mathematics, none of which can be accounted for in naturalist (e.g., psychological) terms.

NATURALISTIC FALLACY The reduction of axiological or moral predicates, such as "good," to natural ones such as "healthy," "welfare-enhancing," or "useful." **a Strong thesis** All of the value judgments, norms, and conventions can be deduced from factual statements, in particular formulas representing natural laws. This view is mistaken, because factual statements tell what is, not what ought to be. **b Weak thesis** Values and moral norms can be analyzed in the light of natural or social science. In principle, there is nothing fallacious about such an attempt to bring values and norms down to earth. Science-oriented value theorists and moral philosophers willingly perpetrate the naturalistic fallacy in its weak version. For example, compassion may be regarded as both a moral virtue and a natural disposition that can be either heightened or weakened by education, reflection, and social experience. ↑**Fact / value gap.**

NATURALIZATION The conversion of a humanistic or social discipline into a natural science. Examples: sociobiology and the inclusion of epistemology and linguistics in psychology or biology. These endeavors are doomed to fail. Sociobiology fails because there are irreducibly social concepts, such as those of social structure and justice. (By contrast, biosociology, or the study of the social channeling of biological needs, is a legitimate enterprise.) Epistemology cannot ignore the social context of learning and inquiry. But it must admit that cognition is a brain process and thus subject to biological constraints. And linguistics cannot dispense with its own irreducible concepts, such as those of grammar and meaning. But it must likewise recognize that speech is a neural process. In sum, while naturalization is not always possible, the building of biosocial sciences is often desirable. ↑**Biologism, evolutionary psychology.**

NATURE a The part of the world that exists independently of any observer, and that humans can improve or degrade, study or ignore, but neither create nor annihilate. **b Philosophy of, or *Naturphilosophie*** Philosophical speculation about nature without the benefit of natural science. Part of the Romantic reaction against the Enlightenment. Most of it is hilariously wrong, particularly the books of Schelling and Hegel on the subject. However, three *Naturphilosophen* did make splendid scientific contributions: Goethe, Oken, and Oersted. Contemporary examples: philosophical anthropology and philosophy of mind. In the recent German philosophical literature, *Naturphilosophie* = Philosophy of natural science.

NATURE / CULTURE In a secular worldview, culture is made, whereas nature is given. However, the distinction between the two should not be exaggerated into a separation, let alone opposition, because work alters nature, and the producers and consumers of cultural products are living beings and thus natural as well as artificial. A strict nature / culture ↑**dichotomy** is typical of all idealist philosophies, which place the spirit or mind above nature instead of in the brain, and accordingly oppose the natural sciences to the cultural ones. ↑**Hermeneutics**, ↑**natural science / cultural science dichotomy**, ↑*Verstehen*.

NATURE / NURTURE Inherited / learned. A special case of the empiricism / rationalism and the environmentalism / geneticism controversies. A wrong ↑**dichotomy**, for we inherit dispositions that can be actualized only through experience. In general, potentialities can be actualized only in suitable environments. And some items cannot be learned if the pertinent brain subsystems are missing or defective. Thus we are all children of our parents and our societies. In general, animal development results from a combination of inherited capabilities, environmental stimuli, and the animal's actions. Something similar holds for evolution, ignored by both nativists and environmentalists. ↑**Nativism**.

NATURE, STATE OF The state of primitive humankind, when everyone followed only their instincts, interests, and desires, unconstrained by any social norms. Fiction imagined by theologians and philosophers who ignore that humans are essentially social and partly self-made, hence partly artificial. Though espoused by such modern thinkers as Hobbes, Rousseau, and Rawls, the myth has its roots in the Greek legend of the Golden Age, and the biblical story of the Fall of Adam and Eve. Modern anthropology and palaeobiology have discredited it.

NAVEL CONTEMPLATION Aprioristic speculation about the world. An example is Edmund Husserl's subjectivist method for exploring the world. It consists in "bracketing" it out, that is, in suspending the belief in its autonomous existence, and concentrating instead on the flow of one's own consciousness or primordial intuitions. Predictably, this method has not produced a single finding in any branch of learning. Still, Husserl and his followers have characterized phenomenology as rigorous philosophy and as the infallible science of essences. ↑**Apriorism**, ↑**conceit, philosopher's**, ↑**omphalism**.

NECESSITY a Logic A proposition is *necessarily true* if it is a tautology or if it follows validly from true premises. A proposition q is a *necessary condition* for a proposition p if $p \Rightarrow q$. Example: Meaningfulness is necessary for truth, not the other way round. A proposition p is *sufficient* for a proposition q if $p \Rightarrow q$. Example: Thinking is sufficient for being alive. A proposition p is both *necessary and sufficient* for a proposition q if $p \Leftrightarrow q$. Example: For a construct to qualify as exact it is necessary and sufficient that it has a precise logical or mathematical form. **b Ontology** A state of a thing or an event is *nomically necessary* (as opposed to ↑**contingent** or ↑**accidental**) if it fits causal laws and is consistent with the constraints of the situation. For example, heat is necessary for water to boil. This concept of nomic necessity is unrelated to that of logical necessity. The claim that ↑**modal logic** elucidates both the logical and the ontological concepts of necessity is just as extravagant as the claim that ring theory holds for wedding rings as well as for algebraic ones.

NECROPHILIA, PHILOSOPHICAL Love of dead philosophical subjects or past philosophers whose work led to dead ends.

NEGATION A basic logical connective. The negation ¬ p of a proposition p is the proposition ¬ p that denies, negates, or contradicts p. If p is true, then ¬ p is false and conversely. But if p is only half-true, then ¬p is true. (For example, the negation of "Aristotle was one meter tall" is true.) The negation of a unary predicate F is definable thus: ¬$F =_{df} \forall x¬ \ Fx$. Negation is at the very center of argumentation. Hence the negation-less or positive logical calculi are useless to analyze arguments. They were originally proposed on the assumption that logic must mirror the world, which in turn is made up of "positive" facts. Indeed, there are no negative facts: there are only propositions that deny the occurrence of facts, the truth of other propositions, and so on. In short, negation has no ontic counterpart. The same holds for all the other ↑**connectives** except for conjunction.

NEGATIVISM Any doctrine circumscribed to denying that certain concepts can be defined, certain hypotheses or inferences can be made, or certain actions can or ought to be performed. Negativism can be logical, semantical, epistemological, ethical, political, etc. *Logical* negativism = ↑**Irrationalism**. Example of *semantic* negativism: the view that the concepts of meaning, synonymy, and truth are either dispensable or cannot be properly defined. Example of *epistemological* negativism: radical ↑**skepticism**. Example of *ethical* negativism: Negative utilitarianism, or the view that the only sensible moral norm is "Do no harm." *Social* negativism = Anarchism, i.e., the doctrine that all power is bad, so that the state should be abolished.

NEOPHILIA Love of novelty, rejection of unnecessary or harmful repetition. A characteristic of Greek classical antiquity, the Renaissance, and modernity. Particularly intense among scientists and technologists of all epochs. **Ant** ↑**neophobia**. Neophilia can be critical or fanatical. The critical neophile assesses the merits of a novelty before embracing it. The fanatical neophile loves novelty for its own sake, just as the neophobe rejects all newness except when it consists in the restoration of an obsolete tradition.

NEOPHOBIA Fear or hatred of novelty. Typical of religious fundamentalism and school philosophies. **Syn** conservativism, **ant** ↑**neophilia**.

NEO-X A doctrine inspired by X. Examples: neo-Pythagoreanism, neo-Platonism, neo-Thomism, neo-Kantianism, neo-Hegelianism, neo-Marxism, neopositivism, neopragmatism. A feature of all neo-isms is that *every* one of them is constituted by rival schools claiming to be the rightful heir to the original doctrine. Some of these rival claims are plausible because of ambiguities in the original texts, and because the only criterion of correctness being used is faithfulness to those texts—rather than, say, compatibility with the science of the day. Every neo-ism has been an attempt to overcome some of the difficulties that beset the original ism without, however, correcting its main flaws—for if it did, it would not have qualified as legitimate heir. This is why all neo-isms have failed just as dismally as all attempts at full political restoration. Even if a philosophical doctrine was the best of its time, it cannot remain correct under greatly changed circumstances.

NEUTRAL MONISM The thesis that mind and matter are different aspects or manifestations of a single "neutral" substance that cannot be known. **Syn** double-aspect thesis. Since by hypothesis the neutral substance is unknowable, the thesis can be neither expanded into a theory nor put to the empirical test. It is thus barren, like most attempted compromises between opposites. ↑**Mind-body problem**.

NEW AGE Old hat. A multibillion-dollar industry that markets superstitions, pseudosciences, and fetishes of all kinds. Part of the commercial culture.

NIHIL EST IN INTELLECTU QUOD PRIUS NON FUERIT IN SENSU There is nothing in the intellect that was not earlier in sensation. The principle of ↑**sensationism**. Counterexamples: the concepts of zero, logical consequence, time, causal relation, knowledge, evolution, prehistory, and deity.

NIHILISM ↑**Negativism**. *Ontological*: Nothing real exists. *Epistemological*: Nothing is knowable. *Semantic*: matters of meaning are at best intractable, at worst meaningless. *Axiological*: Nothing is valuable. *Ethical*: There are no mandatory moral norms. **Syn** ↑**amoralism**. *Praxiological*: Nothing is worth doing.

NOMIC Falling under a ↑**law** or pattern. **Syn** lawful.

NOMINALISM a Ontological The view that there are only ↑**individuals**, that these are either concrete things or signs of such (e.g., words), and that none are conceptual. **Syn** vulgar ↑**materialism**. However, the factual sciences and technologies cannot dispense with such items as molecules, organisms, and social systems, none of which is a collection of individuals. Only the simplest of all things, such as electrons and photons, are thought to be genuine (indivisible) individuals. Nor can science and technology dispense with properties and relations, which the nominalist either avoids or construes as collections of individuals, pairs, etc. (I.e., he confuses ↑**properties** with the corresponding ↑**attributes**, and the latter in turn with their ↑**extensions**. This is mistaken because the property-scope relation is one-to-many, not one-to-one. E.g., all mammals are hairy and conversely, and yet these properties are different.) Moreover, scientists and technologists distinguish ↑**essential** from accidental (or incidental) properties—such as, e.g., the chemical composition of detergents by contrast to their color. **b Semantical** The doctrine that there are no concepts and their kin (such as hypotheses and theories) but only names of entities. There are at least two objections against this view. First, concrete things have no conceptual properties, and concepts do not have any physical, biological, or social properties. Second, ↑**names** cannot replace ↑**concepts**, because (a) one and the same concept is likely to be named differently in different languages; and (b) most objects must remain nameless, if only because the set of names is denumerable, whereas the real numbers and the points in spacetime constitute nondenumerable sets. ↑**Name**. **c Methodological** The methodological prescription that one should refrain from asking questions of the form "What is x?" much less "What is the essence of x?" Instead, one should ask questions of the form "How does x behave?" and in particular "What are the regularities in x's behavior (i.e., x's laws)?" **Ant** ↑**essentialism**. Actually methodological nominalism is the same as ↑**descriptionism**, which in turn is a component of ↑**positivism**.

NOMINATUM The object named, as in "the nominata of numerals are numbers."

NOMOETHICS The branch of ethics that investigates the moral problems raised by the law. Sample of problematics: the relations between human rights and legal rights; the utilitarian approach to criminal law; the limits of contractualism; and the status of such maxims as "The rights of every individual are limited by the rights of others," "Every right implies some duty," and "The moral person has the duty to oppose unjust laws." ↑**Law, philosophy of.**

NOMOLOGICAL Having to do with ↑**laws**, as in "nomological statement." **Syn** lawlike.

NOMOTHETIC / IDIOGRAPHIC ↑**Idiographic / nomothetic.**

NON SEQUITUR A statement that does not follow logically from the premises. Examples: "Everything has a beginning; hence the universe must have been created"; "Science does not explain everything; hence there may well be miracles"; "Computers do many things minds do; hence they have minds."

NONDENOTING A term or concept that has no real referent, such as "unicorn." However, it is confusing to regard the predicate "is a unicorn" as nondenoting. It is better to say that it refers to a mythical animal, so that its ↑**extension** (but not its ↑**reference** class) is empty. If "unicorn" were nondenoting, it would be impossible to describe and paint unicorns.

NONSENSE Expression deprived of ↑**sense** in the language in question. Example: "the representation of my primal presence into a merely presentified primal presence" (Husserl). Nonsense is not to be confused with falsity. Whereas the former is useless or worse, the latter can be discussed and perhaps turned into its opposite, because it has a sense.

NORM a Praxiology. ↑**Rule.** At least four kinds of norm are usually distinguished: technical norms, social customs, legal norms, and moral rules. The emergence, maintenance, and rejection mechanisms of social norms (rules capable of being enforced through reward or punishment) are studied by social science. Practical philosophy is interested in the nature and content of norms, as well as in their interrelations and their relations (or lack of thereof) with scientific laws. ↑**Ethics,** ↑**nomoethics.** **b Statistics** Mode or median: the most frequent value in the distribution of a property.

NORMATIVE OR PRESCRIPTIVE Concerning norms, as in "logic, grammar, and the law are normative rather than descriptive."

NOTATION Representation of constructs by symbols. Notations are linguistic conventions. But, like any convention, a notation may be nimble or cumbersome, suggestive or not, and generalizable or not. For example, the symbol 'aRb', short for 'a is R-related to b', cannot be generalized to an n-adic relation, whereas 'Rab' can, namely thus: $Rab \ldots n$. Another example is the Polish notation for logic, which is convenient to type simple sentences, as is the case with *CCprCrs,* which in the standard mathematical notation reads: $(p \Rightarrow q) \Rightarrow (r \Rightarrow s)$. For complex formulas this notation becomes impossibly cumbersome. Likewise, Newton's dots over function signs become unmanageable for derivatives of order higher than two, and cannot be generalized to derivatives of an arbitrary order. Hence they do not even allow one to write such elementary laws as $D^m D^n = D^{m+n}$ for the differential operator D. A cumbersome notation can slow down or even block progress, as was the case with the Roman numerals in antiquity. Which is one more reminder that conventions need not be arbitrary, much less silly.

NOTHINGNESS Nonexistence. There are several concepts of nonexistence. **a Logic** Nothingness is construed as the prefix "not-something," or $\neg \exists Fx$, which amounts to "all-not," or $\forall \neg Fx$. For example, "Nothing is ghostly" is symbolized as either "$\neg(\exists x)Gx$" or "$\forall x \neg Gx$." **b Mathematics** There are several nothingness concepts in addition to "not-something," among them the empty set, the null element of an algebra, and the number ↑**zero. c Ontology** The null individual is the individual whose concatenation (juxtaposition, physical addition) with any other individual equals the latter. This concept, which mirrors no existent, is needed to state formally the philosophical conservation principle, that nothing comes out of nothing or goes into nothingness. The need for even one such concept of nothingness is an embarrassment for both naive realism and empiricism, because no such concept has a counterpart in reality. Yet we need such concepts in order to account for reality, even in everyday-life terms. For example, of an empty box we say that it contains nothing; and of someone who is idle we say that he does nothing. Hegel made much of nothingness, stating that becoming is the synthesis of being and nothingness—a proposition he did not bother to clarify. Existentialism goes even further, in reifying nothingness. That is, it treats nothingness as an entity, and moreover as a central one. (Recall Heidegger's hilarious "*Das Nichts nichtet.*") Obviously, the no-thing is not a thing. Hence it cannot be attributed any properties.

NOUMENON ↑**Thing in itself**, as it exists independently of the knower.The dual of ↑**phenomenon**, or thing as it appears to a knower. Whereas realists assert the possibility of knowing noumena, empiricists (like Hume) and subjectivists (like Kant) deny it.

NOVELTY Whatever did not exist earlier. Novelty can be absolute or relative: the former if it occurs for the first time in the history of the universe, and the latter if it occurs for the first time in a particular thing. Since the history of the cosmos is unknown in detail, absolute novelty cannot be ascertained. Even the Big Bang, if it did occur, may have occurred more than once at different places in the universe. Novelty can also be *quantitative, qualitative,* or both. For example, expansion and contraction are quantitative; birth and death are qualitative; and development and speciation are both qualitative and quantitative. An alternative partition of novelties is into numerical, combinatorial, and radical. *Numerical* novelty is the repetition or multiplication of similar objects, as in the mass production of a good. *Combinatorial* novelty comes from the combination of preexisting objects, as in the formation of molecules out of atoms, sentences out of words, and melodies out of notes. *Radical* novelty is the emergence of things that keep no traces of their precursors, such as light emitted by atoms, social inventions, and infinity. ↑**Emergence,** ↑**neophilia,** ↑**neophobia.**

NOW Time instant referred to a certain ↑**reference frame** and chosen arbitrarily to coincide with some particular event, such as the beginning of an observation. The partner of ↑**here**. There are as many 'nows' as mutually inequivalent reference frames. When the chosen frame is a subject, 'now' is said to be an ↑**egocentric particular**.

NULL HYPOTHESIS The hypothesis that two given variables are unrelated. The first conjecture to be put to the test in the early stages of an empirical investigation in the less-advanced sciences. The falsification of the null hypothesis calls for guessing some positive hypothesis concerning the relation between the given variables. Only null hypotheses, the most primitive of all, fall under ↑**falsificationism**. ↑**Error c**.

NULL THING ↑**Nothingness**.

OBJECT Whatever can exist, be thought about, talked about, or acted upon. The most basic, abstract, and general of all philosophical concepts, hence undefinable. The class of all objects is thus the maximal kind. Objects can be individuals or collections, concrete (material) or abstract (ideal), natural or artificial. For instance, societies are concrete objects, whereas numbers are abstract ones; and cells are natural objects, whereas words are artificial. Alexius Meinong and a few others have tried to build a single theory of objects of all kinds, concrete and conceptual, possible and impossible. This project failed because concrete objects possess properties (such as energy) that no conceptual objects have, whereas the latter have properties (such as logical form) that no material object can possess. Hence the most radical division of the class of objects is into material (or concrete) and conceptual (or formal).

OBJECT LANGUAGE / METALANGUAGE A language used to refer to nonlinguistic items is called an *object* language. By contrast, a ↑**metalanguage** is a language used to refer to expressions in an object language. The object-meta distinction is relative. Thus any reference to a metalinguistic expression is meta-metalinguistic. The deconstructionists, who hold that every word refers only to other words, ignore—inter alia—the distinction in question.

OBJECTIFICATION a Epistemology To render a subjective event objective via behavioral or physiological ↑**indicators**. **b Ethics** To regard or use people as if they were inanimate objects, that is, disregarding their feelings, interests, and rights.

OBJECTIVE Referring exclusively to items in the external world. For example, "Criminality is on the decline" is an objective statement, though perhaps not a true one with reference to some places and times. By contrast, "I empathize with petty thieves" is not objective, although it may be true for some instances of "I." Science, technology, and the humanities are expected to be objective, whereas art can be subjective. By contrast, mathematics is neither objective nor subjective, for it describes neither the real world nor subjective experiences. This shows that the objective / subjective pair does not coincide with the material / conceptual pair.

OBJECTIVE MIND The name Wilhelm Dilthey gave to culture in and by itself, that is, abstracted from the producers and consumers of cultural objects. **Syn** ↑**world 3**.

OBLIGATION, PERMISSION, PROHIBITION Key praxiological, ethical, and legal concepts. The relations among them are context-dependent. For instance, under political democracy the list of permissions is longer than that of obligations and prohibitions; by contrast, in a totalitarian regime the obligations and prohibitions are more numerous than the permissions. In a society inspired by ↑agathonism, the obligations and permissions would be equally numerous, and few prohibitions would be required because people would be encouraged to act according to the maxim "Enjoy life and help live." ↑Deontic logic.

OBSCURANTIST Any attitude, school, or movement that attacks both the rational and the empirical approaches and promotes the blind adoption of dogmas instead. Whereas some obscurantists, such as Husserl and Heidegger, wrote in cypher, others, such as Nietzsche and Mussolini, wrote clearly. The ↑Enlightenment fought religious obscurantism both directly, by criticizing it, and indirectly, by promoting science and science-oriented philosophy. Present-day humanists pride themselves on being the successors of the Enlightenment. By contrast, the ↑postmoderns belong to the latest wave of ↑Counter-Enlightenment. They are obscurantists because of their combination of ↑constructivism and ↑relativism, a variety of absolute ↑skepticism. However, obscurantism is found even among analytic philosophers. Examples: R. Carnap's principle of tolerance (to any ontology as long as it is logically well formed); W. v. O. Quine's thesis of the inscrutability of reference; N. Goodman's world making; and P. Winch's view that the social studies cannot be scientific.

OBSCURE An idea or symbol is obscure if it is not ↑clear. Examples: ↑*Dasein*, ↑intentionality, ↑intuition, noetic, ↑supervenience, ↑unity of opposites,↑*Verstehen*, ↑world 3, ↑*Zeitgeist*.

OBSERVATION Deliberate perception, as in listening and looking by contrast to hearing and seeing respectively. Not to be confused with experiment, which is planned observation of the effects of the knower's active intervention in the situation concerned. ↑Experiment.

OBVIOUSLY A word preceding an unjustified statement. A rhetorical device intended to persuade or forestall criticism.

OCCULT Imperceptible or hidden. There are two kinds of occult objects: inscrutable in principle, and indirectly scrutable by scientific means. Examples of the former: the occult qualities of matter postulated by the alchemists and the schoolmen; the life force of the vitalists; Adam Smith's invisible hand; the general equilibrium of neoclassical economists; and God's designs. Examples of scrutable items that, though occult to ordinary experience, are accessible to the scientific method: atomic nuclei, proteins, biological evolution, mental processes, and social forces.

OCKHAM'S RAZOR Ockham's principle "Entities are not to be multiplied without necessity." Also called *principle of parsimony*. This principle is reasonable, but it is often misinterpreted as demanding ↑simplicity at all costs and, in particular, at the cost of concepts and hypotheses referring to items far removed from experience. ↑Simplism.

The principle is also interpreted, this time correctly, as favoring the simpler of two hypotheses that account for the same data. This rule is correct only if neither of the rival hypotheses enjoys the support of additional hypotheses. Otherwise further desiderata, such as ↑**depth** and ↑**explanatory power**, must be taken into account.

OMNE QUOD MOVETUR AB ALIO MOVETUR Whatever moves is moved by another. Principle of ↑**externalism**, central to the commonsensical and Aristotelian cosmologies as well as to behaviorism. Falsified by inertia, self-assembly, and spontaneity.

OMNIS DETERMINATIO EST NEGATIO Every determination is a negation. This somewhat cryptic dictum of Spinoza's may be exactified as follows: Let x denote an arbitrary object possessing the property P, i.e., assume that Px. What Spinoza seems to have stated is that if Px is the case, then x fails to have some other properties. (For example, a poor person cannot afford to go on a Caribbean cruise.) Calling W the totality of concrete entities, and $\mathbb{P}$ the totality of (unary) properties, we get the transparent ontological principle: $\forall x\, \forall P\,[x \in W\ \&\ P \in \mathbb{P} \Rightarrow \exists Q\,(Q \in \mathbb{P}\ \&\ \neg Qx)]$. A related principle is this: *Nothing possesses every property.* I.e., $\neg \exists x\, \forall P\,(P \in \mathbb{P} \Rightarrow Px)$, which may be rewritten as $\forall x\, \exists P(P \in \mathbb{P}\ \&\ \neg Px)$. An equivalent but at first sight paradoxical way of saying the same thing is this: The ↑**null thing** has all the properties. This statement may even serve to define the null thing if the concept of ↑**property** is in hand.

OMNISCIENCE Complete and perfect knowledge of everything. A theological fiction predicated of certain deities.

OMPHALISM The family of schools of thought that practice ↑**navel contemplation** as the method for getting to know the world. **Syn** ↑**apriorism**.

ONLINE PHILOSOPHY A philosophy that can participate in an extraphilosophical activity, such as management or policymaking, rather than being extraneous to it. Such interference can be constructive or destructive: it can advance research or block it in various ways, from raising interesting new problems and suggesting new approaches to banning lines of inquiry that question dogmas or conventions. For example, materialism encourages cognitive neuroscience, whereas idealism ridicules it; and while scientific realism favors the scientific study of social facts, hermeneutics bans it.

ONTIC Belonging in or concerning the real world, as in "objective patterns are the ontic counterparts of law statements." Not to be confused with 'ontological': 'ontic' stands to 'ontological' as 'social' to 'sociological.'

ONTOLOGY The sober secular version of ↑**metaphysics**. The branch of philosophy that studies the most pervasive features of reality, such as real existence, change, time, causation, chance, life, mind, and society. Ontology does not study constructs, i.e., ideas in themselves. These are studied by the formal sciences and epistemology. Hence the expression 'ontology of mathematics' makes sense only in the context of objective idealism (such as Pythagoras's and Plato's). By contrast, the question 'What is the ontological status of mathematical objects?' is meaningful in all contexts. But in a fiction-ist philosophy of mathematics it has a simple answer: None. ↑**Mathematics, philosophy of.** Ontology can be split into general and special (or regional). *General* ontology studies all existents, whereas each *special* ontology studies one genus of thing or process—physical, chemical, biological, social, etc. Thus, whereas general ontology studies the concepts of space, time, and event, the ontology of the social investigates such general sociological concepts as those of social system, social structure, and social change. Whether general or special, ontology can be cultivated in either of two manners: speculative or scientific. The ontologies of Leibniz, Wolff, Schelling, Hegel, Bolzano, Lotze, Engels, Mach, W. James, H. Bergson, A. N. Whitehead, S. Alexander, L. Wittgenstein, M. Heidegger, R. Carnap, and N. Goodman are typically speculative and remote from science. So is the contemporary ↑**possible worlds** metaphysics. Warning: the expression 'the ontology of a theory' is sometimes misleadingly employed to designate the ↑**reference** class or ↑**universe of discourse** of a theory. The expression is misleading because ontologies are theories, not classes.

ONUS PROBANDI ↑Burden of proof.

OPEN MIND Readiness to learn and discuss new items and revise beliefs. **Ant** ↑**dogmatism**. Not to be mistaken for a blank mind. An open mind is critical: it is equipped with filters that keep garbage out. ↑**Skepticism**, moderate.

OPERATION Artificial process, conceptual or material, whereby an object is transformed into another. Everyday life examples: cooking, nursing, trading. Mathematical examples: $\neg$, $+$, $\partial/\partial x$. Scientific examples: diluting, heating, observing, measuring, experimenting, computing. Technological examples: drilling, joining, managing, litigating.

OPERATIONAL DEFINITION The characterization of a concept through the operations performed to check it. Example: the characterization of "weight" as that which scales measure, or of "intelligence" as that which IQ tests measure. Since definitions are purely conceptual, there are no operational definitions. On the other hand, there are ↑**indicator hypotheses**, such as "Heart-beat is an indicator of the state of health," and "The sum of the rates of inflation and unemployment is a misery indicator."

OPERATIONALIZATION OF THEORIES The enrichment of scientific or technological theories with ↑**indicator hypotheses**, so as to render them testable. For example, macroeconomic models can be checked only by adding to them such global indicators of economic activity as GDP and volume of retail sales.

OPERATIONISM The pragmatist philosophy of science that prescribes that every construct be introduced via some laboratory procedure. For example, the mass concept is said to be introduced via mass measurement techniques. If this were so, there would be as many mass concepts as mass measurement techniques—which is false. In fact, there are only a few mass concepts, such as those occurring in classical and relativistic mechanics. And these are tacitly defined by the equations where they occur, not by reference to measurement techniques. For example, an analysis of the classical concept of mass shows it to be a function from ordered couples <body, mass unit> to positive real numbers: ↑**magnitude**. Explicit reference to a test procedure t is involved only in stating the measured value of the mass of a body b, as in $\mu(b,u,\ t) = m \pm \sigma$, where u is a mass unit and σ is the standard deviation around the average value m. Thus the measured (or empirical) mass value function μ differs from the theoretical mass value function M. Moreover, m would be meaningless without M, since the purpose of mass measurements is to determine the values of the (theoretical, hence universal) mass function for particular bodies. Because of its attempt to subject theory to measurement technique, operationism has had a crippling effect on the natural sciences in banning high-level constructs that could not possibly be linked to laboratory operations. But for a while, during the 1930s and 1940s, it had a beneficial effect on social studies in discrediting wild speculation. Nowadays operationism survives only in the first few pages of some science textbooks.

OPINION Belief that has not been checked for either truth or efficiency.

OPPORTUNITY Favorable circumstance unlikely to be repeated. Biological ↑**evolution** and human ↑**history** are largely sequences of opportunities seized and opportunities missed.

OPPOSITION a Logic Negation. **b Ontology** Conflict. A key concept in ↑**dialectics**, but a fuzzy one since it is not even clear what kind of factual items can have opposites: things, properties, events? For example, do neutrons and photons have opposites? what is the opposite of temperature? and what is the opposite of a collision? Definition: The opposite (or inverse) of a process in a system is the process that, when succeeding the original process, restores the initial state of the system. Examples: expansion and contraction, absorption and emission, combination and dissociation, concentration and diffusion, growth and decline. Thesis: Only processes can have opposites, and only some of them can actually happen in the real world, namely, the reversible ones.

OPTIMAL The best or most desirable. If optima are identified with either maxima or minima, they are seldom affordable. The reason is that, since every thing is characterized by several features, some of which are interdependent, maximizing one of them is bound to decrease or even minimize others. Therefore, the choice of suboptimal goals is usually advisable. This suggests that optimization theories that equate optimality with maximality or minimality serve at best as rough guides, at worst as recipes for disaster. To avoid such risks the ↑**sectoral approach** should be replaced by a ↑**systemic** one.　　　　　　　　　　　　　　　．

OPTIMISM Philosophical optimism (like pessimism) is a doctrine, and as such must be distinguished from its psychological (temperamental) counterpart. It comes in two strengths: radical and moderate. *Radical* or naive philosophical optimism: Ours is the best of all possible worlds (Leibniz and Wolff, criticized by Voltaire in his *Candide ou de l'optimisme*). *Moderate* optimism or ↑**meliorism** boils down to the following hypotheses: (1) logico-semantical: all ideas can be elucidated, perhaps to the point of formalization, as well as made to constitute internally consistent bodies; (2) epistemological: most epistemic problems can be solved through research; (3) ontological: on the whole, the world is not a bad place; (4) practical: although human beings are half-good and half-bad, evil can be checked through knowledge, discipline, and cooperation; on balance and in the long run, the good and the right can be made to prevail; (5) progress of all kinds is feasible but not necessary: the so-called law of progress is an illusion. The **Enlightenment** thinkers were optimists, whereas the ↑**Counter-Enlightenment** ones were pessimists.

OR Ordinary-language designation of the logical ↑**disjunction**.

ORDER a Mathematics The members of a set can be ordered in different ways. The simplest and strongest order is the *strict* (or serial) ordering, such as that of the points in a straight line: it is induced by an asymmetric and transitive relation. A weaker ordering, and therefore a far more common one, is that of *partial* order: it is brought about by a reflexive, antisymmetric, and transitive relation such as "less than or equal to" and "descends from." Example: a philogeny. Formal definition: $<S, \geq>$ is a *partially ordered set* if, for all x, y and z in S, $x \geq x$, $(x \geq y)$ & $(y \geq x) \Rightarrow (x = y)$, and $(x \geq y)$ & $(y \geq z) \Rightarrow (x \geq z)$. **b Science and ontology** Patterned, as opposed to irregular. **c Social science** The social order prevailing in a society is the power structure of the society, that is, the set of power relations in it. Examples: feudalism, theocracy, authoritarian capitalism (fascism), democratic capitalism, democratic socialism, authoritarian socialism (communism). **Ant** ↑**anarchy**.

ORDERED *N*-TUPLE Finite list of items. An ordered pair is usually defined thus: $<a,b>$ $=_{df} \{\{a\}, \{a, b\}\}$. Hence $<a,b> \neq <b,a>$ unless $a = b$. Ordered n-tuple: $<a, b, \ldots, n>$ $=_{df} <<a, b, \ldots, n\text{-}1>, n>$. A useful tool in ↑**exact philosophy**, particularly to define many-featured items, such as the concepts of ↑**meaning** and ↑**science**.

ORDINARY Customary, familiar, nontechnical, as in '↑**ordinary knowledge**', '↑**ordinary language**', and '↑**ordinary-language philosophy**'. Nonexamples: scientific knowledge and the scientific languages.

ORDINARY KNOWLEDGE The body of knowledge used in daily life. In advanced societies it is being constantly updated with scientific and technological findings. However, it is insufficient in mathematics, science, and technology.

ORDINARY LANGUAGE Any of the "natural" languages used to think or communicate about daily-life matters. These languages are insufficient to do mathematics, science, technology, and the humanities, all of which craft their own artificial languages. This is one of the reasons that the popularization of those research fields is hard or impossible. However, ordinary language evolves along the incorporation of some of the findings in those fields into ordinary knowledge. Still, ordinary language abounds with fossils that occasionally distort scientific language, particularly in the less advanced sciences. Example from psychology: "this brain system is the basis (or substrate) of that mental function"; from social science: "the meaning of that action is such and such."

ORDINARY-LANGUAGE PHILOSOPHY The family of philosophies according to which the resources of a "natural" language, such as English, suffice to state anything, as well as to elucidate any configuration of symbols. This family is split into two mutually opposed genera: ↑**analytic philosophy**, that seeks clarity even at the price of depth, and ↑**hermeneutics**, that avoids it. The mere existence of artificial languages falsifies the central thesis of ordinary-language philosophy. ↑**Mathematics**.

ORGANICISM a Biology The thesis that ↑**life** is an organismic process, and that the focus of biology should be the organism rather than either the biomolecule or the biopopulation. A middle ground between ↑**mechanism** and ↑**vitalism**. **b Social studies** The view that society is an ↑**organism**. **c Ontology** The doctrine that every thing, including the universe, is an ↑**organism**. A part of some magical worldviews. A variant of ↑**holism** and a component of some reactionary ideologies, such as Nazism.

ORGANISM Living being. ↑**Life**.

ORGANIZATION ↑**Structure**, ↑order, architecture. Two wholes or ↑**systems** with the same components may be organized (structured) differently. Examples: isomers, nucleotides in a gene, words in a sentence, government cabinets.

ORIGIN Coming into being, beginning, absolute emergence. Some problems concerning the origin of things or ideas are at the same time scientific and philosophical. Examples: origin of the universe, life, species, mind, knowledge, language, religion, rationality, morals, philosophy, the state.

ORIGINAL Radically new, hence unknown before. The whole point of research is to come up with original findings. The point of erudition is to surround originality with a forbidding crust of unimportant comment. The point of censorship is to prevent the diffusion of original findings. In philosophy censorship is achieved most effectively by ignoring mavericks and exalting colleagues who focus on ↑**miniproblems** or ↑**pseudoproblems**.

ORTHODOXY Strict conformity to a belief system, whether ordinary, religious, political, scientific, or philosophical, usually upheld by some power group. **Syn** ↑**dogma**, received opinion. **Ant** heterodoxy. At first sight, orthodoxy is intellectually comfortable, because it does not require original thinking. On second thought it is not, because no head of school has been consistent throughout his life, unless he stopped thinking at an early age. Hence, the orthodox follower is forced either to overlook the inconsistencies of his hero or to invent contorted justifications for them—unless he chooses to venerate only a part of the master's work. Of all the orthodoxies, radical (or absolute) ↑**skepticism** is the hardest to maintain, since the authentic skeptic is expected to question all authority, even his master's. Indeed, the expresion 'orthodox skepticism' is as much of an ↑**oxymoron** as 'skeptical dogmatism'.

OSTENSIVE Accessible to the senses, so that it can be pointed to. An *ostensive definition* is a purported definition of the form "That, which you see (or hear) over there, is an X." Ostensive "definitions" are useful in the learning process. But they are not ↑**definitions** proper, for these are purely conceptual operations. To give an ostensive "definition" is only to name or point out for didactic purposes.

OUBLIETTE The last resting place of most philosophical ideas.

OXYMORON Juxtaposition of mutually incompatible predicates. Examples: Christian science, concrete universal (Hegel), democratic centralism (Stalin), orthodox skepticism, paraconsistent logic, scientific creationism, selfish morals, true fact.

PANLOGISM The doctrine that the world and the rational mind are one. Upheld by Pythagoras, the Stoics, Proclus, Hegel, and a few other objective idealists. Falsified by the very existence of pure logic and mathematics, neither of which assumes anything about the real world.

PANPSYCHISM The doctrine that everything is mental or has the ability to undergo mental processes of some kind and to some degree. A component of most primitive worldviews. **Syn ↑animism.** Falsified by the finding that only highly evolved animals, in particular vertebrates, have mental experiences. **↑Mind.**

PANTA RHEI Everything flows (Heraclitus). The distinctive principle of all dynamicist (or processualist) ontologies. **↑Processualism.**

PANTHEISM The doctrine of the identity of world and deity. Upheld by Xenophanes, David de Dinant, some German mystics, Spinoza, Toland, and perhaps Schelling and Hegel as well. Condemned by the churches because it sacralizes man and makes nonsense of evil, hence of the battle against it.

PARACONSISTENT LOGIC A calculus that allows for **↑contradiction.** Ontological rationale: Since the world is allegedly "contradictory" (i.e., contains mutually opposed forces and processes), any true account of it must contain logical contradictions. This views boils down to Hegelian wordplays on the words 'contradiction' and 'logic'. Actually, any "logic" condoning contradictions is a contradiction in terms: a conceptual monster and therefore a betrayal of reason. There is only one rational thing to do in the face of contradiction: to remove at least one of the mutually contradictory propositions.

PARADIGM A polysemous term designating "perspective," "paragon," "exemplar," "model to be imitated," "standard approach," "theoretical orientation," "thought style," and more. Example: until the birth of field physics and evolutionary biology, mechanics was held to be the paradigm for all sciences. Nowadays every science has several paradigms. Definition: A *paradigm* $\mathcal{P}$ is a body B of antecedent or background knowledge together with a set H of substantive hypotheses, a **↑problematics** P, an aim A, and a **↑methodics** M. In short, $\mathcal{P} = < B, H, P, A, M >$. A generalization of the concept of an **↑approach.**

PARADIGM SHIFT Radical change in the specific hypotheses, the problematics, or the methodics that constitute a given **↑paradigm.** Examples: Platonism $\rightarrow$ Aristotelianism,

Aristotelianism → Thomism, Kantian ethics → utilitarianism, classical economics → neoclassical economics, creationism → evolutionism, modernity → postmodernity. Whereas rationalists demand that good reasons be given to justify a paradigm shift, irrationalists claim that such a change is just as nonrational as a religious conversion or a fashion change.

PARADOX Contradiction or counterintuitive assumption or finding. The paradoxes of the first kind fall into either of two classes: logical and semantical. The former were found in logic and set theory in the early 1900s, and their study stimulated important advances, such as type theory and axiomatic set theory, that lie beyond the scope of the present work. Some of the semantic paradoxes have been known and investigated for centuries. The most famous of them is the ↑**Liar Paradox**, which can be handled with the help of the language-metalanguage distinction. As for the paradoxes of the second kind—the counterintuitive results—quantum physics is rife with them. Suffice it to recall the EPR and↑**Schrödinger's cat** thought experiments. The first has been solved, but the second is still grist for the mills of academic industry. ↑**Inductive logic**, too, is marred by paradox: ↑**raven's paradox,** ↑**grue paradox.**

PARALLELISM, PSYCHOPHYSICAL Leibniz's doctrine that the mental and brain processes are parallel, that is, synchronous but not interacting. ↑**Mind-body problem**. Parallelism is empirically unfalsifiable, since every time we experience a mental event, its neurophysiological "correlate" may be recorded, at least in principle. ↑**Cognitive neuroscience** rejects parallelism because, although it describes everything, it explains nothing.

PARAPSYCHOLOGY The study of alleged paranormal (extrasensory) abilities and processes, such as telepathy, precognition, and psychokinesis. The only pseudoscience that uses statistics and makes experiments—alas, all of which have proved to be flawed. Empiricists claim that such studies should be continued and improved, for one cannot exclude a priori the reality of such phenomena. Scientific realists contend that this is a waste of time because mental processes cannot be detached from the brain, any more than stones can be made to smile, or smiles can be detached from facial muscles. On this view, the disembodied mind postulated by parapsychology resembles the smile of the Cheshire Cat.

PARETO OPTIMALITY The economic and ethical principle that the state of an economy (or a society) is best in which no one can have more unless someone else has less. But any division of a social pie, however inequitable, satisfies this condition. For example, in the case of two people who are to share a given wealth w, the Pareto condition reads: $x + y = w$, where x and y stand for the parts assigned to the first and the second person respectively. This equation has infinitely many solutions. For example, if x is increased by any given amount, then y must decrease by the same amount if the total w is to remain constant: $\Delta x = -\Delta y$. Yet, Pareto optimality is still being extolled by countless economists and moral philosophers.

PARSIMONY ↑**Ockham's razor.**

PART / WHOLE A key ontological relation to be sharply distinguished from the mathematical concepts of set membership and inclusion. Definition: If x and y are concrete things, then x is a part of y if $x \oplus y = y$, where '$\oplus$' stands for physical addition or juxtaposition. In turn, '$\oplus$' is defined tacitly by postulating that the collection of all things, together with the operation $\oplus$, is a ↑**model** or example of a semigroup. ↑**Associativity**.

PART-WHOLE HELIX The understanding of an item belonging to a given ↑**level** of organization (chemical, biological, etc.) requires either analyzing it into its constituents or embedding it into a higher level—or both. This zigzag between part and whole is often, and misleadingly, called ↑**hermeneutic** circle.

PARTIAL TRUTH Most propositions in factual science and technology are at best good approximations to the truth: they are partial truths, such as the statement that the Earth is an ellipsoid. ↑**Truth**. Partial truths must not be confused with relative (contextual) truths. ↑**Absolute / relative**.

PARTICULAR What holds for a single individual or for a narrow range. **Ant** ↑**universal**.

PASCAL'S WAGER Blaise Pascal argued that, although we do not know for sure whether God exists, it is (practically) rational to wager that He does. This is because, even if the probability of God's existence were vanishingly small, such smallness would be compensated for by a huge gain, namely eternal life. (In other words, the expected utility of believing is enormous even if the probability in question is exceedingly small.) This reasoning contains an assumption that is at once scientifically false, philosophically confused, morally dubious, and theologically blasphemous: namely, that God's existence is a matter of chance. Indeed, to begin with, no science can compute or measure the probability of God's existence. Second, the argument involves the confusion between the ↑**plausibility** of a proposition and the ↑**probability** of a fact. Further, honest religious believers balk at the suggestion that one should believe because it is convenient to do so. And of course theologians hold that, far from being a creature of chance, God is the one necessary Being.

PASSION The complement of reason: what now fuels reasoning, now derails it. There is no great endeavor without passion, and nothing right with passion alone. Information-processing (in particular computationist) psychology ignores passions because computers cannot have them. However, every parent, teacher, and leader knows that nobody learns or performs well unless motivated. The moral problem is not how best to avoid passion but how to keep it under control and put it in the service of inquiry and good causes.

PAST / FUTURE Past events are those that have been but are no longer, and future events are those that may still happen. Hence neither past nor future is real, and neither can act upon the present. What can influence the present are some of the traces left by past occurrences, as well as the forecasts that guide our actions. According to relativistic physics, the past-future distinction, though real, is not absolute but relative to the ↑**reference frame**—not to be confused with the inquirer.

PATHOCENTRIC Obsessed with suffering and death. Examples: Buddhism, Christianity, and existentialism.

PATTERN Regularity, ↑**law**. Patterns can be conceptual or ↑**ontic**, and some of the former (laws$_2$) are hoped to represent some of the latter (laws$_1$). There are many kinds of ontic pattern: spatial (like tilings); temporal (like the succession of days and nights); spatiotemporal (like traveling waves); causal (like treatment → cure); stochastic (like the tendency of a mixture to lose order); and mixed (like the scattering of a beam of quantons by a target); physical, chemical, biotic, social; and so on.

PERCEPTION The most basic of all cognitive processes. It starts with sensing or recording (e.g., I sense that there is something out there), and ends up identifying ("interpreting") the object of sensation (e.g., I perceive a dog walking there). Because perception is the most basic of cognitive processes, the Gestalt psychologists thought that it must be instant and global. Contemporary neuropsychology has shown the enormous complexity of perception, as well as its possible distortions. For example, perceiving "what" can be dissociated from perceiving "where," because each is the specific function of a distinct brain subsystem. Likewise the color, shape, and motion perceptions are each in charge of a different neural system. In short, though cognitively elementary, perception is the synthesis of several complex parallel brain processes.

PERENNIAL Said at some time of certain philosophies, such as Aquinas's, Hegel's, and Husserl's, that have become obsolete. Genuine philosophy renews itself incessantly.

PERFECTION An object is said to be perfect if it cannot be altered without changing its kind. Ant ↑**imperfection**. Example 1: Atoms are perfect; ions are imperfect atoms, because they can be completed if positively charged, or stripped off their extra electron(s) if negatively charged. Example 2: The predicate calculus is perfect in being not only consistent but also complete. Example 3: The great works of art are perfect; thus a poem may be spoiled by changing a single word; a painting by altering but one brush stroke; and a musical score by modifying a chord. In formal science perfection is a desideratum, if seldom achieved. In factual science it is not, and this is not only because the grapes are sour. Also because we want to be able to improve the accuracy of empirical data and to enrich theories with subsidiary assumptions and data capable of accounting for particular facts. A complete theory cannot be so enriched without turning inconsistent.

PERSON An animal, in particular human, endowed with mental abilities. This definition accords with contemporary psychology. But it differs from that of Catholic theology, according to which all fertilized human eggs, and a fortiori human embryos, are persons. Personality = The collection of behavioral, cognitive, and moral repertoires of some animal. Normal newborns are only potential persons: They have the ability to become persons when placed in a favorable environment, not if reared in isolation. The question whether severely handicapped babies have this capacity, or remain unpersons forever, is still under debate in ↑**bioethics**.

PERSPECTIVE ↑Approach, ↑point of view.

PERSPECTIVISM All knowledge is relative to some subject: there is no subject-invariant and universal knowledge. This subjectivist view is false, as shown by the universality of mathematics and science. From the truism that all ↑cognition is personal, it does not follow that its findings (knowledge items) cannot be tested, shared with others, and shown to be objective and even true. ↑Relativism, ↑subjectivism, ↑universalism.

PERSUASIVE An argument likely to be or seem plausible or even compelling by virtue of some combination of its cogency, empirical support, compatibility with the antecedent knowledge, or rhetoric form. "Persuasiveness" is a psychological concept not to be confused with the methodological concept of ↑plausibility.

PESSIMISM, PHILOSOPHICAL The worldview according to which the world, or at least humankind, is essentially wicked and irredeemable, so that people are doomed to suffer. Philosophical pessimism starts with the ancient myths of the Golden Age and the Fall, and it has been worked out by Augustine, Luther, A. Schopenhauer, E. von Hartmann, O. Spengler, M. Heidegger, and others. An obvious rejoinder is that there have been periods of advancement in several regards: well-being, human rights, knowledge, etc. Ant ↑optimism.

PETITIO PRINCIPII ↑Begging the question.

PHENOMENALISM The philosophical thesis that only phenomena (i.e., ↑appearances) matter: that what you see is what you get. There are two kinds of phenomenalism: ontological and epistemological. *Ontological* phenomenalism is the view that there are only phenomena: that every thing is a bundle of appearances to someone, and every change is a human experience. Examples: Berkeley, Kant, Mach, Husserl, and the ↑Copenhagen interpretation of quantum mechanics. *Epistemological phenomenalism* is the view that we can know only phenomena. Examples: Ptolemy, Cardinal Bellarmino, Hume, Comte, and Duhem. Obviously, the first kind of phenomenalism entails the second. In either version, phenomenalism is at variance with modern science and even with ordinary knowledge. Indeed, phenomena or appearances are only the starting point of inquiry. Even in ordinary life we seek reality behind appearances. For instance, we check some of our perceptions to make sure that they not just illusions; we scratch the surface of golden things to find out whether they are not just plated; we watch the deeds of a politician to learn whether they match his promises—and so on. Scientific research seeks realities behind appearances, because the latter are subjective and shallow, whereas scientific knowledge is hoped to be objective and deep. This search for the ↑thing in itself takes us beyond perception, into conception and, particularly, theory. Sometimes we succeed in explaining appearances in terms of hypotheses that posit imperceptible things or processes. Well-known examples are Copernicus's explanation of the apparent orbits of planets; the quantum-mechanical explanation of the glint of metallic objects; the genetic explanation of some phenotypic features; the explanation of behavior and mind in terms of neurophysiological processes; and the psychological explanation of some social behavior. The alternative to phenomenalism is ↑**realism**, the view that there are facts which are not phenomenal, and that at least some such facts can be known—though of course conceptually, not perceptually.

PHENOMENOLOGY a Science Description of facts of some kind without regard to the possible underlying ↑**mechanisms**. A phenomenological theory is one that refrains from hypothesizing mechanisms. **Syn** ↑**black-box theory**. Examples: thermodynamics, electric network theory, and behaviorist learning theory. Dual: ↑**mechanismic** or translucent-box theory. **b Contemporary philosophy** The nonscientific description and examination of ↑**phenomena** and ↑**subjective** experience. In particular, Edmund Husserl's doctrine that introspection and the analysis of appearances is necessary and sufficient to disclose the essence of things. He chacterized phenomenology as "the science of essences," "the science of transcendental subjectivity," and "egology." Unsurprisingly, he made no contributions to psychology. Sample of Husserl's prose: "As primal ego, I constitute my horizon of transcendental others as cosubjects within the transcendental intersubjectivity which constitutes the world." Husserl's star pupil, Martin Heidegger, made phenomenology the starting point of his enigmatic musings about ↑*Dasein*, nothingness, and anxiety. Phenomenology and its offshoots were central to Continental philosophy during the first half of the twentieth-century. It now survives in the United States at the margins of ↑**postmodernism**.

PHENOMENON Appearance to someone. This is the etymologically correct and philosophical usage of the word. However, in ordinary language and in the scientific literature, 'phenomenon' is often (incorrectly) used as a synonym for 'fact'. And yet in all fields appearance is usually contrasted to reality. Thus, admittedly the sky only seems to revolve around us, and a dishonest politician is not really what he appears to be. Since the powers of perception are limited, phenomenal knowledge is limited: it reaches only the exterior of a tiny fraction of the totality of things. Moreover, two different things or events may not be discriminated by a perceptual apparatus. In other words, the set of phenomena is a smallish subset of that of facts. And, since different animals are never in the same state and can never adopt exactly the same standpoint, a fact is bound to appear differently, or not at all, to different animals in different states. In sum, there is no one-to-one correspondence between facts and appearances.

PHILOSOPHER Broad construal: A person who asks philosophical problems, holds philosophical views, or teaches them. **Syn** normal human being past age two. Narrow construal: A person who does original research on philosophical problems. Original philosophers, like mathematicians, discover or invent problems, conduct research, invent new ideas, or discover previously unknown relations among them. But, unlike mathematicians, the ideas that concern philosophers are rather pervasive—so much so, that some of them occur in ordinary knowledge and in many research fields. Witness the concepts of thing, change, novelty, time, life, mind, society, justice, knowledge, meaning, truth, norm, and right. Philosophers are popularly perceived as either sages or cranks. Actually these are only pathological cases: most philosophers are honest and competent scholars. Only a few are madmen or crooks. Still, these are disproportionately influential: ↑**postmodernism**.

PHILOSOPHER'S STONE In alchemy the substance that would transmute base metal into gold. In philosophy the experience or method that would yield deep and infallible knowledge without hard work. Examples: the intuitionist's instant insight, the phenomenologist's *époché*, the hermeneuticist's ↑*Verstehen*, the empiricist's induction, the Hegelian's dialectical method.

PHILOSOPHY The discipline that studies the most general concepts (such as those of being, becoming, mind, knowledge, and norm) and the most general hypotheses (such as those of the autonomous existence and knowability of the external world). *Basic* branches: ↑**logic** (shared with mathematics), ↑**semantics** (partially shared with linguistics and mathematics), ↑**ontology**, and the theory of knowledge or ↑**epistemology**. *Applied* branches: ↑**methodology**, ↑**axiology**, ↑**praxiology**, ↑**ethics**, ↑**political philosophy**, and all the ↑**philosophies of** something. Ant ↑**gnosophobia**. The most demanding philosophies are the ↑**exact** and the ↑**scientific** ones.

PHILOSOPHY OF It is the privilege of philosophers to philosophize on, or attempt to draw philosophical morals from, nearly everything. Hence the many *philosophies of X*, where the blank X can be filled with art, law, politics, religion, science, technology, or what-have-you. Ideally, every philosophy of X should be cultivated only by persons with some competence in both philosophy and X. Regrettably, it is common for any philosophy of X to be cultivated by people ignorant of both philosophy and X. Many philosophers tolerate, and a few prefer, fellow philosophers who write about X without knowing any X: they are less demanding.

PHYSICALISM a Ontology The view that all existents are physical things of various degrees of complexity, so that ↑**emergence** is illusory. Syn vulgar ↑**materialism**, radical ↑**reductionism**. **b Philosophy of science** The program of translating all scientific terms into physical-science ones. Predicated on the assumptions that all the sciences are built on an empirical basis, and that the elements of this basis are protocol statements such as "The pointer came to rest at the zero position." This project is a nonstarter because what distinguishes the various supraphysical sciences is that they study peculiar things with emergent properties, such as dissociation energy, adaptive value, anomie, and fairness.

PHYSICS The fundamental science of matter. All philosophers interested in knowledge have been interested in physics, both because so far it has been the most advanced of factual sciences, and because of the widespread belief that in the last analysis they are all reducible to physics. As it happens, although all the higher-level sciences—chemistry, biology, and social science—presuppose physics, none of them is reducible to it. ↑**Reduction**, ↑**reductionism**.

PHYSICS, PHILOSOPHY OF The philosophical examination of physical categories (such as those of matter, energy, space, time, causation, and chance); of philosophical presuppositions, such as that there are real things behind appearances; of general principles, such as that there are basic or indecomposable things; and of the general problems raised by the experimental and theoretical knowledge of the physical world, such as whether quantum physics is applicable to macrophysical entities and condones subjectivism, and whether general relativity substitutes geometrical objects for material ones—or whether all these are philosophical grafts.

PICTURE VIEW OF LANGUAGE The opinion that languages, far from being ontologically and epistemologically neutral, depict the world. If this were true, it would be impossible to state possibilities, falsities, and fictions. ↑**Reflection theory of knowledge**.

PIECING TOGETHER Making a guess to explain data that at first sight look disconnected or paradoxical. **Syn** putting two and two together.

PLAN An ordered sequence of steps intended to solve a problem, conceptual or practical. A key concept in ↑**praxiology**. Every plan is designed in the light of both some body of relevant knowledge and some strategy or ↑**policy**. Clearly, plans can be more or less realistic and effective, moral or immoral, but not more or less true. To be viable, a practical plan must be ↑**systemic** rather than ↑**sectoral**, because the fragmentation of disciplines is an intellectual artifact. And it should also be elastic, that is, open to revision in the light of the results that are being attained in the course of their implementation. (That is, it should include feedback loops.) Rigid planning is just as vulnerable as improvisation. And no planning at all is a way to serfdom.

PLATONISM The doctrine that ideas ("forms") exist autonomously, i.e., regardless of whether someone thinks of them, and that concrete things are but imperfect copies of ideas. The earliest, most articulate, and most influential version of objective ↑**idealism**. Platonism has flourished in ↑**mathematics** but has failed utterly in all the remaining fields, where inquiry proceeds on the assumption that real things exist on their own, have nonconceptual properties, and cannot be understood ↑**a priori**.

PLAUSIBILITY A qualitative property of propositions (in particular hypotheses), beliefs, and inferences. **Syn** ↑**verisimilitude**. A hypothesis that has not yet been checked, or the evidence for which is inconclusive, may sound plausible in the light of some body of knowledge. How plausible? There is no way of knowing as long as no tests have been conducted. But once the tests have been carried out, if they are conclusive, we say of the hypothesis that it has been confirmed (or refuted), so that it may be pronounced true (or false)—at least for the time being. That is, after a conclusive test we no longer need the concept of plausibility. And before testing we cannot (or ought not to) try and measure the degree of plausibility. In this case, the most we can say is that the conjecture in question is plausible or implausible with respect to some body of knowledge, or that one hypothesis is more plausible than another in the same context. More precisely, let p and q designate ↑**coreferential** propositions, and B a body of knowledge relevant to both p and q. Suppose further that B can be split into an essential part E and an inessential part I, i.e., $B = E \cup I$. (Typically, B will contain generalizations with a good track record, whereas I will contain only empirical data and narrow hypotheses.) We may stipulate that

p is *plausible* w.r.t. $B =_{df} p$ is compatible with every member of B.

p is *more plausible than* q w.r.t. $B =_{df} p$ is compatible with more members of B than q.

p is *essentially plausible* w.r.t. $B =_{df} p$ is compatible with every member of E.

p is *essentially more plausible than* q w.r.t. $B =_{df} p$ is compatible with more members of E than q.

The definitions of the dual concepts of implausibility and essential implausibility are obvious. The following axioms for a calculus of plausibility seem to capture some intuitions about the matter. Assuming a fixed body B of background knowledge, and interpreting '$p \geq q$' as "p is more plausible than q w.r.t B," we assert

A1 $\neg (p \geq q) \Leftrightarrow (q \geq p)$
A2 $p \vee q \geq p$
A3 $p \geq p \wedge q$
A4 $\exists x\, Fx \geq \forall x\, Fx$

Some logical consequences follow. A2 entails

Thm. 1 $(p \Rightarrow q) \geq \neg p$

A3 entails that, of two theories differing only by a finite number of axioms, the simpler is the more plausible. (But, because the simpler theory is the less bold one, it benefits from a lesser number of possible confirming instances. Hence the more plausible theory is not necessarily the more promising one: it is only the one that should be checked first.) A hypothesis h may be said to be *empirically plausible* with regard to a set D of data relevant to h, if the overwhelming majority of D confirms h. And a hypothesis may be said to be *theoretically plausible* if it is consistent with the bulk of the background knowledge relevant to it. Normally, only theoretically plausible hypotheses are put to the empirical test, and only empirically plausible hypotheses are judged to be worthy candidates for some theory. This is how research proposals are written and evaluated. Finally, beware of equating plausibility with ↑**probability** or with improbability. Both identifications are wrong, if only because there is no objective method for assigning probabilities to propositions. ↑**Bayesianism**, ↑**probability**. However, though different, the two concepts are related in an obvious way, namely thus: If a and b are random events, and a is objectively more probable than b, then

Event a will happen $\geq$ Event b will happen.

In particular, if two events are equiprobable, then the corresponding assertions are equiplausible. Caution: Do not confuse the plausibility of hypotheses with the ↑**likelihood** of facts. Many plausible hypotheses concern unlikely events.

PLAUSIBLE REASONING Fruitful reasoning that does not fit the rules of deductive inference. Examples: insightful ↑**analogies** and lucky ↑**inductions** (↑**jumping** to true generalities from a sample). Plausible reasoning is more common than deduction, not only in everyday matters but also in mathematics, science, and philosophy. In fact, only fragments of finished mathematics, science, or philosophy can be cast in the deductive mold: mathematics, science, and philosophy in the making are often logically unclean because they make use of plausible reasoning. But, once a plausible reasoning has been shown to be fertile, it can be taken to the logical cleaners.

PLAYING GOD Altering nature in a deliberate manner—for better or for worse. Examples: mining, damming rivers, domesticating and selecting plants and animals, repairing inborn deformities, vaccinating, flying planes, and doing genetic engineering. Playing God is damnable in the eyes of fundamentalist theologians and radical environmentalists alike. Humanists regard playing God as part of being human, but also as requiring scientific study and public debate over such issues as whether it is appropriate to market genetically modified foods without safety studies.

PLENISM The ontological thesis that all the regions of the universe are filled with ↑**material things** of some kind or other. First proposed by Aristotle, and worked out by Descartes. Endorsed by field physics, particularly quantum electrodynamics. ↑**Vacuum**.

PLOTINUS'S PROBLEM Do we desire what we value, or do we value what we desire? The solution depends on whether or not the value judgment in question is well-grounded. If it is, then desire matches valuation. ↑**Value**.

PLURALISM a General Any view asserting that there is more than one species of objects of a certain category. **Ant** ↑**monism**. Particular case: ↑**mind-body dualism. b Logical** The view that one should admit a plurality of logical theories—e.g., classical and intuitionistic. **c Epistemological** The view that, regarding any subject, one may admit more than one theory. **Syn** ↑**eclecticism,** ↑**relativism. d Metaphysical** Two kinds: substance pluralism and property pluralism. *Substance* pluralism asserts that there are two or more basic and mutually irreducible categories of "substance" or entity, e.g., material and mental. *Property* pluralism affirms that, regardless of the number of basic kinds of substance, every thing has more than one property. Descartes was both a substance and a property pluralist, whereas Spinoza was a substance monist and a property pluralist. So is ↑**emergentist materialism**, for it holds that there are many kinds of material things. ↑**Level**.

PLURALITY OF WORLDS If no distinction is drawn between constructs and concrete things, then none will be made between conceptual and real possibility either. In other words, it will be held that "the world we are part of is but one of a plurality of worlds" (David Lewis). Since these alternative unactualized "worlds" are assumed to be causally isolated from one another, we could not possibly access any such parallel worlds. This gives the metaphysician ample freedom to concoct shallow fantasies that divert the student's attention from the real problems that provoke or assault any normal person in the only world there is.↑**Possible worlds**.

POETRY The art of transmuting feelings and emotions into words. Though philosophy is closer to science than to poetry, it is not far away from it. This is because some ontologies elicit feelings and emotions, and some moral philosophies are rooted in them. No wonder then that there have been philosophical poets, such as Lucretius, Dante, Donne, Goethe, Heine, and Antonio Machado.

POINT OF VIEW Syn perspective, standpoint. Set of assumptions used as a guide to explore, or a benchmark to evaluate something. For example, though the death penalty may be justifiable from an economic point of view, it is barbaric from an anthropological standpoint, and monstrous from a moral one. To be sure, no view is possible without some point of view. However, a standpoint need not be arbitrary or subjective: it should be validated by its aims and fruits, as well as by the body of knowledge it presupposes.

POLICING, IDEOLOGICAL The banning of ideas or practices in the name of philosophical, theological, or political principles. Examples: the Soviet censorship of relativistic physics, regarding it as subjectivistic; the Nazi ban on relativity, quanta, and abstract mathematics for being "Jewish," and on modern art for being "degenerate"; the Christan attacks on evolutionary biology; the current ban on stem-cell research; the millennium-old exclusion of philosophical materialism from university teaching, regarding it as inimical to spiritual values.

POLICY A set of general principles about the goals and means of a formal organization. **Syn** in ordinary language: philosophy. The most efficient policies are those designed on the strength of scientific social studies and humanist moral principles. Every ↑**plan** is designed in the light of some policy. In turn, the soundness of policies is judged by the plans they inspire. (This is a case of ↑**virtuous circle**.)

POLITICAL PHILOSOPHY The philosophical underpinning of political theory and social policy. One of the branches of philosophical ↑**technology**. A political philosophy may be secular or theocratic, realist or utopian, scientific or unscientific, fair or unfair, democratic or authoritarian, popular or unpopular. A ↑**humanist** political philosophy is expected to be secular, realist, scientific, fair, and democratic.

POLITICS The struggle for and administration of power: the individual or collective action aiming at influencing the governance of a social group of any kind or size, from family and gang to firm and government. Politics has multiple relations with philosophy, some direct and most indirect. Some of the direct connections are these. Political democracy tolerates philosophy, whereas dictatorship (secular or religious) allows only philosophical schools favorable to the powers that be. This is no coincidence: genuine philosophizing is critical and requires the free change and exchange of ideas. This is why philosophy proper started only in the ancient Greek city-states along with political democracy and the court of law. Nor is it a coincidence that Stalinism punished every deviation from Marxism, and that Nazism tolerated only irrationalist and idealist philosophies. The indirect connections between philosophy and politics are both explicit and tacit. The former take place in the fields of political, social, legal, and moral philosophy. Indeed, all of these disciplines discuss explicitly the various political regimes, as well as the rights and duties of citizens in them. The tacit indirect connections between philosophy and politics concern the implications of basic philosophy for political programs and plans. For example, because it favors the objective investigation of the social world, a ↑**realist** epistemology favors the objective study of things social, which in turn is necessary for their rational and realistic redesign and management. Another: an ontology asserting that individuals, not groups, are the sources of values, and that persons are or ought to be free to some extent, makes room for political activism; by contrast, a holistic ontology entails the total subordination of the individual to the whole, that is, the powers that be. ↑**Political philosophy**, ↑**politology**.

POLITOLOGY The study of politics. **Syn** political science. Actually, at present this field is composed of political science proper, political analysis, history of political thought, and political philosophy. Only a fraction of what passes for political science is composed of empirical or theoretical studies of particular political processes. Far too many empirical studies are atheoretical, and a disproportionate fraction of the theoretical ones are ↑**rational-choice models** far removed from political realities. It is no wonder then that no politologist has foreseen any of the major political transformations of our time, from the crumbling of the Soviet bloc to the rise of religious fundamentalisms as political powers, and the political power of the great corporations.

POLYSEMY Multiplicity of meanings. **Syn** ↑**ambiguity**.

POP PHILOSOPHY Any collection of popular ill-posed questions, such as "What is the meaning of life?" and maxims that are either trite ("There are two sides to every issue") or egregiously false ("Whatever goes up must come down").

POSIT ↑**Assumption**, ↑**postulate**.

POSITIVISM The family of doctrines requiring that only "positive" facts (experiences) be attended to, and asserting that theories only summarize data and save us thinking. ↑**Dataism**. Although positivists preach ↑**scientism**, they uphold a subject-centered epistemology, and they clip the wings of scientific imagination in demanding that scientists should stick to data. They also claim to shun metaphysics, but in fact endorse ↑**phenomenalism**, which is a subjectivist metaphysics. Main exponents: Ptolemy, Hume, d'Alembert, Comte, Mill, Spencer, Mach, Pearson, Duhem, and the ↑**logical positivists**, in particular R. Carnap and H. Reichenbach. In ethics, most positivists have favored ↑**emotivism**. There are no positivists left in the philosophical community. The only practicing positivists are found in the backward branches of the natural and social sciences, where the main occupation is still data hunting and gathering.

POSITIVISM-BASHING The uncritical attack upon ↑**positivism**, often for the wrong reasons. Currently fashionable, partly because positivism opposes obscurantism, and partly because it is often mistaken for ↑**realism** and ↑**materialism**.

POSSIBILISM The thesis that some ↑**possibilities** are real, not just logical. Opposed to ↑**actualism**. Since the possibilist thesis is an existential proposition, a single case of conversion of possibility into actuality suffices to establish it. For example, although

I am now sitting, I could walk if I wanted to, by activating my walking mechanisms, which are controlled by the brain.

POSSIBILITY What may or may not happen. The power, disposition, or ability to change state or become something of a different kind. Examples: zygotes are potential multicellular organisms; infants are potential speakers; married couples are potential families; armies and big business coalitions are potential governments. **Syn** ↑**potentiality**. The dual or complement of ↑**actuality**. There are two main concepts of possibility: conceptual (or logical), and real (or physical). The two have only the name in common. A ↑**construct** is *logically possible* relative to a given context C if it does not introduce any irrelevancies or contradictions in C. Otherwise it is conceptually impossible—though perhaps writable, such as 'square circle'. Real possibility is radically different, because there is only one real world, which is assumed to be lawful: ↑**lawfulness, principle of**. A fact is *really possible* if it is consistent with the relevant (natural or social) laws. Otherwise it is *really impossible*. For example, it is really possible for a large celestial body to knock the Earth off its orbit. By contrast, travel backward in time is really impossible because macrophysical processes (and some microphysical ones as well) are irreversible. The relation between real possibility and actuality is this: What is or will be, was really possible to begin with. The more robust statements about real possibility or impossibility are those based on laws involving mechanisms. Indeed, a transition from possibility to actuality involves the activation of some latent or "dormant" mechanism. For example, a car is accelerated by pressing the gas pedal. Real possibility confirms ↑**possibilism** and, by the same token, it falsifies ↑**actualism**. Since real possibility has nothing to do with conceptual possibility, no single theory can cover both. This suffices to condemn both Meinong's theory of objects (both possible and impossible) and ↑**modal logic** as futile academic exercises. Science deals with really possible facts but not with whole possible worlds like Leibniz's, which are solely conceptual, hence of no help to ontology, epistemology, or science. ↑**Possible world**.

POSSIBLE WORLD Imaginary alternative to the actual world. For example, in a world different from ours, humans would be the slaves of machines; in another, people would think with their feet; in a third, there would be no people at all—hence no philosophical problems. These imaginary worlds make sense only in a religious worldview, where the deity (or deities), unconstrained by the laws of nature, may entertain and evaluate alternative plans on the eve of creation or re-creation. Speculating on such fanciful possibilities has given rise to a whole possible-worlds metaphysics and semantics based on ↑**modal logic**. Thus one may claim that Aristotle is not the same as the author of the *Nicomachean Ethics*, because in a different world this book might have been written by someone else. But, since all we know concerns only one world, this problem is bogus. Yet the exact handling of this pseudoproblem is the only claim to fame of certain philosophers. Possible-worlds metaphysics and semantics are mere academic games. ↑**Plurality of worlds**.

POST Prefix used to advertise the unborn successor to a school or current of thought deemed to be dead, as in "postmodern" and "postpositivist." Useful to pass old hat for new. **Syn** anti.

POST HOC, ERGO PROPTER HOC After this, hence because of this. An ontological fallacy, for what precedes an event need not cause it.

POSTMODERN A clear concept in architecture, where it stands for the revolt against the modernism initiated by Le Corbusier and the Bauhaus group. Far less clear in other fields, except as a rejection of the intellectual values of the Enlightenment, in particular clarity, rationality, consistency, and objective truth. Deconstructionist literary criticism, "cultural studies," and postmodern philosophy are contemporary versions of age-old irrationalism. Actually, postmodern philosophy—in particular phenomenology and existentialism—is antiphilosophical, for conceptual rationality is a necessary condition for authentic philosophizing as opposed to incoherent rambling. ↑**Counter-Enlightenment,** ↑**continental philosophy.**

POSTMORTEM, PHILOSOPHICAL Exhumation and meticulous dissection of some long-deceased, forgotten, and uninteresting philosophical item. Sufficient to earn an academic degree or a promotion. ↑**Necrophilia, philosophical.**

POSTULATE Initial assumption in a theory or an argument. **Syn** ↑**axiom.** A *postulate* (or *axiom*) *system* is a system of premises from which all the other propositions in a theory follow. It is justified only by its logical consequences. In the case of mathematics, the latter include the standard theorems; in the case of factual science, the consequences are empirically testable theorems. The problem of guessing a set of postulates entailing the standard theorem is of the inverse kind.

POTENTIALITY ↑**Possibility.**

POWER An agent's ability to force something or somebody (self or other) to do her will, possibly against the patient's will. The central concept of ↑**politology.** Power can be biological (as in gender discrimination), economic (as in labor exploitation), political (as in all political orders), or cultural (education and indoctrination). The strength of power can be measured by the size of the resources commanded by those who wield it.

POWER IS TRUTH The powers that be dictate what is true. A slogan of ↑**social constructivism.** The epistemic counterpart of the formula ↑**Might makes right.**

PRACTICAL REASON Reason to value, decide, or act. A central concept of ↑**praxiology.** Practical reasons can be good or bad. Their prior worth is best gauged by technological and moral considerations. However, ultimately their worth will be measured by the consequences of the action in question. Still, this value judgment may be challenged by invoking the occurrence of unforeseen circumstances. Only research can help resolve the question.

PRACTICAL SYLLOGISM Any argument whose conclusion is a recommendation either to act or to abstain from acting. ↑*Modus nolens,* ↑*modus volens.*

PRAGMATICS The embryonic chapter of ↑**semiotics** that studies the use of signs, or the sign-speaker relations. Most philosophers approach pragmatics armed only with their personal linguistic experience together with some logical tools. No wonder that this approach has yielded little more than a typology of speech acts. If it ever gets off the ground, scientific pragmatics will be included in the union of psycholinguistics, sociolinguistics, and ↑**praxiology**. And if this happens, there will be no place for philosophical pragmatics, any more than there is room for philosophical entomology.

PRAGMATISM The philosophical doctrine according to which ↑**praxis** is the source, content, measure, and goal of all knowledge and all value. Accordingly, pure research is either nonexisting or expendable; the test of anything is utility; truth is either a euphemism for practical usefulness or something negligible; belief, even if unscientific, is justifiable if it "works satisfactorily for you"; and altruism is a form of selfishness. Judged from a pragmatist viewpoint, pragmatism is obviously ambivalent. Because it writes off all unpractical ideas, it is a form of philistinism and thus hostile to higher culture, in particular mathematics, basic science, and philosophy—although its founding fathers, C. S. Peirce, W. James, and J. Dewey, were distinguished thinkers. However, pragmatism is occasionally useful to discredit outlandish speculation or inefficient planning. The axiological and praxiological partner of pragmatism is ↑**utilitarianism**.

PRAXIOLOGY Action theory. Along with ethics, axiology, political philosophy, and methodology, a component of practical philosophy, or philosophical ↑**technology**. ↑**Action**. Sample of problematics: What is rational action? What are the relations between policies and plans? How are collective and individual actions related? Is decision theory helpful to plan courses of action? Can a policy science be at the same time scientific and morally committed? Is the laissez-faire policy both economically efficient and morally justified?

PRAXIS ↑**Action** informed by knowledge, as in "medical praxis" and "legal praxis."

PRECONCEIVED IDEA Strictly speaking, an oxymoron. Charitably interpreted, either a ↑**hypothesis** or an unexamined or uncritically accepted idea.

PREDESTINATION The doctrine according to which one's life is predetermined by God before birth. The theological version of ↑**fatalism**. Held by Augustine, Calvin, and Islam. That such a doctrine, which condones undeserved suffering and denies free will, should have followers, is still a puzzle for social psychologists.

PREDICATE Conceptualization of a property. **Syn** ↑**attribute**. Predicates can be unary, like "inhabited," binary, like "loves," ternary, like "between," and in general n-ary. And they can be simple or indivisible, like "divisible" and "poor"; or compound, like "indivisible" and "blue-collar worker." In mathematics, predicate = property. In all the other fields of knowledge, properties are *possessed* by things and *represented* by (or conceptualized as) predicates. Such representation is contextual: it depends on the theory. For example, mass, a basic property of all bodies and particles, is represented by different predicates in different theories. A predicate may be analyzed as a function from individuals, or n-tuples of individuals, to propositions. For example, "rationalist" maps the collection of people into the set of all the propositions containing the given predicate, e.g., propositions of the forms "x is [or is not] a rationalist," and "all rationalists engage in debate." "Loves" is an example of a binary predicate. Indeed, it maps ordered pairs of the form <higher vertebrate, object> into the set of propositions involving that particular predicate—e.g., "Philosophers love abstract ideas," which can be formalized as "$\forall x \exists y (Px \ \& \ Ay \Rightarrow Lxy)$." In general, $P: A \times B \times \ldots \times N \rightarrow S$, where S designates the set of all statements containing P, and $\times$ the ↑**cartesian product** of sets. Warning 1: This analysis is at variance with the standard one, originally proposed by Frege. According to the latter, a predicate F is a function from individuals to truth values. Hence Fb, the value of F at b (for individual b), would be either truth or falsity. This is absurd, because it leads to identifying all propositions with the same truth value. A "Frege predicate" turns out to be the composition of two maps: the P above, from individuals into propositions, and the map V (truth valuation) from propositions into truth values. Warning 2: The analysis of predicates is not always straightforward. For example, "good teacher" is not the conjunction of "good" and "teacher." Instead, it is the conjunction of "teacher," "clear," "accessible," "helpful," "responsible," "stimulating," "inspiring," etc.

PREDICTION / RETRODICTION, FORECAST / HINDCAST, SCIENTIFIC Inference from the known present to the unknown future or past. Grounded statement concerning future or past facts. The ground or basis for a scientific prediction (or retrodiction) is a set of law-statements, or at least trend-statements, and empirical data. (If a trend is invoked, the statement is called an *extrapolation* from present circumstances.) Therefore every scientific forecast (or hindcast) is a conditional of the form "Assuming pattern(s) P and present circumstance(s) C, the state of the thing concerned at time t will be (or was) S." The logical form of predictions and retrodictions is the same as that of ↑**explanations**. The differences are ontological and epistemological: Whereas explanations proper are mechanismic, forecasts and hindcasts may be based on purely descriptive statements such as rate equations and time series.

PREFORMATIONISM / EPIGENETICISM Two rival hypotheses about biological development or ontogeny (in contrast to evolution). According to preformationism, development consists in the unfolding of characters preformed in the germ. The homunculus fantasy, as well as genic determinism (the thesis that everything is in the genetic "code"), are examples of preformationism. Epigeneticism, on the other hand, states that development consists in the emergence of new characters from the unstructured germ. Current developmental biology overcomes the preformation-epigenesis dichotomy: it holds that development is a constructive (or morphogenetic) process steered by both the genome and the environment, and that the germ (egg or zygote) is a complex system rather than an unstructured blob of cytoplasm.

PREJUDICE Unexamined or uncritically accepted idea. Examples: the beliefs that every existent has been created, and that all complex items are mere associations of existents.

PREMISE or PREMISS ↑**Assumption** in an argument or deduction. Premises are evaluated by their logical consequences. In particular, the worth of ↑**axioms** is determined by the theorems they entail.

PRESENTISM The tendency to demean earlier beliefs and practices for not measuring up to present-day standards. Rightly regarded on a par with anachronism. **Syn** ↑**Whiggism.**

PRESUMPTION OF INNOCENCE An important principle in humanistic ethics and liberal jurisprudence. According to it, the burden of proof of guilt must be borne by the accusing or prosecuting party. Under authoritarian regimes everyone is presumed guilty unless they prove innocence.

PRESUPPOSITION An ↑**assumption** that is either hidden or taken for granted: a premise occurring tacitly in an argument. For example, classical mathematics presupposes ordinary (classical) logic; and all of physics, including the quantum theory, presupposes classical mathematics, which in turn presupposes classical logic. Since presuppositions are assumptions which are taken for granted, they are seldom examined. Error or unwanted assumption may lurk in them. An example is the ↑**axiom of choice**, which had often been used inadvertently until it was stated explicitly; and, when this happened, some mathematicians hailed it while others (the constructivists) rejected it. One of the virtues of ↑**axiomatics** is that it involves the unearthing and critical examination of presuppositions. For example, any adequate axiomatization of quantum mechanics will show that it presupposes large areas of classical mathematics, which in turn presupposes ordinary logic. This suffices to disown all the attempts to understand quantum physics in terms of ↑**many-valued logic**, ↑**quantum logic**, ↑**fuzzy logic**, or any other deviant logic.

PRESUPPOSITIONLESS PHILOSOPHY A philosophy that takes nothing for granted. An ideal dreamt by some philosophers, among them Bacon, Hegel, and Husserl. Such enterprise is logically impossible, because all philosophical research is triggered by some problem; and the very statement of any ↑**problem** presupposes a number of more or less tacit premises—e.g., that the object of research may exist (conceptually or materially); that it has knowable properties; that truths about it are (or are not) attainable; and that for some reason the research itself is worthwhile. Although logic can be constructed, though laboriously, without any logical postulates, it cannot dispense with rules of inference—nor with the assumptions that there are propositions and proofs.

PRIMA FACIE On the face of it, at first sight. Preliminary impression or hypothesis, likely to be corrected through a more detailed or deeper examination, as in "Nothing is really what it looks at first sight." For example, prima facie all the norms of a moral or legal code are equally valid. But a conflict between two norms, or two duties, may arise in a particular case, as when a doctor treating an AIDS patient sacrifices patient confidentiality to public health.

PRIMARY / SECONDARY (PROPERTY) A primary property of a real thing is one that is independent of any knower. Examples: position, mass, chemical composition, life, visual acuity, social structure, productivity. A secondary property of a real thing is one attributed to it on the basis of perception, hence it may be judged differently by different subjects. Examples: color (by contrast to wavelength), the size of the rising Moon, taste, beauty, political profile. Physics, chemistry, and biology study only primary properties. Secondary properties are studied by psychology and social science. According to radical ↑**empiricism**, secondary properties are primary. Examples: Mill's definition of a thing as "a permanent possibility of sensation"; Mach's thesis that sensations are the building blocks of the universe; and Carnap's "construction of the world" in terms of perceptions. ↑**Sensationism,** ↑**qualia.**

PRIMITIVE CONCEPT A concept that is basic or not defined in a given context, where it serves to define other concepts. Examples: 0 in ordinary arithmetic, and "time" in physics. The status of primitive is contextual: a concept that is basic in one context may turn out to be definable in another. For example, "time" is definable in ontology in terms of the concept of a changing thing. ↑**Definition.**

PRINCIPIUM INDIVIDUATIONIS Principle of individuation: the property that makes an object different from all other objects. For example, people can be individuated by their genetic "fingerprints." ↑**Individuation.**

PRINCIPLE An extremely general assumption or rule. Examples: the logical principle of noncontradiction; the extremal principles of physics, such as Hamilton's; the ↑**categorical imperative.**

PRINCIPLE / PRACTICE In all walks of life we meet incongruities between principles and action. For example, when falling sick, the religious believer is unlikely to trust in prayer alone; when crossing the street, the social constructivist is unlikely to regard the incoming traffic as a social construction; and when falling in love, the rational-choice theorist is unlikely to try and maximize his expected utilities. To achieve consistency between a principle and the corresponding practice, one may need to modify at least one of them. Principles should be practicable, and actions should be principled—a meta-principle that is easier to state than to implement. ↑**Principlism.**

PRINCIPLISM a General Abiding by a consistent set of explicit principles or norms. **Ant** case-based reasoning, opportunism. There is no merit in principlism other than in the principles it upholds. If some of these are bad, inconsistency is preferable to principlism. **b**↑**Bioethics** The school that favors the principles of autonomy, beneficience, nonmaleficience, and justice. That is: Choose by yourself, help others, do not harm, and shoulder burdens together with benefits. Close to ↑**agathonism.**

PROBABILISM a Ontology The doctrine that all facts are ↑**contingent,** and all laws probabilistic. **Syn** ↑**tychism. b Epistemology** The doctrine that all factual knowledge is "probable," in the vulgar sense of being either plausible or inaccurate, hence uncertain. A kind of ↑**skepticism.**

PROBABILISTIC LAW A law-statement containing a probability function. The basic laws of quantum physics are probabilistic. This shows the need to broaden the concept of ↑**determinism** to include probabilistic patterns. It also forces one to include ↑**predictions** of the probabilistic kind, of the form "The probability that this event will happen within the next hour is such and such." The question whether probabilistic laws are derivable from nonprobabilistic laws has been answered in the negative—until new notice.

PROBABILISTIC PHILOSOPHY a General The use of the ↑**probability** calculus to exactify philosophical concepts. About twenty different philosophical concepts, including those of causation, truth, simplicity, and meaning, have been declared to be definable in terms of probability. Unsurprisingly, only confusion has resulted from extruding an exact concept from its proper context, which is that of the theory of probability plus the family of stochastic models. **b Ontology** At first sight, causation is a special case of probable connection, namely when the value of the latter equals unity. More precisely, the following definition would seem to be adequate: "c is the cause of $e =_{df}$ The conditional probability of e given c equals 1." But this won't do, because of a hidden circularity. Indeed, the notions of cause and effect occur in the definiens: all that is being said is that in certain cases the probability of the cause producing its effect is maximal. **c Semantics** Several philosophers have proposed using the concept of probability to elucidate the notion of truth, either by equating the two, or by defining truth as improbability. These attempts were bound to fail if only because attributing a probability to a proposition is about as reasonable as attributing it an area. Indeed, probabilities are measures of sets—so much so that the advanced theory of probability is a special case of measure theory, which in turn is an exactification and generalization of the intuitive ideas of length, area, and volume. Not being sets, propositions are not measurable, hence they are neither probable nor improbable. They can be more or less ↑**plausible** instead; and some of them are truer than others: ↑**partial truth**.

PROBABILITY Measure of ↑**possibility**. A sketch of the foundations of the elementary abstract probability calculus follows. Underlying theories: Ordinary (classical) logic, naive set theory, elementary algebra, and analysis. Primitive concept: the probability function P, from unspecified sets (called 'events') to real numbers in the unit interval. This function is implicitly defined by the following postulates. Axiom 1: If S is an arbitrary nonempty set, and F a family of subsets of S, then all the unions and intersections of members of F are in F. Axiom 2: P is a function from F into the $[0,1]$ interval of real numbers. Axiom 3: For any A in F, $0 \le P(A) \le 1$. Axiom 4: If A and B are nonintersecting members of F, then $P(A \cup B) = P(A) + P(B)$. Axiom 5: $P(S) = 1$. The theory is semiabstract, because the independent variables of the probability functions are sets of nondescript individuals. Although these sets are often called 'events', they need not represent physical events. Nor do the notions of relative frequency and credibility occur in the axioms. This semantic neutrality allows the application of the probability calculus in all factual sciences and technologies. However, all the legitimate applications involve the notion of objective chance. ↑**Bayesianism**; ↑**chance**; ↑**probabilistic law**; ↑**probabilistic philosophy**; ↑**probability, objective**; ↑**probability paradoxes**; ↑**probability, vulgar notion**; ↑**randomness**.

PROBABILITY, OBJECTIVE Property of things of certain kinds, such as atoms and molecules, as well as of items picked at random from a population. It is conceptualized by theories or models that borrow from the calculus of ↑**probability**. **Syn** ↑**chance** or stochastic ↑**propensity**, as different from causal propensity.

PROBABILITY PARADOXES a Rooted in ordinary knowledge The following paradox should highlight the risks lurking behind the vulgar notion of probability. ↑**Probability, vulgar notion**. Given that there are currently about 6 billion people in the world, the probability that a human being picked at random be the American president is only 1:6 billion = 0.0000000017. Hence it would seem that the following argument holds. (1) If an individual is human, he or she is probably not the American president; (2) John Doe is the American president; (3) therefore, John Doe is (probably) not a human being. Obviously, this is not a valid conclusion. Indeed, its premises are

    A For every x, if x is human, then the probability that x be the American President = 0.0000000017.
    B John Doe is the American president.

However, nothing follows from the conjunction of *A* and *B*. Indeed, by hypothesis, the total population (or sample space) in question is humankind at the present moment. Hence an individual picked at random from this population is necessarily a human like the rest. So, whether such individual is the American president or not is irrelevant: such individual is, by assumption, human. Moral: Beware of ordinary language, particularly when employing the word 'probability'. **b Rooted in the subjectivist interpretation**. ↑**Subjective** (or Bayesian) probability is rife with paradoxes. One of them is the following—which, according to legend, nearly wrecked a conference on theoretical biology. Of three prisoners, Matthew, Mark, and Luke, two are to be executed, but Matthew does not know which. He believes that his own chance of being executed is 2/3. He asks the jailer to give him the name of one man, either Mark or Luke, who is going to be executed. The jailer replies that Mark will be executed. Good subjectivist that he is, Matthew feels somewhat relieved: he believes that this piece of information lowers his chance of being executed from 2/3 to 1/2. Is he right? No, because the individuals to be executed have already been chosen: the problem is alien to chance, hence talk of probability is unjustified. Only if the two prisoners to be executed had been picked at random, the probability of Matthew's being chosen would have been 2/3. And his chance would indeed drop to 1/2 only if his jailers, having condemned Mark, decided to draw lots between Matthew and Luke. But this is not one of the data of the problem. Moral: Beware of subjective probabilities: attaching numbers to hunches does not render these more respectable.

PROBABILITY, SUBJECTIVE a General Subjective probability is said to be a measure of the degree of belief in, or credibility of, a proposition. Hence its **syn** ↑**credence**. It is often resorted to in the face of uncertainty, i.e., the absence of sufficient information. Being subjective, the probabilities that different subjects assign to the same event are likely to be different, yet on the same footing, hence corrigible only in the light of future information. In other words, subjective probability assignments are intuitive and arbitrary, hence nonscientific. Consequently they amount to gambling without knowing the odds—clearly an irrational procedure and one risky in practice. By the same token, playing with subjective probabilities lends itself to endless philosophical games falling in the category of ↑**hollow exactness**. Thus, assigning subjective probabilities to propositions has rightly been called "gambling with truth." Likewise, assigning subjective probabilities to events, as is done in ↑**decision theory** and ↑**game theory**, could be gambling with life and death—unless of course one is only playing an academic game.

PROBABILITY, VULGAR NOTION In ordinary language 'probable' is often identified with either 'likely' or 'plausible'. Both identities are incorrect. The former because, whereas 'probable' designates a quantitative concept, 'likely' is qualitative. And equating ↑**plausibility** with probability is mistaken because a proposition, whether plausible or not, cannot be assigned a probability, any more than it can be priced. ↑**Probability paradoxes**.

PROBLEM A gap in knowledge judged worthy of being filled. A first partition of the set of problems is into *conceptual* and *empirical*. Whereas the former require only conceptual tools, the latter also demand empirical investigation. This distinction is overlooked by the philosophers who attempt to solve psychological problems in an a priori fashion, as well as by the students of society who posit utilities and probabilities without any empirical evidence. The following is a finer partition. *Logical*: demanding only logical analysis. Example: Find out whether the relation of buying is binary, ternary, or quaternary. *Mathematical*: requiring only mathematical knowledge. Example: check the proof of a given theorem. *Scientific*: demanding empirical or mathematical research. Example: the old Molyeneux problem, concerning a man born blind who has learned to distinguish by touch a cube from a sphere: Were he to receive suddenly the gift of sight, would he be able to distinguish those things by just looking at them? *Technological*: demanding technological knowledge and acquaintance with the client's specifications. Example: Design a purely defensive army costing no more than 1 percent of the GDP. *Moral*: requiring moral principles and knowledge of the situation of the people involved. Example: Discuss the pros and cons of legislation restricting the right to reproduce. *Practical*: demanding ordinary or artisanal knowledge. Example: Repair this computer or that hernia. Finally, another classing of problems is into direct and inverse. *Direct* problems are well posed and mostly soluble, and have unique solutions. Examples: given a target and a beam of particles directed at it, predict (probabilistically) how they will scatter; given a person's intentions and circumstances, forecast his behavior. *Inverse* problems are improperly posed, typically have no solutions, and, when they do have solutions, these may not be unique. Examples: given the particles scattered by a target, guess the latter's interaction with the incoming particles; given a person's behavior, guess his intentions and circumstances. Problems are expressed either as questions (e.g., 'What is X?') or as imperatives (e.g., 'Find out X'). ↑**Erotetic logic**, ↑**inverse problem**.

PROBLEM, PHILOSOPHICAL A problem in logic, semantics, epistemology, ontology, axiology, ethics, praxiology, or social philosophy. Typically, a general, bold, and unsettling questioning of a piece of received wisdom that nonphilosophers regard as unproblematic. Examples: Why accept the standard inference rules? What are meaning and truth?, What, if anything, holds the universe together? What are the differences beween computers and brains? and Can we give good reasons for value judgments and moral rules? The mere statement of a philosophical problem presupposes the solution to a number of other problems. For example, asking whether the death penalty is moral presupposes a definition of morality, the admission that the law and ethics intersect, and the acceptance of the canons of rational debate. Much the same holds for the checking of a solution to any philosophical problem: We want to know whether it is clear and logically coherent, whether it jibes with antecedent knowledge, and whether and how it might be tested for truth. In other words, philosophical problems come in bunches (systems), and in definite though changeable contexts. For this reason it is fruitless to tackle philosophical problems one at a time and in a philosophical vacuum—the way they are in ↑**ordinary-language philosophy**. The latter, incidentally, holds that what pass for philosophical problems are just puzzles arising from a careless use of language.

PROBLEM SOLVING Most intellectual activities consist in attempting to solve problems with given means and aims. But once in a while researchers engage in problem finding: they look for gaps in the background knowledge. Computers can help with problem solving but not with problem finding. Hence they cannot replace curious brains. In particular, they cannot replace the trailblazers.

PROBLEMATICS The collection of possible problems in a field of research or action. Examples: the problematics of cognitive neuroscience is the collection of all the possible problems concerning the neural "substrate" of mental processes; that of ontology is the collection of all the possible problems concerning the most general features of reality. The concept of problematics occurs in the characterizations of ↑**science**, ↑**technology**, and other fields of inquiry.

PROCEDURAL Having to do with procedure or form rather than substance. Examples: the procedural view of justice inherent in ↑**legal positivism**; and Joseph Schumpeter's and Karl Popper's procedural conception of democracy as being about votes rather than the common good.

PROCESS A sequence of states of a concrete (material) thing. Examples: motion, change in chemical composition, signal propagation, digestion, perceiving, thinking, working. Formalization in the case of denumerable states: $\pi = <s_1, s_2, \ldots, s_n>$, where the s_i stand for the states of the thing in question. If a process is a continuous sequence, and the state function F of the changing thing is time-dependent, we can set $\pi = < F(t)$ | $t \in T>$, where T is the duration of the process. If two or more processes occur in a thing at the same time (in parallel), more than one state function is needed to describe them. If they are independent, the total process is represented by the union of the partial processes. A *Markov process* is a stochastic (probabilistic) process in which the next state depends exclusively upon the present state and not on the past history of the system concerned. Warning: anatomists use 'process' as synonymous with 'organ'.

PROCESSUALISM The view according to which all things change. Its motto is Heraclitus's ↑*Panta rhei*. Its heuristic metaphor is the river or, more abstractly, the so-called ↑**arrow of time**. Processualism comes in two strengths: radical and moderate. According to the former, as represented by Alfred N. Whitehead, concrete things are bundles of processes. This thesis is logically untenable, because the notion of a process presupposes that of a thing, since a process is defined as a change in the state of a concrete entity. By contrast, the moderate version of processualism is compelling. In fact, all the factual sciences study changeable things, and all the technologies design alterations in existing things, or even wholly new things. In short, the universe is indeed like a river, though not pure flux: what "flows" incessantly is stuff of some kind or other—physical, chemical, biological, social, technical, or semiotic.

PROGRAM a Methodology A collection of scientific or technological research ↑**projects** or ↑**plans** unified by an ↑**approach** and a ↑**goal**. Examples: the programs of current research into the origin of life, the neural "basis" of mind, the search for extraterrestrial life, and the automation of routine work. **b Computer science** A precise instruction for the step-by-step solution of a well-formulated problem. An ↑**algorithm** that, when fed into a computer, guides it from one state to another, in such a way that the data of a problem get transformed into its solution in a "mechanical" way, that is, with neither additional assumptions nor intelligence, let alone intuition. In other words, such an algorithm is a well-defined function $\alpha : D \rightarrow S$. **c Program-as-theory view** The opinion that computer programs are ↑**theories** or equivalent to theories. This claim is mistaken because, whereas a computer program is a sequence of instructions, which are neither true nor false, a theory is a ↑**hypothetico-deductive** system of propositions that can be tested for truth. **d Politics** A statement of society-wide goals, such as either social welfare or the promotion of private enterprise, accompanied by the means deemed adequate to implement them. Political programs are inspired by ↑**ideologies**, hence partly by some ↑**political philosophy** or other.

PROGRESS Process of improvement in some regard and to some degree. Denied by cultural relativism and the mythologies involving the idea of a past Golden Age or Garden of Eden. **a Epistemology** Increase in the truth, depth, coverage, and systemicity of the body of knowledge. Some of the means for epistemic progress are: increased accuracy of empirical data; replacement of unrelated hypotheses by theories, of verbal models by mathematical ones, and of ↑**black-box** theories with translucent-box ones; and interrelation or even merger of previously isolated research fields. **b History of philosophy** Has there been progress in philosophy? Yes, but not in all epochs and not without stagnation and regression. For example, epistemology, ontology, and axiology tackle today problems that were not even on the agenda a century ago, such as whether atomic physics confirms subjectivism; whether things are bundles of events; and whether individual values, such as liberty, can be promoted without implementing social values, such as democracy. **c Ontology and science** Claude Bernard's criterion of biological progress: increasing autonomy vis à vis the environment, which amounts to increasing stability of the organism's internal milieu (homeostasis). All progress is advancement in some regards, never in all. Moreover, it may be conjectured that all progress in a given regard is accompanied by regress in others. For example, increase in the speed of locomotion, whether in animals or in artifacts, is achieved through increased energy spending; increased ease of mechanical computation is accompanied by loss of ability to do approximate mental calculations; and most technological progress causes unemployment. Therefore the idea that biological evolution and human history are always progressive is false. Not even one-sided progress is continual: there are plenty of regressive phases, some of which end up in extinction. In short, the "law of progress" is mythical. **d Ethics** There is moral progress in a society if its members become increasingly honest, solidary, kind, free, tolerant of diversity, and willing to resolve conflicts by peaceful means. **e Social philosophy** A social change is progressive if it improves the quality of life of the vast majority. Examples: environmental protection, family planning, universal health care, and education. A social change is regressive if it causes most people to be worse off than before. A social philosophy, ideology, program, or party can be said to be progressive if it promotes or effects progressive changes.

PROJECT, RESEARCH A ↑**plan** designed to study a particular ↑**problem**.

PROMOTION The sole unconfessed goal of many an academic exercise.

PROOF a Logic and mathematics Logically valid derivation of a theorem from assumptions or definitions with the help of rules of inference. In other words, a formal proof is a finite sequence of statements, such that each of them is either a premise or a consequence of one or more preceding members of the string in accordance with a logical rule of inference. Formal proofs are typical of formal science and of the mathematized sectors of factual science. Proof theory is the nucleus of ↑**metamathematics**. **b Epistemology** It is generally accepted that proofs are the prerogative of mathematicians: that nothing can be proved in factual science or in technology. However, most scientists and technologists do not abide by this radical skeptic view. Thus, they will claim that diffraction proves that light is undulatory rather than corpuscular; that hydrolysis proves that water is a compound; that the effects of drugs and surgery on mental functions proves that these are brain processes; that fossils and vestigial organs prove evolution—and so on. In short, most scientists regard overwhelming and repeated evidence as proof, even though it lacks logical necessity.

PROPENSITY Tendency of a thing to pass from one state to another. Two kinds: causal and stochastic. Moths have a (causal) propensity to fly toward light sources. Excited atoms have a (stochastic) tendency to decay to lower-energy states. ↑**Probability** quantitates stochastic propensity.

PROPERTY Feature, trait, or characteristic possessed by some object, conceptual or material. Properties are conceptualized as ↑**predicates**. The former are possessed, the latter are attributed (correctly or incorrectly). The *scope* of a property is the collection of things that possess it. If human knowledge were perfect, the scope of a property would be identical with the ↑**extension** of the corresponding predicate. *Universal principles* about properties of objects of any kind, whether conceptual or material: (1) Every property is the property of some object: there are no properties in themselves (non-Platonism); (2) every object has a finite (but perhaps very large) number of properties; (3)

some properties are intrinsic and others relational; (4) some properties are essential and others accidental; (5) every property is related to other properties: there are no stray properties. *Ontological principles* about concrete things: (1) every property is either primary (subject-independent) or secondary (subject-dependent); (2) there are neither negative nor disjunctive properties; (3) all properties are changeable; (4) every law of things of a kind is a property of theirs; (5) every property is involved in at least one law: there are no lawless properties. *Epistemological principles* about properties of concrete things: (1) every property is scrutable, however indirectly and partially; (2) every property can be conceptualized as a predicate in at least one manner (the properties-predicates relation is one-many). ↑**Nominalism** rejects properties or construes them as sets (of the individuals that instantiate them). Hence they cannot distinguish properties with the same scope, such as "scarce" and "expensive."

PROPHECY Groundless forecast. Examples: prophecies of the end of the world, history, reason, science, or philosophy. When the prophecies of a cult fail, most of its followers rally rather than defecting. By contrast, when a scientific prediction fails, scientists revise some of its premises (hypotheses or data).

PROPOSAL Invitation, suggestion. Example 1: "It was proposed to investigate the logic of problems." Example 2: Notation conventions, as in "Let n designate an arbitrary whole number." Proposals can be evaluated as interesting, practical, or acceptable, and can thus be discussed rationally. But they are neither true nor false. Not to be confused with ↑**proposition**.

PROPOSITION The simplest meaningful system composed of concepts. **Syn** ↑**statement**. Examples: "2 >1," "Canada is cold," "Antarctica is colder than Canada." The following, a fragment of the ordinary propositional calculus, is one of the possible implicit (more precisely, axiomatic) definitions of the concept of a proposition. A proposition is any formula that satisfies the following conditions (axiom schemata):

P1 $p \vee p \Rightarrow p$ (simplification)
P2 $p \Rightarrow p \vee p$ (addition)
P3 $p \vee q \Rightarrow q \vee p$ (commutativity)
P4 $(p \Rightarrow q) \Rightarrow (r \vee p \Rightarrow r \vee q)$ (interpolation)

However, this definition is incomplete, for it does not include the condition that every instance of a propositional schema has got to have a ↑**meaning**, i.e., a ↑**reference** together with a ↑**sense**. As for ↑**truth**, it is a sufficient but not a necessary property of a proposition. That is, whatever is true or false (in some degree) is a proposition, but the converse is false. ↑**Truth-gap theory**. Warning 1: Propositions are not to be confused with ↑**proposals**—as they often are in everyday parlance, particularly in French. Warning 2: Nor are they to be mistaken for sentences, since every proposition can be designated by one or more ↑**sentences** in some language. The converse is false, for there are sentences that designate no propositions because they have no signification. Examples taken from Heidegger: *Die Sprache spricht* ("Language speaks"), *Die Welt weltet* ("The world worlds"), *Die Werte gelten* ("Values are worth").

PROPOSITIONAL ATTITUDE Any of the mental attitudes to a proposition, as in '*b* believes that *p*', '*b* doubts that *p*', '*b* hopes that *p* will come to pass', and '*b* wishes that *p* were true'. Since propositional attitudes are facts, they should be studied by psychology and linguistics rather than being made the subject of philosophical speculation. ↑**Belief.**

PROPOSITIONALIZATION Transformation of an imperative or an interrogative into a declarative sentence. Examples: Do not kill! → It is immoral to kill; What is to be done? → We are faced with the problem of deciding what to do.

PROTO Prefix suggesting logical or historical precedence, as in "protophysics" and "protoscience." Examples: protophysics studies such ontological items as physical addition and the part-whole relation, as well as such omnipresent scientific concepts as magnitude, dimension, and unit; the social studies are still at the protoscientific stage; and linguistic philosophy is a protophilosophy.

PROXY ↑**Indicator.**

PSEUDOEXACTNESS The use of symbols that designate ill-defined concepts. ↑**Alchemy, conceptual.**

PSEUDOFACT A nonexisting fact mistaken for a fact. Examples: Sightings of angels, flying saucers, "aliens," and positivists. Belief in pseudofacts is often fostered by superstition or ideology. Occasionally it may be suggested by scientific theory too. But in this case the belief, if interesting, may excite the curiosity of others who will try to replicate it, and so eventually the alleged fact will be shown to be a nonfact. The distinction between genuine facts and pseudofacts is alien to antirealists, in particular social ↑**constructivists,** for according to them all facts are artifacts. For this reason, they treat pseudoscience on a par with science.

PSEUDOPHILOSOPHY Discourse that sounds philosophical but isn't, for being nonsensical, trivial, or utterly at variance with the bulk of scientific or technological knowledge. Example: "*Insein* [Being-in] is [. . .] the formal existential expression of the being of *Dasein* [Being-there], which has the essential condition of Being-in-the-world" (Martin Heidegger). Gertrud, are you in the kitchen? Ach so, then you are there. Good, then you are-in-the-world.

PSEUDOPROBLEM A problem concerning a ↑**pseudofact,** or raised by a ↑**fuzzy** idea, or by a knowledge gap. Examples of the first: How does levitation work? How did the universe come into being? Examples of the second: Why is there something rather than nothing? What comes first: existence or action? Examples of the third: the ↑**raven** and ↑**grue** paradoxes. The ↑**logical positivists** dismissed metaphysics, accusing it of dealing only with pseudoproblems, either in being ill-formulated or in not being soluble with the help of empirical data. This is indeed the case with much of metaphysics—including the ↑**phenomenalism** held by the positivists themselves. However, it is possible to formulate some metaphysical problems in an exact manner, and to investigate them in the light of scientific or technological knowledge. ↑**Ontology.**

PSEUDOSCIENCE Doctrine or practice devoid of scientific foundation but sold as scientific. Examples: astrology, graphology, characterology, parapsychology, psychoanalysis, psychohistory, creation science, and neoclassical microeconomics. The pseudosciences are excellent tests for any philosophy of science. Tell me how many pseudosciences you are willing to buy, and I'll tell you what your philosophy of science is worth.

PSEUDOTAUTOLOGY An expression that has the linguistic form of a tautology but not its logical form. Example: 'Enough is enough'. This sentence looks like the tautology "a = a," but actually it is short for "You have said (or done) too much already. Now stop it." This example should be enough to exhibit the shallowness of linguistic analysis. ↑**Language game,** ↑**linguistic analysis**.

PSYCHOLOGISM a General The view that psychology can explain everything human, from logic to society. A popular delusion that underrates nonmental factors, in particular environmental and economic ones; ignores the importance of studying ideas in themselves regardless of who thinks them; and overrates the power of ↑**psychology**. **b Philosophy of logic** The opinion that logic is the study of the laws of thought, and that all ideal (abstract) objects are psychological. The invention of nonstandard logics and the counterintuitive character of many mathematical ideas have falsified psychologism. Although Husserl is often credited with antipsychologism, actually he took it from Frege, who in turn borrowed it from Bolzano, who had learned it from Leibniz, who got it from Plato.

PSYCHOLOGY The study of behavior and mind. **a Folk** The part of ordinary knowledge that attempts to account for behavior and mind. A mixed bag of truths and superstitions. **b Protoscientific: nonbiological** The experimental and theoretical investigation that describes behavioral and mental processes, and tries to discover their patterns. **c Scientific: biological** The scientific search for the biological (in particular neural and endocrine) mechanisms of behavior and mentation. **Syn** ↑**cognitive neuroscience**, psychobiology, physiological psychology, neuropsychology. Philosophical underpinning: ↑**emergentist materialism. d Philosophy of psychology** The logical, semantical, epistemological, ontological, and ethical study of psychological theories and practices, as well as of the interactions between psychology and philosophy. Example 1: Most armchair psychology presupposes the myth of the immaterial soul. Example 2: Behaviorism puts into practice the positivist injunction to stick to data and to refrain from making hypotheses about unobservables. Example 3: Neuropsychology presupposes (and confirms) the materialist doctrine that the mental is neurophysiological. Example 4: The clinical psychologists and psychiatrists who put the mental health of their patients at risk by employing false or untested theories betray the Hippocratic oath.

PSYCHON The smallest neuronal system capable of having a mental experience.

PSYCHOPHYSICAL PARALLELISM The view that mental states are synchronous with brain states, but otherwise unrelated to them. A variety of psychoneural dualism. ↑**Mind-body problem**. Parallelism is popular for the following reasons. First, it jibes with the vulgar idea that, although mind and body are separate, they are somehow related to each other. Second, it allows physicists, chemists, and biologists to go about their business without bothering about the possibility that their own mental processes may influence directly their laboratory operations. Third, it excuses the psychologists who take no interest in the brain. Despite its popularity, parallelism is not scientific, because it is empirically unfalsifiable. Indeed, every time a mental event occurs, it will be found that a concomitant neural event happens. Besides being untestable in the strong sense, parallelism is at variance with the tacit scientific ↑**worldview**, which is ↑**materialist**. Furthermore, along with the remaining varieties of psychoneural dualism, parallelism is an obstacle to the investigation of the neurophysiological mechanisms of the mind.

PURE Polysemous term, signifying now a priori, as in Kant's "pure reason," now disinterested, as in "pure (or basic) science."

PURPORT The purport of a construct in a given context is the set of its entailers in the context. Dual: ↑**import**. The union of the purport and the import of a construct equals the latter's ↑**sense**.

PURPOSIVE ↑**Goal-directed**. Behavior directed to attaining a goal. A feature of some of the behavior of the higher vertebrates. A peculiarity of ↑**anthropocentric** doctrines, in particular theologies, is to attribute a purpose to every thing and every process. ↑**Teleology**.

PUZZLE Trivial question, the tackling of which requires neither technical expertise nor research involving original ideas, and the solution to which does not enrich human knowledge. ↑**Linguistic philosophy**.

Q.E.D. *Quod erat demonstrandum*: which was to be demonstrated. The frequent use of this expression in mathematics suggests that theorems do not drop automatically from axioms and definitions, but have to be guessed before an attempt is made to prove them. Nor do axioms and definitions always suffice: special constructions and lemmas (propositions borrowed from other theories) are usually needed as well.

QUAESTIO FACTI A problem or matter of fact, and thus to be settled with the help of empirical data. For example, whether or not there is free will, and whether or not the market is a morality school, are matters of fact, hence to be investigated empirically.

QUAESTIO JURIS A problem or matter of law or rule, as opposed to one of fact. For example, whether an action conforms to the law of the land, or a procedure fits the scientific method, are matters of law, hence to be solved by checking the corresponding norms rather than any facts.

QUALIA Phenomenal (or secondary) properties, such as colors, sounds, tastes, smells, and textures. Phenomenalists treat qualia as independent entities, as in "this blue" and "that noise." However, this is an abstraction: there are no qualia without sentient organisms. ↑**Phenomenalism,** ↑**primary / secondary properties**. Some philosophers have misunderstood the denial of the independent (subject-free) reality of qualia to mean that the scientific worldview is purely quantitative. This is mistaken, for not all quantities are pure quantities, i.e., numbers such as 7 or π. The values of ↑**magnitudes** are quantities or degrees of qualities or properties.Thus 100 km/hr is an amount of speed. And psychoneural ↑**dualists** claim that qualia cannot possibly be accounted for in neurophysiological terms. How do they know? The current gaps in psychology should not be turned into the pillars of a solid philosophy of mind. And those gaps are being closed by ↑**cognitive neuroscience**, which is gradually unveiling the mechanisms whereby the brain transforms sensations (stimulus detections) into perceptions (qualia). What is true is that, since the neuroscientist cannot see, hear, or taste a quale from the outside, he must rely on the experimental subject's introspective report. Still, this problem is not radically different from the nuclear physicist's, who has no direct access to nuclear processes.

QUALITATIVE Concerning nonquantitative features. Logic, set theory, abstract algebra, and general topology, as well as philosophy, are qualitative disciplines. A *qualitative change* is one involving a gain or loss of properties. Qualitative changes can be represented quantitatively, namely by functions whose values grow from zero or vanish to zero. In a ↑**state space**, qualitative changes appear as the sprouting or pruning of the axes representing the properties in question.

QUALITY a Syn ↑property. b Nonquantitative property, such as existence and beauty. Quality does not oppose quantity. Every quantitative property is the amount, intensity, or degree of some quality. For example, volume is the measure of expanse, pH measures acidity, and the Gini index measures income inequality. **c Law of change of quality into quantity and vice versa** This, the third "law" of dialectics, is a confused way of stating the true ontological thesis that qualitative changes are bound to occur as increases or decreases in the intensity of a quantitative property cross a threshold; and that, once such change occurs, a new pace of growth or decline starts. Calling this a 'transformation of quality into quantity', or vice versa, is characteristic of muddled thinking. **d Praxiology** Grade of a good or service, as in "good-quality car." Quality in this sense is in principle definable in quantitative terms, such as reliability and durability.

QUANTIFIER A logical prefix such as 'some' or 'all'. The former is called 'existential', the latter 'universal'. The name 'existential quantifier', symbolized ∃, is adequate in mathematics: here, existence coincides with someness. For example, when writing an equation of the form "$F(x) = 0$," where F is a numerical function, we presuppose the prefix $∃x$, namely thus: $∃x [F(x) = 0]$. This formula can be read either "There exist zeroes of F" (simpler: "F has [some] zeroes") or "For some values of x, F takes on the value 0." In extramathematical contexts '∃' is ambiguous: it can mean either factual (concrete) existence, or formal (abstract) existence. In these contexts we often need to specify which of the two senses is intended. Moreover, since existence (in some context) is supremely important, it should be regarded as a property. Modern logicians have rejected this claim on the ground that ∃ is not a predicate. But this is begging the question whether "exists" can be formalized as a predicate. In fact an ↑**existence predicate** can be defined in an exact fashion.

QUANTITATION The transformation of a qualitative concept into a quantitative one. Examples: "weight" quantitates "heaviness," and "probability" quantitates "chance propensity." If the concept concerned is a set, its quantitation consists in finding out the cardinality (numerosity) of the set. If the concept is a predicate denoting a quantitative property of real things, its quantitation consists in the introduction of a ↑**magnitude** or numerical function. In the social sciences the ambiguous 'quantification' is used more frequently.

QUANTITY ↑Magnitude.

QUANTON Any of the physical entities that quantum physics accounts for adequately and classical physics does not. Examples: photons, neutrinos, electrons, atoms, molecules, crystals, superconductors, and neutron stars. Dual: Classon. ↑**Quantum mechanics**.

QUANTUM LOGIC Logical calculus that purports to tackle some of the perplexities raised by quantum physics, in particular the fact that an electron does not have at the same time a sharp position and a sharp momentum. However, this is no more paradoxical than that one cannot swim and type at the same time. These are features of reality, and therefore beyond the scope of logic. Moreover, the very idea of quantum logic is rooted in a mistaken conflation between operators and propositions. In any event, no new theorems in quantum physics have ever been deduced with the help of quantum logic. Which is what should have been expected from the start, since quantum theories have classical mathematics built into them, and in turn the underlying logic of classical mathematics is the ordinary predicate logic. In sum, quantum logic is one more academic industry.

QUANTUM MECHANICS The branch of quantum physics that deals with things endowed with mass, such as electrons, but in general lack classical properties such as sharp positions. It is of philosophical interest for several reasons. First, it replaces classical mechanics at the microphysical level—which argues for the objectivity of ↑**levels** of organization. Second, it does not contain the concepts of sharp shape and speed; most properties turn out to be blunt rather than sharp. Third, it contains the principle "Once a system always a system." Fourth, it contains markedly counterintuitive but well-corroborated results, such as ↑**Heisenberg's inequalities** (the sharper the position, the more spread out the velocity, and conversely). For this reason its referents are best given a special name, such as ↑*quantons*, rather than being called 'particles' or 'waves'. Fifth, the theory was initially interpreted as asserting that all microphysical facts are created by acts of observation or measurement: this is the gist of the Copenhagen interpretation, which prevailed in textbooks until recently. This view, which evokes Berkeley's ↑*esse est percipi*, is untenable for the following reasons. First, the axiomatization of the theory reveals that it does not contain the concept of an observer. Second, when posing a theoretical problem that does not involve a measuring instrument, the macrophysical environment is taken for granted and treated classically as a whole instead of being analyzed into microentities. (This point is relevant to the problem of ↑**macro-micro** relations, in particular ↑**reduction**. The need to specify the environment and the global way in which it is described show the failure of radical ↑**reductionism**, hence of methodological ↑**individualism**.) Third, normally, when calculating energy levels, scattering cross-sections, and other quantities, no reference to observation is made. Nor could it be made when calculating spontaneous processes, such as radioactivity, pair "annihilation," or the light emitted by a star. All of this suggests that the positivist or ↑**Copenhagen interpretation** of quantum mechanics is inconsistent with its mathematical formalism, and points to the need for a realist interpretation of it. For example, the usual (semisubjectivist) formulation of Born's postulate is this: "$|\psi(x)|^2 \, \Delta x$ is the probability of *finding* the thing in question in state ψ within Δx upon measuring its position." This formulation is wrong if only because such probability depends not only on the thing but also upon the measurement technique. A realist reformulation of the principle is this: "$|\psi(x)|^2 \, \Delta x$ is the probability that the thing in state ψ *is present* within Δx." Such a reinterpretation not only clarifies and simplifies matters: it also brings the theory in line with the rest of science, and it prevents the use of the theory in support of spiritualism.

QUESTION Linguistic expression of a ↑**problem**. Example: 'What is the composition of x?' 'What are the constituents of x?' and 'The problem is to find the composition of x', as well as their translations into other languages, are equivalent formulations of one and the same problem. Experimental psychologists have shown that subjects behave differently when asked to solve a given problem framed as different though equivalent questions.

QUESTIONABLE An idea is questionable if it is unclear, insufficiently justified, or false. Every time an idea is questioned, it is judged in relation to some body of knowledge that is assumed if only for the sake of the argument: there is no absolute doubting, or questioning in a vacuum. Hence the logical impossibility of absolute (or radical) ↑**skepticism**.

QUOTATION Quoting serves multiple scholarly functions: giving credit, exhibiting evidence, giving the impression of scholarship, flattering, sparing the effort of doing research, and serving as a wheelchair for the intellectually handicapped.

QUOTATION MARKS Single quotes, as in *'love' is a four-letter word*, flag linguistic expressions and kick them up to the metalanguage. Double quotes, as in *"power" is a relation*, serve to distinguish constructs from either words or things.

RADICAL PHILOSOPHY A philosophy that wrestles with deep problems or defends extreme views. Examples: innatism and behaviorism; vulgar materialism (physicalism) and idealism; empiricism and rationalism; utilitarianism and deontologism. The great virtue of radicalism is its consistency; its greatest risk is that it is likely to propose at best only half-true solutions to multifaceted problems. For example, radical empiricism ("Experience is the alpha and the omega of knowledge") and radical rationalism ("Reason is both necessary and sufficient to attain knowledge of any kind") are each only half-true. Again, talk of rights only is just as one-sided as exclusive talk of duties. Caution: in recent times 'radical philosophy' has come to denote a mishmash of marginal philosophies, many of them irrationalist.

RANDOMNESS Syn ↑**chance**. The particular kind of disorder characterized by local irregularity (e.g., individual coin tossing) combined with global regularity (e.g., long-run equal chances of heads and tails). The standard view is that randomness is measured by ↑**probability**. Far from being lawless, the events in a process or in a collection of facts are said to be random if they satisfy ↑**probability laws**, that is, formulas containing concepts drawn from the ↑**probability calculus**. In turn, this calculus applies only to random events. No circularity here: if there is reason to suspect that the events of a certain type are random, one attempts to craft a probabilistic model to represent them. One then checks the model by confronting it not only to the original data but also by checking some predictions made with the help of the model. If the model is empirically confirmed, it is pronounced true—till new notice—and the events in question are pronounced random. But if the model is refuted by the available evidence, there are two possibilities: either the events are nonrandom or the events are random but either the particular stochastic model is false or the checking procedure was incorrect—e.g., for involving an exceedingly small sample. ↑**Chance, probability**.

RANDOMNESS TEST Criterion to decide, at least provisionally, whether or not a collection or sequence of events is random. Any probability distribution or stochastic (probabilistic) model will serve as such a criterion. However, no randomess test is suitable for populations of all kinds. For example, the Poisson distribution is adequate to test large numbers of low-probability events (such as the disintegrations of a small sample of radioactive material), but not for very small numbers, such as scientific discoveries. The problem is still open, as shown by the coexistence of alternative theories of randomness. However, each of these exactifies in its own way the intuitions that

239

(a) randomness comes in degrees; and (b) randomness is complete or perfect when each item in the collection has the same probability (i.e., for a uniform distribution).

RATIOEMPIRICISM Any synthesis of moderate ↑**rationalism** and moderate ↑**empiricism.** Examples: Kant's epistemology, ↑**logical positivism**, and **scientific** ↑**realism.**

RATIONAL-CHOICE THEORY Any ↑**theory** or ↑**model** whose central concepts are those of subjective ↑**utility** and ↑**probability**, and whose key axiom is that everyone behaves (or ought to behave) so as to maximize his or her expected utility. (Expected utility of an action with possible outcome X = probability of X × utility of X.) The general theories of utility, decision, and games, as well as the rational-choice models in economics, sociology, political science, and other fields, are of the rational-choice type. Whereas some scholars regard them as descriptive, others take them to be normative. All of these theories assume that every person has his or her own utility function for goods of every kind; that this function depends only on the quantity of the good in question; that it does not alter with experience; and that all persons, in all circumstances, attempt to maximize their expected utilities. However, the precise form of the utility function is seldom specified: usually it is only subjected to the rather lax condition that it increases monotonously at a decreasing rate. And even when the function is mathematically well-defined, it is rarely checked empirically. Furthermore, the assumption that the outcomes of any action can be assigned a probability is false: outside the casino, human actions are seldom left to chance. Because of such conceptual and empirical flaws, rational-choice theories are hardly scientific. Yet all of them have a true kernel, namely the thesis that human action has a strong self-interest component. ↑**Utility,** ↑**utilitarianism.**

RATIONALISM Recognition of the authority of reason. *Moderate* or *critical* rationalism: Trust in reason to help search for truth or efficiency. In this sense many philosophical schools, from Platonism and Aristotelianism to Thomism to Kantianism to dialectical materialism to logical empiricism, are rationalist. *Radical* or *dogmatic* rationalism: Blind faith in the ability of reason, unaided by perception or action, to unveil reality or even construct it. **Syn** ↑**apriorism.** Radical rationalism is adequate only in ↑**mathematics,** which deals exclusively with ↑**truths** of reason. It is inadequate everywhere else. By contrast, moderate rationalism, when combined with moderate empiricism, is adequate in all inquiries and deliberations concerning matters of fact. This combination is ↑**ratioempiricism,** in particular **scientific realism.**

RATIONALITY The word 'rationality' is polysemous. Hence its indiscriminate use without qualification is an indicator of weak or lazy rationality. Indeed, at least the following twelve concepts of rationality should be distinguished. (1) *Semantical*: minimizing fuzziness (vagueness or imprecision), i.e., maximizing exactness. Example: replacing "most" by a precise percentage. (2) *Logical*: striving for internal consistency, i.e., avoiding contradiction. Example: replacing "yes and no" by "yes in respect A, no in respect B." (3) *Dialectical*: checking for inferential validity, i.e., conformity to the rules of deductive inference. Example: No one has disproved the existence of God; does it follow that God exists? (4) *Erotetic*: posing only problems that make sense in some context. Example: refraining from asking such questions as Where does time go? and Why is there something rather than nothing? (5) *Methodological*: (a) questioning, i.e., doubting and criticizing; (b) justifying, i.e., demanding proof or evidence, favorable or unfavorable; or (c) using only justifiable methods, i.e., procedures that are empirically successful and grounded in well-confirmed theories. Example: Are such-and-such parapsychological experiments methodologically clean? (6) *Epistemological*: Caring for empirical support, and discarding conjectures incompatible with the bulk of scientific and technological knowledge. Example: Has telepathy been shown to exist, and would it be consistent with the scientific hypothesis that mental processes are brain processes? (7) *Ontological*: adopting a consistent worldview compatible with the bulk of the sciences and technologies of the day. Example: Is the belief in an afterlife compatible with biology and psychology? (8)*Valuational*: studying, ranking, choosing, designing, or striving for goals that, in addition to being attainable, are worthwhile. Example: Is it worthwhile trading earthly delights for promises of an afterlife? (9)*Prohairetic*: ranking a set S of alternatives (or options) in such a way that the preference relation $\geq$ is complete (i.e., covers all the pairs of members of S), reflexive ($x \geq x$ for all x in S), and transitive (If $x \geq y$ and $y \geq z$, then $x \geq z$ for all x, y and z in S). (10) *Moral*: adopting, proposing or following moral norms that, in addition to being implementable, are likely to promote individual or social welfare. (11) *Practical*: Adopting means likely to help attain the goals in view. (12) *Economic*: envisaging or carrying out courses of action likely to maximize one's utility without regard to others or even at their expense. Shorter: egoism. (The disguise of selfishness as rationality is one of the great intellectual swindles of the twentieth century.) The first seven concepts may be designed collectively as *conceptual* rationality; the remaining five, *pragmatic*. Any view, plan, or course of action satisfying the first eleven rationality conditions will be said to be *fully rational*, or just *reasonable*. Anything violating one or more of the first eleven rationality conditions will be said to be *partially rational*. The first eleven concepts of rationality distinguished above are not mutually independent but form a system: they are ordered as indicated.

RATIONALITY, INSTRUMENTAL Principle of instrumental rationality: A rational individual engages deliberately in an action M at a certain time if (1) M is one of his goals and M has priority over other goals of his at that moment (in case the activity is its own reward); or (2) he has good reasons to believe that (a) action M is likely to help him attain a goal G to which he assigns priority at the time; and (b) the cost of M (to self or others) is smaller than the benefit derivable from attaining G (in case the activity is only a means to a goal). Instrumental rationality is said to be *objective* if the beliefs involved in the above principle constitute pieces of objective knowledge, i.e., are sufficiently justified. Otherwise it is *subjective*. Vilfredo Pareto assumed that all deliberate human behavior is either objectively or subjectively rational. But this assumption is a ↑**tautology** by virtue of the meaning of "deliberate." (Only arbitrary decisions are both objectively and subjectively irrational.) And the hypothesis that what is ordinarily described as subjective or irrational is so merely because the observers have not discovered the point of view of the actor is unfalsifiable. However, unlike the preceding assumption, this one is fertile: it suggests looking closer at the actor's interests and motives.

RAVEN'S PARADOX A paradox in ↑**inductive logic** proposed by Carl G. Hempel. The empirical generalization "All ravens are black" is formally equivalent to the proposition that all nonblack things are nonraven. (↑**Contraposition**.) Hence finding a blonde would seem to confirm the given generalization—which is paradoxical, not so say silly. This paradox is dissolved upon noting that anyone interested in ravens will start by confining his universe of discourse to birds, so that he would regard meeting a blonde as irrelevant to his concern. In other words, since the maximal reference class of "All ravens are black" is the class of birds, only data about birds are relevant to the hypothesis in question. Any reasonable theory of ↑**reference**, matching the way scientists actually handle predicates, might have avoided the flood of publications generated by this puzzle.

REAL Existing either in the external world (independently of any subject) or in subjective experience. Examples: stars and their perceptions, thought processes and hallucinations. Perception is only a fallible indicator of physical existence. The overwhelming majority of physical things are imperceptible; and sometimes we perceive things that are not there: hence the fallacy of ↑**phenomenalism** and the insufficiency of naive ↑**realism**. Caution: All natural things are real, but the converse is false since concrete artifacts, too, are real. **Ant** fictitious.

REAL DEFINITION Characterization or description of the salient features of a real thing, as in "Man is a tool-making animal." The name is inappropriate because ↑**definitions** proper are constructs (either identities or axiomatic), and obviously a real thing is not the same as any of its descriptions. The closest one can get to a real "definition" is this. Start by postulating the existence of entities of some kind, every member of which is endowed with such-and-such properties, and then introduce a definition that names such entities. Example: There are things endowed with mass, and these things are called 'bodies'. The ordered pair <postulate, definition> may thus be regarded as a modern successor to a real definition.

REALISM a Ontological and epistemological The view that some facts are objective rather than subjective or phenomenal, and that some of them can be known—though of course not perceptually but conceptually. There are three main kinds of realism: idealist, naive, and scientific. *Idealist* (or *Platonic*) *realism* identifies reality with the totality of ↑**ideas** and their shadows. The former are assumed to exist autonomously, in a realm of their own, whereas concrete things would be their shadows or copies. Thus, a circular tabletop would be only a poor copy of a perfect and eternal geometric circle. *Naive realism* regards as real whatever can be perceived and holds that the world is the way we perceive it to be. By contrast, *scientific realism* identifies ↑**reality** with the collection of all concrete things, i.e., things capable of changing in some respect or other. It also holds that things are far more complex than they appear to be, hence to account for them we need theories in addition to empirical data. According to scientific realism ideas, far from being self-existing, are in minds (or brains). The choice between the three kinds of realism depends on the kind of philosophy we want and where we wish to place it. If we care only for speculative philosophy, and accordingly place it in an ivory tower, we should prefer idealist realism because it is internally consistent and it demands the least effort. And if we do not care for the imperceptible constituents of the perceptible things, we can make do with naive realism. But if we want philosophy to be of some use in the quest to understand the real world, we should adopt (and enrich) scientific realism, for it postulates the autonomous existence of the external world, admits that we are largely ignorant of it, and encourages us to explore it further, enriching and deepening the fund of factual ↑**truths**. Although the concept of factual truth is central to scientific realism, this does not involve the assumption that complete truth is always obtainable. It demands only the search for truth, the eventual attainment of approximate truths, and the latter's corrigibility. **b Moral** The metaethical view that there are moral facts and, correspondingly, moral truths and falsities. Examples of moral facts: murder and volunteerism. Examples of moral truths: "Starting a war is the worst crime," and "Volunteerism is good." **c Legal** School of legal philosophy and jurisprudence that regards law as a ↑**sociotechnology** aiming at social control and social reform. ↑**Law, philosophy of**.

REALIST An adherent of ↑**realism**. Not to be confused with 'realistic' or practical. All realistic people are realists, but the converse is false.

REALITY The totality of ↑**real things**. Being a collection, reality is unreal. By contrast, the aggregation (physical addition) of all real things, that is, the ↑**universe** or ↑**world**, is real.

REALITY CHECK The test of a statement to find whether it is true as claimed. Reality checks are routine in everyday life, science, and technology. By contrast, they are absent from religion, pseudoscience, and nonscientific philosophy.

REASON The mental faculty consisting in thinking in a cogent way. The complement of experience and the guide to deliberate action. Trust in reason is called ↑**rationalism**.

REASON / CAUSE At first sight, the reason for doing something is not the same as the cause of the action: whereas reasons are conceptual, causes are physical. For example, the sudden shower caused me to take cover, but the reason for doing so was to avoid getting soaked. On second thought, reasons are efficient only when they become causes rather than remaining items of pure thought. But in this case the causes are internal: they occur in the agent's brain. So, the reason / cause distinction does not amount to a dichotomy.

REASONABLE Polysemous term. Rational, in agreement with the known facts, and taking the situation (or constraints) into account. Meek, conformist, in agreement with me. ↑**Rationality**.

REASONING a Psychology A thought process triggered by some problem and which ideally reaches a conclusion in "real time." **b Logic** A chain of propositions from premises to conclusions. **Syn** ↑**argument**.

RECEIVED VIEW Prevalent view adopted without fresh investigation. **Syn** ↑**dogma**.

RECONSTRUCTION, RATIONAL Transformation of an untidy body of knowledge into a well-organized one. In particular, ↑**formalization** and ↑**axiomatization**.

RECURRENCE, ETERNAL The cyclical repetition of the states of the world. An impossible process. ↑**Irreversibility**.

RECURSION A function from nonnegative integers to nonnegative integers is defined by recursion if it is introduced by two or more equations, one of which holds for 0, and the other(s) specify the manner in which any further values of the function are computed. Example: the factorial function ! is defined recursively as follows: $0! = 1$, $(n+1)! = (n+1)n!$ These two formulas are necessary and sufficient to compute any value of !, such as $3! = 1.2.3 = 6$.

REDUCTIO AD ABSURDUM A standard method of proof that involves the discovery of a contradiction and its subsequent removal. Sketch: Assume that p, and that, if p, then q. Suppose now, for the sake of the argument (i.e., pretend), that not-q. Then by ↑*modus tollens* it follows that not-p. But p was asserted (assumed to be true) to begin with. Hence not-q proves to be false. And, if ordinary logic is admitted, "not-not $q = q$" holds, whence q has been proved. ↑**Intuitionist** mathematicians do not accept the ↑**double negation** principle, hence cannot avail themselves of this proof method, which, when applicable, is the easiest.

REDUCTION a Concept An epistemic operation and, more precisely, a kind of analysis whereby the reduced object is conjectured or shown to depend on some other, logically or ontologically prior to the former. If A and B are both either constructs or concrete entities, to reduce A to B is to identify A with B, or to include A in B, or to assert that every A is either an aggregate, a combination, or an average of As, or else a manifestation or an image of B. It is to assert that, although A and B may appear to be very different from one another, actually they are the same, or that A is a species of the genus B, or that every A results somehow from Bs—or, put more vaguely, that A "boils down" to B, or that "in the last analysis" all As are Bs. Examples of *conceptual reduction*: whole numbers are either primes or sums of primes; statics is a chapter of dynamics; optics is a chapter of electromagnetic theory. Examples of *ontological reduction*: heat is random molecular motion; mental processes are brain processes; and social facts result from individual actions. **b Logic of reduction** We must distinguish four cases of reduction: of concepts, propositions, theories, and explanations. To reduce a *concept A* to a concept B is to define A in terms of B, where B refers to a thing, property, or process on either the same or on a lower (or higher) ↑ **level** than that of the referent(s) of A. Such a definition may be called a *reductive definition*. (In the philosophical literature reductive definitions are usually called "bridge hypotheses," presumably because they are often originally proposed as hypotheses. History without analysis can be misleading.) Three kinds of reductive definition of a concept: (a)*same level*, as in "Light $=_{df}$ electromagnetic radiation"; (b) *bottom-up* or *microreductive*, as in "Heat $=_{df}$ random molecular motion"; and (c) *top-down* or *macroreductive*, as in

"Natural selection $=_{df}$ Elimination of individual organisms by environmental pressure." The reduction of a *proposition* results from replacing at least one of the predicates occurring in it with the definiens of a reductive definition. For example, by virtue of the reductive definition "Formation of linguistic expressions $=_{df}$ Specific activity of the Wernicke area," the psychological proposition "Mary was forming a linguistic expression" is reducible to the neuroscientific proposition "Mary's Wernicke area was active." An *explanation* will be said to be reductive if at least one of its explanans premises is a reduced proposition. For example, the explanation of the formation of a system in terms of the self-assembly of its components is of the microreductive (or bottom-up) kind. Work on an assembly line, or on the origin of life, induces explanations of this kind. By contrast, the explanation of the behavior of a system component in terms of the place it holds or the role it performs in the system is of the macroreductive (or top-down) type. The car mechanic and the social psychologist typically resort to explanations of this type. Finally, the analysis of theory reduction may proceed as follows. Call T_1 and T_2 two theories (hypothetico-deductive systems). Assume that both share some referents, and call R a set of reductive definitions, and S a set of subsidiary hypotheses not contained in either T_1 or T_2. Our stipulation is that (1) T_2 is *fully* (or *strongly*) *reducible* to $T_1 =_{df} T_2$ follows logically from the union of T_1 and R; and (2) T_2 is *partially* (or *weakly*) *reducible* to $T_1 = $ df T_2 follows logically from the union of T_1, R, and S. **c Limits on theory reduction** Ray optics is strongly reducible to wave optics by way of the reductive definition "Light ray = df Normal to light wave front." In turn, wave optics is strongly reducible to electromagnetism by virtue of the reductive definition (a) above. On the other hand the kinetic theory of gases is only weakly reducible to particle mechanics because, in addition to the reductive definitions of the concepts of pressure and temperature, the former includes the subsidiary hypothesis of the random initial distributions of positions and velocities. Likewise quantum chemistry, cell biology, psychology, and social science are only weakly (partially) reducible to the corresponding lower-level disciplines. Even the quantum theory contains some classical concepts (e.g., those of mass and time), as well as hypotheses about macrophysical boundaries, so that it does not effect a complete microreduction. Likewise, no microeconomic activity can be adequately described without specifying such macroeconomic features as the going discount rate and the political situation. The microreduction attempted by neoclassical microeconomics is unsuccessful precisely because it makes no room for the macroeconomic environment. Nor are many other reduction claims justified. By contrast, the ↑**merger** of disciplines into ↑**interdisciplines**, such as biochemistry, neuropsychology, and political sociology, is far more common and has been very successful. ↑**Reductionism**.

REDUCTIONISM The research strategy according to which the complex is best explained by reduction to (or decomposition into) its constituents. **Syn** nothing-but-ism. Examples: ↑**atomism** in physics and chemistry, ↑**mechanism** in biology, ↑**biologism** and ↑**economism** in social science, and ↑**sociologism** in epistemology. *Radical* reductionism denies ↑**emergence**, and therefore claims that reduction is both necessary and sufficient to account for any complex item. Examples: Human sociobiology and the belief that the completion of the Human Genome Project solved once and for all the enigmas of human nature. *Moderate* reductionism holds that one should reduce as far as possible, but acknowledge (and explain) emergence when encountered. Ontological counterpart: ↑emergentist materialism.

REFERENCE Every ↑predicate and every well-formed proposition refers to, or is ↑about, something or other. For example, "viscous" is about some fluid, and "metabolites" concerns organisms. The collection of referents of a predicate or proposition is called its *reference class*. For example, "mass" refers to all bodies, and so does "harder than." Incidentally, these two examples show that the reference class of a predicate need not coincide with its ↑extension. Indeed, whereas "harder than" refers to bodies, its extension is the collection of ordered pairs of bodies for which the relation actually holds. In obvious symbols, $\mathcal{R}$(harder than) = B, $\mathcal{E}$(harder than) = { $<x,y> \in B \times B|$ x is harder than y} $\subset B \times B$. The gist of a theory of reference follows. Let P be a unary ↑predicate representing a ↑property of objects of some kind A. Clearly, P refers to As. This statement can be reworded in the following way, which lends itself to generalization to n-ary predicates. A unary predicate P may be analyzed as a function from the pertinent set A to the set S of statements containing P. That is, $P: A \rightarrow S$. The assertion that P refers to A amounts then to the statement that the *reference class* of P is the domain A of the function P, i.e., $\mathcal{R}(P) = A$. The generalization to the n-ary predicate $P: A \times B \times \ldots \times N \rightarrow S$ is: $\mathcal{R}(P) = A \cup B \cup \ldots \cup N$. Note the contrast with the extension of P, which is included in the cartesian product of the factors of the domain of P.

REFERENCE FRAME ↑Frame of reference.

REFERENT The object referred to by a ↑construct: that which the latter is about. A member of the ↑reference class of a construct.

REFLECTION THEORY OF KNOWLEDGE The thesis that true factual knowledge "reflects" reality in a more or less distorted way. Syn naive ↑realism, commonsense realism. Distinctive of dialectical materialism and of the early Wittgenstein. This view holds for such simple statements as "The cat is on the mat," but it fails for statements involving unobservables, such as "possible," "electron," "decision," and "class struggle." The failure of naive realism does not affect scientific ↑realism, which holds that most scientific constructs represent imperceptible things or properties.

REFLEXIVITY Reference to oneself, as in "I am sorry for myself." Syn ↑self-consciousness.

REFUTATION The invalidation of an argument by showing either that some of its premises are false, or that they do not entail the conclusion in accordance with the laws of deductive logic. ↑Falsifiability.

REFUTATIONISM ↑Falsificationism.

REGRESS, LOGICAL To go up from consequences to premises, from present to past, or from effects to causes. A legitimate conceptual operation as long as it is finite. However, every regress is conjectural, for it purports to solve an ↑**inverse problem**, and inverse problems have either no solution or more than one. Hence, there can be no regress ↑**algorithms**.

REGULAR The property of a process of being uniform, repetitive, or patterned (lawlike). In a strict or narrow sense, stochastic (probabilistic) and chaotic processes are irregular. In a broad sense, they are not, since they satisfy laws.

REGULARITY A polysemous term that covers ↑**law**, association or concomitance, strong ↑**statistical correlation**, social or moral ↑**norm**, and even mere ↑**trend**. A main goal of scientists is to find regularities.

REIFICATION The treatment of a property, relation, process, or idea as if it were a thing. Example: "I have worries" instead of "I am worried"; the popular notions of energy, mind, justice, and beauty as entities; the ideas that language (rather than a speaker) is creative and grows in the mind; and the theses that biospecies are individuals, and that lineages are historical entities. Dual: ↑**ideaefication**.

REISM The thesis that the world is composed exclusively of things. **Syn** ↑**materialism**.

RELATA The terms of a relation. Example: The relata of the teaching relation are teachers and students. If R holds among the relata $a, b, . . ., n$, one writes: $Rab. . .n$. In this statement, R is distinguished but not separated from the relata it holds together. There are no relations without relata, and no relata without relations. This refutes both ↑**individualism** (relata precede relations) and ↑**holism** (relations precede relata).

RELATION a Logic Correspondence between two or more sets, the members of which are called ↑**relata**. The correspondence or matching may be one-to-many, many-to-one, or one-to-one. In either of the last two cases the relation is called a ↑**function**. The simplest relations are those between two sets: they are called 'binary' or 'dyadic'. Examples: "less than" and "acts on." The next in order of complexity are the ternary or triadic ones. Examples: "between" and "gives." In general, one speaks of n-adic or n-ary relations or predicates. Relations may be pictured as ↑**arrows**. The *domain* of a relation is the set where the arrow originates, and its *codomain* the set of tips of the arrow. For example, the domain of the relation of selling is the set of sellers, and its range that of buyers. Ancient logic ignored relations and attempted to reduce all relations to unary (monadic) predicates. This is an impossible task. By contrast, unary properties can be defined in terms of dyadic ones, namely thus: $Px =_{df} \exists y Rxy$. Example: x is married $=_{df}$ $\exists y$ (x is the spouse of y). This suffices to refute ↑**individualism**, which assumes that bare individuals precede related individuals. Relations have often been regarded as unreal, perhaps because of that flaw of ancient logic and the concomitant subject-predicate grammar. But of course intrinsic properties raise the same problem. Actually neither unary properties nor relational ones exist by themselves. In reality there are only things with properties and related to other things (except for the universe as a whole, which is a thing but is unrelated to anything else). The standard explicit definition of an n-ary relation is that it is a subset of a cartesian product of n sets. Hence if Rxy, one is asked to write $<x,y> \in R$. This extensional construal fails for the basic concepts of identity and set membership. ↑**Extensionalism**. Besides, the construal in question is utterly useless in the case of concrete things, for these are not sets. For example, a bond or link between two molecules, persons, or organizations is a relation but not a subset of a cartesian product. It is preferable to define relations axiomatically, and to say that only the ↑**extension** of an n-ary predicate is a subset of the cartesian product of its domain and its range. Thus, e.g., for a binary relation R with domain A and codomain B, $\mathcal{E}(R) \subseteq A \times B$, and $<x,y> \in \mathcal{E}(R)$. **b Science** Most of the (intrinsic and relational) properties of real things are conceptualized as relations, in particular functions. For example, the concept of GDP is a function from couples <nation, year> to dollars. ↑**Property**, ↑**predicate**.

RELATIONAL A joint property of two or more objects, one of which may be either a frame of reference or an observer. Examples: positions, velocities, and forces in classical physics; distances, durations, and temperatures in relativistic physics; all the ↑**secondary properties**, such as color, smoothness, and sweetness; and all the values, such as health, fairness, and beauty. Caution: everything subjective is relative, but the converse is false. For example, poverty is relative (to the poverty line of a region) but not subjective.

RELATIVE a Logic A construct is relative to another if it can only be characterized (e.g., defined) in terms of the latter. Example: "small" only makes sense relative to some quantity taken as a baseline. Thesis: All constructs are logically relative (or relational). **b Ontology** ↑**Relational** properties, such as height, energy, and wealth, are those whose values are relative to some reference frame or other. Some physical properties, such as electric charge and entropy, are absolute (frame-independent); others, such as position, force, and field intensity, are relative (frame-dependent). **c Epistemology** All ↑**secondary properties** are relative to some sentient being. ↑**Absolute / relative**.

RELATIVISM a Ontological The view that everything is ↑**relative**. This view is incompatible with modern science, which teems with absolutes, such as invariant properties and laws, along with relative ones. All the other relativisms are special cases of ontological relativism. **b Anthropological** The opinion that all cultures are equivalent, so that there is no such thing as social development, and consequently no objective justification for social reform. Ironically, relativism is proffered as intersubjectively and universally true. **c Epistemological** The application of anthropological relativism to the pursuit of knowledge. That is, the view that every truth is relative to some individual, social group, or historical period. In other words, there would be no objective ("absolute") and universal (cross-cultural) truths. The mere existence and success of international scientific and technological publications and meetings, with their underlying international standards of truth tests, is a tacit refutation of relativism. **d Axiological** The doctrine that all ↑**values** are subjective and local, or bound to places or epochs, hence they are neither objective (subject-free) nor universal (cross-cultural). This view has a grain of truth: some values are indeed relative to place and time. For example, hope in the afterlife, military valor, nobility of the blood, equality, civic conscience, and the taste for classical music are far from universal. By contrast, life, reciprocity, honesty, loyalty, solidarity, knowledge, justice, security, and peace are universal or nearly so. Moreover, it may be argued that those who do not share these universal values are misguided and harm themselves or others. Secular ↑**humanism** postulates these universal values, but it does not oppose relative values as long as their implemetation is harmless. **℮ Ethical** The family of ethical doctrines which deny that there are universal norms. Relativism comes in several strengths. The most radical is ethical ↑**nihilism**, according to which moral norms cannot be vindicated in any way other than as survival devices. A slightly moderate kind of ethical relativism is the one included in cultural relativism. According to it, every culture (or society) has its own morality, and no morality is better than any other. (Example: one should not oppose the death penalty in barbaric nations.) Moderate ethical relativism holds that, whereas some moral rules are absolutely good, others are absolutely bad, and the worth of still others is relative to individual, group, or circumstance. Example of the former: "Give Caesar his own." Example of the second: "Help others whenever you can." Example of the third: "Use violence only to protect lives, and then only with restraint." **Ant** ↑**absolutism**.

RELATIVITY PRINCIPLE The ↑**metanomological statement** that the basic physical laws are absolute, that is, independent of the frame of reference (in particular the observer), provided it is inertial (not accelerated). The principle does not hold for the derived laws, which are frame-dependent, but in any event it is consistent with scientific ↑**realism**.

RELEVANCE Object A is relevant to object B if A makes some difference to B, or B depends upon A. Relevance relates facts, constructs, or constructs and facts. Examples: Biology is conceptually relevant to psychology (C-C); the economy is factually relevant to politics (F-F); light is referentially relevant to optics (F-C); economic theory ought to be pragmatically relevant to business (C-F).

RELEVANCE LOGIC Any logical calculus that attempts to avoid two features of classical logic: that a contradiction entails any proposition, and that a tautology is entailed by an arbitrary proposition. The existing relevance logics do not accomplish this goal because they include the principle of ↑**addition**. The only way to avoid irrelevancies is to restrict the universe of discourse from the start and to proceed axiomatically. ↑**Axiomatics**.

RELIGION System of untestable beliefs in the existence of one or more supernatural beings and the accompanying practices, mainly worship and sacrifice (of self or others). Some influential belief systems, such as original Buddhism, Jainism, Taoism, and Confucianism, are not religions proper according to the above definition, for they do not include beliefs in deities. Whereas some religions promise afterlife, others do not; and only some threaten hell. Hence belief in afterlife and in eternal reward or punishment are not defining features of religion. ↑**Theology**. Religions are seriously studied by psychology, sociology, history, and philosophy. The *psychology* of religion studies the ways religious ideas are acquired and the manner in which they change as a result of experience or mental sickness. It also studies the roles of religious belief, e.g., in coping with helplessness, unpredictability, fear of death, and guilt feelings. The *sociology* of religion studies the social functions and dysfunctions of religious beliefs and religious communities, such as their contribution to social cohesiveness and divisiveness, and their use as a tool of social control. The *history* of religions studies their emergence and transformations in relation with other aspects of social life, such as the economic and political ones. The philosophy of religion may be an adjunct to theology or independent of it. In the former case it lacks the intellectual freedom inherent in philosophical research. In particular, it cannot afford to question the existence of God(s) or any other essential dogmas of the religion in question. Therefore a theologically committed philosophy of religion is not authentically philosophical. A genuine philosophy of religion will examine the logical, semantical, epistemological, ontological, and ethical problems raised by the hypothesis of the existence of deities. In particular, it will examine (a) the question whether religion is compatible with ↑**rationality** in any of the senses of this term; (b) the areas of scientific research that can be affected by religion; and (c) the constraints of religious belief on ethics. The first question is easily answered in the negative, since all religions demand blind faith. As for the second question: Religion need not interfere with research in logic or mathematics. Nor does it affect research into most problems in the factual sciences—except when, as in the cases of Paul and Augustine, it actively discourages such research in being heathen and irrelevant to personal salvation anyway. But, particularly if organized and militant, religion is bound to affect research into problems whose solution is likely to contradict religious dogma. Examples: reality of miracles and faith healing, efficiency of prayer, history of the cosmos, origin of life, evolution through random genic change and natural selection, nature of mind, origin of religion and its role as a social control mechanism. Religion is also bound to affect research into some philosophical problems, such as those of the limits of human reason; the evidential value of religious experience; the "meaning" of human life, suffering, and death; whether allegiance to God or church should prevail over allegiance to humankind; and whether it is possible to be moral without religion. Which brings us to the third question. The problem of the influence of religion on morals is an empirical one. The empirical evidence is ambivalent. In a few cases religion favors prosocial behavior—in particular compassion and solidarity, at any rate among coreligionists. But at other times religion condones crime or even inspires it—as is the case with holy wars (in particular crusades and jihads) and the persecution of infidels and heretics. Likewise, whereas in some cases religion inspires abdication of personal responsibility, at other times it does the opposite. Moreover, whereas some religious believers are humanists (though of course not secular ones), others are zealots who do not hesitate to use violence against unbelievers. (But the same holds for some militant atheists.) Therefore secular ↑**humanists** can, and in fact often do, work alongside some religious believers to promote humanitarian causes. And, even while not respecting religion because it is an instance of magical thinking, humanists should tolerate believers and defend their right to worship. As for the nonempirical problems in the philosophy/religion interface, suffice it to mention the following: Is something good because God approves of it? What is the relation between positive law and ↑**natural law**? Is all evil man-made?

RELIGION AND ETHICS The traditional view on this matter is that there can be no ethics without religion. This opinion is contradicted by the existence of nonreligious moral philosophies, such as those of Jainism, Confucianism, and secular ↑**humanism**. Humanism and religion handle moral questions in radically different ways, and in most cases give them different solutions. For one thing, religious moralities are dogmatic and therefore box moral debate inside the rigid frame of accepted norms, whereas humanists are expected to handle moral problems in the light of reason and experience. For another, because they rely on allegedly perennial principles, religious moralities can seldom cope with new problems, aspirations, and sensibilities: witness the debates on human rights, social justice, family planning, the death penalty, and war.

RELIGION AND SCIENCE In principle, there are four possible views on this question: Science is included in religion; religion is included in science; they are mutually disjoint; and they overlap in some regard. The first view, upheld by some fundamentalists, is patently false: no religious scripture contains, say, quantum theory or evolutionary biology. The second view is that of natural theology, which sought the imprint of divine design in nature. But of course natural science has found no divine fingerprints. The third view, that religion and science are disjoint, hence compatible, is false as well. Indeed, (a) both religion and science refer to the world and ask some of the same questions about it, particularly problems about origins—of the world, life, man, mind, religion, etc.; but (b) to answer these common questions scientists employ the scientific method, whereas religionists resort to either grace or allegedly sacred scriptures; and (c) not surprisingly, the conclusions reached by scientists and religionists are mutually incompatible, as highlighted by the controversies over the nature, origin, and evolution of life, mind, and society. In conclusion, religion and science have a small but important overlap: the set of ↑**big questions**. ↑**Double-truth doctrine**.

REPRESENTATION a Ordinary knowledge A polysemous term. **b Cognitive science** Perception, as in "the representation of the visual features of an external object." **c Semantics** A conceptual, visual, auditory, or artifactual translation of an object (material or ideal). Examples: functions represent their domains into their codomains; Venn diagrams represent sets (mostly metaphorically); lattices are representable by trees; individual factual propositions, such as "The door is open," represent facts; law-statements represent stable objective patterns; architectural blueprints represent actual or possible buildings; circuit diagrams represent actual or possible electric circuits; maps represent parts of planets; computer simulations represent real things or mathematical models of them. Idealists have no use for the concept of representation. Moreover, some of them—particularly the constructivists— conflate map with territory. This is why the very notion of representation is absent from the standard semantic theories. And this is also why these theories are useless to analyze scientific and technological discourses. Naive realists (e.g., dialectical materialists and the early Wittgenstein) believe that true representations "mirror" facts and are thus unique: ↑**reflection theory of knowledge**. This is not true of artistic representations: think of photography, painting, or sculpture. A fortiori it does not hold for scientific and technological representations. These are symbolic, not mimetic or iconic, in particular pictorial. So much so that any given fact or pattern may be represented in different ways. For example, a process may be represented by a block-and-arrow diagram, a finite-difference equation, a differential equation, or an integral equation. Moreover, some representations, such as the diagrams of certain electric circuits, are physically equivalent despite being visually different.

REPUBLIC Commonwealth, or the system of public (nonprivate) goods ordinarily administered by the state or government. The ultimate goal of ↑**politics** is to gain access to such administration.

RES COGITANS / RES EXTENSA Thinking thing / extended thing. Descartes's way of describing the alleged mind / matter opposition. Neuropsychology has refuted this dualism, asserting instead the identity of the thinking thing and the brain—which of course is extended. Only constructs in themselves are unextended. ↑**Mind-body problem**.

RESEARCH Epistemic exploration: Methodical search for knowledge. Not to be confused with either bibliographic search or net surfing. Original research tackles new problems or checks previous findings. Rigorous research is the mark of science, technology, and the "living" branches of the humanities. It is typically absent from ↑**pseudoscience** and ↑**ideology**. **Syn** investigation, ↑**inquiry**.

RESEARCH PROJECT In general, one starts research by picking a domain *D* of either facts or ideas, then makes (or takes for granted) some general assumptions (*G*) about them, collects a body *B* of extant knowledge about the *D*s, decides on an aim (*A*) and, in the light of the preceding, picks or invents the proper method (*M*). Hence, an arbitrary research project π may be sketched as the ordered quintuple π = <*D, G, B, A, M* >. The general assumptions *G* of a *scientific* research project include the hypotheses that the items to be investigated are material, lawful, and scrutable, as opposed to immaterial (in particular supernatural), lawless, or inscrutable.

RESPONSIBILITY a Ethics and praxiology An agent is morally responsible for an action if the action is morally justified, and if he can perform it whereas no one else in sight can. The abdication of a responsibility can be just as grievous as the commission of an antisocial action. **b Law** An agent is legally responsible for an action if he has been charged with it according to some contract, and he has accepted to execute it. In modern legislation, only able adults are deemed to be legally responsible. ↑**Duty / right**.

RESULTANT A property of a system is said to be *resultant* if some of its components possess it; otherwise it is called ↑**emergent**. For example, having energy is a resultant property of a cell, whereas being alive is an emergent property of it. Radical ↑**reductionists**—in particular physicalists and methodological individualists—hold that all properties are resultant. Hence they focus on the composition of ↑**systems** and overlook their ↑**structure**, as a consequence of which they cannot control them.

REVELATION Alleged message from a deity. Only professional religionists are qualified to certify revelations. When a layperson claims to have had a revelation, he is suspected of delusion or deceit.

REVERSE ENGINEERING The tackling of ↑**inverse problems** in artifact design. Example: given the specification for the desirable features of an artifact, invent a device complying with it. In other words, given the desired function, invent a mechanism capable of realizing it.

REVERSIBLE The property of a process, of returning a thing to its initial state. Examples: the turning of a wheel, a periodic oscillation. Some microphysical and most macrophysical processes are irreversible. This holds in particular for radioactive disintegrations, deformations of plastic bodies, heat transfer, life processes, and evolutionary and historical processes. Hence the eternal regress (or recurrence), postulated by some religions and philosophies, is impossible: the world never returns to a previous state.

REVISIONISM The practice of revising (or reviewing) a body of knowledge as doubts arise about its truth, cogency, or relevance. Typically, historians are revisionist: they rewrite history as new documents come to light or new approaches are invented. Unfortunately, the people who perpetrate historical forgeries—such as nationalist historians and Holocaust deniers—have given revisionism a bad name. These are historical revisionists rather than revisionist historians. Leninists have used the epithet 'revisionist' to insult and punish deviant Marxists.

REVOLUTION, EPISTEMIC A *rupture épistémologique* (Gaston Bachelard) or *scientific revolution* (Thomas S. Kuhn, Paul K. Feyerabend) is said to make a clean break with extant knowledge. So much so that the new theory is claimed to be ↑**incommensurable** (incomparable) with the old one. This idea has a grain of truth: a radical original discovery or invention has no antecedents. Examples: field physics, molecular biology, mathematical economics, exact philosophy. However, even such breakthroughs have roots. For example, field physics deepened and extended action-at-a-distance theories; molecular biology was the offspring of biochemistry and genetics; and exact philosophy is an application of mathematics. Besides, if a radically new idea is admitted, it is either because it proves to be truer than the earlier ones on the same subjects or because it initiates a new fertile field, as were the cases with field physics and nuclear physics. Furthermore, tradition is often a stepping stone for epistemic novelty. This holds in particular for the formal tools employed in science in technology. Thus the seventeenth-century Scientific Revolution was considerably helped by the legacies of Greek mathematics and medieval logic. Arguably there have been only two scientific revolutions: the birth of science in antiquity, and its rebirth in the seventeenth century. In conclusion, most great epistemic novelties are breakthroughs rather than revolutions. ↑**Discontinuity, fallacy of,** ↑**rival views**.

RHETORIC The art or technique of persuasion regardless of truth. Much appreciated by politicians, marketing experts, speechwriters, and postmodern academics who write about the "rhetorical turn."

RIGHT, n Ethics A permission to think or do something, as in 'the right to life' and 'the right to vote'. Rights can be moral (like the right to work), legal (like the right to own property), or political (like the right to run for public office); and whereas some rights are local, others are universal. All rights have changed along history, and some of them are the object of political debate and fight. Individualists hold rights and duties to be individual, whereas holists claim that some or even all rights are collective. A systemic approach sheds light on this controversy, in treating rights along with duties, on the principle that every right induces a duty and conversely: ↑**agathonism**. This suggests that rights are bestowed on individuals in certain circumstances but not in others; similarly for duties: they may be required of individuals in some cases but not in others. For example, the voluntarily unemployed able persons have no moral right to public support; and healthy people on welfare have the duty to do some mandated socially useful work. ↑**Duty / right,** ↑**human right.**

RIGHT / WRONG, adj a General A dichotomy applicable to ideas and actions of all kinds. Examples: the pairs clear/obscure, valid/invalid, precise/imprecise, true/false, good/bad, and just/unjust. It is an open question whether a general and nontrivial theory of right and wrong is possible. **b Philosophically right / wrong** Given the variety of philosophies, the qualifiers 'philosophically right' and 'philosophically wrong' make sense only within a given philosophy. However, a philosophical idea may be judged from outside philosophy—e.g., as resisting exactification or as inconsistent with factual science. ↑**B test.**

RIGOR Abidance by agreed-on rules. Rigor can be formal (logical), methodological, epistemological, moral, or practical. Formal rigor boils down to ↑**exactness,** ↑**consistency,** and ↑**validity.** Methodological rigor is compliance with the ↑**scientific method.** Epistemological (or empirical) rigor is methodological rigor together with compatibility with the bulk of the best available knowledge. Moral rigor is strict abidance by whatever moral code one has adopted, regardless of circumstances. Whereas logical and epistemological rigor are worthy goals, moral rigor (or inflexibility) can lead to cruelty. Finally, practical rigor is compliance with the best relevant technological knowledge.

RIVAL VIEWS Two or more views about matters of fact are mutually rival if they account in different ways for roughly the same facts. Examples: creationism / evolutionism, idealism / materialism, individualism / holism. Since they are rival, they can be compared with one another. ↑**Incommensurable,** ↑**revolution, epistemic.** When evaluating rival views concerning a domain of facts, one should check which complies best with the following requirements. (1) *Intelligibility*: Is the view clear or foggy? If somewhat obscure, can it be elucidated and eventually formalized, or is it inherently fuzzy and therefore not susceptible to development? (2) *Logical consistency*: Is the view internally consistent or does it contain contradictions? If it does contain inconsistencies, can these be removed by altering or dropping some of the assumptions without giving up the most important ones? (3) *Systemicity*: Is the view a conceptual system (in particular a theory) or part of one, or is it a stray conjecture that cannot enjoy the support of any other bit of knowledge? If stray, can it be expanded into a hypothetico-deductive system or embedded in one? (4) *Literalness*: Does the view make any literal statements or is it just a metaphor? If an analogy, is it shallow or deep, barren or fertile? And is it indispensable or can it be replaced with a literal account? (5) *Testability*: Can the view be checked conceptually (against previously accepted items of knowledge) or empirically (by observation or experiment), or is it impregnable to criticism and experience? (6) *Evidence*: If the view has been tested, have the test results been favorable, unfavorable, or inconclusive? (7) *External consistency*: Is the view compatible with the bulk of knowledge in all the fields of scientific research? (8) *Originality*: Is the view novel? And does it solve any outstanding problems? (9) *Heuristic power*: Is the view barren or does it raise new and interesting research or application problems? (10) *Philosophical soundness*: Is the view compatible with the philosophy underlying scientific research? That is, is the view naturalist or does it posit ghostly items such as immaterial entities or processes beyond experimental control? And is it epistemologically realistic or does it involve subjectivism or apriorism (e.g., conventionalism)? ↑**Mind-body problem e, f.**

ROMANTICISM The complex cultural movement that was started by Vico and Rousseau and culminated with Hegel. Progressive in art (especially literature and music), regressive in philosophy, and ambivalent in politics. Main characteristics: irrationalist, holist, unruly, obscure, subjectivist, fantastic, excessive, nostalgic, and wishing to join natural history (rather than science) with philosophy, religion, and art.

RULE Prescription for doing something, whether manual, intellectual, or social. Kinds: conventional, logical, empirical, scientific, technological, and moral. Etiquette, grammatical, and ↑**notational rules** are *conventional*. Hence they can be altered if found obsolete or inconvenient. *Logical* rules are of two kinds: conventions concerning well-formedness, and rules of ↑**inference**. Every system of logic consists of a set of axioms plus a set of rules. Without the latter nothing can be deduced. For example, the conditional "If A, then B" leads nowhere even adding either that A is true or that B is false. Only adding explicitly the ↑*modus ponens* rule can one detach (assert separately) B or A, as the case may be. *Empirical* rules are adopted as a result of trials believed to be successful. They are sometimes altered following scientific experiment. *Scientific* and *technological* rules are framed on the basis of natural or social laws. Unlike empirical rules, the scientific and technological ones are based on laws : ↑**Rule based on law**. However, these, too, are adopted or rejected on the strength of their performance. *Moral* rules are norms of conduct toward others. Metanorm: Moral rules should be set up in the light of scientific knowledge, and adopted or rejected by their practical consequences.

RULE BASED ON LAW Any ↑**law-statement** that can be put to use is the scientific basis for two rules: one which prescribes what to do in order to attain some goal, and its dual, which prescribes how to act to avoid such result. For example, a law-statement of the form "If C happens, then E will occur" is the basis for the rules

R^+ = To get E, do C.
R^- = To avoid E, abstain from doing C.

This duality is the root of the moral ambivalence of much of ↑**technology**.

RULE WORSHIP Conformism, uncritical acceptance of rules. Examples: linguistic, moral, political conformism; and Wittgenstein's thesis that playing any "language game," such as doing mathematics, is just "following rules." A constructive skeptic will propose altering or even dropping any rules that are illogical, impractical, or which cause unnecessary harm.

RUPTURE, EPISTEMOLOGICAL ↑Revolution, epistemic.

SACRALISM The ↑**worldview** according to which the universe is ↑**sacred**, and therefore to be contemplated and worshiped rather than studied and transformed. Modernization involves desacralization.

SACRED Pertaining to the divinity or its worship. Secular humanists have no use for this concept except in its metaphorical or moral sense, that is, as something nonnegotiable, such as human rights. **Ant** profane.

SALTATIONISM The view that biological and social evolution are sequences of leaps or qualitative discontinuities. Ant ↑**gradualism**. All the factual sciences know of both leaps and gradual changes.

SALVA VERITATE Preservation of ↑**truth-value** under substitution, as in "0 < 1" and "1 > 0." It has been claimed that this is a criterion of sameness of meaning. However, it is not even a necessary condition, as shown by the case of the propositions that have not yet been assigned a truth-value or, a fortiori, are ↑**undecidable**. Intersubstitutability *salva veritate* does not guarantee meaning invariance. For example, upon replacing "humans" with "birds," and "hominids" with "reptiles," the true proposition "All humans descend from some hominids" turns into "All birds descend from some reptiles" *salva veritate*, but not *salva significatio*. Two constructs have the same ↑**meaning** if and only if they coincide in both their senses and their referents. In this case, the corresponding linguistic expressions are inter-translatable. ↑**Translation**.

SATISFACTION A key concept in ↑**model theory**. An abstract formula or theory is said to be *satisfiable* if it has an interpretation in a known domain. For example, the formula "ab–ba = 0" is satisfiable in the domain of real numbers, whereas "ab + ba = 0" is satisfiable by matrices and vector products. The philosophical significance of the concept of satisfiability is that it occurs in the definition of mathematical ↑**truth** as satisfiability in some model.

SAWDUST PHILOSOPHY The philosophy resulting from analyzing stray philosophical ideas or crumbling philosophical systems. **Ant** ↑**systemism**. ↑**Analytic philosophy**.

SCALA NATURAE Ladder of nature. ↑**Chain of being**. Modern successor: ↑**level** structure.

SCHEMA Sketch or list of salient properties, such as "bachelor, young at heart, non-smoker." Pl. schemata.

SCHOLAR Broad construal: A well-educated specialist, in contrast to a narrow one. Narrow construal: One who disguises obscurity as profundity, quotes platitudes in a dead language, and footnotes other people's original ideas.

SCHOLASTICISM Commentary on some texts, sacred or profane, important or insignificant, ancient or modern, that is not expected to solve any significant problem other than that of keeping a religious or academic job. Typically, the schoolman— whether medieval or contemporary—will study what author X says about the pronouncements of authority Y on subject Z, instead of addressing Z directly. Scholasticism, which was supposed to wither away with the emergence of modern philosophy, dominates the contemporary philosophical scene.

SCHOOL PHILOSOPHY The philosophy of a dogmatic school, movement, or sect. A proved recipe for founding a school philosophy is this: "Take a half-truth (if absolutely necessary, even a full truth) and proclaim it to be the sole truth." Examples: From the fact that some processes involve conflict, conclude that all processes are dialectical; from the fact that some choices are rational, conclude that all of them are; from the fact that knowledge requires experience, conclude that experience is the root and the flower of knowledge; from the fact that the advancement of knowledge involves criticism, conclude that criticism is the engine of scientific progress; from the fact that research is socially conditioned, conclude that every item of knowledge has a social content; from the fact that some social relations are subject to contract, conclude that everything social and moral is contractual. School philosophies die hard either because they hold a grain of truth or because they are sustained by social movements.

SCHRÖDINGER'S CAT A thought experiment that highlights a peculiarity of ↑**quantum mechanics**. The peculiarity in question is that ↑**quantons**, the referents of quantum physics, are normally in states that are superpositions of "sharp" states (or eigenstates of an operator representing a property, such as energy or spin). For example, an electron's spin is normally a linear combination of the "up" and "down" states. When the electron enters a magnetic field, the superposition "collapses" (projects) onto one of the two "sharp" states. Actually, this happens whether the external field occurs naturally or has been set up by an experimenter. However, according to the positivist or ↑**Copenhagen interpretation** of quantum mechanics, the collapse occurs only as a result of an observation. Now extrapolate all this from quantons to either macrophysical systems, such as measuring instruments, or supraphysical things, such as organisms. Lock up a cat for a while in a steel cage containing a tiny bit of a radioactive substance and a vial containing a powerful poison that will be released if struck by a product of the disintegration of a radioactive atom. If this happens while the cat is caged, it will die almost instantly. But it may not happen. What state is the cat in while unobserved in the cage? If quantum mechanics held for cats, the unfortunate creature would be in a linear combination of the states "alive" and "dead." That is, it would be half-alive and half-dead. When the lid of the cage was lifted and the cat observed, the superposition of states would collapse onto either of the two sharp states. Thus far the thought experiment devised by E. Schrödinger with the intention of showing that there is something basically wrong with quantum physics. However, this conclusion must be wrong, since the theory accounts with marvelous precision for a multitude of physical facts. What is wrong is to extrapolate it to macrophysical things, particularly if endowed with supraphysical properties, such as life. It is also wrong to talk about the states "alive," "dead," and "half-dead" as if they were physically well-defined. In the context of quantum physics they are empty words, because they are not solutions of the Schrödinger equation for a cat—an equation that nobody has written, let alone solved. The situation does not improve if the cat is replaced with a measuring apparatus, because such a device is macrophysical and therefore beyond the reach of the quantum theory. Furthermore, there are no universal measuring instruments, and therefore the general quantum theory of ↑**measurement** is just hand-waving. Every type of measurement instrument calls for its own special theory.

SCIENCE The critical search for or utilization of patterns in ideas, nature, or society. A science can be *formal* or *factual*: the former if it refers only to constructs, the latter if to matters of fact. Logic and mathematics are formal sciences: they deal only with concepts and their combinations, and therefore have no use for empirical procedures or data—except as sources of problems or aids in reasoning. By contrast, physics and history, and all the sciences in between, are factual: they are about concrete things such as light beams and business firms. Therefore they are in need of empirical procedures, such as measurement, along with conceptual ones, such as calculation. The factual sciences can be split into *natural* (e.g., ↑**biology**), *social* (e.g., ↑**economics**), and *biosocial* (e.g., ↑**psychology**). With regard to practicality, science can be split into ↑**basic** or pure and ↑**applied**. And neither is to be mistaken for ↑**technology**.

SCIENCE AND RELIGION ↑Religion and science.

SCIENCE, APPLIED The search for new scientific knowledge of possible practical utilization. Examples: mathematicians, physicists, chemists, biochemists, pharmacologists, clinical psychologists, and sociologists apply science to the extent that they engage in original scientific research of possible use in industry or government. If they only use scientific findings in a professional capacity, they rank as highly skilled craftsmen or servicemen. Applied science is the bridge between basic (or pure) science and technology. Examples: materials science, solid-state physics, pharmacology.

SCIENCE, BASIC The disinterested search for new scientific knowledge. Examples: physics, chemistry, biology, sociology, and positive economics. The basic sciences constitute a system. The *system of factual scientific research fields* is a variable collection, every member $\mathcal{R}$ of which is representable by a 10-tuple

$$\mathcal{R} = <C, S, D, G, F, B, P, K, A, M>,$$

where, at any given time,

(1) C, the *research community* of $\mathcal{R}$, is a social system composed of persons who have received a specialized training, hold strong communication links among themselves, share their knowledge with anyone who wishes to learn, and initiate or continue a tradition of inquiry (not just of belief) aiming at finding true representations of facts;

(2) S is the *society* (complete with its culture, economy, and polity) that hosts C and encourages or at least tolerates the specific activities of the components of C;

(3) the *domain* or *universe of discourse D* of $\mathcal{R}$ is composed exclusively of (actual or possible) real entities (rather than, say, freely floating ideas) past, present, or future;

(4) the *general outlook* or *philosophical background G* of $\mathcal{R}$ consists of (a) the ontological principle that the world is composed of concrete things that change lawfully and exist independently of the researcher (rather than, say, ghostly or unchanging or invented or miraculous entities); (b) the epistemological principle that the world can be known objectively, at least partially and gradually; and (c) the ethos of the free search for truth, depth, understanding, and system (rather than, say, the ethos of faith or that of the quest for sheer information, utility, profit, power, consensus, or good);

(5) the *formal background F* of $\mathcal{R}$ is the collection of up-to-date logical and mathematical theories (rather than being empty or formed by obsolete formal theories);

(6) the *specific background B* of $\mathcal{R}$ is a collection of up-to-date and reasonably well confirmed (yet corrigible) data, hypotheses, and theories, and of reasonably effective research methods, obtained in other fields relevant to $\mathcal{R}$;

(7) the *problematics P* of $\mathcal{R}$ consists exclusively of cognitive problems concerning the nature (in particular the regularities) of the members of D, as well as problems concerning other components of $\mathcal{R}$;

(8) the *fund of knowledge K* of $\mathcal{R}$ is a collection of up-to-date and testable (though rarely final) theories, hypotheses, and data compatible with those in B, and obtained by members of C at previous times;

(9) the *aims A* of the members of C include discovering or using the regularities (in particular laws) and circumstances of the Ds, systematizing (into theories) general hypotheses about Ds, and refining methods in M;

(10) the *methodics M of* $\mathcal{R}$ consists exclusively of scrutable (checkable, analyzable, criticizable) and justifiable (explainable) procedures, in the first place the general ↑scientific method.

(11) There is at least one other *contiguous* scientific research field, in the same system $\mathcal{R}$ of factual research fields, such that (a) the two fields share some items in their general outlooks, formal backgrounds, specific backgrounds, funds of knowledge, aims, and methodics; and (b) either the domain of one of the two fields is included in that of the other, or each member of the domain of one of the fields is a component of a concrete system in the domain of the other.

(12) The membership of every one of the last eight components of $\mathcal{R}$ *changes*, however slowly at times, *as a result of inquiry* in the same field (rather than as a result of ideological or political pressures, or of "negotiations" among researchers), as well as in related (formal or factual) fields of scientific inquiry.

Any field of knowledge that fails to satisfy even approximately all of the above twelve conditions will be said to be *nonscientific* (examples: theology and literary criticism). A research field that satisfies them approximately may be called a *semiscience* or *protoscience* (examples: economics and political science). If, in addition, the field is evolving toward the full compliance of them all, it may be called an *emerging* or *developing science* (examples: psychology and sociology). On the other hand, any field of knowledge that, being nonscientific, is advertised as scientific, will be said to be *pseudoscientific*, or a *fake* or *bogus* science (examples: parapsychology, psychoanalysis, and psychohistory). Whereas the difference between science and protoscience is one of degree, that between protoscience and pseudoscience is one of kind.

SCIENCE, PHILOSOPHY OF The study of the nature of science, its differences from other modes of knowledge, its philosophical presuppositions, and the philosophical problems it raises. Sample of its problematics: What is science and how does it differ from ordinary knowledge? What are the commonalities and differences between science and technology? What are the marks of pseudoscience? Does science presuppose the autonomous reality and lawfulness of the world? How do scientific theories relate to reality and to experience? Can science go beyond phenomena and relations among them? Is it possible to describe real things in the minutest detail and with perfect accuracy? What are scientific laws and scientific explanations? Does the inclusion under a generalization qualify as a scientific explanation, or is the description of a mechanism needed as well? What is the role of mathematics in factual science? Do relativistic and quantum physics subscribe to subjectivism? Has chemistry been reduced to physics? Is genetics a chapter of biochemistry? Is evolutionary biology testable? Does progress in psychology depend upon neuroscience? Is sociology reducible to psychology? Are there social laws? Are rational-choice theories precise and, if so, have they been empirically confirmed? Are there ways out of the rationalist-empiricism and individualism-collectivism dilemmas? What if any is the role that philosophy plays in scientific research? Is basic science morally committed? Are there limits to the advancement of science? The problematics of the philosophy of science varies along both science and philosophy. Every philosophy proper has its own philosophy of science. And the worth of any philosophy of science should be gauged by the faithfulness of its portrayal of current scientific research, its fruitfulness in helping evaluate research projects, and its efficacy in warning against unpromising projects. Unsurprisingly, there are no Kantian, Hegelian, phenomenological, existentialist, Wittgensteinian, or deconstructionist philosophies of science. ↑**B test**.

SCIENCE, RELEVANCE TO PHILOSOPHY Because science studies everything that exists or may exist, whether conceptual or material, natural or social, it should be relevant to all the branches of philosophy except logic. But in fact most philosophical schools are indifferent to science when not hostile to it. This is their loss, for their views on being, knowing, or doing are then bound to be obsolete. Examples: the current mainstream philosophies of mind and language.

SCIENCE WARS The philosophical and sociological controversies caused by the revival of ↑**constructivism** and ↑**relativism** in the mid-1960s.

SCIENTIFIC PHILOSOPHY Philosophy that, in addition to being ↑**exact**, agrees with the bulk of the sciences and technologies of the day. Examples: a philosophical theory of space and time compatible with general relativity; a theory of novelty (or emergence) consistent with evolutionary biology; a philosophy of mind compatible with cognitive neuroscience. Caution: Scientific philosophy ≠ Philosophy of science. Caution 2: ↑**Logical positivism** called itself 'scientific' but it was not because it was beholden to phenomenalism (hence subjectivism) and inductivism. Its love of science was thus unrequited.

SCIENTIFICITY The property of being scientific, as in "evolutionary biology is scientific," and "present-day evolutionary psychology is not scientific." There are several scientificity criteria. A necessary condition for an item (hypothesis, theory, or method) to be scientific is that it be both conceptually precise and susceptible to empirical test. This condition disqualifies the rational-choice models that do not specify the utility function or that rely on subjective probability estimates. However, the condition is insufficient, for it is satisfied by the hypothesis of the creation of matter out of nothing. What disqualifies the latter is that it is incompatible with the bulk of physics, in particular the set of conservation theorems. The following criterion answers these concerns: A hypothesis or theory is scientific if (a) it is precise; (b) it is compatible with the bulk of relevant scientific knowledge; and (c) jointly with subsidiary hypotheses and empirical data, it entails empirically testable consequences. ↑**Science, basic**.

SCIENTISM The view that scientific research is the best way to secure accurate and deep factual ↑**knowledge**. Not to be confused with the views that scientific research is the only source of knowledge or that all scientific findings are true and final. A component of both ↑**logical positivism** and scientific ↑**realism**. Scientism has encouraged the attempts to transform some chapters of the humanities into sciences: recall, e.g., the origins of contemporary anthropology, psychology, linguistics, and the social sciences. The term was used pejoratively by F. Hayek and others to designate the aping of natural science in social studies. He and other members of the "humanist" (armchair) camp in social studies view scientism, rather than antiscience or pseudoscience, as their main enemy.

SCRUTABILITY The ability to be scrutinized or examined. Such ability is a joint property of the object being scrutinized and the knower, for it depends on the latter's means of observation and analysis. Example: atoms, the hereditary material, and mental processes became empirically scrutable only in the twentieth century. ↑**Scientism** denies the existence of inscrutable things other than those that have disappeared without leaving perceptible traces. By the same token, obscurantists assert the existence of inscrutable entities (such as deities) and incorrigible statements (dogmas). This is why they feel free to write at length on the many wonderful properties of such pseudothings and pseudotruths.

SECOND-ORDER LOGIC Any logical calculus that admits quantification over predicates, as in "All properties are properties of something" and "Some properties hold only for abstract objects." First-order logic (the ordinary predicate calculus), which admits only quantification over individuals, is a particular case of second-order logic. The latter is required to handle such key philosophical theses as Leibniz's principle of the ↑**identity** of individuals, and mathematical principles such as that of mathematical ↑**induction**.

SECONDARY PROPERTY A property that, far from inhering in a thing, is possessed by the thing as perceived. Examples: color (by contrast to wave length), taste, beauty. All such properties are conceptualized as object-subject relations. The predicates representing secondary properties occur in the propositions that describe ↑**phenomena** (appearances). ↑**Primary / secondary**.

SECTORAL APPROACH The approach typically adopted by the specialist who overlooks the systemic nature of the world and of our knowledge of it. Suitable only for tackling what appear to be narrow problems, such as unblocking a pipe and taking (but not "reading") a lung X ray. **Syn** tunnel vision. **Ant** ↑**systemic approach**.

SECULAR Worldly, earthly, free from supernatural (otherworldly) beliefs and organized religions. **Ant** otherworldly, religious.

SECULARISM Nonreligious approach, belief, or practice. Science, technology, most of the humanities, and the constitutions of nearly all the advanced countries, including the United States, are thoroughly secular. Secularism is characteristic of both pre-Socratic and modern philosophy. In particular, dialectical materialism, Hegelianism, Kantianism, and positivism are thoroughly secular. Religious fundamentalists fight openly the secular state. When they adopt gradualist tactics, they usually start by attempting to reinstate religious teaching and prayer in public schools, ban the teaching of evolutionary biology, and "cleanse" public libraries.

SEDUCTIVE INFERENCE Nondeductive ↑**inference**, in particular analogical and inductive. Seductive inferences obey no rules because they depend critically on the subject matter. We can only hope that they suggest plausible hypotheses.

SELECTION Sorting, whether blind or deliberate. Examples: natural selection and personnel selection. The conscious selection in the light of definite criteria, as in artificial selection and quality control, is usually called ↑**choice**. ↑**Natural selection**.

SELF-ASSEMBLY The spontaneous aggregation of things into a system, in one or more steps. Examples: polymerization, formation of a crystal out of a solution, synthesis of DNA molecules from their precursors, formation of ↑**psychons** out of neurons, emergence of street-corner gangs. To be distinguished from ↑**self-organization**.

SELF-CONSCIOUSNESS Consciousness of oneself, in contradistinction to awareness of external objects. ↑**Consciousness**.

SELF-CORRECTION The distinctive ability of science, or rather the scientific community, to correct whatever errors it detects. Actually this holds only for mathematical and experimental errors. The correction of errors of other kinds may require the help of philosophy. This holds in particular for errors of omission, such as the absence of the brain in much of psychology; semantic errors, such as mistaken interpretations of mathematical formulas in physical theories; and moral errors, such as helping design offensive weapons in exchange for research grants.

SELF-DETERMINATION a Ontology A thing or process that determines itself instead of being determined by something else. Examples: the motion of bodies and light in a vacuum once they start moving and until they meet an obstacle; exothermic chemical reactions; trains of abstract thought; the universe as a whole according to any naturalist ontology. The notion of self-determination was inherent in ancient atomism; it acquired scientific citizenship in the form of the principle of inertia, and it occurs in all contemporary sciences. But it is alien to most philosophies, which are ↑**externalist** in regarding ↑**matter** as passive. ↑**Self-assembly,** ↑**self-organization. b Ethics** Personal autonomy: the right of adult individuals to choose their own lifestyle. Unconditional according to egoism, nonexistent according to holism, and bounded by the rights of others according to a systemist moral philosophy such as ↑**agathonism. c Politology** The right of nations to rule themselves. This right is bounded by international obligations. It poses the problem whether the fight for self-determination should displace all other concerns or should be subjected to a reasonable cost-benefit analysis. **Syn** national sovereignty.

SELF-DETERMINATION, PARADOX OF If a person were fully self-determined, she would be unable to accomplish everything she needs and desires, because she would not seek the help required to overcome her limitations and resist external pressures. Hence, rather than attempting to maximize self-determination, we should try to balance individual initiative with cooperation, and rights with obligations. The same holds, mutatis mutandis, for national self-determination.

SELF-FULFILLING PROPHECY Prediction bound to be borne out for influencing behavior of self or alter. Example: a government's announcement that the economy is about to enter a period of recession may trigger the recession, for it prompts firms to fire employees in anticipation of lower sales.

SELF-ORGANIZATION ↑**Self-assembly** resulting in a system composed of subsystems that did not exist prior to the onset of the self-assembling process. Example: morphogenesis, or the formation of an embryo's organs. To be distinguished from mere ↑**self-assembly**.

SELF-REFERENCE a Semantics The property of a sentence of referring to itself, as in 'This is an English sentence' and 'This sentence is true', where 'this' names the sentence itself. Self-reference must be handled with care because it may lead to paradox, as with the case of the ↑**Liar paradox. b Biology and social studies** Misnomer for 'feedback', 'self-regulation', and 'homeostasis', as well as for people's ability to refer to themselves and judge themselves in the light of other people's opinions.

SEMANTIC ASSUMPTION Specification of meaning, in particular of reference. Example: In the formula "$pV = $ const.," p and V stand for the internal pressure and the volume of a gas respectively—or for the price and quantity of a merchandise. The full description of a mathematized scientific ↑**theory** includes a set of semantic assumptions alongside a mathematical formalism. This is why the same mathematical constructs, such as the linear and the exponential functions, occur in nearly all sciences and technologies: because, being neutral, they can be assigned different meanings in different contexts.

SEMANTICS a Ordinary language A mere matter of words. **b Linguistic** The discipline that investigates the way speakers assign meanings to linguistic expressions and the ways they translate them, as well as the causes of their misunderstanding. **c Mathematical** The study of the notions of ↑**model** (or example) of an abstract formalism such as Boolean algebra. **d Philosophical** The discipline that studies the concepts of ↑**reference**, ↑**intension**, ↑**sense**, ↑**meaning**, ↑**representation**, ↑**interpretation**, ↑**translation**, ↑**definition**, ↑**truth**, and their kin. The results of this study should help scientists decide what certain theories refer to, as well as ↑**exactify** some of the intuitive concepts they use, such as those of content, context, and partial truth.

SEMIOTIC SYSTEM A concrete system including signs that signify something to someone. More precisely, a semiotic system is a system with

Composition = A group of people using a collection of ↑**symbols** (artificial signs) to communicate with one another;

Environment = A community or society;

Structure = Syntactic, semantic, and phonological relations among the symbols, and other relations between these and their users as well as social relations among these;

Mechanism = Communication (through speech, writing, or body language).

The first component of this quadruple (composition) hardly needs elucidation. The second (environment) only serves as a reminder that semiotic systems do not exist in a vacuum and, moreover, that some signs stand for natural or social items. As for the structure of a semiotic system, the key nonsocial relations in it are those of signification or sign-signified relations. There are two such relations, ↑**denotation** and ↑**designation**, according as the object signified is material or conceptual. Finally, the fourth component (communication) tells us how symbols "come to life" and make a semiotic system "work" and change in the process. Neither of the last two components occurs in ↑**languages** when studied in themselves, i.e., as abstract systems, regardless of individual language users and linguistic communities. A language may thus be regarded as an uninhabited semiotic system.

SEMIOTICS The study of ↑**semiotic systems**, in particular texts and ↑**languages**. It is composed of ↑**syntax** (the study of structure), ↑**semantics** (the study of meaning), and ↑**pragmatics** (the study of the use of signs). Semiotics is still largely programmatic: so far only syntax (logical and linguistic) is well developed. General semiotics is the doctrine that everything is, or is reducible to, a collection of signs—whence confusions such as those of meaning with intention, and politics with political discourse. **Syn** ↑**textualism, hermeneutics**.

SENSATION Blurry and indiscriminate ↑**perception**, as in sensing a sound before identifying its kind or source, and feeling pain without knowing where exactlly it hurts, let alone what caused it.

SENSATIONISM a Epistemology The view that sense ↑**data** are all there is (ontological sensationism) or all we can know (epistemological sensationism). The former is a variety of ↑**subjectivism**, whereas the latter is a variety of ↑**empiricism**. Berkeley,

Mach, and the young Carnap were ontological sensationists; Ptolemy, Hobbes, Condillac, Comte, and Mill were epistemological sensationists. Both schools conflate sensation with perception and underrate the power of reason. **b Technology** Though dead in philosophy and moribund in psychology, sensationism is alive and well in ↑**artificial intelligence**. Indeed, it underlies the program of building machines that become intelligent, and even autonomous, as they interact with their environment via sensors and effectors. This program ignores the fact that sensory inputs are insufficient to pose or solve conceptual problems, such as those involving the concepts of imperceptibility, void, time, truth, or proof.

SENSE a Ordinary language Polysemous term, as shown by the many ways in which "That makes sense" can be read: "That expression is intelligible," "That hypothesis is plausible," "That action is adequate to its goal," etc. This ambiguity is one of the roots of the ↑**hermeneutic** thesis that the goal of social studies is to unveil the sense (or meaning) of human actions. **b Semantics** The sense or content of a construct is the union of the items of the same type that ↑**entail** or are entailed by it. I.e., $S(c) = \{x|$ $x \vdash c\} \cup \{y \mid c \vdash y\} = \mathcal{A}(c) \cup \mathcal{P}(c)$. The first term in the right-hand side is called the *purport* or logical ancestry, and the second the *import* or logical progeny of c. Related concept: ↑**intension**.

SENSE DATUM Knowledge provided by the senses, as in "that stinks" and "this hurts." Such knowledge of subject-bound (or egocentric) particulars lends itself to low-level generalizations such as "Garlic stinks" and "Fire hurts." Subject-invariant generalizations, such as "Force equals mass times acceleration" and "Globalization increases the vulnerability of national economies," go beyond sense data. The view that we have access only to sense data, not to the external events that cause them, is called ↑**phenomenalism**.↑**Sensation**.

SENTENCE A linguistic expression that, if intelligible, is the linguistic counterpart of a ↑**proposition**. That is, propositions are designated by sentences. Example: 'Katzen sind selbstsüchtig' and 'Los gatos son egoístas' designate the proposition that cats are selfish. Thus, one and the same proposition can be designated by different sentences in a single language and, a fortiori, in different languages. (Shorter: The designation function, that maps symbols into constructs, is many-to-one.) However, some sentences are just noises. Example: '[T]he immediate "I," already enduring in the enduring primordial sphere, constitutes in itself another as other' (E. Husserl). ↑**Nominalists**, who do not admit constructs for fear of Platonism, talk of 'sentences' when referring to propositions, and to the 'sentential calculus' when referring to the propositional calculus. The confusion between a construct and its linguistic wrappings is mistaken because constructs are not married to any particular language, let alone to grammatical rules, which are not universal. Nominalists cannot account for ↑**translation**, for this involves ↑**meaning** invariance, and meanings are not symbols but whatever sense and reference symbols convey.

SENTENTIAL CALCULUS Nominalist name of the ↑**propositional calculus**. ↑**Sentence**.

SEQUENCE A finite or infinite set together with an order relation, such as ≤ . Examples: 0,1,2, . . .*n* , . . .; the steps in a complex chemical reaction; the words in a sentence; a life history; a stream of consciousness. Standard notation: $S = <x_i \mid i \in \mathbb{N}>$. **Syn** list, string.

SERENDIPITY Finding one thing through seeking another: accidental discovery. Its importance should not be exaggerated, because the unprepared explorer is unlikely to notice anything out of the ordinary.

SET A collection of items with a fixed membership. The membership may be arbitrary, as in the case of $S = \{3, \text{America}\}$, or not, as in the case of the set of integers (which is actually a system). A set may be abstract (with nondescript members), as in any general set-theoretic formula, such as $A \subseteq B \Rightarrow A \cap B \neq \varnothing$. Or the elements of the set may be designated (described), as in "the real line" or "the set of humans who are alive right now." The concepts of set and set membership are the central (and undefined) concepts of ↑**set theory**.

SET THEORY The theory that studies abstract ↑**sets**. Actually there are several set theories: for instance, with and without the ↑**axiom of choice**, and with and without the continuum hypothesis (↑**infinity**). Hence there are as many meanings of "set" as set theories. Yet, elementary (or naive) set theory suffices for most purposes, and it is a powerful tool of philosophical analysis. For example, it allows one to ↑**exactify** the semantic notions of ↑**extension** and ↑**intension**; the ontological concepts of ↑**natural kind** and ↑**process**; and the axiological notions of ↑**value** and ↑**utility**. All rigorous set theories are axiomatic. However, none of them is known to be consistent. Some set theory or other, together with the underlying first-order classical predicate logic, is still usually regarded as the foundation of nearly all of mathematics. However, ↑**category theory** is an alternative foundation. This shows that the foundation of mathematics is neither single nor permanent, let alone uncontroversial.

SEXUALISM The program of explaining all animal behavior in terms of sex drive (or its repression) and reproduction. Examples: psychoanalysis and sociobiology. ↑**Biologism**.

SHOULDERS OF GIANTS, ON THE Abbreviation of the famous aphorism coined by Bernard de Chartres in the twelfth century: "We are like dwarfs sitting on the shoulders of giants, and so able to see more and see farther than the ancients." Knowledge is cumulative in some respects, and even modest investigators can contribute to it through using findings of geniuses. Still, it takes hard work to climb on the shoulders of a giant, and good brains to see farther once there.

SIGN Thing that "stands for" or represents another object. ↑**Designation**. Two kinds of sign are usually distinguished: natural and artificial. The former are symptoms of states or changes of state of concrete things. For example, dark clouds and dark looks are signs of rain and anger respectively. By contrast, artificial signs are conventional artifacts crafted and utilized to evoke factual items or to name constructs. Examples: linguistic expressions, items of body language (such as winks), logos, diagrams, and numerals. Natural signs, such as a haloed moon or a violent food riot, are such only by way of hypothesis. By contrast, artificial signs are such only by virtue of convention. That is, natural signs are perceptible ↑**indicators** of imperceptible things, properties, or events. Hence they are nonsignificant. Therefore, talk of their "meaning" is at best metaphorical, at worst plain wrong. In particular, it is mistaken to think of social life as a text or "like a text" just because people "interpret" social behavior, i.e., make ↑**hypotheses** concerning its intention or goal: ↑**hermeneutics**, ↑**textualism**. To forestall confusion one should use the word ↑**symbol** to stand for the concept of artificial sign such as a numeral or a road sign. Accordingly, the expression 'status symbol' should be replaced with 'status indicator'.

SIGNAL A signal is a process (or ↑**sequence of states**) in some concrete system, such as an organism or a society. Signals can be linguistic or nonlinguistic (such as the courtship dance of fruit flies). A linguistic signal is a process whereby a message of some kind (information, question, order, etc.) is transmitted from one person or machine to another. Caution: Not every linguistic signal signifies something. Example: Heidegger's pseudodefinition of "spirit" in his infamous 1933 rectoral address: "Geist ist ursprünglich gestimmte, wissende Entschlossenheit zum Wesen des Seins." This suggests that Whorf and Sapir were wrong in stating that every language has a conceptual content which influences the way its speakers think. The fact that one can express meaningless as well as meaningful sentences in any given language shows that language is a neutral tool for communicating and thinking—as well as for simulating thought. And this suffices to draw a sharp distinction between ↑**semiotic** and ↑**conceptual systems**. If no such distinction existed, it would be impossible to express alternative ideas, much less mutually incompatible ones, in the same language. Consequently, rational debate would be impossible.

SIGNIFICANCE a Ordinary language Importance. The significance of an idea is measured by the number of ideas it is related to. Hence significance increases with ↑**systemicity. b Statistics** A value of a variable is said to be *statistically significant* if it is definitely larger or smaller than could be expected by chance. The *statistical significance level* is the probability that an observational result is not a random artifact. In biomedical research, psychology, and sociology, the standard statistical significance level is p = 0.05. This means that 5 out of 100 data are fortuitous coincidences. In particle physics the criterion is p = 0.0001, or 99.99 percent. This is 500 times more demanding, because it means that only one out of 10,000 similar experiments is a statistical fluke. ↑**Error**.

SIGNIFICATION Object signified. The essential property of symbols is that they signify something to someone, in that they either ↑**designate** or ↑**denote** something. The structure of the concept of signification is a relation of the third degree: x signifies y to z. Two symbols are equisignificant if they designate or denote the same object, as is the case with '3,' 'three', and ' | | |'.

SIMPLICITY Simple = without parts. Examples: photons, letters, prime numbers. **Ant** ↑**complexity. a Conceptual** All basic concepts in a given context are simple, in that they are undefined in the context. However, definability is contextual (relative to some theory). Hence simplicity is contextual as well. Exceptions: the concepts of ↑**object** and ↑**identity** are irreducible or undefinable. **b Factual** All of the quanta of the various fields, in particular photons and electrons, are assumed to be simple in that they have no parts. Practical consequence: they are indecomposable. However, compositional simplicity does entail simplicity in other regards. In fact, the elementary "particles" have a number of unusual properties; they are normally in complex states—i.e., in states that are superpositions of infinitely many simple states (or eigenstates); and they are described by some of the most complex theories in history. **c Practical** A procedure is simple if it can be carried out with little effort, though it may be lengthy.

SIMPLISM The view that the simplest hypotheses, theories, or methods are always to be preferred. Its motto is "Less is more." Given the complexity of the real world, the only justifications for simplism are poverty, ignorance, and laziness. Indeed, the history of knowledge is, on the whole, one of increasing ↑**complexity**. However, unnecessary complexity is to be shunned because it is wasteful and pretentious. ↑**Ockham's razor**, ↑**simplicity**.

SIMULATION Anything that represents symbolically another thing. For example, a chess game simulates (at least originally) a battle; a maquette simulates a construction; and some computer programs represent particular features of things—such as buildings—or processes, such as the traffic flow in a city. If the simulated thing is real, its simulation may help analyze and predict its behavior. In the case of a blueprint or a mathematical model, such analysis and prediction may exhibit some of the flaws in the design or model, and thus point the way to improvement. Caution 1: A simulation of x must not be mistaken for x itself. For example, a simulation of a living thing is not alive—hence the claim that a computer program is alive, or thinks, is as wrong-headed as the claim that Donald Duck is actually chasing his nephews. Caution 2: Simulation cannot replace experiment, because it does not confront the model with the facts it refers to. A simulate and the object simulated are obviously different. Otherwise there would be no point in simulation. Yet, both are sometimes confused, as when certain computer programs are said to be alive, to think, or to play chess, while actually only the programmer-programmed system can do any such thing. ↑**Artificial intelligence,** ↑**artificial life**, ↑**computationism**.

SITUATIONAL Dependent on the particular situation or state of the system concerned, as in "reasonable decisions are situational." Emphasis on the situation or circumstance is needed to avoid inflexibility and cruelty in practical (e.g., moral, legal, medical, and political) matters. Overemphasis on them is to be avoided because it accompanies loss of principles.

SITUATIONAL LOGIC No such thing.

SKEPTICISM a Axiological The view that value judgments cannot be grounded or even disputed about: that no good reasons can be given for or against them. While this may be true of untutored sensory taste, it is doubtful about aesthetic valuations, and definitely false about moral judgments. Indeed, there are solid reasons for preferring honest work to theft, bargaining to resorting to violence, and so on. Moral judgments are subject to empirical test because they steer actions with observable consequences. ↑Realism, ↑values. b Epistemological The family of doctrines according to which some or all knowledge is dubious or even false. Two varieties: systematic and methodic. *Systematic*, total, or radical skepticism is the doubting of everything. *Methodic* or moderate skepticism uses doubt as a check on new ideas. Systematic skepticism, such as that of Pyrrho, Sextus Empiricus, or Francisco Sánches, is impracticable because every idea is evaluated or checked against other ideas. Whereas doubt paralyzes the systematic skeptic, it spurs the methodic skeptic. This is why methodic skepticism is the norm in all rational pursuits: one doubts only when there is some reason to doubt; and when there is, one investigates. ↑Skeptic's paradox.

SKEPTIC'S PARADOX The radical skeptic doubts everything equally. In particular, he puts all ↑hypotheses, scientific or nonscientific, on the same level. For example, he is likely to rank psychokinesis (the moving of material objects by the mind) together with the principle of conservation of energy, which contradicts psychokinesis, since this involves the creation of energy. Consequently he will plead for tolerance or even support for speculations or experiments concerning psychokinesis. Thus in practice radical skepticism may encourage gullibility. ↑Anything goes, ↑anything is possible, ↑open mind, ↑skepticism.

SKETCH ↑Schema.

SLIPPERY SLOPE A common argument for conservatism in debates about moral, medical, legal, and political norms. For example, "If you legalize this practice (e.g., abortion), you'll condone the next-worse one (e.g., mercy killing), and so on. We must draw the line early on: Otherwise we will slide down a slippery slope that ends up in hell." To be sure, a line must always be drawn between permissions and prohibitions. However, the line is vague and shifting, and it should not stop progress. Remember that John Locke, in his letter on toleration, banned atheism; and that England punished theft by hanging until the early 1800s.

SOBRIETY, PHILOSOPHICAL Conceptual discipline and verbal moderation. To be avoided: wild fantasy, such as Hegel's, and riotous prose, such as Husserl's and Heidegger's.

SOCIAL Belonging to or concerning a social group. Examples: trading, voting, teaching, healing, organizing. Prosocial actions promote the ↑common good, whereas antisocial actions harm it.

SOCIAL PHILOSOPHY The branch of philosophy that deals with the various doctrines on social order: their general features, epistemic ground, and moral justification. To be relevant, a social philosophy must be close to ↑social science and ↑social technology. However, this should not be an obstacle to the crafting of social ↑utopias.

SOCIAL SCIENCE The disinterested scientific study of social systems and social action. Main branches: anthropology, sociology, economics, politology, culturology, history, and their various combinations (such as socioeconomics and historical sociology). Not to be mistaken for the "humanist" or armchair social studies, such as phenomenological sociology, critical theory, and cultural studies, neither of which offers empirical evidence for its claims—many of which are cryptic to boot. Not to be confused either with ↑**social technology**, which is concerned with controlling or changing society rather than explaining it. Social science research can be empirical or theoretical (in particular mathematical). Following the positivist tradition, only the former is regarded as scientific. Philosophical and ideological influences are stronger, and seldom to the good, on social studies than on any others. Witness the idealism-materialism, individualism-holism, subjectivism-realism, and market-state controversies. ↑**Social science, philosophy of**.

SOCIAL SCIENCE, PHILOSOPHY OF Investigation of the philosophical problematics raised by social research. Sample: What kind of thing is society: fictitious or real, spiritual or material? Is there a way out from the individualism-holism dilemma? Are there social laws or only temporary trends? What are the engines of history? What are the commonalities and differences between the social and the natural sciences? Are the social sciences ↑**idiographic**, ↑**nomothetic**, or both? Do historians make history? What is ↑**Verstehen** and what if any is its role? How true are the principles of mainstream economic theory? Can social science be morally neutral? What is the relation between social science and ↑**social technology**?

SOCIAL TECHNOLOGY, or SOCIOTECHNOLOGY The design of policies and plans for the maintenance, repair, or construction of social systems, private or public, on the basis of social science. Main branches: management science, resource management, normative macroeconomics, social work, jurisprudence, criminology, normative demography and epidemiology, and city planning. Sample of problematics: How best to combine technical expertise with self-government? How to attain full employment without parasitism? Why and how to make medicare universal? How to stimulate consumption without causing inflation? How to avoid inflation without increasing unemployment? How to ensure security without repression? How to promote civic responsibility? How to protect the public from cultural garbage without censorship? Are there viable alternatives to capitalism and socialism?

SOCIETY A system composed of animals of the same species, occupying the same territory, and held together by bonds of some kind. A human society is characterized by a social structure composed of artificial bonds: economic, political, and cultural. ↑**Individualism** denies the very existence of society, whereas ↑**holism** holds society to be everything, and persons nothing. ↑**Systemism**, an alternative to both individualism and holism, conceives of human society as a supersystem composed of ↑**systems** that are set up, maintained, reformed, or dismantled by individual action. According to it, the atomic person of individualism is just as fictitious as the impenetrable whole of holism. Hence the study of society is irreducible to either the study of individuals or the study of social wholes without regard to their composition. The concept of society is a philosophical (in particular ontological) category because it is common to all social and biosocial sciences and technologies. Also because its study raises many important epistemological and ethical problems, such as those of the adequacy of ↑hermeneutics, and whether social science is ↑value-free or value-bound.

SOCIOBIOLOGY The attempt to reduce social science to evolutionary biology and genetics. Not to be confused with biosociology, or the study of the impact of society on human biological processes—e.g., the effect of poverty on height and mental development. ↑Biologism, ↑naturalization.

SOCIOLOGISM a Sociology The view that individual human action is exclusively determined by either social structure or culture. A variety of ↑holism, sociologism ignores the inner springs of action, such as individual needs, beliefs, and aspirations. b Epistemology The view that all knowledge is produced collectively and moreover has a more or less explicit social content or social utility. It underrates truth and ignores curiosity and the fact that neither mathematics nor natural science have a social content. ↑Constructivism, ↑relativism.

SOCIOLOGY a The synchronic social science that focuses on social structure regardless of its source (biological, economic, political, or cultural). It intersects partially with all the other social sciences. In particular, there are social anthropology, sociolinguistics, economic sociology, political sociology, social history, legal sociology, medical sociology, and sociology of knowledge. b Sociology of philosophy The almost nonexistent branch of sociology that studies the impact of social circumstances on philosophy, and the latter's reaction on society. Example of the first: a study of the attack of Nazism on rationalism, positivism, and materialism. Example of the second: a study of the philosophical components of any ideology, such as the rationalism inherent in traditional liberalism. c Sociology of science and technology The sociological study of the social stimuli and inhibitions upon scientific research and technological research and development. Examples: study of the social conditions of the favorable reception of scientific and technological novelties in the seventeenth century, and of the negative impact of regressive politics on the funding of contemporary social studies.

SOCRATIC METHOD Teaching through questioning and analyzing rather than delivering information. Effective teaching combines both methods. The Socratic method might be suitable for tapping the know-how of craftsmen. Imagine what a Socrates might learn about the details of industrial processes if he worked as an engineer, a mid-level manager, or a supervisor in a modern factory. ↑Knowledge.

SOLIDARITY Propensity to help others. Along with equality, respect for the person, and reciprocity, solidarity is a pillar of any sustainable human social system. Exaggerated by ↑holism and threatened by radical ↑individualism. By extension, used as synonym for the mutual dependence of the components of a ↑system of any kind.

SOLIPSISM a Ontological The belief that only the subject or knower exists. The most radical and only consistent version of subjective idealism. No solipsist of this kind has been found outside psychiatric wards. **b Epistemological** The belief that I alone am in the possession of all truths. **Syn** delusion of intellectual grandeur. **c Methodological** The principle according to which, in order to investigate the mental, I should ignore other people. This principle is endorsed by phenomenology, which Husserl defined as egology or the study of the self, and moreover a study involving the ↑**epoché** (or bracketing out) of the external world. No psychologist accepts this fiction, since psychology is the objective investigation of other people's mental processes. **d Moral** The belief that only I matter to myself and others. **Syn** selfishness.

SOME Quantifier lying between "none" and "all." Formalized by the "existential" quantifier ∃, as in "∃x ($x^2 = 1$) and "∃x (x is an angel & x protects me)." It would be mistaken to read ∃, in either formula, as real (material) existence. ↑**Existence predicate**.

SOPHISM Logically invalid statement or argument. Examples: the Taoist principle "weakness is strength"; Spinoza's (and Engels's) definition of "freedom" as the knowledge of necessity; the utilitarian characterization of altruism as enlightened selfishness.

SOUL The theological ancestor of ↑'**mind**'. An allegedly immaterial and immortal entity, and moreover one inaccessible to science. Parapsychologists, psychoanalysts, and many philosophical psychologists believe in immaterial souls though not in their immortality. Contemporary psychology knows no soul. The history of the humanities is to a large extent the history of the soul.

SOUNDNESS An argument (reasoning) is sound if, besides being formally ↑**valid**, its premises and conclusions are true.

SPACE a Mathematics Any structured set may be regarded as a space. If this structure is determined by a distance function, the space is metric. There is an unlimited number of conceivable mathematical spaces, hence of geometries. **b Physics** In contrast to the multiplicity of mathematical spaces, there is a single physical space, which is a feature of the real world. A physical geometry is constructed by suitably interpreting a mathematical geometry. Example: *Int* (line) = light ray, *Int* (surface) = light wave front. Unlike mathematical geometries, which are tested only for internal consistency, physical geometries must be subjected to empirical tests too. There is nearly universal agreement that Euclidean physical geometry holds far away from massive celestial bodies, whereas Riemannian geometry, inherent in the general theory of relativity, holds in their vicinity. By contrast, there is no universal agreement on the very nature of physical space—an ontological question. **c Ontology** An ontological theory of space attempts to answer the question: What is space? It should not be committed to a definite metric, but should leave this problem to physics, because only measurements can help determine the coefficients of the space (or space-time) metric. There are two main views on the nature of space: the absolutist and the relational ones. According to the former, physical space is the self-existing stage where the cosmic drama unfolds: it precedes, lodges, and labels physical entities. This view is strongly suggested by the way we use spatial coordinates to place entities: we often start by building a spatial grid.

By contrast, according to the relational theory, physical space is the collection of changing things together with the relation of betweenness. This view is strongly suggested by general relativity. In fact, according to it, space (or rather space-time) is intimately connected to matter. This connection is so intimate that, if there were no matter of some kind, however subtle, there would be no physical space left. ↑**Geometry, philosophical,** ↑**space-time**.

SPACE-TIME The synthesis of space and time as effected by relativistic physics, according to which the where depends on the when and conversely. Caution: space and time are intimately related but cannot get transmuted into each other. For example, the rate of change w.r.t. time is not the same as the rate of change w.r.t. position. Space-time may be taken to be the basic structure of the collection of all ↑**events**, or changes of state of material things. Hence, no matter, no space-time. This view is inherent in the general theory of relativity, which is the standard theory of gravitation—though by no means the only possible one. Indeed, the central formula of this theory is "$G = \kappa T$," where the tensor G describes the structure of space-time, whereas the tensor T describes the distribution of matter (inclusive of fields other than the gravitational field). If $T = 0$ everywhere, G describes purely mathematical four-dimensional spaces, since there are no physical entities left in whose terms the geometric concepts occurring in G can be interpreted. To find out the structure of the space-time surrounding a piece of matter, such as a star or a light beam, one must start by specifying the corresponding stress-energy tensor T. Since space-time and matter are intimately connected, they coevolve. Moreover, according to quantum cosmology, space-time emerged when the universe expanded to the size of about a hydrogen atom. However, this theory is highly speculative and therefore likely to be short-lived.

SPECIES A collection of things sharing some basic properties. Examples: chemical and biological species. The first rung in a classification. More inclusive concepts: genus, family, kingdom. The relation between a genus and its species are these: A genus is the union ($\cup$) of its species; every one of these is included ($\subseteq$) in its genus; and every individual is a member ($\in$) of a single species. The view that species are concrete individuals ignores this analysis because it mistakes the membership relation with the part-whole relationship. ↑**Natural kind,** ↑**taxonomy**.

SPECIESISM The view that humans are superior to all other animals in all respects, not just intellectually and morally; and that this alleged superiority entitles them to use other species as they see fit. Speciesism is as difficult to justify as to escape. ↑**Animal rights**.

SPECIFICATION a Precise description of an object. In particular, (a) characterization of an organism as a member of a well-defined species; and (b) condition that an artifact, such as a house or a social program, is expected to meet. **b** Imprecise description, as in "Gene g specifies protein p," or "Gene g specifies where the eyes are to develop." A convenient word to disguise ignorance of the specific mechanism in question.

SPECULATION The framing of conjectures without caring, at least for the time being, for their factual truth. There is no philosophy, mathematics, science, technology, or even rational action without some speculation. But the outcomes of speculation ought to be checked for internal and external ↑**consistency** and, if need be, with fresh evidence as well. This distinguishes serious and fruitful from wild and barren speculation. Idealists have held that unchecked speculation is the prerogative of authentic philosophy. Scientific realists require that philosophical speculation be checked against the body of relevant mathematical, scientific, or technological knowledge. ↑**B test.**

SPEECH ACT An utterance believed, rightly or wrongly, to have a practical effect. Examples: proposals, promises, warnings, threats, prayers, oaths, cheers. The study of speech acts constitutes a small fragment of ↑**linguistics** (in particular sociolinguistics), ↑**anthropology**, the ↑**sociology** of communications, and ↑**pragmatics**. So far it has neither raised nor solved any interesting philosophical problems. Given the heterogeneity of speech acts, it is doubtful that a general and nontrivial theory about them may be constructed.

SPIRIT Immaterial being, individual or collective, capable of acting upon material things. The central concept of ↑**animism**, ↑**idealism**, and ↑**spiritualism**. Not to be confused with *mind*, which is always personal.

SPIRIT OF THE TIMES The ruling ideas of an epoch. **Syn** ↑*Zeitgeist.*

SPIRITUALISM In the past, identical with ↑**idealism**. Nowadays, belief in spirits or souls floating around and accessible to rare individuals endowed with paranormal abilities. A popular cult and a modest but steady industry.

SPIRITUALITY Polysemous term. In religion and idealist philosophy, the opposite of material or carnal. Seldom used by naturalists and secularists, who prefer to speak of disinterested cultural concerns, such as music, mathematics, or philosophy.

SPONTANEOUS Self-initiated, not in response to external stimulation, uncaused. Examples: some neuronal firings, self-organizing systems, and radioactivity. A property that ↑**machines**, in particular computers, lack. ↑**Aseity.**

STATE a Ontology and science The state a concrete thing is in at a given instant, and relative to a given reference frame, is the totality of its properties at that time and relative to that frame. Each state is representable by a particular value of a ↑**state function**. Calling F a state function for a thing of some kind (and relative to some reference frame), the state of the thing at time t is representable by $F(t)$. **b Philosophy of mind** The expression 'mental state' is frequently used but never clearly elucidated in the philosophies of mind that are not parts of science-oriented ontologies. Thus it is sometimes said that the brain *causes* mental states—which is like saying that the atmosphere causes weather states. Things do not cause states but are in states. Only events (changes of state) can cause or render probable other events.

STATE FUNCTION A function whose values represent the possible states of a concrete entity. Examples: the list of the thermodynamic variables p, V, and T; the state (or wave) function in quantum mechanics; the list of demographic variables that characterize a human population. In ontology it is convenient to define a state function F for the individuals of a given natural kind, relative to some reference frame, as an ordered n-tuple of the form $F = <F_1, F_2, \ldots, F_n>$, where each component is a time-dependent function representing a property shared by all the members of the kind. As t varies, $F(t)$ may take on a sequence of values, the totality of which represents the history of the thing over the interval concerned. The state functions in ↑**quantum mechanics**, usually designated by ψ, are functions of the space and time coordinates. ↑**State-space**.

STATE-SPACE The set of all states that the things of some kind can be in: the space spanned (swept) by a ↑**state function**. This is an abstract ↑**space** whose dimensionality depends on the theory. The state-spaces in classical physics, as well as in biology and social science, have a finite number of dimensions, whereas in quantum physics they are infinitely dimensional.

STATE-SPACE APPROACH The approach consisting in focusing on ↑**state functions** and their ranges. Employed throughout science and technology, and used occasionally in exact philosophy. In the latter no particular state functions need be defined: only their existence must be assumed. This suffices to define an event as a pair of states, a process as a sequence of states, and a qualitative change as the jump of the tip of the state function to a subspace of a different dimensionality.

STATEMENT ↑**Proposition**.

STATISTICAL PROBABILITY The name positivist philosophers give to the long-run ↑**frequency** of events of a kind. The expression 'statistical probability' is misleading because every ↑**probability** is the probability of an individual state or event, whereas every frequency (long-run or otherwise) is a collective property of a collection or sequence of states or events. Besides, it is mathematically incorrect to equate probabilities with frequencies.

STATISTICS The scientific study of large groups of facts of some kind, such as births and automobile accidents. Some typical statistical concepts are those of sample, average, mode, and variance. Statistics can be descriptive or analytical (mathematical). The former is of central importance to all social sciences and technologies. Mathematical statistics, an application of the probability calculus, is the study of the concepts and methods employed in descriptive statistics, such as those of representative sample and confidence interval. This discipline is of philosophical interest because it deals with ↑**emergent** properties such as the distribution of a feature over a population, the design of observations and experiments, empirical tests of low-level hypotheses, ↑**inductions** from sample to population, and correlation as an indicator of possible causation.

STOCHASTIC Chancelike. ↑**Randomness**, ↑**probability**.

STOICISM Ancient naturalist and humanist philosophy. Stoicism is known above all for its ethics, which recommends fortitude in the face of misfortune.

STRUCTURALISM a General concept Emphasis on the ↑**structure** of ↑**systems** at the expense of their composition and environment. Example: Marx's pseudodefinition of an individual as a set of social relations. This definition is incorrect because relations do not precede their relata. **b Special concept** The attempt to understand society as a ↑**semiotic system**. The French version of ↑**textualism** or ↑**hermeneutics**. It has the great advantage that it substitutes talk of symbols for the study of real people, and talk about conventions for the empirical investigation of trends, norms, and laws. This literary approach is cheap but barren. **c Philosophy of science** The idealist view that the referents of scientific theories are mathematical concepts—e.g., that a system of particles is identical with a certain relational system (rather than being represented by the latter). ↑ **Models muddle.**

STRUCTURE A property of all ↑**systems**, whether conceptual or material, natural or social, technical or semiotic. The structure of a system is the set of all the relations among its components, particularly those that hold the system together. Examples: the structure of a sentence is the order of the types of its constituents, such as Subject-Verb-Object in the case of "Socrates drank hemlock"; the structure of a theory is the relation of entailment; the structure of a DNA molecule is the sequence of the nucleotides that compose it; the structure of a culture includes the relations of learning and communication; the structure of an army consists of the relations of command, supply, communication, and combat. In the last example, command belongs in the internal, and supply and combat in the external structure of an army—or *endostructure* and *exostructure* respectively. Structures are properties of systems: there are no structures in themselves. Therefore the expression 'agency-structure relation', common in social studies, should be understood as meaning the relation between individual agents and the social systems in which they act. Recipe for a catchy book title: start it with "The structure of."

SUBCONCEPT A ↑**concept** whose ↑**extension** is included in that of a wider concept. That is, if c and C are concepts, then $c \le C =_{df} [\,\mathcal{E}(c) \subseteq \mathcal{E}(C)\,]$. Examples: Equilateral triangle $\le$ Triangle, Hominid $\le$ Primate, Prosocial $\le$ Social.

SUBJECT a Logic and linguistics The object(s) of which something is predicated. In ancient and medieval logic, every subject was single; in modern logic it may be multiple. For example, the subjects of 'Abelard and Héloise loved one another' are Abelard and Héloise. **Syn** ↑**referent**. **b Psychology** Experimental animal. **c Epistemology** Knower. **d Praxiology** Agent.

SUBJECTIVE Having to do with a ↑**subject** (knower or agent) and her inner life. For example, "She feels depressed" is subjective because it expresses a subject's present mood. However, in principle such feeling can be described in ↑**objective** terms, ideally in terms of the value of the concentration of serotonin in the subject's mesolimbic system. The nonbiological psychologies deny the relevance or even possibility of such objective study, whereas neuropsychologists and biological psychiatrists are carrying it out.

SUBJECTIVE IDEALISM The doctrine that everything revolves around the knowing subject. Radical version (ontological constructivism): The subject constructs the world. Moderate version (epistemological relativism): Things are the color the subject sees them. ↑**Constructivism,** ↑**idealism,** ↑**phenomenalism,** ↑**relativism,** ↑**subjectivism /** **objectivism.**

SUBJECTIVISM / OBJECTIVISM According to subjectivism, everything exists and must be described relative to some knower. Prime examples: Protagoras, Berkeley, Mach, and the constructivism-relativism currently fashionable in the philosophy and sociology of science. According to objectivism (realism), the external world exists on its own and it should be described in an objective manner, that is, without referring to the subject's state of mind. Science and technology are tacitly objectivist. Hence someone who claimed, e.g., that earthquakes happen because he wills them, or that they should only be described in terms of the terror they cause, or that geologists should be blamed for them, would not be taken seriously by anyone—not even by subjectivist philosophers when outside their studies. ↑**Idealism,** ↑**phenomenalism,** ↑**realism.**

SUBMERGENCE The disappearance of things or processes of some (natural) kind. The dual of ↑**emergence.** Examples: extinction of biospecies, disappearance of institutions, and obsolescence of philosophies. ↑**Evolution,** whether biological or social, is punctuated by submergence as well as by emergence.

SUB SPECIE AETERNITATIS From the point of view of ↑**eternity** in the theological sense of this word, i.e., as intemporality. This is how ideas in themselves, in particular mathematical ideas, are usually regarded: as intemporal objects.

SUBSTANCE In medieval philosophy, that which remains unaltered underneath change. In contemporary philosophy, substantial individuals are concrete or material things— hence changeable ones. A category absent from empiricism.

SUBSTRATE Material, stuff, as in "the amygdala is the neural substrate of fear"—an unnecesary circumlocution for "the amygdala is the organ of fear."

SUBTHEORY A theory whose ↑**reference** class is included in that of a wider theory. Examples: statics ⊆ dynamics, optics ⊆ electromagnetic theory, theory of natural selection ⊆ theory of evolution. Caution: An arbitrary subset of formulas of a theory is not a theory: to qualify, the collection in question must be closed under deduction. ↑**Sub-** **concept.**

SUBTLETY Discrimination, refinement, or depth. There is no recipe for attaining either. On the other hand, there are tools for refining ideas. Two of them are logic and mathematics. However, ↑**linguistic philosophers** claim that mathematical logic cannot capture the subtleties of ordinary language. ↑**Conjunction** would be a case in point. For instance, in ordinary language, 'smart but dishonest' is not the same as 'dishonest but smart'. A logician might rejoin that this example makes no dent on logical conjunction, but exemplifies instead the hidden assumptions made in using ordinary language. Indeed, the LHS of the above inequality can be analyzed thus: 'x is smart and dishonest. And, since x is dishonest, one should be on guard when dealing with x'. On the other hand, the RHS abbreviates 'x is dishonest and smart. And, since x is smart, one may learn something from x'. Thus, analysis can capture the subtle difference between 'and' and 'but'. It is an unstated principle of applied logic that all the subtleties of ordinary language can be analyzed in like manner. ↑*Esprit de finesse*.

SUFFICIENT a Logic A proposition p is a *sufficient condition* for a proposition q if p ⇒ q. Example: it is sufficient for a number to be divisible by 2, that it be divisible by 6. **b Ontology** First principle of sufficient reason: "Every event has a cause." **Syn** ↑**causal principle**. This principle can still be held to be true of a great many events. But its range has shrunk as a result of the discovery of such ↑**spontaneous** events as radioactivity and ↑**self-assembly**. **c Epistemology and praxiology** Second principle of sufficient reason: "A reason must be given for every opinion and every decision." Corollary: "Groundless opinion or decision is unacceptable." A pillar of ↑**rationalism**.

SUMMUM BONUM The highest good. For Christians, the *summum bonum* is everlasting life; for utilitarians, happiness; for agathonists, welfare of self and others.

SUPERNATURALISM Belief in supernatural entities, whether secular such as ghosts, or religious such as angels and devils. **Ant** ↑**naturalism**. All religions involve belief in the supernatural.

SUPEROGATORY Said of actions that go beyond the call of duty. They are performed daily by ordinary people, but do not occur in the utilitarian balance sheet.

SUPERSTITION Groundless and persistent belief or belief system, such as ↑**supernaturalism**, ↑**spiritualism**, ↑**parapsychology**, psychoanalysis, and homeopathy. Not to be mistaken for mere falsity, which is bound to occur in the course of any research—until spotted and repaired or discarded.

SUPERVENIENCE Dependence of one set of properties on another, as in "mental characteristics are dependent, or supervenient, upon physical characteristics." In vogue in the philosophy of mind but unknown to scientists, and a mushy version of the exact concept of ↑**emergence**. Talk of supervenience is Platonic talk of properties in themselves, i.e., properties detached from the things possessing them. The standard account of supervenience, due to Jaegwon Kim, involves negative and disjunctive properties, which nothing concrete can possess, and which are suggested by the confusion of ↑**property** with ↑**attribute**. Contrary to the concept of emergence occurring in science and in ↑**emergentist materialism**, that of supervenience is symmetric and static. In short, a useless notion that has muddied the debate over the nature of the mind.

SURREALISM, PHILOSOPHICAL Any collection of groundless philosophical views. Examples: Plato's theory of ideas, Leibniz's doctrine of monads, Berkeley's immaterialism, dialectical "logic," possible-worlds ontology and semantics, epistemological anarchism, and social constructivism.

SUSPENSION OF BELIEF The methodological ↑**skeptic** refrains from assigning truth values to propositions in the absence of strong (preferably conclusive) evidence in their support. He adopts the ↑**truth-gap theory**.

SYLLOGISM Special kind of deductive argument cast in predicate logic. Example: All As are Bs, and all Bs are Cs, whence all As are Cs. The word is often used erroneously as a synonym of deductive inference, which actually includes plenty of nonsyllogistic inferences, such as "What holds for any holds for all."

SYLLOGISM, PROPORTIONAL A useful nondeductive reasoning like this:

f percent of all As are Bs.
This is an A picked at random

The probability that this is a B equals f.

If the condition that the individual in question has been picked at random is omitted, the reasoning is invalid, because talk of probability is legitimate only with reference to randomness, which in this case inheres in the sampling process. ↑**Probability**.

SYMBOL Artificial sign. Examples: linguistic expressions, diagrams, logos, road signs, architectural blueprints, maps, numerals, logical and mathematical signs. A symbol is a sign produced or used either to designate a concept or some other ↑**construct**, or to denote a nonconceptual item, such as an individual material thing or another symbol. We may call them *designating* and *denoting* signs respectively. Example of a designating sign: a numeral (which designates or names a number). Example of a denoting sign: a proper name. The relations of designation (symbol-concept) and denotation (symbol-thing) can combine with the relation of reference (or aboutness), as in the following diagram:

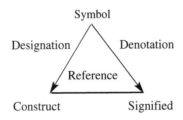

The designating-denoting and the symbol-nonsymbol splittings do not coincide because, whereas some symbols stand for constructs, others don't. Thus the numerals '4' and 'IV' designate the number four, which is a pure concept, whereas proper names and place-names denote concrete things. Likewise, the symbol '$5' denotes a five-dollar banknote (or check or money order) or its equivalent in commodities. Symbols are perceptible entities, not abstract ones like concepts and propositions: think of readable sentences, visible drawings, and audible words. However, only iconic (or representational) symbols, such as most road signs, are directly interpretable. The non-iconic signs cannot be read without an accompanying, though often tacit, code. Think of the letters of the alphabet and the words they compose, in contrast to hieroglyphs. Or think of maps, musical scores, graphs, circuit diagrams, organization charts, or architectural blueprints. Symbols can be "read" (interpreted) only with the help of (explicit or tacit) codes or semiotic conventions, such as: "Letter s → Sibilant sound," "Blue patch on a map → Water body," "Serrated line in an electric circuit diagram → Ohmic resistance," "$ → dollars," and "Money → commodities." In other words, whereas nonsymbolic signs are purely material artifacts, symbols are material artifacts.

SYMBOLPHRENIA Obsession with symbols, on the assumption that everything is a symbol for something else. Characteristic of magical thinking, psychoanalysis, and postmodernism, in particular deconstructionism.

SYNCATEGOREMATIC A symbol devoid of meaning when taken in isolation from other symbols. Examples: punctuation signs, parentheses, articles, prepositions.

SYNERGY Effective ↑**cooperation** in either nature or society. For example, every evolutionary novelty requires synergy among the pertinent genes; and the success of any business enterprise depends critically upon the synergic interaction among its departments. **Ant** anarchy.

SYNONYMY Two terms are mutually synonymous if they have the same ↑**meaning**— in particular if they designate the same concept. This definition is meaningless to anyone who, like a nominalist, claims to dispense with ↑**concepts**.

SYNTAX a Linguistics The study of the grammatical structure of sentences and texts. Sentence parsing (into noun phrases, verb phrases, and the like) belongs in syntax. **b Philosophy** The logical analysis of concepts, propositions, and conceptual systems, in particular theories. At one time the ↑**logical positivists** held the ↑**formalist** view that philosophy consists in syntax, with total disregard for content. Some logicians liked this view because it made them into instant ontologists, epistemologists, and ethicists.

SYNTHESIS The assembly or combination, natural or artificial, of objects of different kinds, as in "the synthesis of biomolecules out of their precursors," and "analytic geometry is a synthesis of algebra and geometry." In Hegelian and materialist ↑**dialectics**, the (impossible) merger of opposites, as in "becoming is the synthesis of being and nonbeing."

SYNTHETIC A PRIORI A synthetic a priori proposition is one that refers to facts (or experiences) and is a priori, that is, prior to experience. According to idealism, all propositions that refer to the world are synthetic a priori. Empiricists deny this thesis on the evidence that modern science was accompanied by the rejection of apriorism and an explosion of observation, measurement, and experiment. It is true that all scientific propositions are ultimately a posteriori, in the sense that, even when not suggested by experience, they must be empirically testable and eventually checked against facts. But the philosophy underlying scientific research does contain synthetic a priori propositions, such as the principles of the reality, lawfulness, and intelligibility of the real world. These principles are synthetic for referring to reality, but they may also be regarded as a priori for being tacitly assumed by anyone who engages in the scientific exploration or alteration of the world.

SYSTEM a Concept Complex object every part or component of which is related to at least one other component. Examples: an atom is a physical system composed of protons, neutrons, and electrons; a cell is a biological system composed of subsystems, such as organelles, which are in turn composed of molecules; a business firm is a social system composed of managers, employees, and artifacts; the integers constitute a system bound together by addition and multiplication; a valid argument is a system of propositions held together by the relation of implication and the rules of inference; and a language is a system of signs held together by concatenation, meaning, and grammar. We may distinguish the following basic ↑**kinds of system**: concrete and conceptual, as exemplified respectively by an organism and a theory. In turn, concrete systems are natural, social, or artificial (human-made). **b CESM analysis** The simplest analysis of the concept of a system involves the concepts of composition, environment, structure, and mechanism. The *composition* of a system is the collection of its parts. The *environment* of a system is the collection of things that act on, or are acted upon, the system's components. The *structure* of a system is the collection of relations (in particular bonds or links) among the system's components, as well as among these and environmental items. The former may be called the *endostructure* and the latter the *exostructure* of the system. The *total structure* of a system is thus the union of these two sets of relations. We may define the *boundary* of a system as the collection of the components of the system that are directly linked with items in its environment. (Two items are directly linked if they are linked and nothing else interposes between them.) Note the difference between boundary and shape. Whatever has shape has a boundary but the converse is false. Indeed, there are shapeless things, such as light atoms and business firms, that have boundaries. The boundary of an atom is the collection of its outer electrons, and the boundary of a business firm is constituted by its sellers, buyers, marketers, lawyers, and public relations agents. Finally, a system's *mechanism* is constituted by the internal processes that make it "tick," that is, change in some respects while conserving it in others. Obviously, only material systems have mechanisms. We are now ready to define the concepts of subsystem and supersystem. An object is a *subsystem* of another if and only if it is a system itself, and if its composition and structure are included in the composition and structure respectively of the latter, whereas its environment includes that of the more encompassing system. Examples: statics is a subsystem of dynamics; a chromosome is a subsystem of a cell; a social network is a subsystem of a society. Obviously, the relation of being a *supersystem* of a system is the dual of that of being a subsystem. For example, everyone of us is a system of organs, and these are in turn supersystems of the component cells. The universe is the maximal concrete system: the supersystem of all concrete systems. A realistic model of a system of a concrete system should involve its main features: composition, environment, structure, and mechanism. In other words, we should model the system s of interest, at any given time, as the ordered quadruple: $\mu(s) = <C(s), E(s), S(s), M(s)>$. As time goes by, any or all four components are bound to change. It is less obvious but also true that, except in microphysics, we do not need to know, and in any case we cannot know, the ultimate components of every system. In most cases it will suffice to ascertain or conjecture the composition of a system at a given level. (The concept of composition of a system s at level L is defined thus: $C_L(s) = C(s) \cap L$.) Thus, the social scientist is not interested in the cellular composition of his agents. Furthermore, more often than not, his units of analysis are not individuals but social systems, such as households, business firms, schools, churches, political parties, government departments, or entire nations. What some social scientists call the *world system* is the supersystem of all the social systems on earth. The above analysis of the concept of a system shows clearly why the ↑**systemic approach** is preferable to its rivals, every one of which overlooks at least one of the four distinguishing features of a system.

SYSTEM, CONCEPTUAL A *conceptual* system is one composed of ↑**constructs**. The simplest of all conceptual systems are propositions, such as "Humans are sociable." For purposes of analysis it is convenient to formalize this particular proposition to read: "For all x, if x is human, then x is sociable." The *components* of this minisystem are the logical concepts "for all," "if-then," the blank x, and the extralogical predicates "is human" and "is sociable." The *structure* of a proposition is its logical form, best displayed with the help of predicate logic. In the above case, it is $(\forall x)(Hx \Rightarrow Sx)$. And the *environment* of a proposition is its setting or context, i.e., the more or less heterogeneous and untidy set of propositions that are or may be logically related to the given proposition. Two of the members of the environment of the above example are "All humans are animals," and "Sociality is necessary for human welfare." Outside such context, the given proposition would not be such, for it would be devoid of sense. Indeed, the sentence designating (or expressing) a proposition would be incomprehensible in isolation. Since propositions are systems, systems of propositions, such as systems of equations and hypothetico-deductive systems, are supersystems, i.e., systems composed of subsystems. Nor are these the only kinds of conceptual system. Other kinds are ↑**context**, ↑**classification**, and ↑**theory**.

SYSTEM, FUNCTIONAL A set of properties (or their respective predicates) related by laws (or their respective law-statements). For example, the various bodily functions hang together: they constitute a functional system. Indeed, any change in one of them, such as a sudden drop in blood pressure, affects several others, such as mental lucidity. Since a functional system cannot be detached from the concrete system it inheres in, talk of functional systems is elliptical. For instance, the various mental functions (e.g., cognitive, affective, and volitional) are not disembodied, but are functions of the brain. A formalization of the concept with the modest resources of the predicate calculus follows. If $\mathbb{P}$ designates the collection of all possible properties of concrete things, then $\mathcal{F}$ is a functional system if
$$\mathcal{F} = \{P, Q \in \mathbb{P} | (\exists x)(\forall P)(\exists Q)[x \text{ is a concrete system } \& Px \& Q \in \mathbb{P} \& (Px \Rightarrow Qx)]\}.$$
↑**Function**.

SYSTEM, KINDS OF The following basic kinds of system may be distinguished:

1 *Conceptual,* such as classifications, hypothetico-deductive systems, and legal codes.

2 *Material*
    2.1 *Natural*, such as atoms, the solar system, nervous systems, and organisms
    2.2 *Social*, such as families, schools, business firms, and social networks.
    2.3 *Technical*, such as machines, road networks, and TV networks.
    2.4 *Semiotic*, such as languages, musical scores, and maps, together with their users.

This is not a ↑**classification**, because (a) most social systems are artificial as well as social: think of hospitals, banks, or armies; (b) some social systems, such as farms, contain not only people but also machines, animals, and plants; (c) all ↑**semiotic systems** are artifacts; and (d) all modern social systems involve semiotic systems. Still, the above typology is a rough representation of the salient objective features of the systems that compose the world. Quick (and therefore vulnerable) definitions of the five above concepts follow. A *conceptual* system is one composed of concepts. A *natural* system is one whose components, as well as the bonds among them, belong in nature— i.e., are not man-made. A *social* system is one some of whose components are conspecific animals, and others are artifacts (inanimate like tools, or living like domestic animals). A *technical* system is one constructed and operated by people with the help of technical knowledge. A *semiotic* system is one composed of people using artificial signs such as words and figures. An *artificial* system is one containing made things. The class of artificial systems equals the union of all the nonnatural systems.

SYSTEM, MATHEMATICAL A system constituted by mathematical objects or their theories. Examples: geometrical figures, determinants, number systems, systems of equations, groups, Boolean algebras, categories, manifolds. A plane triangle is a system composed of three sides, and characterized by ↑**emergent** properties (such as area and conservation of shape under rotations and reflections) that neither of its components possess. Moreover, a change in the length of any of its sides results in a different system.

SYSTEM OF HUMAN KNOWLEDGE At first sight human knowledge is a mosaic without any discernible patterns. A closer look reveals underlying unity. This unity is effected by bridges of at least six different kinds: (a) ↑**logic**, the canon of rational reasoning and an elementary tool of conceptual analysis; (b) ↑**mathematics**, which is portable across research fields because, like logic, it lacks ontological commitments; (c) the ↑**scientific method**—the most demanding research strategy—which is applicable in all fields of inquiry, from physics to ethics and management science; (d) ↑**reduction**, which is less common than usually thought; (e) the ↑**merger** of initially disjoint disciplines, as in the cases of biochemistry, cognitive neuroscience, political sociology, and other ↑**interdisciplines**; and (f) the digging up and elaboration of the philosophical ideas involved in science and technology, such as those of system, emergence, and truth, and the principles of the reality, lawfulness, systemicity, and intelligibility of the world. Because of the existence of these bridges, every science is a member of the system of human knowledge. Once the ↑**systemic** character of human knowledge is realized, explicit use of it can be made in research. ↑**Systemic approach**, ↑**systemism**.

SYSTEM, PHILOSOPHICAL A system (as opposed to a heap) of philosophical ideas. Aristotle's was the earliest, most comprehensive, and most influential of all philosophical systems. Other important philosophical systems have been those of Aquinas, Descartes, Spinoza, Leibniz, Kant, Hegel, and Marx and Engels. The failure of all past philosophical systems, and the ease with which they became ossified and turned into obstacles to philosophical advancement, have served as excuses for not attempting to build any new systems, and for leaping from one ↑**miniproblem** to another instead. As a consequence most contemporary philosophies are unsystematic: ↑**sawdust philosophy**; ↑**fickleness, philosophical**. The reason for building philosophical systems is that all of the important philosophical ideas come in bundles and cross disciplinary borders. Hence no branch of philosophy, with the doubtful exception of logic, is self-sufficient. Every philosophical problem belongs in at least two of the major philosophical disciplines: logic, semantics, epistemology, ontology, and ethics. For example, a modicum of logic and semantics is required to tackle epistemological problems, some of which raise the ethical problems of the utilization of knowledge for practical purposes. The price paid for unsystematicity is patchiness and shallowness—sometimes inconsistency as well.

SYSTEM, SOCIAL A system whose components are gregarious animals, in particular but not exclusively human beings. Examples: anthill, flock, family, gang, learned society, religious community, firm, government. ↑**Society**.

SYSTEM, TECHNICAL A social system where advanced technology is used prominently. Example: contemporary industrial plants, armies, and hospitals.

SYSTEMATICS The ↑**classification** of things, such as molecules and organisms, with the help of the explicit rules studied in ↑**taxonomy**.

SYSTEMATIZATION The transformation of a collection into a ↑**system**. In particular, the formation of an inductive generalization out of data, and the transformation of a group of inductive generalizations into a theory.

SYSTEMIC Being or belonging to a ↑**system**. Ant stray, isolated.

SYSTEMIC APPROACH a Concept The ↑**approach** informed by the principle that everything is either a ↑**system** or a component of such, hence it must be studied and handled accordingly. Opposed to the **individualist** (in particular ↑**atomistic**), ↑**sectoral**, and ↑**holistic** (nonanalytic) approaches. **b Contrast with rivals** Every one of the rival approaches misses at least one of the four distinguishing features of systems: composition, structure, environment, or mechanism. Thus ↑**holism** tackles every system as a unit and refuses to analyze it into its composition, environment, and structure; consequently it overlooks its mechanism(s) too. ↑**Individualism** refuses to admit the very existence of systems over and above their components, and consequently it misses structure and mechanism. ↑**Structuralism** ignores composition, mechanism, and environment, on top of which it involves the logical fallacy of postulating relations without relata, above them, or prior to them. Finally, ↑**externalism**, too, overlooks the internal structure and mechanisms of systems, and therefore leads to overlooking the inner sources of change. **c Advantages** The adoption of a systemic approach is theoretically advantageous because every thing, except for the universe as a whole, is connected to some other things. For the same reason it is practically advantageous as well. In fact, it spares us the costly mistakes incurred by the expert—scientist or technologist, policymaker or manager—who overlooks most of the features of the real system he studies, designs, or steers. For example, the plans for economic recovery or development devised by the International Monetary Fund fail more often than not because they are ↑**sectoral**, not systemic: they ignore the biological, cultural, and political costs of the readjustments they recommend regardless of the type and degree of development of the society.

SYSTEMICITY The property of being a ↑**system** or belonging to one. Examples: atoms, bodies, cells, machines, sentences, and schools are systems. By contrast, the stars in a constellation, the components of a garbage dump, and Wittgenstein's aphorisms are nonsystemic.

SYSTEMISM a Ontological The ↑**worldview** according to which the world is a system of systems rather than either a solid block or an aggregate of individuals. It views the cosmos as the supersystem of all lawfully changeable things, and our knowledge of it as a supersystem of ideas. More precisely, systemism postulates that *every concrete thing and every idea is a system or a component of some system*. Like ↑**holism** and ↑**processualism**, but unlike other cosmologies, systemism is not committed to any hypothesis concerning the stuff systems are "made" of: it is essentially a structural (though not a structuralist) view. Hence, systemism is consistent with idealism as well as with materialism, and it can be adopted by religious believers as well as by unbelievers. Therefore it is an incomplete cosmology, one that can be used as a scaffold for building alternative cosmologies. **b Epistemological** Ontological systemism has epistemological consequences. One of them is that ↑**reduction**, though necessary, is insufficient; the other is the need to exhibit and reinforce the links among all the fields of inquiry beneath their diversity: ↑**interdiscipline**. ↑**Atomism** suggests that every system be explained only by analyzing it into its parts: the research strategy of atomism is microreduction. ↑**Bottom-up/top-down.** For example, we understand a cell by decomposing it into organelles and other components. True, but this understanding is only partial, because the specific function of each organelle in a cell can be understood only in relation to the overall functions of the cell. For example, the chemistry of a DNA molecule is not enough to understand the regulating functions it performs in a living cell. To attain an adequate understanding of the cell we need to combine the top-down strategy with the bottom-up one. Nor is the need for this combination restricted to cell biology. We need it in physics to explain, e.g., the behavior of the electrons inside a solid. In chemistry to explain, say, the function of a group of atoms in an organic molecule. We need it in psychology, to understand, e.g., the roles of motivation and emotion in learning. And we need it in social science to explain, say, how individuals modify their social environment and how the latter shapes their behavior. The combination of the two strategies is necessary because wholes happen to be composed of interacting components, and because the behavior of the latter can be understood only in relation with one another and with their contribution to the whole. (Note, incidentally, that epistemology has ontological roots, hence it cannot be developed independently from ontology.) A second epistemological consequence of the systemist cosmology is that, since the world is a system, so must be our knowledge of it. In other words, because there are no stray things, our knowledge of the world cannot be a mere aggregate of disjoint bits, but must be a system. Yet the current fragmentation of knowledge is a well-known if often deplored fact. How can such fragmentation of knowledge be explained and remedied? It can be explained by the excessive division of scientific labor that started at the beginning of the nineteenth century, and by the concomitant loss of a philosophical perspective. Ours is a culture of specialists, each with his own sectoral vision. This vision suffices to tackle narrow problems, such as measuring reaction velocities. But the more interesting problems, such as those of explaining why the reaction speed decreases with increasing age, require the collaboration between disciplines, in this case neuroscience. ↑**Interdiscipline**, ↑**unity of science**. A third epistemological consequence of the systemic worldview is that the knower, far from being self-reliant, is a member of an epistemic community, which in turn depends on society at large. **c Synopsis** Let us finally pull together the two main strands of systemism. The ontology of systemism may be compressed into the principle that every object is either a system or a component of a system. The epistemological counterpart of this postulate is that every inquiry into an object ought to include a study of its environment, which in turn requires embedding the study in the ↑**system of human knowledge**. These two axioms taken together entail the following consequence: Studying, designing, or operating any items as if they were simple and isolated, or working in a discipline as if it had no relatives worth looking into, can get us only so far—or may even lead us astray.

SYSTEMS THEORY A family of theories straddling ontology and engineering. They study concrete systems in general, that is, regardless of the stuff they are made of, hence the peculiarities of their structure. There are two sorts of systems theories: hard and soft. The former involve mathematics and are technology-oriented. Examples: automata theory, control theory (cybernetics), statistical information theory, linear systems theory, and synergetics. By contrast, the systems "theories" of the soft kind are nonmathematical. Actually, they are old ↑**holism** in new garb.

TACIT KNOWLEDGE ↑**Knowledge** that is not explicit, and is usually acquired by doing. **Syn** know-how. For example, knowing how to bicycle, speak, eyeball, or even make routine calculations. Tacit knowledge is important in all fields, even in intellectual pursuits. But, ↑**intuitionism** notwithstanding, know-how is not superior to explicit knowledge. This is so because, being tacit, it can hardly be analyzed, evaluated, improved upon, and communicated. An interesting problem for administrators is how to tap worker's know-how in order to scrutinize it, refine it, and make it available to others. ↑**Socratic method.**

TARSKI'S DEFINITION OF TRUTH Alfred Tarski's thesis that the idea of factual ↑**truth** is exactified by the biconditional: '*p*' is a true sentence if and only if *p*. Here, '*p*' names *p*, whence it belongs to a ↑**metalanguage** of the language in which *p* is couched. The example used ad nauseam is this: 'Snow is white' is a true sentence if and only if snow is white. One of several objections is that the biconditionals in question only relate sentences to their names (or languages to their metalanguages), so that they remain on the linguistic (or conceptual) level. By contrast, the aim of any genuine ↑**correspondence theory of truth** is to relate sentences (or rather the propositions they designate) to their factual referents. For example, the proposition "The cat is on the mat" is true if and only if, in fact, the cat is on the mat. ↑**Truth.**

TASTE The evaluation of certain items is said to be a matter of taste, or aesthetic, if it does not depend on either truth or usefulness. Some philosophers, and most mainstream economists, have held that tastes are "stable" (unchangeable) and therefore beyond dispute: ↑*de gustibus non est disputandum*. By contrast, any parent, teacher, or psychologist knows that most tastes (and aversions) are acquired.

TAUTOLOGY A proposition true by virtue of its logical form and regardless of its content. **Syn** logical truth. Example: "not-(*p* and not-*p*)." Two logical theories are (basically) the same if they share the same tautologies. In this case they may also be said to be two different *presentations* of the same theory. Two logical calculi are *different* if they differ in at least one tautology. For example, ordinary and intuitionistic logic are different because they do not share the principle of the third excluded. This shows that tautologousness is relative and, more precisely, logic-dependent. However, there is one exception, namely the principle of noncontradiction. Any "logic" that does not contain this principle, whether as an axiom or as a theorem, is bogus, for the paramount normative function of logic is to spot inconsistencies and help remove them. Since ↑paraconsistent logic makes room for contradictions, it does not qualify as a logic. ↑Cryptotautology, ↑pseudotautology.

TAUTONYMY A sentence true in a language by virtue of the meanings of the terms occurring in it. Examples: "Bachelors are unmarried," "Manometers are pressure gauges." Syn semantical truth. Ant heteronymy or semantic falsity. ↑Analytic.

TAXONOMY The methodology of ↑systematics: the investigation of the principles of ↑classification, particularly in biology. These are: (1) every member of the original collection is assigned to some class; (2) there are two types of class: simple (species) and composite (e.g., genus), the latter being the union of two or more simple classes; (3) each simple class is composed of some of the members of the original collection; (4) each class is a set whose membership is determined by a predicate or a conjunction of predicates; (5) each class is definite: there are no borderline cases; (6) any two classes are either mutually disjoint, or one of them is contained in the other: if the former, they are said to belong to the same rank, otherwise to different ranks; (7) only two logical relations are involved in a classification: the membership relation $\in$, holding between individual and class, and the inclusion relation $\subseteq$, which relates classes of different ranks; (8) every composite class equals the union of its subclasses of the immediately preceding rank; (9) all the classes of a given rank are pairwise disjoint (do not intersect); (10) every partition of a given rank is exhaustive: the union of all the classes in a given rank equals the original collection. If condition (9) is not met, one has to do with a ↑typology, not a classification proper. ↑Species.

TECHNIQUE Special method, such as microscopy, electrophysiology, chromatography, magnetic-resonance imaging, and computer-aided design. Regrettably, most of the training of graduate students in the sciences consists nowadays in learning techniques at the expense of substantive ideas, as if techniques were more than means.

TECHNOETHICS The branch of ethics that investigates moral problems raised by ↑technology. Sample of problematics: environmental and social impact of megaprojects, labor-saving machines and devices; the use of high-tech means for barbaric goals; and the moral justification of social policies and plans. If medicine, biotechnology, jurisprudence, and resource management are regarded as technologies, then ↑bioethics, ↑nomoethics, ↑business ethics, and ↑environmental ethics must be included in technoethics.

TECHNOLOGY The branch of knowledge concerned with designing artifacts and processes, and with normalizing and planning human action. Traditional technology—or technics, or craftmanship—was mainly empirical, hence sometimes ineffective, at other times inefficient or worse, and only perfectible by trial and error. Modern technology is based on science, hence it is capable of being perfected with the help of research. Main kinds: physical (e.g., electrical engineering), chemical (e.g., industrial chemistry), biological (e.g., agronomy), biosocial (e.g., normative epidemiology), social (e.g., management science), epistemic (e.g., ↑artificial intelligence), and philosophical (↑ethics, ↑methodology, ↑political philosophy, ↑praxiology). Technology should not be confused with applied science, which is actually the bridge between basic ↑science and ↑technology, since it seeks new knowledge with a practical potential. Technologists are expected to design, repair, or maintain artifacts, such as machines and industrial or social processes. And they are expected to serve their clients or employers, who seek their expertise to further economic or political interests. (Whistleblowers are few and easily disposable.) This is why technology can be good, evil, or ambivalent. ↑Technoethics.

TECHNOLOGY, PHILOSOPHY OF The ontological, epistemological, and ethical study of technology. Sample problems: What is an artifact? What are the similarities and differences between technology and science? Can technologists invent new laws? What if any are the philosophical presuppositions of technology? How does technology relate to art? Is technology morally committed? Should the professional codes include moral norms concerning public welfare and environmental protection? Some philosophers of technology mistake artifact for technology, and are either technophiles or technophobes. Technology is an artifact only in the sense that it is made rather than found. And, since there are bad technologies and good ones, both technophily and technophobia are unwarranted.

TELEOLOGY The doctrine that there are final causes. Teleology can be ↑immanent or ↑transcendental, as well as radical or moderate. *Immanent* teleology is the view that (some or all) things have intrinsic natural goals—e.g., that all organisms strive toward perfection. *Transcendental* teleology holds that the goals that guide a thing are both external to it and supernatural. Whereas transcendental teleology is part of theology, immanent teleology is compatible with a naturalist if prescientific cosmology. Aristotle's final causes were immanent; so were Aquinas's with reference to nature, though not to man. *Radical* teleology holds that everything from electron to man, society, and cosmos has some goal or other. Modern science and philosophy reject radical teleology with reference to nature. For example, the colorful flowers are not "made" to attract bees, for these animals do not distinguish colors. And evolution, far from being targeted, is open-ended. The domain of final causation is that of conscious behavior, hence its study is restricted to human psychology and social science. Talk of final causes in any other discipline is just an anthropomorphic relic.

TELEONOMY New name for ↑teleology.

TENSE LOGIC Classical ↑logic enriched with the operators "past" and "present." A useless toy, because any predicate can be tensed by including the time variable. For example, "it was dry" can be construed as "it is dry at a time t prior to the present time t_0." Thus, the statement "The shirt was dry" can be formalized as "$\exists t \, (Dst \, \& \, t < t_0)$." Since this is a particular case of a formula in the predicate calculus, tense logic is unnecessary. This result should come as no surprise, given that factual science and technology have always dealt with past, present, and future, without requiring a change in logic.

TERTIUM NON DATUR ↑Excluded middle: *p* or not-*p*.

TEST Check. Ideas are tested for well-formedness, meaningfulness, truth, or fruitfulness. Artifacts and plans are checked for viability, effectiveness, efficiency, cost-effectiveness, user-friendliness, etc. Actions are checked for compliance with technical and moral norms. And norms are checked for both efficiency and compatibility with higher-level norms.

TESTABILITY The property of a proposition or theory of being able to be put to a test intended to either confirm or infirm it. For example, the statements that 7 is a prime number, that aspirin reduces pain, and that free trade is beneficial are testable. Examples of untestable propositions: there are forever undetectable material entities; heaven exists; the stronger a man's Oedipus complex, the stronger its repression; all the discoveries made by particular scientists would sooner or later have been made by others; there are worlds other than the only one we live in. A necessary condition for testability is conceptual precision (minimal ↑**vagueness**). Testability is necessary for a proposition to be subjected to actual tests and thus eventually to be attributed a truth value. Hence, contrary to the claim of theologians, untestable propositions cannot be true, let alone eternally so. Testability can be purely conceptual (as in mathematics), empirical (as in daily life and protoscience), or both (as when a theory is put to the test by checking some of its consequences in conjunction with suitable empirical data). Empiricists equate testability with confirmability, whereas rationalists equate it with falsifiability: ↑**confirmation**, ↑**falsifiability**. Unmindful of philosophical strictures, scientists and technologists care for both positive and negative evidence: the former because they are truth indicators, and the latter because they indicate falsity. A few unfavorable cases may suffice to shoot down a new hypothesis but not a well-established one: in the latter case one conjectures something else to account for the exceptions. (However, such ↑**ad hoc hypothesis** should be independently testable.) Nor is strong inductive support sufficient to conclude that a generalization is a ↑**law**, for it may be just a temporary ↑**trend**: ↑**induction**. Theoretical support, too, is required to confer such status: The hypothesis should belong in a hypothetico-deductive system, and it should be compatible with other theories. In sum, full testability is confirmability *cum* falsifiability.

TEXTUALISM The view that everything is a text or "like a text," hence understanding anything is subjecting the corresponding text to interpretation. To regard the universe as a book or a library would seem to be a librarian's nightmare worthy of Anatole France, Italo Calvino, or Jorge Luis Borges. Yet this view is implicit in Heidegger's writings as well as in ↑**hermeneutic** philosophy, poststructuralism, deconstructionism, general semiotics, the idealist wing of ethnomethodology, and the ↑**constructivist-relativist** sociology of science. Thus Heidegger: "*Im Wort, in der Sprache werden und sind erst die Dinge*"; J. Derrida: "There is no outside-the-text"; and S. Woolgar: "reality is constituted in and through discourse." Of course, none of these authors has bothered to offer even a shred of evidence for his extravagant claims. Hermeneuticists take textualism literally, not metaphorically, while claiming at the same time that all knowledge is metaphorical. Ordinary folks, by contrast, distinguish words from their referents; they know that writing was invented only five millennia ago; and they realize that atoms, stars, plants, people, societies, and things lack syntactic, semantic, and phonological properties. This is why we cannot read or interpret such things. This is why we study them experimentally and build mathematical models of them without waiting for the semiotician to tell us what they are. To be sure, scientists expound and discuss their problems and findings, but—unless they happen to be linguists or literary critics—their discourses refer mostly to extralinguistic things, not to other texts. Not even our ideas about things can be identified with their linguistic wrappings. In particular, scientific theories are not texts: they have logical, mathematical, and semantic properties, not linguistic or literary ones. This is why scientific theories are studied by scientists, logicians, and philosophers, not by hermeneuticists, linguistic philosophers, or literary critics.

THEISM Belief in a personal supreme being in charge of the world. All the major religions are theistic. To be distinguished from ↑**deism**.

THE MORE, THE BETTER The dogma of consumerism.

THEOLOGY The religious study of ↑**religion**. It includes fantasies about the objects of religious worship, the justification of religious practices, and criticisms of rival religions, heterodoxies, and atheism. Because in these matters there are no truth criteria other than compatibility with the canonical scriptures, and because any nonscientific text can be interpreted in alternative ways, there are more theologies than religions. In particular, the Christian, Hindu, Jewish, and Moslem religions have been the object of a large number of rival theologies, from mystic to rationalist. Ironically, theological controversy has fostered the study of logic, which was eventually used against theology. The importance of interpretation in such matters has led to ↑**hermeneutics** even in secular matters. Every theology is an ↑**ideology**, but the converse is false, for there are secular ideologies, such as liberalism and socialism.

THEOREM A logical consequence of a set of premises (axioms, definitions, and lemmas). Theoremhood is, like the axiom status, purely logical. So much so that a theorem in one theory may occur as an axiom in another. Barring the ↑**undecidable propositions**, mathematical truth is the same as theoremhood. By contrast, a theorem in theoretical factual science, such as physics or economics, may be factually false. Most theorems are first conjectured, then proved—sometimes long after they have been guessed. Note that theorems are not the property of mathematicians: anyone working on a theory is expected to conjecture, prove, or use theorems in it. This holds, in particular, for theoretical physics and philosophical theories.

THEORETICAL ENTITY Concept occurring in a scientific theory or hypothesis, and denoting a thing, property, or process inaccessible to ordinary observation. Examples: planetary orbit, atom, enzyme, gene, evolution, hominid, aggregate demand. Strictly speaking, the expression is an oxymoron, for theories are not precisely entities (real things). The correct name is 'theoretical concept'.

THEORIFICATION A hypothesis or set of hypotheses becomes theorified when included in, or expanded into, a ↑**theory**. For example, Newton theorified the laws of motion of Galileo, Kepler, and Huyghens by turning them into special cases of his mechanics.

THEORY Hypothetico-deductive system: i.e., a system composed of a set of assumptions and their logical consequences. In other words, every formula of a theory is either an assumption or a valid consequence (theorem) of one or more assumptions of it: $T = \{t \mid A \vdash t\}$. Again: a theory is a set of propositions closed under deduction (i.e., including all the logical consequences of the axioms). Most people, even some philosophers, confuse theory with ↑**hypothesis**. This is a mistake, because a theory is not a single proposition but an infinite set of propositions. Therefore it is far more difficult to confirm or to falsify than a single hypothesis. (Analogy: a net is stronger than either of its component threads, hence harder to make and to rip.) Another serious confusion is that between theories and ↑**languages**. This is a mistake because theories make assertions, whereas languages are neutral. The mistake is part of ↑**formalism**, the mathematical component of ↑**nominalism**. A theory may refer to objects of any kind, nondescript or well-defined, conceptual or concrete, and its assumptions may be true, partially true, false, or neither. The condition of logical deducibility from the initial assumptions confers formal (syntactical) unity upon the theory. This allows one to treat theories as (complex) individuals. These individuals possess emergent properties that none of their components (propositions) possess, such as consistency (noncontradiction). Example 1: Set theory, graph theory, and Boolean algebra are abstract (uninterpreted) theories. Example 2: Number theory, Euclidean geometry, and the infinitesimal calculus are interpreted mathematical theories. Example 3: Classical mechanics, the theory of natural selection, and neoclassical microeconomics are factual theories. Nonexample: The assumptions "All As are Bs," and "All Cs are Ds," where the predicates A, B, C, and D are not inter-definable, do not constitute a system, hence do not generate a hypothetico-deductive system. Indeed, no consequences derive jointly from them.

THEORY-LADEN OBSERVATION Observation conducted in the light of some hypothesis or theory, and thus likely to involve some conceptual bias. **Ant** naive observation. Some philosophers have claimed that all observation is theory-laden. This thesis is false: only sophisticated scientific observations are conducted in the light of theories proper. What is true is that all scientific observations are prompted by hypotheses and colored by expectations.

THEORY-PRACTICE CONNECTION According to common sense, theory is the opposite of practice. By contrast, Marxism recommends the unity of theory and practice, and even talks of "theoretical praxis." Neither view is correct, for much theory is irrelevant to practice: think of pure mathematics, cosmology, paleontology, or archaeology. What is true is that rational action is informed by (sound) theory. Thus the construction of a hydroelectric plant follows designs guided by electrodynamics, elasticity theory, etc.; likewise the design of intelligent social policies is based on sound social theory. In a perfect world all political actions would be guided by social science, social philosophy, and ethics.

THESIS Hypothesis or doctrine proposed, defended, or to be justified, as in "Spinoza's thesis of the identity of God and nature." **Ant** ↑**antithesis**. Any thesis-antithesis pair constitutes an ↑**antinomy**. Hegel claimed that every thesis combines with its antithesis to produce a synthesis, but he did not disclose the secret of this alchemy.

THING An object other than a construct. Examples: atoms, fields, persons, artifacts, social systems. Nonthings: properties of things (e.g., energy), changes in them, and ideas considered in themselves. According to ↑**materialism**, the world is composed exclusively of things, only very few of which are persons.

THING IN ITSELF, or *DING AN SICH* Thing existing independently of the knower. **Syn** noumenon. Nonexistent according to Berkeley and the ↑**Copenhagen interpretation** of quantum mechanics; unknowable according to ↑**phenomenalism** (e.g., Kant and Hume); and both existent and partially knowable according to scientific ↑**realism** (e.g., Galileo and Einstein).

THOUGHT a Broad concept Cognitive process. **b Strict sense** Rational process, as in attribution, comparison, generalization, instantiation, invention, deduction, computation, and design.

THOUGHT-EXPERIMENT An experimental design that has not yet been implemented, or that cannot be carried out because it runs counter to some law of nature. Examples: trying to catch up with a light beam in a vacuum, and attempting to reverse a life history. Although thought-experiments prove nothing, they may have heuristic value. They may also be misleading. ↑**Experiment,** ↑**computer simulation.**

TIME A fundamental ontological category shared by all disciplines except mathematics and neoclassical microeconomics. The concept of time is slippery and has therefore been the subject of much nonsense. For example, the popular metaphor that time flows is nonsensical because time is not a thing: ↑**arrow of time**. What "flow" (change) are real things. Time is, to speak very loosely, the pace of change of real things. (That is, time is not absolute but relational.) But time is not a property of any particular real thing: like space, time is "public," that is, shared by all things. (More precisely, the times relative to any given reference frame are shared by all the things that can be connected with that frame through electromagnetic signals.) Two main concepts of time are distinguished: physical (or ontological) and perceptual (or psychological). Physical time is usually regarded as objective, whereas psychological time is, by definition, time (or rather duration) perceived by a subject. Physical time is objective but it does not exist by itself, detached from everything else. So much so, that time is measured by observing some process or other, e.g., a swinging pendulum or the disintegration of radioactive material. And, strictly speaking, time is imperceptible. We can only perceive or feel some processes. And such perception depends critically on our participation in such processes. Thus the subjects of experiments on sensory deprivation soon lose the count of time. There are three main views on the nature of physical time: that it does not exist (achronism); that it exists by itself (absolutist conception); and that it is the pace of becoming (relational theory). Achronism has become an anachronism.

According to the absolutist view, time is independent of changing things, so that there would be time even if nothing changed, and even if the universe were hollow. The first important change in the conception of time came with Eintein's special theory of relativity (1905). It welded time to space (though keeping them distinct) to constitute the concept of space-time; and it distinguished two time variables in every physical situation: the proper time, attached to the physical thing of interest, and the relative time, attached to the adopted reference frame. Prior to the inception of general relativity (1914), physicists had presupposed the absolutist conception, as shown by the fact that they chose a rigid ↑**space time** grid (or reference system) prior to representing the physical thing or process of interest. Since then it is generally agreed that, in regions of high concentration of matter (hence intense gravitational fields), the values of the coefficients of the space-time metric depend on the distribution of matter, and therefore have got to be determined experimentally. There is no theory (hypothetico-deductive system) of absolute time. By contrast, there are a few general (philosophical) theories of relational time, some subjectivist and others realist. The simplest of the latter takes the time order in a thing to map the sequence of states of the thing, and duration as a sequence of events in the same thing. Its axioms are: For any three point events e, e' and e" relative to a given frame of reference, $T(e, e') = - T(e', e)$, and $T(e,e') + T(e', e") = T(e, e")$. ↑**Space**.

TO BE IS TO PERCEIVE OR TO BE PERCEIVED George Berkeley's subjectivist empiricism and ontological phenomenalism in a nutshell. It survives in the ↑**Copenhagen interpretation** of quantum physics, according to which existence consists in either measuring or being measured. Berkeley's dictum is widely believed to be irrefutable. However, it flies in the face of everyday experience, in particular work experience, from cobbling to running a hydroelectric plant. It also fails to match laboratory practice, which consists in observing, manipulating, or transforming things that preexist the scientist.

TOLERANCE a Ethics Respect for other people's rights. All moral and legal codes enshrine tolerance in some regards, particularly in the private sphere, whereas they restrict it in others, particularly in the public sphere. Since there are limits to rights, tolerance must be limited too. It is debatable whether radically intolerant ideologies should be tolerated in a democratic society, especially if they infringe upon human rights or incite to murder. It is less debatable that cultural swindle, such as New Age, should not be tolerated in public schools. **b Praxiology** The imprecision, or discrepancy, between actual value and ideal value that one is willing to put up with for the sake of keeping costs down.

TOP-DOWN ↑**Bottom-up/top-down**.

TRADITION, PHILOSOPHICAL The corpus of philosophical ideas since the time of the pre-Socratics. Tradition is more important in philosophy than in any other discipline. This is not only because philosophical progress has been slow, partly because of ideological interferences. It is also because many of the big philosophical problems have not yet been solved satisfactorily. For these reasons no serious philosopher breaks totally with tradition, and every serious philosopher engages in silent dialogues with some of his predecessors. (True, ↑**linguistic philosophy** owes nothing to tradition. But is it philosophy?) Like the composer Gabriel Fauré, we "should like to take a line that is both classical and modern, sacrificing neither contemporary practice to hallowed traditions nor traditions to the fashion of the moment."

TRANSCENDENTAL a Transphenomenal, behind appearances. **b** Beyond the scope of both reason and experience, but presumably within the purview of religion or subjective idealism. ↑**Naturalism**, ↑**pragmatism**, and ↑**humanism** have no use for this concept of transcendence. ↑**Immanent / transcendental. c Transcendental idealism** The view, held by Vico and Kant, that the mind can only think what it constructs, hence the ↑**things in themselves**, if they exist at all, are unknowable.

TRANSITIVITY A binary relation R is transitive in a set S if, for all x, y, and z in S, Rxy & $Ryz \Rightarrow Rxz$. Examples: =, ~, >, ⊂, part-whole, precursor, successor, power. Nonexamples: ∈, similarity, friendship, collective preference.

TRANSLATABILITY The ability of a text in a language to be faithfully translated into another language of comparable expressive power. Translatability is a test of the cognitive meaningfulness of ordinary-language expressions. By contrast, most mathematical formulas are untranslatable into ordinary-language sentences—which falsifies a central thesis of ↑**ordinary-language philosophy**. Gobbledygook is untranslatable, hence not universal. Example taken at random from Heidegger's famous *Sein und Zeit*: *"Verstehen ist das existenziale Sein des eigenen Seinkönnen des Daseins selbst, so zwar, dass dieses Sein an ihm selbst das Woran des mit ihm selbst Seins erschliesst."* There are as many "translations" as "interpretations" of this string of words. This is a reminder that not every ↑**sentence** designates a ↑**proposition**.

TRANSLATION Consider two ↑**sentences** in different languages. Each is a faithful translation of the other if both sentences designate the same ↑**proposition**—that is, if both have the same ↑**meaning** (sense cum reference). Neither verifiability nor sameness of truth value should be required for translatability, because some sentences designate untestable or as yet untested propositions, hence they cannot be attributed truth values except tentatively.

TREE, LOGICAL A ↑**graph** representing logical relations and operations. Example: a two-element lattice $\mathcal{L} = <\{0,1\}, \lor, \land>$:

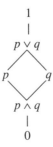

$$1$$
$$|$$
$$p \lor q$$
$$p \qquad q$$
$$p \land q$$
$$|$$
$$0$$

In words: the propositions p and q at the center are implied by their conjunction $p \wedge q$, which in turn is implied by an arbitrary contradiction 0; moreover, the original propositions imply their disjunction $p \vee q$, which in turn implies an arbitrary tautology 1, such as $p \vee \neg p$.

TRIAL AND ERROR Procedure whereby something is tried and perfected until it attains the preset goal. Trial and error may proceed either blindly or intelligently. The former occurs in nature under the pressure of natural selection; in artifacts, by virtue of negative-feedback devices; and in daily life, when checking ideas of procedures more or less haphazardly. Intelligent trial and error comes in two varieties: algorithmic (as in the mathematical methods of successive approximations), and nonalgorithmic (as in checking plausible solutions, and in carrying out scientific experiments and technological tests). The ↑**scientific method** may be regarded as an instance of intelligent and nonalgorithmic trial and error. Its most obvious nonalgoritmic components are finding the problem and the solution candidates.

TRILEMMA Problem of choice among three options that are prima facie mutually exclusive. Philosophical examples: individualism-holism-systemism, rationalism-empiricism-realism, and deontologism-utilitarianism-agathonism. Every moral problem is a trilemma, because it presents a choice among inaction, right action, and wrong action.↑**Dilemma**.

TRUTH The word 'truth' designates a family of concepts that are mutually irreducible (not interdefinable). We distinguish the following: formal, factual, moral, and artistic. **a Formal** A formula in abstract mathematics (e.g., set theory, general topology, and group theory) is formally true if it is ↑**satisfiable** in some domain (or under some interpretation). For example, the commutative law "$x \otimes y = y \otimes x$" is satisfiable by number multiplication (but not by either matrix or vector product). And if a formula in a nonabstract mathematical theory (e.g., number theory, Euclidean geometry, and the calculus) is a theorem in it, then it is true in the same theory. In short, barring ↑**Gödel** pathologies, formal truth equals either satisfiability or theoremhood. **b Factual: semantic concept** Factual truth has traditionally been characterized as the adequation or fitting of ideas to reality. (By extension, pictures, photos, and films can also be assigned truth or falsity.) For example, a proposition asserting the occurrence of an event e will be said to be true iff e happens. (↑**Tarski's definition of truth** fails to capture the idea of adequation of proposition to fact, since it relates sentences to their names, and thus remains on the linguistic plane.) **c Factual: ontological concept** In addition to the realist (semantic) conception of the truth of a proposition, we need a materialist (ontological) notion of a true thought. This can be loosely described as the matching of a sequence of neural events in the knower's brain with facts in his (external or internal) world: it is an objective (though not necessarily faithful) fact-fact correspondence, rather than a construct-fact one. Example: the successive firings of neurons in the subject's visual cortex in response to a sequence of flashes in the room. But neither of the preceding sketches is a definition, let alone a theory. Nor do we have a satisfactory link between the two concepts: all that is still in the works. In addition to a definition and a theory of the concept of truth as correspondence, we need a truth criterion, i.e., a rule for deciding whether a given factual proposition is true or false (completely or to some extent). ↑**Truth criterion. d Moral truth** This concept belongs in ↑**moral realism**. For example, "Oppression is evil" is a moral truth in a humanist morality, and "Impiety is sinful" is a moral truth in a religious morality. **e Fictional truth** In the context of *The Merchant of Venice*, it is true that Othello kills Desdemona. But of course these are fictional characters, so that fictional (in particular artistic) truth is not factual. Nor is it formal, because plays are not mathematical theories. But it can be moral, as is the case with some biblical parables.

TRUTH CRITERION A suitable criterion is this: the proposition p is factually true if (a) p is compatible with the background (antecedent) knowledge, and (b) p is consistent with the best empirical evidence for p. Factual truth and factual falsity, full or partial, are attributes of propositions concerning facts. We assign any such attribute on the strength of empirical tests such as a run of observations. The result of such operation is a metaproposition such as "Proposition p describing fact f is true in the light of test t." In short, the path from a fact in the external world to truth (or falsity) and belief looks roughly like this: External fact $f \rightarrow$ Thought of f (brain fact) $\rightarrow p \rightarrow$ Test of p $\rightarrow$ Evaluation of $p \rightarrow$ Belief or disbelief in p. A test of p involves a piece of knowledge about test procedures (e.g., chromatography) that does not occur explicitly in the preceding chain. Likewise, the evaluation of the outcomes of the test procedure involves a further bit of knowledge (e.g., the theory of errors of observation or of statistical inference). The following truth criteria are employed in the advanced experimental sciences. An empirical proposition e is true just in case it is a reading of a well-calibrated high-precision instrument. And a theoretical proposition t asserting that the value of a property is true, if the discrepancy between t and the best empirical estimate is less than the admissible error.

TRUTH-GAP THEORY The thesis that not all propositions are either true or false; hence the valuation function—i.e., the function that maps propositions into truth values—is a partial function. Examples of propositions lacking a truth value: (a) the hypotheses that are untestable or that, being testable, have not yet been tested, such as all those concerning the future; (b) the undecidable propositions in certain mathematical systems.

TRUTH, KNOWLEDGE OF According to Platonism, all propositions are true or false whether we know it or not, and even whether or not they have been thought up by anyone. This is not the realist view. According to the latter, truth and falsity are not intrinsic and inborn properties of factual propositions, but attributes we assign them on the strength of tests. Hence factual propositions are not true or false whether or not we know it. So much so, that an untested proposition has the same truth status as an ↑**undecidable** proposition: it is neither true nor false. A fortiori, propositions have no truth value unless they have been thought, since before that they did not exist. For instance, before the birth of paleontology, the proposition "Dinosaurs became extinct 65 million years ago" was neither true nor false, because it did not even exist. At first sight this sounds like the operationist thesis that physical properties, such as mass, only emerge as a result of measurement. This appearance is deceptive, because mass is possessed by bodies whether or not they are measured, as can be shown from the way mass is conceptualized, namely as a function from bodies to positive real numbers. By contrast, the truth value v of a proposition p concerning a fact f is assigned relative to both the antecedent knowledge and some test procedure t. Hence a change from t to an alternative test procedure t' may force us to replace v with a different truth value v'. Hence, the thesis that propositions lack a truth value before being tested is unrelated to operationism. In short, according to scientific realism, statement precedes testability precedes actual test precedes truth value. More precisely, the assigment of a truth value is the last step of the following sequence of operations:

(1) state an untried proposition p;

(2) examine p in the light of a body B of relevant knowledge, to ascertain whether p is plausible w.r.t. B; if p is found plausible, proceed to the next step:

(3) perform test(s) of p to find out whether p is T to some extent; if the test(s) outcome D passes inspection,

(4) evaluate p in the light of B and D : $V(p, B \cup D) = v$.

When p is first stated, there need be no implication that it is true: it is proposed for inspection. It is only when p is declared to be true on the strength of some tests that we can legitimately assert it. ↑**Truth-gap theory**.

TRUTH, PARTIAL A truth value comprised between (total) falsity and (total) truth. That is, a truth value greater than 0 but smaller than 1. For example, "Aristotle was an Indian philosopher" is a half-truth, since it is the conjunction of a true statement and a false one. "The current world population is four billion" is two-thirds true, because the actual population is (approximately) six billion. And "The value of π is 1" is one-third true because actually $\pi \approx 3.14$, where $\approx$ stands for approximate equality. Partial truth is the norm in inordinary knowledge, applied mathematics, factual science, and technology. Approximation theory, a branch of mathematics, is a family of methods for calculating successive approximations to the total truth (or the exact value). They are utilizable when the exact value is mathematically well-defined but unattainable, as is the case with most integrals and nonlinear differential equations. No generally accepted theory of partial truth is available—a large gap in philosophy. Caution: the concept of partial truth is often mistaken for that of relative (or contextual) truth. A statement may be completely true in (relative to) a theory but false or even irrelevant in another. Partial truth has also been mistaken for ↑**plausibility**. Since truth comes in degrees, so does ↑**falsification** (or refutation).

TRUTH-TABLE Technique or ↑**decision procedure** for determining the truth value of a composite proposition by assigning in succession the values T and F to its constituents. Example:

p	q	$p \vee q$	$p \,\&\, q$	$p \Rightarrow q$	$p \Leftrightarrow q$
T	T	T	T	T	T
T	F	T	F	F	F
F	T	T	F	T	F
F	F	F	F	T	T

TRUTH VALUE The degree of truth or falsity assigned a proposition. The standard doctrine is that every proposition has a truth value, which is either truth (or 1) or falsity (or 0). However, what right do we have to assign a truth value to a proposition that has not yet been tested or that has been proved to be untestable (or undecidable)? This suggests that truth valuation is a partial function on the set of propositions: ↑**truth-gap theory**. And the existence of half-truths, such as "There are only two sexes" (while actually there are four) suggests that the codomain of the truth valuation function should include more values than 0 and 1. ↑**Truth, partial**.

TURING MACHINE An ideal computer that exactifies the intuitive notion of an ↑**algorithm**. A Turing machine is formally characterized by a next-state (or transition) function that maps the collection of <internal state, stimulus> pairs into the set of internal states of the machine. This function is subject to the condition that, in the absence of a stimulus, the machine stays in its initial state. That is, the machine lacks initiative or ↑**spontaneity**. It thus exemplifies the Aristotelian doctrine of change, as well as ↑**behaviorism**: no response without stimulus. The theory of Turing machines is part of ↑**metamathematics** and theoretical computer science. It is also the root of the ↑**computationist** view of brain and mind.

TURING TEST A test purporting to distinguish minds from computers by comparing their outputs. It lacks validity because it focuses on computation and function (net overt behavior). It disregards the nonalgorithmic mental operations, such as problem finding, as well as their neurophysiological mechanisms. ↑**Argentine room**.

TWO-BY-TWO DESIGN Research into the possible correlation between two distinct items, such as properties or events. For example, suppose we wish to find out whether epistemological relativism is empirically favored by egalitarianism or by individualism. To this end we set up, fill with empirical data, and analyze the table

Relativists & Egalitarians	Relativists & Inegalitarians
Universalists & Egalitarians	Universalists & Inegalitarians

↑**Causal analysis**.

TYCHISM The doctrine that chance is real and more basic than causation. **Syn** ↑**probabilism**. Modern science combines causalism with tychism rather than adopting either. For example, it calculates and measures unconditional probabilities, as well as the probabilities that certain events may cause others.

TYPE THEORY The logic that includes quantifications of all orders: first (over individuals), second (over predicates), third (over second-order predicates), and so on. The *hierarchy of types* is the family of all quantification domains: individuals, first-order predicates, second-order predicates, etc. So far, only members of the first three rungs occur in philosophy, science, and technology.

TYPE / TOKEN Every particular dollar bill is said to be a token, copy, or occurrence of the "one-dollar" type. Like species, types are concepts, whereas tokens can be material, conceptual, or semiotic. For example, every occurrence of the symbol "2" in a mathematical text is a token of the type "2." The type / token distinction occurs prominently in some versions of the psychoneural identity hypothesis, which I do not profess to understand.

TYPOLOGY Grouping of objects of a kind into ↑**ideal types**. Example: The division of humankind into pure races, disregarding evolution and miscegenation. Not to be confused with ↑**classification**. Typological thinking was discredited in biology with the emergence of evolutionary theory and population genetics. But it is still going strong in social studies. Caution: In the biological literature "typological" is sometimes used interchangeably with "essentialist." This use is misleading because, whereas the first concept implies the second, the converse is false. Indeed, ↑**essentialism** does not involve the hypothesis that types (species) are fixed, or that the current types are degenerate descendants of (unknown) originary types (urtypes).

ULTIMATE Basic, unanalyzable, or definitive. Sometimes predicated of things, concepts, questions, methods, assumptions, etc. In view of the historical record, skeptics are wary of conferring such status except contextually. ↑**Perennial.**

ULTIMATELY In the final analysis, or in the last instance, or basically, or at the root. For example, economicists claim that everything social is ultimately economic, whereas politicists hold that everything cultural arises from or serves the struggle for power. An obvious rejoinder is that invoking such final analysis is empty without a ↑**decision procedure** for determining that such analysis has actually been performed. Consequently, many of the propositions of the form "X is ultimately Y" are untestable. They are acceptable only if proposed as research projects.

UNANTICIPATED CONSEQUENCES OF PURPOSIVE ACTIONS Every deliberate action has unforeseen and even unforeseeable consequences. Some are favorable, others unfavorable (or "perverse"). Many side effects are of this kind. Possible sources: chance (in its two senses); the fact that every action alters one or more components of a system; unpredictability in principle, ignorance, error; ignorance of one's own real interests; willful disregard for other people's interests; and tunnel (as opposed to systemic) vision.

UNCERTAINTY Doubt arising from the knowledge that one's knowledge is imperfect (incomplete or inaccurate). The dual of information in the sense of Shannon's theory: as information increases, uncertainty decreases. ↑**Decision theory** and other ↑**rational-choice theories** claim that uncertainty is tamed upon being quantitated, namely by equating the degree of reasonable belief in a proposition as the latter's probability. But since this probability is subjective, hence arbitrary, the taming in question is illusory. No machinery other than research can turn ignorance into knowledge and thus reduce uncertainty. Caution: Uncertainty, a mental state, should not be confused with ↑**indeterminacy**, an objective condition. ↑**Uncertainty relation.**

UNCERTAINTY RELATION Misnomer for ↑**Heisenberg's inequalities.**

UNDECIDABLE PROPOSITION A proposition that can be neither proved nor falsified within a mathematical theory. ↑**Decision, insoluble.** ↑**Gödel's** discovery that there are undecidable propositions in every sufficiently rich theory caused a commotion among philosophers, many of whom interpreted it as a sign of the weakness of reason. However, it does not seem to have deprived any mathematician of his sleep; so much so that it has not been an obstacle to the sensational advancement of mathematics since it was published in 1931.

UNDERDETERMINATION Scientific hypotheses and theories are said to be underdetermined by the empirical data relevant to them, because in principle alternative hypotheses or theories could account for the same data. For example, my thinking of my daughter just at the moment when she telephoned me can be explained either as a coincidence or as a case of telepathy. But further considerations, for example about the validity of ↑**parapsychology**, will help decide between the two hypotheses. This method—the recourse to external ↑**consistency**—is not available to empiricists. They are stuck with uncertainty. ↑**Duhem-Quine thesis**.

UNDERSTANDING A psychological category that applies to facts, symbols, and constructs. To understand an idea is to fit it into a known network of ideas; to understand a symbol is to discover its referent; and to understand a fact is to understand its explanation. In ↑**hermeneutic** philosophy 'understanding' is an ill-defined term. ↑*Verstehen*.

UNIFACTORIAL / MULTIFACTORIAL An approach, doctrine, or theory is said to be unifactorial if it holds that only properties, forces, or processes (in particular mechanisms) of a single kind matter. Examples: mechanism, culturalism, and economism. The complexity of the world is such that unifactorial views are at best approximately true, and even so in very special circumstances (e.g., in experiments where the variables of other kinds are held constant). Therefore, they are eventually replaced with multifactorial views. ↑**Sectoral approach**, ↑**systemic approach**.

UNIFICATION Epistemological unification consists in bringing together two or more research fields. There are two main unification procedures: ↑**reduction** and ↑**merger**. Neither is superior to the other: both can be extremely fruitful, particularly in combination.

UNITY OF KNOWLEDGE ↑**System of human knowledge**.

UNIVERSAL Property possessed by all the members of a collection. More precisely, if *C* designates a collection, and *P* designates a property (whether intrinsic or relational) or a predicate, then *P* is *universal in C* = $_{df}$. Every member of *C* is a *P* (or is *P*-related to some other individual). Examples: all material entities possess energy, and every construct is meaningful in some context. **Ant** particular. Objective idealism notwithstanding, ↑**universals** are not entities but properties of either constructs or things. Hence there are no universals *ante rem*, that is, without particulars or detached from them. For example, geometric circularity is a property of all individual circles. The distinction between universal and particular is all-important but does not amount to a separation. There are no more universals in themselves than there are bare particulars, that is, individuals devoid of properties. However, this should not prevent anyone from building abstract theories of individuals devoid of intrinsic properties, or theories concerning properties and relations in themselves. The treatment of universals as if they were things, or as if they existed apart from particulars, is the fallacy called ↑**reification**. Examples: Saying 'I have a job' instead of 'I am employed'; Plato's fuzzy ideas of the good and of justice as existing before things; treating energy and information as entities; regarding beauty as an entity embodied in beautiful things.

UNIVERSAL GRAMMAR The grammar underlying the particular grammars of all the 6,000 plus known languages. The El Dorado of linguistics. Its existence is yet to be established by exhibiting a handful of nontrivial universal grammatical rules, and showing empirically that they are common to a representative sample of the collection of "living" languages. As long as this breakthrough does not occur, universal grammar will continue to be a subject of fanciful papers and books in theoretical linguistics and the philosophy of language.

UNIVERSAL STATEMENT A proposition beginning with "all" or "every." Example: "Every sustainable social group is ruled by some moral code." ↑**All / some**.

UNIVERSALISM The thesis that some truths, values, and norms are or ought to become universal. A component of ↑**humanism**. Ant particularism, ↑**perspectivism**, ↑**relativism**, tribalism.

UNIVERSALIZABILITY The property of being extensible to all humans. Not to be confused with Americanizability, aka globalizability. **a Epistemology** Universalizability is characteristic of genuine science and philosophy. Thus, there is no such thing as German physics or ↑**feminist philosophy**. By contrast, not all technologies are suitable to all regions: some are more adequate than others. **b Ethics** According to Kant and ↑**agathonism**, a property required of all moral norms. ↑**Categorical imperative**.

UNIVERSE The system of all existents (real or material things). Syn ↑**world**, ↑**cosmos**. The universe has some peculiar properties: it is unique and self-existent; it does not lie between two other things; it has no environment; it does not interact with anything else; it is eternal (notwithstanding the groundless equation of the Big Bang, or beginning of the expansion, with the birth of the universe); it occupies all space; and the known part of it is expanding. It is not yet known whether the universe is spatially finite or infinite. Since this is an empirical question that may eventually be solved by physical cosmology, one should not favor dogmatically either hypothesis. The hypotheses that the universe had a beginning and will have an end are theological, not scientific. It is not just that there is no evidence for either event, but that no physical laws involve either a manufacture or an expiration date.

UNIVERSE OF DISCOURSE The collection of the possible referents of a discourse, that is, the ↑**reference class** common to the predicates occurring in the discourse.

USE / MENTION When uttering or writing a linguistic expression we make use of it. Example: the preceding sentence. By contrast, when mentioning an expression, as in '*love* is a four-letter word', we had better distinguish it by enclosing it in quotation marks or writing it in italics. Unless this precaution is taken, misunderstandings may occur. Example: the expression 'the word processor' is ambiguous, for it can mean either "the word-processor" or "the word 'processor'." In the first case, "word-processor" is being used, in the second the word 'processor' is being mentioned. ↑**Language level**, ↑**object language / metalanguage**.

UTILITARIANISM The family of humanist axiological and ethical theories that equate "good" with "useful" (or pleasurable, or conducive to happiness). The central concept of these theories is the fuzzy one of subjective value or ↑**utility**. Their central rule is: "Always behave so as to maximize the expected utility." There are two versions of utilitarianism in moral philosophy: redneck (or J. Bentham's) and highbrow (or J. S. Mill's). The former conflates all pleasures and ranks them equally, whereas the latter rates intellectual and aesthetic pleasures much higher (more valuable) than the others. In social philosophy two varieties of utilitarianism are distinguished: individualist (or selfish) and social (or altruistic). The former recommends maximizing the agent's own utility, whereas the latter favors maximizing the social or total utility. However, the aggregate utility is not well-defined, if only because utilities are not additive. ↑**Happiness**. From a methodological point of view one must distinguish act from rule utilitarianism. The act-utilitarian evaluates each action on its own merit, without positing any special rules. The rule-utilitarian demands that certain rules be followed—but so far no such rules have been proposed. Hence the philosophical discussions of rule utilitarianism resemble theological speculations. The merits of utilitarianism are marred by the fuzziness of the concept of subjective ↑**utility**. The metaphysical and epistemological partner of utilitarianism is ↑**pragmatism**.

UTILITY Subjective value, or usefulness for a subject. The gain—material, aesthetic, or moral—accruing to an action or attributed to a thing or process. **Ant** disutility. The *expected utility* of the outcome of an action is the product of the subjective utility by the probability of the outcome. This concept applies only to gambling. Besides, whereas economic utility is often well-defined (namely as profit or gain in dollars), the general concept of utility is not. Two different concepts (or rather families of concepts) of utility are usually distinguished: ordinal or qualitative, and cardinal or quantitative. *Ordinal utility* is similar to preference: it is an antisymmetric and transitive relation. (That is, for any three objects a, b, and $c : a > b \Rightarrow \neg(b > a)$, and $(a > b) \& (b > c) \Rightarrow a > c$.) Some versions of ↑**utilitarianism**, and most ↑**rational-choice** models in social studies, particularly in microeconomics, employ the concept of *cardinal* (or quantitative or numerical) *utility*, regarded as the quantitation of subjective or perceived gain. However, this concept is seldom well-defined. When it is, the adoption of any given utility function is not empirically justified. Being subjective, utility may eventually be elucidated by scientific psychology. ↑**Rational-choice theory**, ↑**value**.

UTOPIA, SOCIAL Blueprint for a better society. A utopia may or may not be based on social-science findings. A science-based blueprint would be realistic and might inspire and steer a social movement aiming at correcting some of the present social ills, as well as constructing a perfectible society rather than a perfect one. The construction and discussion of utopias belongs in ↑**social philosophy**. **Ant** dystopia.

VACUUM Until the mid-nineteenth century, a vacuum was conceived of as a region of space devoid of massive matter. From then on it was recognized that every region of space is the seat of a number of force fields, such as gravitational and electromagnetic fields. Moreover, even if the latter are switched off, a residual fluctuating field remains, though of null average intensity. The electromagnetic vacuum can pull an atomic electron in an excited state down to a lower energy level ("spontaneous" radiative decay). Thus, since it has physical properties, "empty" space is not quite void. This should have profound implications for any science-oriented ontology. Indeed, it corrects ↑**atomism** and partially vindicates ↑**plenism**, suggesting a sort of synthesis of the two. Above all, it suggests that space, being changeable, is material.

VAGUE Imprecise, ill-defined. Vague concepts do not necessarily satisfy standard logic. ↑**Fuzzy**.

VALIDATION Any process aiming at checking the ↑**validity** of an idea or procedure. Whereas the validation of a logical or mathematical idea is purely conceptual, that of factual hypotheses, experimental and technological designs, and moral norms involves empirical research.

VALIDITY a Logic The property of a reasoning or argument, of fitting the rules of inference of some logical calculus. Logical validity is independent of truth: the propositions involved in a valid argument may not have been attributed any truth values. However, if the premises of a valid argument are true, then its conclusions are true as well, and the argument is said to be ↑**sound**. ↑**Entailment. b Epistemology** A scientific hypothesis or theory is validated if it is shown to match the relevant empirical evidence, the bulk of the background knowledge, and the philosophical presuppositions of scientific research. **c Methodology** A measurement or test technique is valid if it actually measures or checks what it purports to measure. For instance, some intelligence tests are invalid because they assess information rather than creativity. **d Ethics** A proposal, policy, plan, or action is morally valid if it satisfies the moral norms that have been adopted. Its validation is usually called foundation, ↑**justification**, or ↑**vindication**.

VALUE a Mathematics and science If *f* is a function that maps a set *A* into a set *B*, then the value of *f* at the point or element *a* in *A* equals *f(a)*, the image of *a* in *B*. Examples: the value of the sine function at $\pi/2$ equals 1; the value of the speed of light in a vacuum is roughly 3.10^{10} cm/sec; the truth value of a tautology equals 1. **b Axiology and praxiology** Worth of an item, as in "The market value of that computer is $1k," and "Placebos have some therapeutic value." Values can be *intrinsic* or *instrumental* (i.e., means for the realization of other values). Health is an intrinsic value, and in most societies money is one of the means for keeping healthy. Values can also be *objective* (or intrinsic) or *subjective* (or personal). Examples: aesthetic values are subjective, whereas social values are objective. Objective values can be objectively assessed and rationally argued about. By contrast, for the time being subjective values (utilities) cannot be so handled. ↑**Utility**. Values are not entities but objective properties of things, states, or processes. However, they are relational and not intrinsic properties. Indeed, the simplest analysis is this: "*w* is valuable to *x* in regard *y* in circumstance *z*," or *Vwxyz* for short. A set-theoretic concept of value can be defined as follows. If an action is necessary and sufficient to bring about certain positive effects *P* along with the unavoidable negative side effects *N*, the value of the action α may be set equal to the set-theoretic difference between *P* and *N*. I.e., $V(\alpha) = P \setminus N$.

VALUE-FREE / VALUE-BOUND A classical controversy in social science and its methodology is whether the study of society can and ought to be value-free. Whereas Marx thought that it cannot be, Weber taught that it must be. The distinction between basic ↑**science** and ↑**technology** helps to solve this dilemma: Whereas basic social science is value-free (even when it studies valuation), social technology is not, because it is triggered by social issues involving valuations, and because it recommends social policies whose implementations are likely to affect different social sectors. For example, while "positive" macroeconomics is value-free, normative macroeconomics is not, because it designs policies and plans hoped (or feared) to alter such social features as employment rate, consumer confidence, and social expenditures. However, social technology will be ineffective or worse unless based on solid basic social-science research—hence the need for value-free research along with value-bound policymaking.

VALUE JUDGMENT A statement about the value of an attitude, proposal, or action. Examples: "Racism is despicable," "Sexual advances to minors are immoral," and "Violence is bad except in self-defense." The popular view is ↑**emotivism**, according to which all value judgments are subjective: that they are matters of taste, feeling, or personal convenience. This empiricist view seems adequate to aesthetic values, not to practical or moral ones. In the latter cases, value judgments are expected to be justified by prudence, morals, or both. For example, oppression is bad not only because it degrades the oppressed (moral ground), but also because it may provoke their rebellion (practical ground). This suggests a ↑**value theory** combining the cognitive with the emotive. ↑**Fact / value**, ↑**value theory**.

VALUE THEORY The family of theories of ↑**value**. **Syn** axiology. Main varieties: absolutist and relativist, objectivist and subjectivist, emotivist and cognitivist. Axiological *absolutism* holds that all values are eternal, cross-cultural, and independent of circumstances—all of which relativism denies. *Objectivism* maintains, and subjectivism denies, that all values are objective. According to *emotivism,* all valuations are affective rather than cognitive—a thesis denied by cognitivism. Axiological *realism* borrows a bit from all these contrasting views. It holds that whereas some values, such as enjoyable life, are absolute, others, such as truthfulness, are relative; that some, such as welfare, are objective, whereas others, such as happiness, are subjective; and that some values, such as solidarity, are cognitive as well as emotive.

VARIABLE a Logic *Individual* variable: unspecified subject(s) of a predicate, as in "*x* is valuable" and "*x* is more valuable than *y*." *Predicate* variable: Unspecified predicate of an individual, as in "For all *P*: if *Pb*, then ∃*x Px*." **b Mathematics and science** Whatever can take on a numerical value, as in *Card S = n*, and "*y* = *x*²." Examples: numerosity, distance, time, blood pressure, reaction velocity, price, and GDP. When two variables are functionally related, an arbitrary value of the argument is called the *independent* variable, and the corresponding value of the function the *dependent* variable. For example, in the formula *y = f(x)*, *x* is the independent, and *y* the dependent variable. Caution: only the increments Δ*x* and Δ*y* can be interpreted as cause and effect respectively—and even so provided neither variable stands for time.

VENN DIAGRAM ↑Euler-Venn diagram.

VERIFIABILITY a Methodology Old name for ↑**testability**. **b Semantics** Verifiability principle: the thesis that the ↑**meaning** of a proposition depends upon the way it is verified (tested). A central thesis of ↑**logical positivism** and, in particular, ↑**operationism**. The thesis is false for two reasons. First, concepts are meaningful but not verifiable. Second, meaningful propositions must be constructed before any empirical procedures aiming at testing them can be designed: it is impossible to design a test, much less carry it out, unless one understands the proposition to be tested. (Try testing "The d'Alembertian of the vector potential equals 4π times the electric current density" without understanding what this means.) In short, meaning precedes test, not the other way around. ↑**Testability**.

VERIFICATION The procedure whereby the truth value of a hypothesis is established. Nowadays displaced by 'test'. ↑**Confirmation**, ↑**falsifiability**.

VERISIMILITUDE ↑**Plausibility**. Not to be confused with either ↑**probability** or partial ↑**truth**.

VERSTEHEN A key though ill-defined term in ↑**hermeneutic** philosophy and social studies. Usually translated as either 'interpretation', 'understanding', or 'comprehension'. In W. Dilthey, *Verstehen* = empathy. In M. Weber, *Verstehen* = conjecture about the intention of an actor or the aims of his action. A main tenet of the historico-cultural or hermeneutic school is that social scientists must seek to verstehen ("understand," "comprehend," or "interpret") social facts, not to explain them. Since such understanding is subjective, hence free from objective and rigorous standards, the social studies cannot claim to attain more objective truth than the interpretation of religious scriptures. Certainly, in scientific social studies *Verstehen* may suggest hypotheses. But these ought to pass the requisite tests before being accepted.

VICIOUS CIRCLE Repeating in the definiens a term occurring in the definiendum, as in "a thing is alive if it is endowed with a vital impulse." Vicious circles are to be avoided, not so ↑**virtuous circles**.

VIEW An ambiguous word that designates ↑**approach**, ↑**hypothesis**, or ↑**opinion**.

VINDICATION ↑**Justification** or ↑**validation** of a method or a norm. Neither of these can be said to be either logically valid or factually true.

VIRTUAL Unreal, imaginary, simulated. Examples: virtual optical images, virtual forces, computer ↑**simulations** of real processes. "Virtual reality," at first sight an oxymoron, denotes any device that produces a visual simulation of a real thing or process. Hence it is not the opposite of reality but part of made reality.

VIRTUE Disposition to do good to self or others. Examples: compassion, curiosity, fairness, fortitude, goodwill, honesty, industriousness, ingenuity, intelligence, judgment, justice, love of truth, loyalty, moderation, prudence, rationality, rectitude, reliability, sincerity, solidarity, tolerance. *Intellectual virtues*: those conducive to acquiring knowledge. *Moral virtues*: those conducive to helping others. *Civic virtues*: those conducive to improving the social order. All virtues are both intrinsically and instrumentally valuable: their exercise is a part of becoming a decent person, and it helps others. Some virtues, such as uprightness, are personal; others, such as solidarity, are social; still others, such as justice, are both personal and social.

VIRTUOUS CIRCLE A process whereby the validity of a proposition, norm, technique, or set of either is made to depend on another, which in turn depends upon the former, in such a manner that progress results. Example 1: Mathematics depends on logic, which in turn is justified by its performance in mathematical reasoning. Example 2: A philosophy is sound only if it is compatible with the bulk of scientific and technological knowledge, which in turn rests on certain philosophical principles: ↑**B test**. Example 3: Moral norms are vindicated by their practical consequences, which in turn are evaluated in the light of the former.

VISUALIZATION a Construction of a visual analog (or iconic model) of an abstract object. Examples: decision tree, deductive tree, diagram of a portion of a lattice, ↑**Euler-Venn diagram**, ↑**graph**, ↑**tree, logical. b** Imaging of invisible things or processes, such as electron trajectories by sensitive photographic plates, and mental processes by fMRI (functional magnetic resonance imaging).

VITALISM a Biology The ↑**idealist** and ↑**holist** doctrine that what distinguishes living beings from nonliving ones is a peculiar immaterial entity ("entelechy," vital force, life-giving "principle," *élan vital*, constructive force, etc.). Since the essence of life is assumed to be immaterial, it lies beyond the reach of normal science, so that it must remain forever mysterious. Vitalism is an instance of property / stuff ↑**dualism**, and of the explanation of the obscure by the more obscure. Vitalism was killed by biochemistry at the beginning of the nineteenth century. It was revived in recent years as the view that life is ↑**information** of a special kind, namely genetic information. This view is false because 'genetic information', far from being an immaterial substance, is nothing but the order of nucleotides in genes. No stuff, no genetic information. ↑**Informationism. b Philosophy** The epistemological and ethical view, held by Nietzsche, according to which only that which helps live deserves being believed or done. A version of ↑**pragmatism** and a form of ↑**anti-intellectualism.**

VOID Empty space. A key concept in ↑**atomism**, according to which all there is, is atoms and their combinations in the void. According to contemporary physics, the void is full. ↑**Vacuum.**

VOLUNTARISM a Ontology The thesis that the world is a blind will to live. **b Epistemology** The view that the basic statements are chosen as a result of arbitrary decisions. **c Ethics and social philosophy** The thesis that every action, far from being determined by external circumstances, is a result of voluntary decisions. This thesis is a half-truth: we shape our own life histories ("destinies"), though both constrained and stimulated by our milieu.

VOODOO PHILOSOPHY Any philosophy that includes such mysteries as the existence of multiple parallel universes, the social construction of the world, the generation of theories by empirical data, the attainment of truth through sheer criticism, the emergence of moral norms in a social vacuum, or the infallibility of certain texts.

WAR a Ontology The struggle of opposites central to ↑**dialectics. b Politics** The ultimate crime. According to traditional political theory and ethics, there are just wars as well as unjust ones. Actually all wars are unjust because they involve mass murder and other violations of ↑**human rights**. There can be only a just side in a war, namely that of the victim of an unprovoked aggression. However, sides may shift. For example, if the victim wins and takes revenge on the aggressor as a whole, it becomes unjust. The Roman adage, "If you wish peace, prepare for war," is a recipe for war. The recipe for peace is "If you wish peace, live in peace." ↑**Science wars**.

WELFARE Well-being: being and feeling healthy and reasonably happy. A key concept of ↑**social philosophy**. What politicians and political philosophers usually call the 'welfare state' is actually a relief state. A ↑**good society** would make it possible for the vast majority to attain welfare through work, mutual help, and social services rather than charity.

WELTANSCHAUUNG ↑Worldview.

WFF Well-formed formula. A formula that fits the relevant formal conventions. Examples: "*p* and *q*" is a wff, whereas "*p q* and" is not; "length of pencil in cm = 20" is a wff, whereas "length of pencil = 20" is not. The formulas in factual science must satisfy the condition of *dimensional homogeneity*: the two members of an equality must have the same dimensions, e.g., $L.T^{-2}$ (the dimension of acceleration). This condition is often ignored in social studies.

WHAT-IF QUESTION A ↑**counterfactual** question, such as "What would have happened to ethics if the French Revolution had not occurred?"

WHIGGISM ↑Presentism.

WHOLE Complex object. A whole can be either a collection, an aggregate, an undifferentiated blob, or a ↑**system**. Emphasis on the absolute priority of the whole is called ↑**holism**.

WHY IS THERE SOMETHING RATHER THAN NOTHING? The ultimate ontological question according to Heidegger. Actually it is a theological question, for it makes sense only upon being rephrased as "Why did God create the world?" In a secular context one takes the existence of the world for granted, and explores it or attempts to control parts of it.

WILL Disposition to act deliberately. A capacity of the primate frontal lobes, which can be either heightened or diminished by experience, drugs, and surgery. ↑**Free will**, ↑**goodwill**.

WISDOM *Practical wisdom* or *phronesis* = Good judgment concerning practical problems. That is, knowledge cum prudence. *Theoretical wisdom* = Good judgment concerning theoretical problems. That is, knowledge cum intellectual intuition. Theologians oppose theological wisdom to scientific knowledge. They hold that the former is deeper and more secure than the latter, in being based on eternal verities, namely those proclaimed by prophets, sacred scriptures, or church authorities. But they offer no evidence for this claim. Moreover, the wiser among them admit that everything religious and theological is ultimately a matter of faith or revelation, not of empirical evidence or rational debate.

WORD Element of an ordinary (natural) language. Words are letters or concatenations of letters of a language. The set of words of a language is called its *vocabulary.* The vocabulary of every modern language contains technical terms as well as terms in general use. The formation of sentences out of words is a case of ↑**emergence**. The difference between a ↑**language** and its vocabulary illustrates the concept of a ↑**system** in contradistinction to an unstructured collection (such as a vocabulary).

WORD-TO-THOUGHT RATIO An indicator of the content of a text. Low in exact philosophy and high in pseudophilosophy.

WORK The action that sustains human life and makes the social world tick. It is studied by ergonomics, economics, industrial sociology, praxiology, moral philosophy, and social philosophy. The concept of work used to be central to classical economic theory, from Smith to Marx. By contrast, it is the great absent from rational-choice theories, in particular neoclassical microeconomics, which deals with the exchange of goods as given. From Locke on, one of the moral and social problems involving the concept of work is whether workers are entitled to the fruits of their labor. ↑**Socialism**.

WORLD ↑Universe.

WORLD MAKING The delusion consisting in believing that thinking is making. A hobby of madmen and subjectivist philosophers. ↑**Constructivism**.

WORLD 3 Karl R. Popper's name for the "world" of ideas in themselves, as distinct from both the "worlds" of material things (or World 1), and that of mental processes (or World 2). Anticipated by Hegel and Lenin. A double fiction, since (a) ideas are not self-existing; and (b) they do not constitute an overall "world" or system, but come together into distinct regional "worlds" (systems), such as those of mathematics and archaeology. **Syn** ↑**objective mind** (Wilhelm Dilthey), culture in and by itself over and above people. ↑**Culture**.

WORLDLY Material as opposed to spiritual, otherworldly, or supernatural.

WORLDVIEW a General A schema of all there is. **Syn** *Weltanschauung*, philosophical cosmology. A worldview may be coarse or refined, sketchy or detailed, fuzzy or clear, consistent or inconsistent. It may be magical or naturalist, religious or secular; idealist, materialist, or dualist. It may be ordinary or science-oriented; fertile, barren, or obstructive—and so on. And it may also be a mixed bag of scientific and magical views. Worldviews are not the private property of philosophers and theologians. Ethologists assure us that every animal forms a representation or map of its immediate environment, which allows it to navigate in it and survive. Anthropologists and psychologists know that every human being has some worldview or other, if usually coarse and tacit rather than sophisticated and explicit. The difference between the cosmologies imagined by intellectuals and those held by others is that the former are explicit and therefore subject to analysis, criticism, and correction. Every reasonably comprehensive cosmology must contain answers to such basic questions as: Are there deities? If so, do they still tamper with the world or have they retired? Did the world have an origin, and will it have an end, or is it eternal? What is the stuff of the cosmos: matter, energy, information, idea? What holds things together? What takes things asunder? Is radical novelty possible? Is the cosmos qualitatively flat or organized in levels? What is life? What is mind? What is a person? Is there destiny or fate? What is society? What is history? Will there be an end to history? **b Functions** Every philosophical cosmology discharges both a conceptual and a practical function. Its *conceptual* function is that of providing a framework where every fact and every idea may fit or "make sense," i.e., cohere with the rest. The *practical* function of a cosmology is to provide guidance in life: to help formulate goals, choose means, design plans, and evaluate all that. **c Twelve worldviews** There are at least a dozen influential worldviews: ↑**holism**, which views the world as an animal or like one; ↑**hierarchism**, which regards it in the image of a ladder; ↑**atomism**, the metaphor for which is the cloud; ↑**processualism**, which views the world as a river without banks; ↑**mechanism**, according to which the cosmos is a clock; ↑**materialism**, which equates "thing" with "material object" and "real entity"; ↑**tychism** (or probabilism), which views the world as a casino; ↑**agonism**, for which the cosmos is a battlefield; ↑**idealism**, which proclaims that ideas either constitute or rule the world; ↑**sacralism**, which regards the cosmos as a temple; ↑**textualism**, which views the world as a book or a library; and ↑**systemism**, for which the cosmos is the system of all systems. Nearly every one of these worldviews contains a grain of truth or has made a positive contribution. Thus, holism has taught us that, indeed, wholes have (↑**emergent**) properties of their own. Hierarchism was eventually transmogrified into the idea that the world is not qualitatively flat but is organized into ↑**levels**. We owe atomism the idea that there are indeed simple or indivisible things, such as electrons and quarks. The basic idea of processualism has become commonplace. Mechanism was the first worldview based on a scientific theory. Tychism is appealing because the basic laws of quantum theory are probabilistic. And agonism would be right if it only held that some processes, not all, are conflictive. But none of these views is free from serious flaws. Thus, holism notwithstanding, the universe is not a block: it is often possible to isolate some things from others, at least in some respects, to some extent, and for a while. Nor is it true that analysis is impotent to yield some knowledge of wholes. Hierarchism has been replaced by the evolutionary view that the lower precedes the higher, not in power or dignity, but just as precursor. Atomism is wrong in minimizing interactions and emergence. The radical processualist view that change precedes substance is mistaken, for every change is the change in the properties of some concrete thing. Mechanism is far too narrow: we need not only mechanics but hundreds of other disciplines as well. Tychism is too extreme, because even the basic probabilistic laws involve causal concepts. (Thus, one calculates the probability that a given external field will cause the scattering of an incoming particle within a certain solid angle; besides, there are plenty of non-random processes, such as earthquakes and the reading of this entry.) Agonism overlooks the pervasivenes of cooperation, without which there would be no concrete systems to begin with. Besides, it has been formulated in a cryptic fashion. As for materialism, it is the worldview tacitly adopted by all scientists and technologists when not on philosophical forays. Indeed, they deal only with concrete things—some of them thinking ones—never with disembodied ideas. For this reason idealism is incompatible with science and technology; besides, it is a serious obstacle to the scientific study of the mental. But at least it rightly emphasizes the great importance of ideas in human affairs. In short, every one of the first eight worldviews contains some falsities along with some truths. By contrast, sacralism and textualism are utterly false, hence useless in the best of cases. Indeed, the former suggests replacing science with theology, or at least ignoring their incompatibility, and giving up any beliefs in freedom and responsibility. Textualism is utterly false because concrete things have neither linguistic nor literary properties. And it is disabling because it leads to conceiving of students of reality as mere readers. **d Systemist synthesis ↑Systemism**, the twelfth worldview in the above list, is a sort of synthesis of the valuable components of the first eight worldviews. It conceives of the world as the supersystem of all systems, and it regards our knowledge of it as a supersystem of data, hypotheses, theories, and methods. It boils down to the postulate that every object is either a system or a component of some system. Put negatively: There are no strays. Systemism is inherent in science, technology, and more. In fact, we all discover or invent, utilize, analyze, or design more or less complex systems, such as atoms and cells, nervous systems and social organizations, number systems and spaces, or languages and theories. Nothing can be understood in isolation. Thus, we understand a word in a sentence, and a sentence in a discourse; we understand individual behavior in its social context, and the latter within its natural matrix—and so on. The systemic nature of both the world and knowledge suggests the adoption of the ↑**systemic approach**.

ZEITGEIST Literally, spirit of the age. Broadly, body of prevailing beliefs and problems in a given society at a given time. Typically, holists claim that all thought is a predictable product of the contemporary *Zeitgeist*. This thesis is untestable, for it encompasses nonconformism as well as conformism. Hence it should not occur in a scientific ↑**culturology**.

ZENO'S PARADOXES Zeno of Elea's arguments against the reality of change. The best known is "Achilles and the Tortoise." Achilles runs ten times as fast as the tortoise, but has a handicap of h stadia. When he reaches the tortoise's starting point, the latter has already walked h/10 stadia ahead of him; by the time Achilles has reached this second position, the tortoise is h/100 stadia ahead, and so on ad infinitum. The total distance that Achilles must run to overtake the tortoise is the infinite series $h + h/10 + h/100 + \ldots + h/10^n + \ldots$ Now, the ancient Greeks thought that every sum of infinitely many terms, like this one, must be infinite. But we know that the given series converges to $h/[1 - (1/10)] = 10h/9$. This dissolves the paradox. Its only interest for our time is that it exemplifies the thesis that many a philosophical puzzle ends up by being solved with the help of science. Other examples are the causalism / tychism dilemma (solved by quantum mechanics), the vitalism / mechanism controversy (terminated by biochemistry), the ↑**mind / body problem** (solved by cognitive neuroscience), and the ↑**nature / culture** dichotomy (destroyed by the biosocial sciences).

ZERO The most important natural number, since it is the only one needed (as primitive or undefined) to construct all the others. Vulgar materialists and radical empiricists should refrain from using the number 0, because it has no counterpart in either reality or experience. True, some ↑**magnitudes** take the 0 value for certain states of real things, such as the entropy of a perfectly orderly aggregate, the electric resistance of a superconductor, the age of an organism at fertilization, and the salary of an unemployed person. But having zero P-ness is not the same as being P-less: the former condition may change, not so the latter.